TEACHING
High School Social Studies

HARPER'S SERIES ON TEACHING

Under the Editorship of
Ernest E. Bayles

TEACHING
High School Social Studies

PROBLEMS IN

Reflective Thinking

AND

Social Understanding

Maurice P. Hunt   Lawrence E. Metcalf
Fresno State College   *University of Illinois*

Second Edition

HARPER & ROW, PUBLISHERS
New York, Evanston, and London

TEACHING HIGH SCHOOL SOCIAL STUDIES
Problems in Reflective Thinking and Social Understanding
SECOND EDITION

Contents

v

Preface

WHEN AUTHORS revise a book, they have to decide whether the first effort was essentially correct. If they decide it was not, they start the second edition from the beginning. The reader will find in this second edition very little in the way of fundamental change. The basic idea of reflective study of cultural problems has been retained.

An attempt has been made to simplify and concretize the approach originally presented. Readers of the first edition sometimes complained about its difficulty for the beginning student. It was also felt that insufficient attention had been given to how-to-do-it aspects. We have tried to cope with these deficiencies, but are quick to admit that the book is still difficult enough to challenge the teaching ability of any instructor of methods.

The prologue, with which this edition begins, is intended to give the reader a graphic, dramatic, and impressionistic view of the kind of teaching our basic theory requires. We hope that this device will give the reader an "easier" introduction to our basic concept of teaching.

This is followed by two chapters on purposes of social studies education and the nature of learning, and then by five chapters in instructional theory. We now believe that methods of instruction cannot be deduced from learning theory alone, although a sound method of teaching cannot ignore what is known about learning. A knowledge of the nature of subject matter and the logical aspects of teaching are also necessary for development of a theory of instruction. In chapters 4, 5, and 6, we clarify our understanding of the nature of subject matter as we distinguish among three kinds of content—concepts, generalizations, and values. It is also our view that each kind of content calls for a somewhat different logical treatment. In the chapter on concepts, for example, we try to make it clear that the logical treatment of concepts must take into account the nature of concepts. We do the same in the chapters on generalizations and values. What is the nature of a generalization? Of a value? What is the proper logical treatment of each? In all three chapters we present many, many examples in the hope that this will solve certain how-to-do-it problems.

The section on basic theory concludes with a chapter on the teaching of history, which tries to make clear a certain conception of the nature of history, and the necessity within that conception to adapt one's logic to the peculiarities of concepts, generalizations, and values. The first edition was criticized for its scattered treatment of the teaching of history. We have placed all that we have to say about history in one chapter—Chapter 7.

The section on a basic theory of method is followed by four chapters on technical problems. These chapters are essentially the same as ones in the first edition. A reading and study of these chapters is important to instructors who want to emphasize solutions to how-to-do-it problems.

Finally, we have updated the chapters on problematic areas of the culture. These were called the closed areas in the first edition. We have retained the idea of closed areas but we use the broader and less forbidding label, problematic areas, because we recognize that an area can be problematic without being closed. We do not, however, wish to "play down" the importance of getting closed minds to reflect. This section on problem areas includes a new area, Power and the Law, which was not treated at all in the first edition.

In order to make space for the chapters on concepts, generalizations, values, and history we had to drop from this edition treatment of materials of instruction, academic freedom, and the teaching of subjects other than history. We regret the necessity to do this, but the book already threatens to reach encyclopedic proportions.

M.P.H.
L.E.M.

October, 1967

Acknowledgments

THE AUTHORS are indebted to many persons both living and dead. Throughout the book, the influence of the thinking of John Dewey will be evident. An immense debt is also owed the late Boyd H. Bode, with whom both authors were privileged to take courses. The imprint of H. Gordon Hullfish's thinking will also be visible, particularly in the authors' interpretation of moral conflicts as representing choices between competing goods. Alan Griffin, a student of Boyd Bode, helped the authors immeasurably in their understanding of Dewey's meaning for social studies education. The influence and direct help of Professor Ernest E. Bayles have been of incalculable value. He read carefully the theoretical sections of the manuscript and through his suggestions, both content and style were greatly improved.

We wish to thank the following publishers for permission to quote material in Chapter 11: McGraw-Hill Book Company for test exercises drawn from *Appraising and Recording Student Progress*, by Eugene Smith and Ralph Tyler and Houghton Mifflin Company for test items drawn from *The Construction and Use of Achievement Examinations*, by Herbert E. Hawkes, E. F. Lindquist, and C. R. Mann. We also wish to thank the University of Chicago Press for permission to quote material from *Generalization in the Writing of History*, edited by Louis Gottschalk.

Deep appreciation goes to our wives, Mabel and Barbara, who helped to prepare the manuscript for publication. The authors, of course, take full responsibility for whatever shortcomings the book possesses.

M.P.H.
L.E.M.

October, 1967

TEACHING
High School Social Studies

PROLOGUE

A Classroom in Action

THE PROLOGUE is intended to involve readers in a strategy for selecting and communicating content in high-school social studies. We have designed it to raise questions about what good teaching is and to serve as a prelude to the more theoretical material to follow. The prologue is a fictionalized account of what might happen in a world-history class. It is presented in dialogue and portrays a situation in which discussion is the primary classroom tool of the teacher. The topic (or unit) is *revolution in its most general sense;* the teacher uses a chapter in the textbook which treats the American and French revolutions of 1776 and 1789 as a "springboard" for getting into the subject.

The following account is idealized in the sense that it makes certain assumptions and contains omissions that reduce its "real life" qualities. We have done this so the material will make its point with a minimum of words. The assumptions and omissions are as follows:

1. It is assumed that the teacher is more effective than the average social-studies teacher, particularly a teacher of history. It is not necessarily assumed that the students are better than average. We presume that a typical class of high-school students contains at least a half-dozen students who are not merely competent but who enter into class discussion regularly; we presume, also, that in any class the number of active participants will increase as interest builds. We do not at any time indicate specifically how many *different* students are participating.

2. Although we have depicted a teacher who is probably doing a better job than one usually sees in high-school history, it should not be taken that the teacher is so talented that any prospective or in-service teacher who reads this book could not emulate him (her, if you prefer). What he is trying to do will become more understandable to readers as they proceed through the book.

3. The school, like most, does not have a library adequate for study of revolution in its broadest ramifications; there is a public library nearby, as well as a state college library—both of which are accessible to students. The school, like most, is administered under the assumption that there is a given amount and type of subject matter to be covered in each course each year. In the academic courses, this subject matter usually is defined by a syllabus or textbook.

4. Omitted from the example of teaching which follows is any refer-

ence to the usual distractions which tend to interrupt classes. Likewise omitted are facetious, irrelevant, and labored contributions to discussion; also deleted are lengthy detailed explanations such as would be necessary to treat the topic at the level on which it is here treated. In real life, a great many more words would be expended to get the job done. What follows, therefore, is much more compact and direct than a teacher could expect to achieve in a real class. The object of the example only is to show what can be done and how.

The teacher is designated by "T"; students by "S," except in some instances where it reads better to use a fictitious first name.

DAY 1

T: We are now ready to begin study of the chapter in our textbook entitled, "Two Revolutions That Threatened the Old Order," which was your assigned reading for today and tomorrow. But since in this course we have not yet considered seriously the meaning of revolution, I propose that we treat the subject more broadly than does this textbook chapter. This means we may want to re-read some material which has come before and some which comes later, as well as dip into other kinds of resource material. Class, what purpose do you think will be served by studying the subject of revolutions?

S: We should understand revolutions better.

T: What do you mean by understand?

S: I mean what we have meant all year by the term. To understand a statement means to see its relatedness to other statements—like facts to theories and theories to facts—and also to have an idea as to the use to which the statement can be put outside of school.

S: Yes, but to carry it further—to understand a concept like revolution means to be able to identify specific cases that have occurred and to describe the characteristics of a specific case so that if you encounter a new instance you will know how to classify it. If you know that a new happening is a revolution, you should be able to predict—or forecast—the results of behaving toward it in a given way.

S: Would it be simpler and equally correct to say that if we understand the meaning of revolution we know when one is occurring and what to do about it?

T: I think that at least some class members have the point well enough. To get down to business, then, what does the word revolution mean?

S: I looked in the textbook index under "revolution," and couldn't find any place where the authors give a general definition.

S: I did the same, and all I could find were references to certain revolutions, such as the American, French, and Russian.

S (with book open to index): The book refers to revolutions in different countries. But it also refers to "industrial revolution."

S: I would think the best way to define revolutions is to say they are what Communists start.

S: Do you think people like Thomas Jefferson, John Adams, Patrick Henry, and Thomas Paine were Communists?

S: America was an exception.

T: In more recent times, there may be a connection between Communist movements and certain kinds of revolutions. Let's save that question until later. What I'm interested in now is classifying revolutions as to general type.

S: What, then, about what the book calls the industrial revolution? Maybe there is a two-way classification: political and industrial.

T: I think it is time for us to use our imaginations—to play some hunches. Maybe there are several kinds of revolutions which are political only in their side effects—revolutions which have the *general pattern* of the industrial revolution. What might be some examples?

S: I don't think I understand the industrial revolution yet.

(The teacher gives the class a concise definition of the industrial revolution.)

S: That is simple enough, but I'm still not sure what you are trying to get at.

T: Suppose I said that one very general meaning of the word "revolution" is a drastic change—a turning over of the established pattern. We have named two—political and industrial. What might be other examples?

S: Then anything would be a revolution if it more-or-less turns things upside down? I would think you could say there has been a scientific revolution.

S: Related to this would be a revolution in medicine.

S: I think there has been a revolution in the way people behave. My grandmother would have fainted if she had seen a bikini or a miniskirt.

S: Along this same line there has been a major change in how people talk. It seems that nowadays no subject is thought bad or shameful to discuss. Even preachers talk about sex in their sermons.

T: Do you think there has been a revolution in the way our schools are run?

S: I haven't lived that long. But to hear dad talk about it there has been a lot of change—mostly for the worse.

S: I just thought of one—the way men and women behave toward each other. My dad once always gave a woman his seat if a bus was crowded. And he would take off his hat in elevators. He doesn't any more. Women now act more like men and men more like women.

T: I think we have made the point. These gradual, spread-out revolutions—which affect our social life, or science or industry—do they cause fighting? I mean real bloody fighting—armed warfare?

S: Not usually or for every long. Mainly there is a lot of talk by the old folk about the world going to the dogs.

T: It appears that several of you at least have some good ideas. I think that perhaps our greatest need now is for more information. It may be that an unabridged dictionary would point the way a little. After that, perhaps the encyclopaedias. Don't forget the *Encyclopaedia of the Social Sciences*—there's a set in the college library. Most of the books on the subject are pretty hard for students at your grade level. Probably the easiest is Crane Brinton's *Anatomy of Revolution*—which is about the general characteristics of revolutions of the kind described in our textbook chapter—those which have a strong political element. This is in paperback and available in all the libraries. Another good book, but much harder, is George Pettee's *The Process of Revolution*. There is at least one copy of this in the college library and possibly one in the public library. Also, you can always see what you can dig out of the periodical literature.

We have out in the open the idea that the term "revolution" has more than one meaning. But I don't want you to stop there. I want you to be able to classify the American and French revolutions beyond just their political implications. And even more, learn something about their form or pattern—something which might apply to other revolutions in other times and places.

DAY 2

T: What have you come up with, class?

S: I looked in Webster's unabridged dictionary for meanings of "revolution." The first meaning given is a surprise.

S: It is the encircling of one body by another—one complete encirclement—like when we say that in 365 days the earth makes one revolution around the sun.

S: That doesn't help much.

S: The most useful thing I could get from the dictionary was "a fundamental change in political organization or in a government or constitution."

S: I looked into the encyclopaedias that are in the school library. *Britannica* doesn't have an article on revolution. I had better luck with *Americana*. It has a short article in which the writer seems to make a distinction between real or genuine revolutions and social changes which actually are not revolutions. He defines revolution like this: ". . . a term used to designate a fundamental change in the government or the political constitution of a country, mainly brought about by internal causes and effected by violence and force of arms on the part of a considerable number of individuals. . . ." The article went on to say that a revolution should not be confused with a *coup*—whatever that is—or an insurrection, mutiny, rebellion, or revolt. The article made the point that a revolution causes the ruling power of a country to pass from one economic class to another. I don't understand all of this, but it seems to me we can get more help out of this definition than anything in our text or the dictionary.

T: To save time, I will give you an idea of what some of those words mean. *Coup* is a French word which literally means a blow or stroke. All of the words above are related, in that they refer in some way or other to a sharp, sudden, action of some sort.

S: I looked into the book by Brinton. I also found a copy of the book by Pettee at the public library—it's too hard for me. I did try to wade through its preface and first chapter. I think both authors are writing about revolutions like the American and French. I got the idea of a distinction we haven't mentioned. It's the distinction between a *major* revolution which turns a country upside down in only a few years and other kinds of revolutions which work much more slowly and peacefully.

T: Very good. Yesterday, we named several of the last kind.

S: Maybe the words "violent" and "peaceful" would be good to distinguish one general kind of revolution from another.

S: Could we say that if a change in something is slow enough it is likely to be peaceful but if it is rushed it may become violent?

T: And either kind of change could be labeled a revolution? Do all of the political revolutions you have heard of include violence?

S: I haven't read ahead in the book, but I think I can remember from other reading—or maybe from a TV program—that the Russian Revolution was a pretty messy affair. Wasn't there a kind of war within the country, with extremists squared off against moderates? I can't remember much about it.

T: I suspect we get a little off the track if we dwell too much on violence. It is a common feature of major revolutions which occur in a hurry, but probably it is no more important than a number of other features of such revolutions. What might be some other features of major revolutions which set them off from the long-range, evolutionary changes we have mentioned?

S: Most people were unhappy. Especially in France.

S: Yes, there is something in the book about the peasants being hungry.

S: In each of these revolutions a completely different group ended up with the political power. In America it was the colonists and in France Napoleon and his supporters.

S: I think a main point to remember is that both of these revolutions were political. They caused a change not only in who governed but in the form of government.

S: That ties in with the statement quoted earlier this period from the *Americana* article. I forget just now how it went, but it included a change in political power.

T: Eleanor, could you re-read the quote?

ELEANOR: It says that revolution is a ". . . term to designate change in the government or the political constitution of a country . . ." and goes on to mention internal causes and the use of force by a considerable number of people.

T: Tomorrow let's consider this matter of internal causes, numbers of persons involved, and who it is that become revolutionaries. I wonder if it would be well at this point if we organized ourselves better for study. I want to make sure certain reading gets done. I have here several textbooks which are designed for college level but they aren't so very hard. Who will take these and see what he can dig up on revolutions which have happened? . . . . Oh, fine, then Fred, Andy, June, and Sharon—take these. Now I definitely want someone to go to the college library and read the article on revolution which is in the *Encyclopaedia of the Social Sciences*. The article is entitled "Revolution and Counter-Revolution." Okay, Eleanor—this article is heavier and longer than the *Americana* article, but I think you can get something out of it.

S: I would like to look further in the book you mentioned by Pettee. My father owns a copy.

S: It must be great to have a father who is a political science prof. at State—especially when we are studying a topic like this.

T: Maybe it's lucky for all of us. Go to it, Jackie. If you get hung up, why don't you see if your father can bail you out? What I want you to do particularly is see what the author considers to be the prior conditions and steps that have characterized, and are an essential part of, all major political revolutions. I think we could stand a fairly careful report on Brinton's book. Any takers? No? Well, how about you, Paul and Barbara? I think you are up to it. You can work together as a team.

(By now the teacher has exhausted his resources—he has given assignments to all the good readers in the class. The others all read at or below their grade level and can handle only relatively popularized treatments.)

T: Will the rest of the class see what material they can find in our own text about revolutions other than those of America and France? Some of you may be willing to go to our school library and look in the *Readers' Guide to Periodical Literature* for references.

DAY 3

T: Let's take up where we left off yesterday. Remember we are discussing revolutions which are basically political, which involve a whole nation rather completely, which are somewhat sudden, and which in many cases are accompanied by violence—what Professor Pettee calls in his book, "major revolutions." What I want to get out into the open is what various historians of revolution think are *common* background conditions of revolution and *common* steps which occur during revolution—the *process* of revolution, you might say. Or, if I may use a fancy but better term, the *morphology* of revolution. Now —what does anyone have that is new?

S: It has been mentioned before, but the common people are starving. We ought to emphasize that.

S: I don't know about that. Where has anyone shown that the American colonists were starving?

S: Well, maybe not the Americans. But the French peasants were.

S: I have managed to struggle through quite a bit of Brinton's book. He gives the impression that the important fact about the period before a revolution is widespread discontent. People don't have to be starving or even hungry to feel discontented. Students were discontented last fall because the football team did poorly, but I noticed even the most disgusted of them didn't miss any meals.

S: Maybe people are discontented when they think the situation could be better than it is at the time. To someone else, they may not appear to have much to be discontented about. But they are unhappy because they think things *could be improved but nothing is improving.*

S: This ties in with revolutionary situations. In both America and France, the revolutionary leaders were mainly middle or upper-middle class. Some of them were pretty upper class—like Washington, Jefferson, and Lafayette.

T: Are there any cases where the revolutionary leaders are getting better off all the time but still want to start a revolution?

S: Yes, that was surely the case in the American colonies.

S: We seem to have it established that there is widespread discontent, even though that does not necessarily mean people are suffering. I would like to add another point: people have lost confidence in their government. They think it won't do what needs to be done if continuing progress is to be made.

S: Besides losing confidence, there is another group in existence which the people think can do a better job of leading—the revolutionary leaders.

S: Then most of the people want a change of government—from the old group of leaders who aren't leading very well, to a new group.

T: How does this new group of political leaders capture the following of the people? Is it because they are of better character?

S: No, they have a plan—a lot of promises.

S: They promise some kind of paradise on earth, if people will only turn from the old leaders and follow them.

T: What do Brinton and Pettee call this imaginary paradise?

S: It is called the revolutionary myth.

S: I got the impression that without a myth the middle-class revolutionary leaders would have an awfully hard time persuading the poor people to fight for the new government.

T: What is the nature of a revolutionary myth?

S: Well, it presents a picture of an ideal government and economic system.

S: A whole way of life—it is worded so it sounds as if everyone will be better off. The myth is very high sounding. It plays down the fact that people may have to make a lot of sacrifices.

T: Would you say the Declaration of Independence was a pretty persuasive revolutionary myth?

S: It must have been. It surely stirred up the colonists.

T: To get back to the theme of discussion, we have a state of discontent, a new political group demanding control of the government, and a myth with which this new group arouses the masses of people. What follows?

S: The old government has to show real incompetence—the old government pretty much has to break down. The army—or part of it—may desert to the side of the revolutionary group. Everyone loses confidence.

S: The old government also is not in touch with the people. Communication breaks down.

T: When will the revolutionary leaders feel in a position to try to take power? How far do things have to go?

S: When they think almost everyone is behind them—when enough of the regular army or militia are behind them so they can form a military force.

S: I should think that sometimes they might form their own military force. But they would have to be pretty sure the regular army wasn't very eager to fight the new revolutionary forces.

S: I think at the same time, or maybe as a necessary earlier condition, the old ruling group will have lost its morale. Some of the key people in government may even have fled. I doubt if the old government is functioning very well—if at all.

T: What is it like when the revolutionary group seizes control—that is, what happens?

S: They try to grab control of what they need the worst in order to establish themselves.

T: What do they need the worst?

S: Control of an army—this is essential for success.

T: What else would the revolutionary leaders need to control?

S: I should think the communications system: TV, radio, the press, the telephone system, etc.

T: What happens with respect to government?

S: The old political leaders are kicked out of office, and revolutionary leaders take their place.

S: The revolutionary leaders execute the old political leaders.

S: I don't think always. I haven't read anywhere that anyone was executed in the American Revolution.

T: Time doesn't permit us to pursue this point right now. In any case, it is time for an assignment. An easy one first: There is a TV documentary scheduled for tonight. It is entitled, "Cuba—the Forgotten Revolution." I assume from the previews that it is a rundown on what has happened in Cuba in recent years. Station KHIST at 9—this is for all of you.

Now—I would like to assemble a special team of students to put on paper a progress report of findings up to now plus what we haven't got to yet. What I would like is a compilation of material which properly could be entitled, "The Conditions and Steps of a Major Revolution." What do you think I want treated?

S: When you say conditions—I should think that would mean the kind of situation which has to exist before a revolution is possible.

T: What do you think I meant by steps?

S: A treatment of the developments, in the order in which they appear. That is, what happens first, what second, and so on.

T: Good enough. I want a few pages prepared on these subjects. I wonder how we could best organize to do it?

S: I don't know enough about the subject—don't include me.

T: I think we can find something for everyone to do—but obviously not everyone can be included on a team to prepare this material. It's pretty hard for a committee to paint a picture, and too many coauthors get in each other's way.

S: I nominate Jackie—she's an eager beaver.

S: What about Eleanor?

S: And Paul and Barbara.

T: If the four who have been suggested are willing, then they have the job.

JACKIE: We will need to have some ideas on format.

T: Why don't you consult with each other and also get the opinions of other class members? I want this to be "hand-out" material. When you get the material drafted—let's see—you are a good typist, Joan. Would you like to put the stuff on ditto masters? And maybe Howard and Fred would like to run them off on the school ditto machine. Let's try to have this ready to hand out by day after tomorrow.

DAY 4

T: Eleanor, I know you are involved as a member of the writing team. But I suspect you have some notes concerning the article which I asked you to read in *Encyclopaedia of the Social Sciences*. Will you brief the class on what you found out?

ELEANOR: That was not an easy assignment. I couldn't understand a lot of it. I do think this article adds something to our definition of revolution—insofar as I can make sense of it. It breaks what we have called major political revolutions down into two types.

T: What are they?

ELEANOR: Bourgeois revolutions and proletarian revolutions. A bourgeois revolution is a political revolution which places in power a group which wants to establish a capitalist state—free enterprise I suppose you might call it.

T: And a proletarian revolution?

ELEANOR: That is when there is already a capitalist state which isn't working very well—it usually has a government which is dictatorial and a landholding system which is very feudalistic—and the workers and peasants revolt and establish their own government. The article refers to the French Revolution as bourgeois and the Russian as proletarian.

I don't know for sure what all this means but it sounds potent; I'll quote: A revolution occurs in a ". . . society torn by an internal antagonism between a smaller upper class which by virtue of its proprietary claims to certain sources of income receives a considerable portion of the social product and a large lower class which performs all the manual, routine labor and subsists in relative poverty."

S: What are proprietary claims?

T: The claims a person has on income because he owns or controls property—if I rent my house, you could say I have a proprietary claim to the rent.

S: Then all that statement means is that the upper class has enough property so it receives most of the income—and everyone else is poor.

ELEANOR: Yes, the author seems to make a big point about how the masses are suffering and the rich live in idle luxury.

S: I don't think this checks out with what we have already said. I thought we agreed that the real leaders of a revolution were usually middle-class people.

ELEANOR: If we are referring to what this author calls bourgeois revolutions, then I don't see that there is any argument.

S: Then you would have to describe a Communist revolution differently—it occurs when most people are poverty stricken and it is lead by workers and peasants. Or is it?

ELEANOR: The article has an answer for this.

T: I think the class should try to straighten itself out on this point. Just what role, if any, does the middle class play in a Communist revolution? Let's see what our writing team ends up saying about this. Eleanor, what else did you find in this article which might be of interest?

ELEANOR: The article I've just been reporting will help our writing team in analyzing the part played by the middle class. But to get onto something new, there is some stuff which is right up our alley. There is a topic on conditions before the outbreak of revolution. A number of points are given—many of which we have already mentioned. This list of conditions seems to apply equally to a bourgeois or proletarian revolution.

T: Anything else?

S: There seems to be quite a bit on counterrevolutionary movements.

S: What is a counterrevolution?

S: It is a political and often military move made either to prevent the revolution from occurring or to unseat the new revolutionary rulers. It may occur before, during, or after a revolution.

T: What would be an example of a counterrevolution?

S: I was reading in one of the college textbooks that you handed out. It treats the American and French revolutions a lot more thoroughly than our textbook—and a number of revolutions not mentioned in our book. I got interested in what happened for several years after the American revolution and read some in a United States history text I found in the library. It seems to me that some of Alexander Hamilton's ideas were opposed to what most colonists thought they were fighting for. But the best example, I thought, was in the administration of John Adams. The attempt to suppress all criticism of government by the people. Some famous laws were passed which limited freedom.

T: You probably refer to the Alien and Sedition Acts of 1798. We could carry this a lot farther. But what about counterrevolution in France?

S: I found a book in the college bookstore on the French Revolution and other revolutions that were attempted in the first half of the 1800s. There is a pretty good chapter on the French Revolution. The writer says counterrevolutionary acts by the king and others high in the old government brought the revolution to a head. Until the king was executed, the monarchy kept opposing the developing revolution at every turn.

S: I think I've got something useful here in my notes—I found a book in the library on the world since 1914. It has some good stuff on the Russian Revolution. It tells for one thing how, in the early stages, a new government was set up—controlled by the Constitutional Democrats. Today, I guess you would call them moderates.

T: Probably Alexander Kerensky's short-lived government.

S: I got an idea that this government was pretty popular for a time. But on the other side were the Soviets who wanted to change everything—they were the extremists. They were well organized and gained the support of large sections of the army.

T: Then?

S: Well, it seems that the most radical group was called Bolsheviks and a man named Lenin controlled them. They staged a *coup* and seized power. Soon they had control of the whole country.

S: We were talking about counterrevolutions. Where did that come in?

S: Counterrevolutionaries appeared all over the place. They included the nobles, clergymen, some army officers, the moderates with democratic ideas, and even some of the Allies in World War I—like the United States—who sent men, money, and guns to put down the Bolsheviks.

S: I remember hearing about the "White Russians." What did they have to do with this?

S: This was the name given to organized counterrevolutionaries who tried to establish local or regional governments. They made a big blunder, though— they acted as if they wanted to bring back the old feudalistic system. Most peasants went over to the side of the Bolsheviks. A kind of civil war developed.

T: Were the Bolsheviks a nice group of people?

S: They began a reign of terror.

ELEANOR: Of course. Revolutionaries always resort to terror when threatened by counterrevolutionaries. It was the same in the French Revolution—and others. After they feel secure, they may simmer down.

T: There is one thing we haven't got around to yet. Remember that TV program I assigned last night?

S: I didn't think it was very exciting. It was kind of a rehash of what we have been over in our current events discussions.

S: It told how Castro at first fooled everyone by pretending to be a liberal democrat. He had the support of the middle class for a time—and even of the United States government.

S: And then he became a Communist. And began cracking down—especially on the middle class.

T: How did he crack down?

S: He had a lot of people shot and imprisoned. Then finally he let them leave, and now most of them are in the United States.

T: I wonder if we can tie Castro's revolution to some of the others. Would you call it a bourgeois or a proletarian revolution?

S: It developed into a proletarian revolution. At least, I got the impression that a lot of workers and peasants must have been behind it.

T: Were there a lot of very impoverished people in Cuba before Castro gained power?

S: The TV program didn't make much of a point of this. It made things sound pretty good under the old government—the guy named Something.

S: Batista—he was a dictator and a crook.

T: Was there a counterrevolution in Cuba?

S: I guess you could call the Bay of Pigs invasion an unsuccessful attempt.

DAY 5

T: Our writing team came through. Here are several pages, dittoed and stapled, for each of you.[1] No one claims that there aren't any mistakes in it. Everyone should be a critical judge. But don't criticize unless you have some facts to go on. Jackie, Eleanor, Paul, and Barbara—and our typist Joan—put a lot of work into this.

What I want you to do with this is study it carefully. Make marginal notations of anything you disagree with. But keep in mind that this is to *use*—not to hide away somewhere. Read it carefully for tomorrow—which is probably the last day we can give now to the study of revolution. Tomorrow I am going to ask you to apply these ideas to some situations we have not discussed yet—some current situations that you should be interested in.

As for today, I'm going to let you study this, and, if you want, you can spend time checking up on its accuracy. Anyone who would like a library permit can have it. Some of you have books with you.

S: You mean this is to be a study period?

T: Yes, and I mean *study*. If you don't read this carefully today, you may have a strong feeling of ignorance tomorrow.

DAY 6

T: Mike, you just turned eighteen, I think. Have you registered for the draft?

S: Sure. What does this have to do with revolution?

T: Maybe we can tie it in. Do you think you will be drafted?

S: I reckon so. I can't qualify for college entrance.

T: Do you want to be a member of the armed forces?

S: I guess the food wouldn't be any worse than at home. But I don't exactly like the idea of coming home with an arm or leg missing.

T: You know where you would likely end up in the army, don't you?

S: I don't like much to think about it—but I guess it would be the infantry in Vietnam for me.

T: If you do end up in the infantry, what do you think you would be fighting for?

S: I don't know. Just for the honor of the United States, I guess.

S: I think Mike is mixed up. The world has to be saved from communism.

S: Have you forgotten all we've been studying the past five days? Anyone who gets involved fighting in Asia on our side is a counterrevolutionary. Those countries are having proletarian revolutions. They have an unworkable combination of capitalism and feudalism. Besides that, Asiatics don't like us for historical reasons.

---

[1] This material is included in the Appendix, at the end of the chapter.

S: I'd like to see some discussion on a little more rational basis. I'd like to know more of the facts—instead of propaganda.

T: I'm curious to know the extent to which you can identify what's going on in various parts of the world—using our dittoed material as a guide. It contains a lot of useful concepts and generalizations relating to revolution.

S: I think the main thing on everyone's mind is Vietnam. But how does understanding the French Revolution and others help much in understanding Vietnam?

JACKIE: Maybe there is a major revolution going on there. If so, all or most of the conditions and steps that have been typical historically ought to apply.

S: Keep talking.

S: Well, the revolution hasn't really occurred yet because of the strength of counterrevolutionary forces, but I think the preliminary conditions are all there. There certainly has been a long period of discontent among the poor— and probably among many of the middle class too, such as Buddhist leaders and intellectuals. The National Liberation Front, with the help of the North Vietnamese, has provided pretty effective revolutionary leadership. The myth is present—the future Communist paradise plus the hope of shoving the whites out of Asia. There have been a succession of pretty ineffective bourgeois governments. The army desertion rate is high.

S: Jackie, you have this down too pat. You say the United States is a counterrevolutionary force. I think in a proletarian Communist revolution of this kind, there *needs* to be a powerful counterrevolutionary force. We don't want Southeast Asia to become Communist do we?

JACKIE: That wouldn't be my first choice. But neither is an indefinite war that no one can win. Would you want to come home a corpse in a war to prevent a country from moving from feudalism into the twentieth century?

S: Naturally not. But I think we have to fight Communism, everywhere, with everything we've got.

T: I'm not sure we are remembering very well the steps that major revolutions take. I can't say I would be happy about it, but suppose the United States withdrew from Asia and suppose Vietnam—and perhaps Thailand and other countries—came under the rule of Communist dictatorships. What do you think would happen over the long run? At this point you ought to be able to make a reasonably intelligent forecast.

S: There would probably be a blood bath—a reign of terror.

S: That would be an expected reaction against internal counterrevolutionary forces.

S: When the terror ends, we could expect the consolidation of the revolution. A new constitution. Maybe a reasonable sort of civilian government. Probably reforms would occur that have been needed for a thousand years.

S: You talk like a Communist.

T: It seems to me that irrationality is getting the upper hand. Much of the world still has a strong feudalistic heritage. These countries will have to enter the twentieth century sooner or later. Some may not make it until the twenty-first century. Could we let it rest that much of Asia is in a revolutionary situation? And most of Africa? And parts of South America? By now you ought to be able to forecast with better than a 50-50 chance of being right where the next revolutions will develop and their general form.

S: Is the day of bourgeois revolutions over?

T: That is for you to figure out. Maybe by the time the course is over, you will have a pretty good idea.

S: What about the risk of most of the backward countries having successful Communist revolutions sooner or later? Could a democratic United States survive in a world like that?

T: I have no answers. I think by now you have a sufficient background of concepts and generalizations about revolution to do some intelligent thinking about this subject.

S: I wonder how many of us males will be alive five years from now?

T: Don't forget that all a study of history can do is help us make informed guesses—and they may all be wrong. At least, most of you seem much more interested in revolution now than you were a week ago. There is just one more question I want to raise—maybe with more success than the earlier question about the outcome of our involvement in Southeast Asia. We have to be brief because there isn't much time.

On the basis of what you know now about the conditions necessary for a revolution, do you think there is likely to be one in the United States in the foreseeable future?

S: It seems to me the risk is great. The government is riddled with Communists—well, at least they are in key spots.

S: My dad is certain there is a conspiracy behind the scenes. As we brought out in discussion, if a group of conspirators can seize control of the communication system, the press, and worm their way into control of important segments of the army—then they have it made. It's just one short step to taking over the office of president and controlling the Congress.

T: I think some of you are ignoring—or forgetting—all the work done by a few students who put on paper the necessary conditions that have existed prior to all major revolutions in the past. Some of you seem committed to the so-called "conspiracy theory" of revolution. I don't know of any experts on the revolutionary process who think this theory is any good. Now try to apply what we have learned to the United States.

S: There has to be very widespread discontent. It seems to me Americans generally are awfully contented. They are complacent. Oh, they may worry some about the foreign situation, but I think what they think about mostly is how to get a promotion at work, eating and drinking, sleeping, recreation, sex, the family—stuff like that.

S: There also has to be a well-organized group of revolutionary leaders with an appealing myth to peddle.

S: It seems to me the "liberals" in the Democratic Party fill that bill.

S: That's nonsense. The resemblance is too superficial—you aren't really seeing the difference between them and the kind of revolutionary leaders in the countries we have studied.

S: What about all those right-wing Republicans? And the extremist groups —like the Minutemen?

T: Have any groups that you indicated shown much willingness to die for their cause, or even put forth a cause that would capture the imagination of a majority of the people?

S: I don't think so. I don't know who has described a "brave new world" for us that has gotten people very excited. We have had New Deals, Fair Deals, New Frontiers, and so on—but how could anyone call them effective revolutionary myths?

T: What about the Communist Party—we have one, you know—as potential revolutionary leaders? We will study this more thoroughly later in the course, but perhaps someone has some ideas now.

S: Some people think there is a Red under every bed—but I don't know much about them.

S: Some politicians call all northern Democrats Communists.

T: I guess I couldn't expect your factual knowledge on this to be very strong as yet. You sound about as well informed as the general public.

S: Whenever you say that, we know you are being sarcastic.

S: It looks as if there is no widespread discontent, no revolutionary leadership, no exciting myth. It seems to me people are "nuts" who get heated up about the possibility of a revolution of the kind we have been studying happening here.

S: If we had a revolution here, it would be a Hitler-style kind of thing—no bourgeois or proletarian revolution in the old sense. The reason I think this is. . . . (The closing bell ends discussion.)

APPENDIX

FOLLOWING *is a verbatim reproduction of the dittoed material that the four-student writing team, with the help of a student typist, prepared for distribution among the class. A professor of political science who is interested in the subject of major political-economic-social revolutions would find superficialities and perhaps some errors of fact in it. His chief criticism might be that it is something of a Procrustean bed—that no particular revolution ever followed this pattern with precision. Nevertheless, we present it for whatever it may be worth.*

"The Conditions and Steps of a Major Revolution"

NECESSARY CONDITIONS FOR A REVOLUTION TO OCCUR

1. A long period of discontent (maybe a century or more). The middle class thinks its condition, which may be good, can be greatly improved. Workers

and peasants may or may not really be suffering, but they, also, believe things could be much better.

2. Effective revolutionary leadership arises. Usually it is the more rebellious and able of the middle class with an occasional defector from the ruling class which makes up the revolutionary leadership. On rare occasions, persons from the lower class rise to become members of the "revolutionary elite." The revolutionary leaders are usually well educated and "cut out" for their role. Some are skilled military strategists.

3. Development of a "revolutionary myth." This is a statement of the political, economic, and social goals of the revolution. It is an idealized picture—a kind of paradise with something good promised for everyone (except the old ruling class). It makes people willing to sacrifice and die for the revolution.

4. The government shows incompetence to govern. Increasingly the old ruling class seems unable to carry on the ordinary functions of government; even the basic services that have always been expected are neglected. Often the leaders lose communication with the common people and the middle class.

5. Demoralization of the ruling class. As the above situations develop, the more intelligent of the ruling class see their situation as hopeless and may flee the country. Others seem to remain blind to the situation until it is too late. By this time there is a general collapse of the government.

6. Revolutionary leaders take final steps. By this time the revolutionary elite at least has the *consent*, if not always the active support, of enough of the people to make a successful take-over of government seem likely. By this time either large segments of the army have defected to them or they have put together their own military force. They have become organized and have decided who will be responsible for what.

THE TAKE-OVER

1. The revolutionary blow (*coup*). The revolutionary leaders seize military control—sometimes at first only locally or regionally. They are able to neutralize what military forces remain loyal to the old ruling class. They then seize control of communications. Once this was the press. In modern times, radio broadcasting; now, television would be important. They also seize the major transportation facilities—roads, bridges, railroads, etc.

2. The transformation of government. The old leaders who remain are deposed and often killed or exiled. At first, the new political leaders are usually "moderates" of middle-class origin. A new constitution is put into effect. The new assembly (or parliament or congress) is in an ambiguous position. As moderates, its members may feel the revolution has gone far enough. They are trusted neither by those who are still loyal to the old government nor by the more radical revolutionaries who think more drastic changes are needed.

3. First counterrevolutionary attempts. If enough of the old ruling group remain around, if they have some military support left (or can get the promise of help from a neighboring government), and have the nerve, they strike back and try to destroy the new revolutionary government and reinstate themselves.

There are many cases where they succeeded (e.g., the series of European revolutionary attempts between the time of Napoleon and 1848). Or they may fail.

4. The terror. The threat of counterrevolution puts the new government in a difficult position. Often the new government consists of kindly, gentle men who are bound together by idealism. But if the counterrevolutionaries win, they lose everything—including their lives, probably. They usually yield to the demands of the extremist revolutionary elements—generally hard and cynical men—who end up capturing the government from the moderates. The moderate revolutionaries as well as all suspected counterrevolutionaries may be slaughtered. This is a period of great hysteria and fear.

5. Mopping up. This may be called the "consolidation of the revolution." Widespread social and economic changes are made. The constitution may once more be rewritten. The old landed aristocracy and other remnants of feudalism are largely wiped out (exception: the slaveholding states of the southern United States). There may be widespread redistribution of property. Enough of the "revolutionary myth" is put into effect to make the masses feel victorious. Often the revolutionary leaders rally patriotic fervor by a policy of military aggression.

6. The period of relaxation, or the *Thermidor*. The latter word comes from the French term meaning a new calendar announced during the French Revolution. The decline of the French terror, associated with the fall of Robespierre, was on July 27, 1794, or the ninth *Thermidor*, Year II, of the new French calendar. The terror is ended, the crisis is over, the revolution seems mainly successful, and most people begin to relax.

LATER COUNTERREVOLUTION AND REVOLUTIONARY SUCCESS

1. Counterrevolutions of a later period. As long as members of the old regime or their sympathizers live, whether in their own country or in exile, they may plot to restore their former position of power and wealth. The delicate balance of power in France during much of the nineteenth century is a good example. The Civil War in the United States in the 1860s was an attempt by the North to complete the unfinished bourgeois revolution of 1776 and by the South to retain a feudalistic system. Some delayed counterrevolutions succeed, as when Franco destroyed the Spanish republic and restored many of the aspects of a feudal monarchy.

2. Revolutionary successes of a later period. Most major revolutions remain unfinished for many years, maybe a century or two. Whatever Jefferson really meant by his statement, "All men are created equal," people have taken it to mean that everyone should have equal opportunities. The United States has never achieved this aim so you could say that the American Revolution is still unfinished. Present-day counterrevolutions are those which reject the main aims of an earlier revolution; those who are still trying to put these aims into effect could be considered the revolutionaries of the latter twentieth century. Some important "unfinished business" of the revolution of 1776 has been tackled only recently through civil rights legislation and Supreme Court decisions.

DISCUSSION QUESTIONS AND EXERCISES

1. Try to arrange for visits to a few high-school history classes in your community. Then write a brief essay comparing or contrasting the teaching you have seen with that just described.
2. Most history teachers say they relate the past and present when they teach. Usually they do this by making comparisons or analogies. They show similarities between a historical and a current event, but do not strive for theoretical statements. Do students learn anything useful from this?
3. The teacher in the above example devoted a lot of attention to concept formation and the making of generalizations (theoretical statements). He did not stress memorizing large quantities of descriptive fact. Is this good practice?
4. It has been said that one reason the Greeks, between the fifth and third centuries, B.C., built such a remarkable civilization was because they had no history. How do you react to such a statement? Why?
5. Try writing, in dialogue form (somewhat like the above) a "unit" in history. Select something controversial, such as the rise and meaning of science, the development of religious thought, war, relations between the sexes, courts and the law, etc.
6. The teacher in the above example deliberately pitches his teaching on a rather demanding level. He tries to challenge students in the upper third or quarter of the class and hopes for the best with respect to the others. What is your opinion of this?
7. At the end, the teacher intentionally did not "wrap up" the unit with neat conclusions. He left a lot hanging. Is this good or bad?

REFERENCES

ARENDT, HANNAH, *On Revolution,* New York, Viking, 1963.

> Miss Arendt is one of today's most brilliant political scientists. This book is theoretical and extremely scholarly. Some critics complain that she makes too many generalizations from intensive study of two revolutions—the American and French. The book contains much more of interest, however—such as Chapter 1, "The Meaning of Revolution." Highly recommended for teachers and high-school students of extraordinary ability.

BRINTON, CRANE, *The Anatomy of Revolution,* New York, Vintage, 1952.

> This is probably the easiest theoretical book to read of all in the list. Better high-school students can handle it. It is also perhaps the most interestingly written. Highly recommended for teachers and students.

CARR, EDWARD HALLETT, *Studies in Revolution,* New York, Macmillan, 1950.

> As usual, Carr has produced a short book that says a great deal. A "must" for teachers, who should review it for those students whose background and read-

ing level make it too difficult. This book is highly readable and better high-school students can handle it.

CARR, EDWARD HALLETT, *The New Society*, Boston, Beacon, 1957.

A classic, especially good on the influence of Rousseau on the development of the Communist "people's democracies." Should be in every teacher's library. Available in low-cost paperback.

Encyclopaedia of the Social Sciences, New York, Macmillan, 1937, "Revolution and Counter Revolution," pp. 367 ff.

Nine pages of fundamental analysis. Very good for its length. (See also the article in *Encyclopedia Americana* on "Revolution"—a short entry on p. 445 of vol. 23.)

HOBSBAWM, E. J., *The Age of Revolution, 1789–1848*, New York, Mentor, 1964 (c1962).

Professor Hobsbawm considers this sixty-year period a crucial one: a period in which, in spite of major counterrevolutionary efforts, the "bourgeoisie" (businessmen) finally came into their own. The conduct of diplomacy, war, government, trade, and methods of industry changed drastically. In short, even though the revolutionists of the far left failed, great gains were made by the middle class in displacing the old feudal way of life.

HOUSEHOLD, GEOFFREY, *Things to Love*, Boston, Little, Brown, 1963.

One of the better novels on the "anatomy of revolution" in South American countries. Fiction which contains much truth.

HUBERMAN, LEO, and PAUL SWEEZEY, *Cuba: Anatomy of a Revolution*, New York, Monthly Review Press, 1960.

A sympathetic portrait of the Cuban revolution, written by a journalist and a well-known economist. It is highly readable and presents the "other side."

JACKSON, BARBARA WARD, *Five Ideas That Change the World*, with a foreword by Kwame Nkrumah, New York, Norton, 1959.

This book of Mrs. Jackson's (the former Barbara Ward) is of special relevance to the subject of revolution. She addresses her message particularly to small, uncommitted countries and makes a plea for pushing revolution in a democratic direction. The book is written under five main heads: nationalism, industrialism, colonialism, communism, and internationalism. Quite readable.

KOHN, HANS, *Revolutions and Dictatorships*, Cambridge, Harvard University Press, 1939.

This scholarly tome is a collection of Kohn's essays. It subjects the American and French revolutions to analysis and also treats Turkey and Zionism. An excellent book. Too hard for students, but good for teachers.

KOHN, HANS, *Living in a World Revolution: My Encounters with History*, New York, Affiliated (a division of Pocket Books), 1965.

Another scholarly work by Dr. Kohn, but unlike the title listed above, it focuses more on contemporary situations. Highly recommended reading for teachers and an occasional high-school student.

LACY, DAN, *The Meaning of the American Revolution*, New York, New American Library-World, 1964.

> Although Mr. Lacy treads on much familiar ground, his theme is novel to many social-studies teachers—namely, that the few years following 1776 did not complete the American Revolution, but that the revolution has been under way ever since, and still has a great distance to go.

PETTEE, GEORGE S., *The Process of Revolution*, New York, Harper & Row, 1938.

> A short but richly laden book by a Harvard professor. One of the best books available on the subject and should be in every social-studies teacher's library. Very well written, but too difficult for any but the best high-school students. A gold mine for teachers.

POLANYI, KARL, *The Great Transformation*, New York, Holt, Rinehart & Winston, 1944.

> Polanyi tries to show why the world is becoming socialist, although not necessarily by violent means. He uses England as his chief case study, and draws heavily from cultural anthropology. A superbly reasoned book, and destined to be a classic. Now available in a reasonably priced paperback edition. "Must" reading for teachers.

SEERS, DUDLEY, *The Economic and Social Revolution*, Chapel Hill, University of North Carolina Press, 1963.

> Seers, a long-time correspondent in Latin America, edits a symposium written by four university professors—one American, two Chilian, and one English. It is mainly a statistical study of what has happened in Cuba since Castro gained power. Seers and colleagues feel that although Communism in Cuba has not been a glowing success, the average Cuban is somewhat better off than before.

SHAPLEN, ROBERT, *The Lost Revolution*, New York, Harper & Row, 1966.

> An old Asia hand writes a book on Southeast Asia covering a time span of twenty years, ending in 1965. He forecasts that the time is long past for the United States to have any significant effect on the course of events in that part of the world. He says,". . . a revolutionary condition existed in IndoChina all along, one that should have been regarded from the start by the Western nations for what it was. . . ."

SZULC, TAD, *The Winds of Revolution: Latin America Today and Tomorrow*, New York, Praeger, 1963.

> According to Szulc, Latin America is in a revolutionary ferment which cannot be bought away by American economic aid. The revolution is a search for a new ideology—a new "myth"—more than it is a search for food. Americans don't seem to understand this yet, and much of our effort is waste. A provocative book.

PART I
Why Teach the Social Studies

CHAPTER I

The Social Studies and American Society

I N EVERY society, education is regarded as the transmission from one
generation to another of that part of the culture which is considered
of ongoing value. Although a culture has material as well as non-material
aspects, it is chiefly the nonmaterial with which education is concerned:
attitudes, beliefs, knowledge, values, concepts, ideas, myths, skills, techniques, and habits. Education is the process by which the young are helped
to develop or acquire the ideational and symbolic equipment believed
necessary by adults to carry on a chosen way of life.

Almost every social-studies teacher believes that preservation of the
cultural heritage is one of his chief purposes. But simply to say that the
American heritage is to be preserved leaves many questions unanswered.
Under this slogan, social-studies education can take many forms. Teachers may vary widely in the content they emphasize and the methods of
instruction they employ. Such variety is almost certain to be the case in a
society such as ours, with conflicts over the meaning of the good life as
one of its defining traits. In an abstract sense, an appropriate education
depends upon what kind of society is desired in the future. Without clarity on this question it is not possible to say what features of present culture possess continuing value. In our conflict-ridden society, teachers and
other adults differ in their perception and understanding of present-day
culture, and in their definitions of what would constitute cultural improvement. Teachers differ among themselves as much as they differ with
lay publics.

It now appears to be the case that great uncertainty has developed in
the United States over the kind of education we should have. Some of our
most hotly debated and least intelligently considered issues relate to curriculum and methods of teaching in our schools. So great is the confusion
that many Americans at this point in the twentieth century favor educational practices which would destroy those aspects of the culture which
they claim to prize most highly. Like moths impelled by their tropisms to
fly into a flame, they seem bent on destroying the very things they say
they cherish.

Problematic Areas of American Culture

Certain aspects of American culture are especially relevant to any discussion of social-studies education. It has come to be granted that American culture is beset with problems. Problems seem to accumulate at a rate faster than we can solve them. It is our contention that this problematic aspect has not been well understood. It has not been understood that problems of social conflict exist not only as issues between individuals and groups, but also as sources of confusion within individual personalities. Neither has the existence of *closed areas* as one of the attributes of a problem area been widely recognized. It is one thing to say that American culture includes a "race problem." But it says a great deal more to observe that this problem exists not only between Negroes and whites, but within each, and that rational solutions are difficult to achieve because race is treated in the culture as a closed area. In our curriculum proposals as set forth in Part IV of this book, we argue for reflective studies of the problematic aspects of American culture, including elements of personal and social conflict that are sometimes closed to rational examination. The closures may arise from community taboos or personal prejudice.

TWO KINDS OF SOCIAL CONFLICT

Large-scale conflict is a trait of any culture that has reached our stage of development. But compared with many other cultures, ours is particularly conflict-ridden, and with good reasons. Settled by peoples of diverse origins and outlooks, the United States has been, ever since its founding, the scene of competing political, economic, and social beliefs. Add to this diversity the factor of industrialization. The change from agrarian-rural to industrial-urban society has generated some of our greatest conflicts. Industrialization speeds change with a result that from generation to generation beliefs undergo marked alteration. Gulfs are created between children and parents, parents and grandparents. Industrialization also fragmentizes society into specialized occupational and other economic groupings, each with its own version of the general welfare. "What is good for business is good for the country" is met or countered by the cry, "Our nation's welfare depends upon the freedom of the working man." And finally, we must add to our list of causes of conflict the fact that industrialization is taking place at an ever more rapid rate generation by generation, and consequently we seem to be falling farther and farther behind in our adjustments. A nation that has not brought its beliefs into line with the first Industrial Revolution now finds itself confronted by a second.

Students of present-day social conflict have found two levels of conflict, *interpersonal* and *intrapersonal*. Interpersonal conflict is exemplified by individuals or groups with sharply opposed beliefs. Such conflicts are usually referred to as "controversial issues." Persons on each side of an interpersonal conflict may be quite consistent in their own outlooks, even though in sharp disagreement with an opposing position. When the advocates of school integration clash with the proponents of racial segregation, we witness interpersonal conflict. Interpersonal conflicts rage in our culture between capital and labor; among social classes; among racial, religious, and ethnic groups; between the sexes; among age groups; and most tragically of all, among nation states, each of which knows that today's advanced weaponry has the capacity to obliterate the human race.

It is not unusual for an interpersonal conflict to become internalized within individual personalities so that people are at war not only with one another but with themselves. Caught in a culture in which interpersonal conflict is always present, they often accept as true and good both sides of many issues, thus incorporating cultural conflicts into their own personalities. When individuals become aware of their own incompatibilities of outlook, the resulting internal struggle produces intrapersonal conflict. Although the content of an intrapersonal conflict may be no different from that of an interpersonal one, it is more difficult to handle and may exact a greater toll as it leads to disintegration of personality.

Although these two kinds of conflict are different, they are often present at one and the same time. Disputants on opposing sides of an issue may be possessed of intrapersonal conflict, making self-understanding and compromise difficult to achieve. The interrelationship of these two kinds of conflict and their bearing upon moral problems has been best expressed by Myrdal in his discussion of American race relations:

The American Negro problem is in the heart of the American. It is there that the interracial tension has its focus. It is there that the decisive struggle goes on. This is the central viewpoint of this treatise. Though our study includes economic, social, and political race relations, at bottom our problem is the moral dilemma of the American—the conflict between his moral valuations on various levels of consciousness and generality. The "American Dilemma," referred to in the title of this book, is the ever-raging conflict between, on the one hand, the valuations preserved on the general plan which we call the "American Creed" where the American thinks, talks, and acts under the influence of high national and Christian precepts, and, on the other hand, the valuations on specific planes of individual and group living, where personal and local interests; economic, social, and sexual jealousies; considerations of community prestige and conformity; group prejudice against particular persons or types of people; and all sorts of miscellaneous wants, impulses, and habits dominate his outlook. . . .

The Negro problem in America would be of a different nature, and, indeed, would be simpler to handle scientifically, if the moral conflict raged only between valuations held by different persons and groups of persons. The essence of the moral situation is, however, that the conflicting valuations are also held by the same person. *The moral struggle goes on within people and not only between them. As people's valuations are conflicting, behavior normally becomes a moral compromise. There are no homogeneous "attitudes" behind human behavior but a mesh of struggling inclinations, interests, and ideals, some held conscious and some suppressed for long intervals but all active in bending behavior in their direction* [1]

Moral dilemmas are not restricted to the area of race relations. They abound in all areas of cultural existence. Consider the following: We have a great number of norms, or standards, to which individuals are expected to accede—success, friendliness, honesty, sexual purity, and a certain degree of gentility. Under given conditions these norms may conflict, as in the case of one who perceives honesty as a barrier to his economic success. Current efforts of the television industry to balance the extravagance of sponsor claims with serious and responsible treatment of news events represent one kind of compromise between competing ideals. Another kind of conflict is between ends and means. Culturally imposed barriers of physical and social conditions make it difficult or impossible for many to achieve the goals implied by their culturally learned ideals—for example, the inability of those whose lot is poverty to achieve economic success.

CLOSED AREAS

Individuals in our culture who have acquired intrapersonal conflict are increasingly uncertain as to what to believe or value. Individuals who are inconsistent or uncertain, cannot engage in morally responsible behavior based upon intellectual understanding and personal commitment. The continued existence of uncertainty and inconsistency on a large scale can be explained only as one turns to the factor of *closed areas*.

Certain areas of conflicting belief and behavior are largely closed to thought. In these areas, people usually react to problems blindly and emotionally. Closed areas are saturated with prejudices and taboos. Inconsistency or mutual contradiction in beliefs and values rule behavior in any closed area. There is usually a reluctance to examine certain ideas because it is believed that they are "impractical, theoretical, or in violation of common sense." Those areas of belief which are most important to individuals are likely to be those in which rational thought is least valued. In

[1] Gunnar Myrdal, with the assistance of Richard Sterner and Arnold Rose, *An American Dilemma: The Negro Problem and Modern Democracy*, Harper & Row, 20th Anniversary Edition, 1962, pp. lxxi–lxxii. Italics in original.

our culture, irrational responses commonly occur in such areas as power and the law; religion and morality; race and minority-group relations; social class; sex, courtship, and marriage; nationalism and patriotism; and economics. The problematic aspects of each of these areas will be discussed in Part IV.

The pedagogical significance of these closed areas is not well understood by most teachers of social studies. If a teacher were intent upon a reduction of prejudice, it would be necessary for him to address his efforts at beliefs and values in closed areas. Any belief that has not been subjected to rational examination is by definition a prejudice no matter how correct or incorrect it may be. Yet teachers rarely invade any closed area, even though every closed area can be opened by skillful, tactful, fair, and objective teachers.

Allusion to the "common sense" of the American people usually refers to their dominant beliefs in one or more of the closed areas. Failure to examine these beliefs in a social-studies classroom has certain effects upon the learning and motivation of students. Students do not learn in any significant and relevant sense the subject matter of history, economics, sociology, anthropology, political science, and geography. These are the very subjects teachers of social studies are hired to teach; but since the knowledge in each of these subject fields conflicts at many points with beliefs that predominate in the closed areas, teachers who take their teaching seriously are placed in a quandary. Many search desperately for items of information that have no bearing upon what students regularly believe, and proceed to teach these rather than basic concepts that would awaken or disturb latent conflicts of students. Students commit to memory names of all state capitals along with other items of information readily available in the reference volumes of any good library. But concepts such as cultural lag, ethnocentrism, deficit financing, gross national product, judicial review, to mention only a few, the meaning of which throws light upon the common sense of students, are either omitted entirely from the curriculum, or given the kind of treatment that leaves their relevance to society and its problems unclear.

Students from this kind of classroom express their boredom by complaint against the necessity of taking courses in the social studies. It is not unusual to find students from a culturally disadvantaged environment attending a social-studies course in which no attention is given to problems of caste and class as root causes of poverty. These students are expected to solve their problems of poverty by learning a trade. Teachers frustrated by this kind of situation often turn to a search for new techniques rather than significant content in order to increase student motivation. Symposia on programmed instruction or team-teaching become popular in-service training. Students who retain genuine intellectual interests pursue them outside school, and pretty much on their own.[2] Unfortunately, very few students retain an intellectual interest in social-scientific content after having been drugged over the years by a safe and sane social-studies education that specializes in an avoidance of issues in closed areas.

Our closed areas change from one historical period to another. Sex is now much more open to reflective study than it was fifty years ago, whereas comparative socioeconomic ideologies (including the issue of Communism) is more nearly closed to rational examination than even twenty years ago. At any given time, some of the closed areas we have listed will be much more tightly closed to reflection than will others; and all have their open aspects, facets which are relatively free of prejudiced belief.

At the same time, certain ideas remain immune to rational consideration from generation to generation. The current view that criticism of American policy in Vietnam gives aid, comfort, and hope to Hanoi reminds one of past criticisms of any dissent expressed during time of war.

Our closed areas exist as sources of totalitarian belief and practice in a culture that strains in two directions, democratic and authoritarian. The term *totalitarian* is appropriate here because the behavior of the American people with respect to closed areas is akin to behavior of leaders of totalitarian states. Each closed area has a set of sanctioned (albeit often irrational and inconsistent) beliefs that everyone is expected to follow, and which we try to inculcate in the minds of the young through propaganda; no one is taught to rely upon independent thinking for his answers, but on tradition, the church, or political leaders. People who get out of line find themselves in deep trouble; and severe pressure, both social and legal, may be placed on persons who have original ideas in these areas.

Closed Areas, Social Issues, and Mental Health

It is hardly surprising that our sharpest intrapersonal conflicts occur in closed areas. Conflicts in areas of belief such as sex, religion, and race are not only common but often sufficiently intense to cause severe emotional disturbance. Many newspaper readers have been impressed by the "madness" of individuals who oppose equal rights for Negroes. In areas open to free thought, conflicts are frankly faced and resolved—if not easily, at

[2] By intellectually serious students we do not refer to those grade-grabbers and credit-chasers seeking entrance into a university who seem to abound in the habitat of suburbia.

least without undue tension. But in closed areas, every problem is likely to be troublesome simply because of the barriers to examining it.

During recent decades it has come to be widely recognized among social scientists and mental hygienists that discrepancies in a culture may have an eroding effect on the mental health of its members. We are told that "A well-integrated culture will presumably not produce as many maladjusted personalities as a disintegrated one. Cultures that are full of glaring inconsistencies will produce more than their share of personality difficulties."[3] Therapists who would reach the root causes of the difficulties faced by their patients dare not ignore the data and concepts of social-science disciplines.

Horney in pointing to cultural conflict as the root of certain personality problems has said, "When we remember that in every neurosis there are contradictory tendencies which the neurotic is unable to reconcile, the question arises as to whether there are not likewise certain definite contradictions in our culture, which underlie the typical neurotic conflicts."[4]

Jung observed that "We always find in the patient a conflict which at a certain point is connected with the great problems of society."[5] Since Jung's day we have witnessed the emergence of an entirely new discipline called social psychiatry.

Some cultural conflicts are more basic than others and cut across all our closed areas. Horney perceives three conflicts at the heart of American culture. One is between "competition and success, on the one hand, and brotherly love and humility on the other." Another is to be found in the tendency of our culture to stimulate needs far beyond the point where they could possibly be fulfilled. A third is between the individual's alleged freedom of choice and all the limitations our culture places upon him.[6]

In the first case, the ideology of competition and success pushes one to be aggressive and assertive, willing to shove others out of the way. Christian ideals, on the other hand, insist that one should be unselfish and humble, willing to turn the other cheek, and prepared to accept the legacies of the meek.

The second conflict mentioned by Horney depends partly for its life blood upon the advertising industry. Advertisements encourage conspicuous consumption and keeping up with the Joneses. But great numbers of Americans find it impossible to fulfill the needs created by the advertising industry, and in Horney's words experience "a constant discrepancy be-

---

[3] Francis E. Merrill and H. Wentworth Eldredge, *Culture and Society*, Prentice-Hall, 1952, p. 180.

[4] Karen Horney, The Neurotic Personality of Our Time, Norton, 1937, p. 287.

[5] C.J. Jung, *Two Essays on Analytical Psychology*, Dodd, Mead, 1928, p. 23.

[6] Horney, *op. cit.*, pp. 287–289.

tween their desires and their fulfillment." This conflict would, however, probably exist without any assistance from advertisements. Our general culture stimulates individuals to want what they are not supposed to have. Adolescents, for example, are submitted to a variety of influences all of which seem to have sexual arousal or titillation as their aim. These influences often originate with respectable, nonpornographic, and nonobscene sources. These same adolescents are told, on the one hand, that sex before marriage is immoral, and on the other, that 50 percent of teen-age marriages end in divorce and that they should complete their education before marriage. Movies that deal sensitively and maturely with sexual problems are labeled "adult" and therefore officially off limits to teen-agers. Another type of movie, designed especially for teen and subteen clientele, narrates crudely and without artistic merit stories that involve prurient and lascivious themes. Only a confused culture, or a mad one, would ban the first kind of movie, and actively promote the second. An objective measure of prurience would no doubt find that teen-age movies are among our "dirtiest" and least edifying.

The third major conflict in our culture concerns any individual who learns to believe that "he can get what he wants if he is efficient and energetic." The counterpart of this belief attributes failure in any endeavor to individual rather than societal deficiencies. Individuals who learn this belief also learn that even such basic choices as occupation and mate are hemmed in by a variety of social limitations. Very few Americans are free to decide what their life is to be. The occupations of sons are often limited by the opportunities of fathers. And marital choices continue to be functions of propinquity, social class, and proper religious faith. An individual who is caught somewhere between free will and determinism is likely to waver "between a feeling of boundless power in determining his own fate and a feeling of entire helplessness."

Lynd has elaborated upon Horney's list of conflicts and has mentioned such contradictions as those "between saving and spending; between playing safe and 'nothing ventured, nothing gained'; between 'you've got to look like money in order to make money' and spending your money for the things you really want; between (if you are a woman) having 'brains' and having 'charm'; between things that are 'right in theory' and 'wrong in practice'; between change and stability; between being loyal and 'looking out for Number One'; between being efficient and being human; between being democratic and 'getting to know the right people'." [7]

Not everyone who grows up in a culture of contradictions becomes mentally disturbed. It is true that some authorities feel that, since certain conflicts are central to our culture and tend to be reflected in most per-

---

[7] Robert S. Lynd, *Knowledge For What?*, Princeton University Press, 1948, p. 103.

sonalities, there is a common neurotic type expressive of the times. Whether this is the case or not, there is no doubt that a substantial proportion of Americans—including the most sensitive, responsive, and intelligent—find it very difficult to come to terms with the conflicting pressures put upon them. Hullfish and Smith have argued convincingly that the mental practices of rationalization and compartmentalization are absolutely necessary to thousands of Americans who otherwise would be unable to deny or avoid conflict, and its concomitant heavy load of guilt.[8]

A social-studies education that helped young people to openly and rationally examine their conflicts in beliefs and values within closed areas would probably reduce rather than increase the incidence of neurosis. An intellectually rigorous as well as permissive and non-threatenening examination would enable young people to progress toward solution of their problems of self-esteem, identity, anomie, alienation, and self-actualization, while at the same time acquiring many of those cognitive understandings possessed by social scientists.[9] Although such study of social issues would be desirable at all grade levels, it probably is most feasible in junior and senior high school. By the time students reach junior high school many are capable of the kind of propositional thinking necessary to a certain kind of social understanding.

Capacity to examine ideas in the closed areas depends very much upon the character of early childhood experience. Some homes and elementary schools provide children with a largely emotional basis for believing that certain outlooks are the only proper views of man and society. Many children are crippled mentally by schools and homes which provide them with rigid attitudes that act as blocks to their reflective development. Elementary schools need to decide whether their pupils can understand the big social issues. If it is decided that most of them cannot, then these issues should be omitted from the curriculum. Indoctrination of "right" social attitudes is least justifiable with a clientele that is said to be incapable of understanding the issues. A lack of analysis plus indoctrination of fixed attitudes is almost certain to produce the kind of student who finds it impossible to entertain new ideas.

INTELLECTUAL DEVELOPMENT AND LIFE ADJUSTMENT

A common issue in curriculum development is whether intellectual growth is the only purpose of public education. This issue is sharpened on one side by those who view a mental-hygiene curriculum as an alternative to an intellectual one. We have just experienced a period in the history of

[8] H. Gordon Hullfish and Philip G. Smith, *Reflective Thinking: The Method of Education*, Dodd, Mead, 1961, pp. 54–56.
[9] Louis E. Raths, Merrill Harmin, and Sidney B. Simon, *Values and Teaching* Merrill, 1966. See chaps. 1, 2, 3, and 4 for a significant theory of values.

education marked by stringent criticism of so-called life-adjustment education. This was a kind of education intended to help young people solve
their personal problems. It was attacked by those advocates of subject
matter and rational thinking who saw in it an antiintellectual emphasis.
The charge was not without merit in that much of what passed as life-
adjustment education did neglect the study of ideas. Students would discuss their dating problems without delving into the cognitive dimensions
of such problems. Dating choices of young people are no doubt influenced in part by social-class concepts of which they are not consciously
aware. A life-adjustment education that clarified the role of social class in
the life choices of adolescents would foster both intellectual development
and personal adjustment. It would support free play between affective
and cognitive domains, and in doing so would exemplify a curriculum
cognizant of the unity of man.

It was a mistake for certain critics of life-adjustment education to
create a conflict between intellectual development and personal adjustment. These two educational aims are not only compatible but indivisible.
Any suggestion that neurosis is fertile ground for intellectual activity
probably originates with the observation that many of our most creative
people have been, if not rather mad, at least, not very happy people. It
does not follow that making children unhappy, or paying no attention to
their personal problems, is the best way to develop their intellectual capacities. Neither does it make sense to teach subject matter in a way that
guarantees lack of personal relevance or meaning. Cognition and personal
adjustment are not competing educational goals if we can assume that
personal problems have roots in conflicting concepts, propositions, values,
and ideologies. To mention only one example, if a high-school youth
comes to believe that sex before marriage is immoral, if his sex drive
reaches a peak during his high-school years, if his culture stimulates sexual
interests and responses, if he is encouraged to postpone marriage until he
finishes his education, if his school treats sex as a closed area, and if society places under heavy ban every possible sexual expression ranging
from masturbation to homosexuality, how does he handle his conflicts and
frustrations? In a day and age when monasteries are no longer popular
mountain retreats, he can find solutions and come to terms with himself
and others only by facing, and thinking through, basic conflicts in the
sexual ideology of American culture. This ideology has a history, and the
content of social science bears upon its meaning. A school that would
help him to explore intellectually those beliefs which concern him emotionally would not be cognitively sterile, or psychologically irrelevant.

An attempt to deal with the intellect and its development out of all relationship to conflicting ideologies would be as fruitless as an attempt to

solve the personal problems of life adjustment without serious study of ideas.

Conflict Resolution in Democratic Societies

The method by which culture is transmitted from generation to generation differs from society to society. We can illustrate this generalization by examining how education functions in two contrasting types of societies.

Education in a Modern Totalitarian State. An educational system designed to serve the needs of dictatorship will differ fundamentally from an educational system designed to serve the interests of a democracy. One of the most significant facts of dictatorship, from the standpoint of education, is the existence of a body of doctrine which functions as a national ideology. This group of beliefs may be fairly consistent internally and pervade all areas of the culture. Its central ideas could be relatively unchanging over long periods of time, whether they revolve around racial supremacy or around the beliefs of Marx and Lenin. If the ideology does undergo change, it must first change within the thinking of totalitarian leadership, after which the new ideology is purveyed to the masses through the educational system.

The function of education in a dictatorship is the uncritical transmission of an official belief structure. The subject matter of education is thus predetermined and essentially the same in every school. The method of instruction is likewise uniform; it is the method of prescription and indoctrination. The "correct" beliefs are taught by withholding or slanting evidence. Doubt and reflection are rigorously excluded from classrooms, because in a dictatorship these are the truly subversive influences. It is particularly the case that reflection will be discouraged in the social sciences and moral philosophy.

In any culture, schools must take some stand with respect to how conflict and doubt are to be treated in classrooms. In a dictatorship, schools try to minimize both interpersonal and intrapersonal conflict by teaching an official ideology and by allowing students, so far as possible, to perceive only one side of questions which in a democracy would be regarded as highly controversial. In short, school authorities hope that suppression of free intellectual inquiry will reduce conflict to an innocuous level. Even so, in a dictatorship some conflicts are bound to appear, for many of the same reasons that they appear in any culture. When interpersonal conflicts arise, attempts are made to remove them from sight through use of propaganda and terror. If either interpersonal or intrapersonal conflict appears in the classrooms of a dictatorship, teachers have no alternative but to tell students what to believe and to try to gain assent through use of rewards and punishments.

In summary, a foremost task of education in dictatorships is uncritical transmission of sanctioned features of the culture, achieved by suppressing intelligence and by dealing forcefully with controversy wherever it threatens to unsettle the social order.

Education in a Democratic State. Although a democratic culture does not have an official ideology in the sense that a dictatorship has, it is assumed that, if a democratic society is to survive, there will have to be general agreement among its members as to central values. While peripheral values may remain in flux, a democracy is in peril if its citizens cannot agree on the meaning of core values such as dignity and worth of the individual, freedom, liberty, and equality. If agreement is absent at this level, survival of the society is still possible provided there is agreement on a method of inquiry by which to explore differences in the meaning and truth of propositions and the justifiability of values. In a democratic society the preferred intellectual method, sometimes called the method of intelligence, consists of logic and scientific investigation. If there is failure to establish agreement on core values, conflicts among individuals and groups and disintegration of personalities are likely to reach unmanageable proportions.

Some students of American culture feel that it is approaching a state of possible breakdown and disintegration because of a growing inability to agree on central values. It is thought that in addition to conflict normally attached to dispute over peripheral values, conflict is developing over fundamental ends. We are ceasing to be a community, as this term is used by sociologists.[10]

A challenge now before American education is to help the American people find consensus on the meaning of democracy—but in ways consistent with the requirements of democratic society. To say that the schools of America should teach children the American heritage, or that, whatever is meant by the American heritage, it should be taught to the young as something absolutely true and good, is an oversimplification. Any school in the United States which tries to transmit the cultural heritage uncritically, in the same manner in which officially supported beliefs are transmitted to the young in a dictatorship, finds itself in a difficult position. *There is not one heritage in the United States; there are many heritages.* The competing traditions that to some extent have always

[10] See Joseph K. Hart, *Education in the Humane Community*, Harper & Row, 1951. Also W. O. Stanley, *Education and Social Integration*, Columbia University Press, 1953.

characterized our history and culture have had their conflicts accentuated by an accelerated rate of change during the past century. Uncritical transmission of all of them can do little but compound confusion and intensify conflict.

Consensus building has become synonymous with resolution of conflict. The means used to achieve consensus determine whether our society shall move in authoritarian or democratic directions. The achievement of consensus through reflective thought should mean two things: general agreement among individuals and inner harmony of individual personalities. An apt term for describing the unique task of education in a democracy is "creative resolution of conflict." By this we mean achievement, by disputing persons and by individuals suffering inner turmoil, of "third alternatives," that is, new positions which, although perhaps to some degree compromise competing outlooks, also include genuinely new values which effectively erase conflict and place life on a level of deeper insight. It is assumed that creative resolution of conflict can occur only in an atmosphere which is reflective and in which ego defenses are reduced to a minimum.

In summary, we say that the chief role of education in a democracy is intelligent or critical transmission of cultural heritages, during the course of which disagreements among individuals and incompatibilities in personal outlook are exposed and resolved creatively. Social-studies education gets to the heart of the matter when it recognizes that our many heritages include a totalitarian or authoritarian one. The most troublesome of present issues are over the question of whether we are to become more democratic or more authoritarian in our core values. To become more democratic is to expose closed areas to rational study. To close down further on inquiry in these areas is to move away from our democratic heritage and toward the authoritarianism we delight in denouncing when practiced by foreign powers.

Learning Theories and Classroom Practice

Whether a teacher believes that education can and should foster creative resolution of conflict in problematic and closed areas depends upon his learning theory as well as his social philosophy. Teachers are not always clear on the relevance of learning theory to objectives and classroom practice. A basic source of confusion lies in the fact that the *products* of learning are several in number and appear *on the surface* to differ greatly from each other. We then get different theories for each of the products. Some argue that classical conditioning is the best theory for explanation of attitudes and tastes. Problem solving and concept attainment, it is argued, can best be understood by use of some other theory. Kuhn, for example, believes that conditioning theories are inadequate for explanation of the learning of concepts.[11] It appears that whether any single theory can explain all products of learning or whether one must vary his theory with his product, is a significant point of difference among present-day theorists.

One of the oldest theories of learning is known as *associationism*. This theory holds that "we connect things in memory, in thought, and in all mental life, simply because they were connected in our original experience with them." [12] Although associationism dates as far back as Aristotle, Thomas Brown (writing in the early nineteenth century) gave it its first modern expression. He devised the celebrated "secondary laws of assocation," which have a decidedly modern ring: the principles of (1) duration, (2) liveliness, (3) frequency, and (4) recency. Over the centuries this theory has evolved through behaviorism to present-day connectionist and reinforcement theories. Most of the early laws of association have been adopted by connectionists, but stated now in terms of stimulus-response relationships. The language of psychology changes more easily than its concepts.

An alternative to various theories of connectionism is field psychology. Field psychology incorporates many of the features of early Gestalt, or configurational, psychology. This psychology is markedly similar to the pragmatic philosophy of John Dewey and Boyd Bode. It was Bode who waged heavy warfare in the 1920s against the reflex-arc concept common to biology at that time. Field psychology, instead of viewing learning as the connecting of formerly unrelated stimuli and responses, sees learning as the discovery of meaning in a perceptual field. (This is commonly called insight.) Tested insights may lead to generalizations which enable a learner to behave intelligently in confronting similar situations of the future.

Within the framework of field psychology, learning is always accompanied by *understanding*, or *grasp of meaning*. This is said to be true of all types of learning, whether habits, skills, attitudes, or knowledge. Although most field theorists would not maintain that all learning stems only from problematic situations, they give much more attention to problem solving as a source of learning than do associationist psychologists. According to field theorists, problems are solved by bringing to bear meanings (insights) gained in previous learning situations. But in the process, the earlier meanings are enlarged and refined, so that the learner

[11] Alfred Kuhn, *The Study of Society: A Unified Approach*, Dorsey Press, 1963, pp. 116–118.

[12] Gardner Murphy, *Historical Introduction to Modern Psychology*, Harcourt, Brace & World, 1942, p. 26.

achieves a reconstruction of his cognitive pattern. This type of learning is usually called reflective.

At present, experimental evidence is adduced to support both associationist and field conceptions of learning. In selecting its data, each school of thought has apparently preferred to focus on certain products of learning to the exclusion of others. Associationists have devoted much research to the learning of motor skills and the memorization of verbal associations. Field theorists have given their major attention to concept attainment and problem solving.

It is significant to know that one may control learning experiences in such a way as to emphasize one product of learning over another. Situations may be so arranged that either verbal associations or concepts may be the chief end in view. This does not mean that either of these can be taught in complete isolation from the other. Learning is all of one piece. Even the learning of a mechanical motor skill can be accompanied by change in a student's values or concepts. But the *emphasis* can be thrown toward one or the other, *particularly in subjects like the social studies*. In the social studies, students can *learn to say* what the the teacher requires as correct response, and to the extent that this is all that happens the students are learning a motor skill that may be explained by the laws of associationism. But if students are to learn whether to believe and act upon certain propositions—that is, if they are to *learn that* certain ideas are indeed true—then, field psychology offers better clues as to appropriate classroom practice. Consider, for example, students who have learned to say that prices are determined by the law of supply and demand. Under a teacher who provides repetitive drill and practice as classroom experience, students may successfully learn to repeat by rote the law of supply and demand and yet not know whether all prices, most prices, some prices, or no prices are actually so determined. They have no way of understanding this so-called law, or whether it is indeed a law. Under a teacher who provides classroom experience consistent with a field theory of learning, and who does not emphasize memorization of isolated content, students will have been launched into the concept analysis and empirical investigation necessary to a determination of whether certain prices in their community were actually the result of competitive conditions as per the law of supply and demand.

Teachers who are aware of differences in learning theory can choose to promote one kind of learning over another. Without knowledge of alternatives, choice is impossible. Unfortunately, teachers' colleges give little attention to issues in learning theory. Textbooks in educational psychology, rather than treat learning theory as such, tend to stress classroom application of assumed psychological principles. Principles can be assessed only in terms of a theory. It is also the case that most of the textbooks in educational psychology give slight attention to cognitive objectives such as concept attainment. They stress the kind of mental hygiene that relies upon proper environment rather than intellectual analysis to cure the mental ailments of pupils. Any attention given to learning problems is eclectic in its assumptions, or dominantly connectionist.

The situation in educational psychology is not helped very much by what occurs in education courses other than psychology. In many of their education courses, prospective teachers encounter a philosophy that implies a field psychology; most are not aware that this philosophy is inconsistent with the connectionist psychology they learned in educational psychology courses. Those who are aware of the conflict but who lack a basis for making a choice become victims of ambivalence. They find it impossible to move in any direction without a sense of sin. The upshot, then, is that students of education either fail to learn that there are more or less contradictory explanations of learning, each resting upon different assumptions about human nature, and each having its distinctive educational and social implications, or having learned all this do not see what can be done about it.

PEDAGOGICAL CONFUSION

Suppose a teacher does not understand the educational and social implications of alternative learning theories. What would be the effect upon his classroom practices? We venture the following as predictable consequences:

1. Teaching would not be dominated by clear purpose. Where teachers are not guided by a clearly *understood* and *chosen* theory of learning, we would expect their teaching to suffer from aimlessness. Aimlessness is not the same as planlessness. Teachers without conscious purposes could still develop and follow elaborate plans. These plans could even be prefaced by statements of purpose and still lack real point. Such plans would give themselves away as soon as one got past the initial statements of purpose; not being rooted in an understanding of learning theory, the procedures called for would probably not bear much relationship to the stated purposes. Like some insurance policies, everything would be all right until one got to the fine print. Nor does aimlessness imply lack of activity. We may imagine classes in which everyone worked diligently, even breathlessly, toward an end which escaped both teachers and students.

2. Students would be engaged in busywork much of the time. By busywork is meant the pursuit of tasks which are not clearly related to purpose. Busy work is the inevitable result of teaching which is not consciously purposeful. There would be textbook recitation in which arbitrary learnings were required, current-events periods in which students read news reports they did not understand or relate to the purposes of the

course, films which were irrelevant to anything else the class was studying, and workbook assignments given for the purpose of keeping students
quiet while at their desks.

3. Emphasis on *techniques* would dominate classroom practice. By a
technique we mean a practice having to do with skill in performance. A
technique is supposed to foster smoothness and efficiency of execution. A
technical emphasis in education means that teachers give a great deal of
attention to what has sometimes been called "method," without corresponding attention to purpose. Put another way, teachers devote much
time to developing a "bag of tricks."

No matter what conception of learning dominated teaching, firm
mastery of technique would be desirable. But in a situation where no
clearly formulated learning theory dominates teaching, an inordinate
emphasis on techniques sometimes fills a vacuum. Teachers who lack a
clear sense of purpose may make a fetish of tricks of execution. One type
of content serves as well as any as a medium on which to practice their
techniques.

4. Without conscious intent teachers would stress repetitive drill in
their classes. An associationist outlook has historically favored this approach. It has called for memorization of verbal associations relatively
low in meaning (the so-called textbook-recitation method as traditionally
conceived). Most present-day teachers have been schooled in this sort of
environment on elementary, high-school, and college levels. Teachers
without a clearly formulated alternative are likely to drift into an associationist practice, and any formal exposure to associationism will almost
certainly reinforce any such drift.

Under this kind of drift and influence, teachers concentrate on teaching a number of verbal associations usually referred to as "right answers,"
or "the facts." Students, for instance, are taught that Columbus discovered America in 1492, that Andrew Jackson invented the spoils
system, that slavery was a major cause of the Civil War, and that the first
colonists came to America to escape religious persecution. These responses are retained until they have served their purpose at examination
time and are then discarded. It is difficult for any teacher to break from
this pattern without a clearly understood alternative before him. So long
as educational psychologists teach associationism, teachers are unlikely to
change from the traditional format of recitation and drill. Yet associationists regularly decry this traditional concept of teaching.

5. Social-studies education would ignore value conflicts in the culture.
Uninfluenced by a clear conception of learning, teachers who encountered a conflict in the classroom would lack the necessary methodology
for dealing with it. They could fall back on an indoctrinative approach
which is implied in associationist theory. But they might have been

sufficiently influenced by their education courses to find this method of
handling controversy unpalatable. They could, of course, try letting
students "hash over" problems in a highly permissive atmosphere; but,
without teacher guidance based upon an understanding of how students
learn and upon the nature of democratic education, such a class would
not be likely to resolve value differences.

The upshot would almost certainly be that, lacking a satisfactory way
of dealing with controversial issues, teachers would simply stop trying.
They would stick to content in textbooks, workbooks, course outlines,
and similar sources of noncontroversial content. And they would try to
confine what controversy they permitted to enter students' thinking to
peripheral rather than central issues.

6. Finally, it can be expected that attempts to be "progressive" would
meet with failure. In most teachers' colleges and university departments
of education a great deal of pressure is put on teachers to adopt modern
or progressive practices. Since not to try to practice the ideas associated
with leading figures such as John Dewey, Boyd Bode, or Jerome Bruner
is to be labeled old-fashioned, most teachers do seriously try—at least to
some degree.

Teachers who are not well grounded in a field theory of learning are
likely to allow their attempts at "progressive" teaching to degenerate into
some form of rote memory work. Without a solid base in a field theory
of learning, those who claim to favor a problem-centered curriculum, a
democratic atmosphere, and a stress on thinking as a way of understanding social controversy would have difficulty in seeing the real point of
many potentially constructive measures and little chance of extricating
students when the new practices flounder in aimless confusion.

The Issue Drawn

The issue posed in this chapter may be sharpened by reviewing briefly
what has been said. Two features of American culture should be understood by every teacher of the social studies: the widespread presence of
conflict and the existence of areas largely closed to rational inquiry.
These two aspects of the culture are closely related. In closed areas, conflicts are more intense and more difficult to resolve than in areas relatively
open to scientific inquiry.

The decisive differences between modern totalitarian and democratic
societies lie in the methods of handling conflict and in the relative number
of areas closed to rational thought. Again, these two are related. A culture
which is consistently democratic resolves conflict in all areas reflectively,

whereas a totalitarian culture tries to suppress conflict and to preserve its many closed areas.

The present is a time of moral crisis in that large numbers of persons in some nominally democratic nations have come to question certain ideas traditionally associated with democracy. They are afraid of their own creed. This fear shows primarily in a tendency to reject the method of critical inquiry in the realm of social affairs. There seems instead to be a growing disposition to flee to some sort of authoritarian principle in areas of pressing conflict.

The schools are implicated in this crisis. In any society, the schools serve as an arena in which typical methods of handling conflict are perfected and demonstrated. In a democracy, the schools must remain a sanctuary for creative resolution of conflict, which in turn requires the practice of critical inquiry in a democratic environment.

How well the schools discharge their function of perfecting and demonstrating the method of intelligence depends in part on how well teachers understand alternative learning theories. At present, teachers are not learning from teachers' colleges or university departments of education that they have a choice between the kind of learning that arises from reflection and the kind that arises from recitation and drill of the most repetitive and mechanical type. They have not come to see the social and educational relevance of the kind of teaching that emphasizes the reflective testing of acquired beliefs and values.

The existence of closed areas coupled with a connectionist theory of learning has resulted in uncritical transmission of values and beliefs from one generation to another. It is not possible for this practice to continue indefinitely. The growth of science, the spread of the scientific spirit, and the growth of democracy imply that we bring many of our traditions under critical scrutiny. The emergence of a field theory of learning gives impetus to this emergent spirit of social criticism. The many inconsistencies involved in beliefs and values within closed areas as well as a tendency for certain beliefs to clash with facts established by modern, scientific disciplines such as medicine, psychiatry, and social science, mean that increasingly, as Myrdal predicted more than twenty years ago, beliefs in these areas come under attack. Such attack against old and honored belief means, too, that many of our traditional values have come to be questioned, even the values of democracy. This criticism of traditional values is likely to continue with only temporary setbacks. The attempts by McCarthyism or Birchism to label subversive any criticism of traditional values illustrate the kind of temporary setback that has as its only consequence a fostering of greater degrees of moral uncertainty, confusion, and cynicism.

The process of extending the method of scientific inquiry into closed areas seems likely to continue. If it does, old, uncritically accepted values will lose much of their force. This does not mean that values will be rejected simply because they are old, but those that survive reflection are likely to have new meanings. New postures more critical even toward newly developed norms will prevail. In short, we could have a future with fewer closed areas—which is the same as to say that people would have become more reflective and democratic.

To reach such a condition involves a great deal of stress and strain. The birth of a more open-minded approach to issues in closed areas will not be easy. Many persons will feel that they can find security only by destroying freedom of thought and by turning to an authoritarian pattern of living as an escape from the troubles of transition.

Stated, then, in its barest form the issue we have tried to develop is this: American society is in *turmoil, transition,* and *crisis.* The resolution of great conflicts can go either way—democratic or authoritarian. We think it is more likely to go democratic. But there is nothing inevitable about the survival of freedom.

Teachers of social studies can help to tip the scales in one direction or another by the kind of learning they choose to promote. Choice, not drift, should determine our future. Learning which consists primarily of conditioned responses is not consistent with the needs of democratic citizenship. Although to be expected in any dictatorship, its presence in any American school is an anomaly and a mockery. Learning in the associationist tradition is quite suited to the requirements of a totalitarian state, where closed areas are held inviolate and conflicts are erased or suppressed through an education based upon propaganda and indoctrination. The democratic alternative is much greater emphasis upon the development of higher thought processes, with all that this implies for reflective examination of critical social issues.

DISCUSSION QUESTIONS AND EXERCISES

1. It is generally assumed that Communism is a major threat to the survival of democratic values. If this assumption is correct how do you explain the fact that study and discussion of Communism is widely feared and opposed in America? What assumptions are made by those who appear to feel that survival of democracy requires that Communism remain a "closed area"?
2. Would there be any closed areas in a fully democratic society? Would the ideas of democracy in themselves constitute a closed area in the sense that people would be discouraged from critical study of them? Do we have to indoctrinate something when we teach?
3. How do you react to the claim that most Americans are confused in their

beliefs and values? Are they more confused than at any other time in our history? Do we face a moral crisis in America?

4. Compile a list of subjects which in your community are not freely discussed in the public or private schools. Could any of these topics be discussed in classes taught by courageous, fair, and objective teachers? Should all these topics be studied and discussed by high-school students?

5. In what ways have attitudes in closed areas changed in your lifetime?

6. Why do we have associationist teaching in the schools of a democratic society?

REFERENCES

BIGGE, MORRIS, *Learning Theories for Teachers*, New York, Harper & Row, 1964.

A comparative study of learning theories, and what each means for classroom teaching. The treatment of field theory is particularly systematic.

BODE, BOYD H., *Conflicting Psychologies of Learning*, Boston, Heath. 1929.

This old and out-of-print volume is one of the best introductions to learning theory. It compares favorably with Bigge's more recent work. Bode later treated the same problem in *How We Learn*, which is a revision of *Conflicting Psychologies*. In the opinion of many, the revised work is not as good as the original, but serious students will want to read both works.

DEWEY, JOHN, *Democracy and Education*, New York, Macmillan, 1937.

This classic is now available in a paperback edition. See Chapter 7 for a non-political definition of democracy. Two criteria are set forth as basic to the meaning of democracy.

GRIFFIN, ALAN, *Freedom, American Style*, New York, Holt, Rinehart & Winston, 1940.

This book, too, is out of print, a fact that should deter no one from borrowing it from a good library. Brilliant writing is organized around a definition of teaching and a study of freedom in a democratic society.

HORNEY, KAREN, *The Neurotic Personality of Our Time*, New York, Norton, 1937.

Discusses the cultural basis of neurosis.

KUHN, ALFRED, *The Study of Society: A Unified Approach*, Homewood, Illinois, Dorsey Press, 1963.

An attempt to synthesize several social-science disciplines for the purpose of studying society. Has some interesting material on concept formation, concept attainment, and learning theory. Good discussion of the nature of science and scientific method.

LYND, ROBERT S., *Knowledge For What?* Princeton, Princeton University Press, 1948.

Deals with cultural patterns in America, and the role of social science in American culture. This book is famous for its concept of cultural discrepancy, and the need to study the inconsistencies of a culture in transition.

LYND, ROBERT S. and HELEN M., *Middletown*, New York, Harcourt, Brace & World, 1929.

LYND, ROBERT S. and HELEN M., *Middletown In Transition*, Harcourt, Brace & World, 1937.

Two studies of cultural conflict and transition in a typical American community. Students will find these books useful in their descriptions of conflicts in the closed areas.

CHAPTER 2

Development of Insight

THE FIELD theory defines learning as development of insight. What does this theory say about the nature of insight and how it is acquired? How would a teacher develop insight in the social studies? What is the difference between good insight and bad?

Perception and Insight

All learning is rooted in perception, and experiments in perception undoubtedly support field assumptions. A person's understanding of his environment, hence his capacity to learn, is based upon his interpretation of what comes to him through his senses. Experiments in perception suggest that perceptions are not literal descriptions of an environment. When a person perceives, he does not merely "photograph" what is there to be seen. Each act of perception has its creative element. What a person "sees" seems to be a product of at least three factors: (1) the influence of past experience, (2) one's purposes at the time of perception, and (3) the object or process in the environment toward which perception is directed.

It follows that it is rare for two persons ever to have the same perception. Each may give the same name to what he perceives, but the *meaning* of what is seen is different for every individual. Kelley and Rasey say it well: "When we behold a tree, we see it in the light of all our tree experience. The plainsman sees one thing, the woodsman another. No two people see precisely the same thing, and in no individual case does perception actually correspond with the tree. It is an interpretation made by the individual in the light of his experiences and purposes." [1]

In short, we see in each situation what we are in the habit of seeing and what we want to see, and not merely what is "really there." Another way of putting it is to say that we see what we are able to see. Good teaching aims to improve our perception by helping us to see what our habits and purposes prevent us from seeing.

[1] Earl Kelley and Marie Rasey, *Education and the Nature of Man*, Harper & Row, 1952, p. 32.

Although most interpretations of the physical features of our everyday world may be presumed to be relatively accurate, when we move into areas where intense purpose and strong emotional sets characterize behavior, perception becomes increasingly undependable. In closed areas, we tend to be governed by habit and desire rather than by "the facts." Confronted with complex evidence, we select evidence supporting beliefs to which we are attached. Teachers of social studies frequently note that their students have beliefs and attitudes on social issues which cause them to make highly subjective and, from the standpoint of a social scientist, often inaccurate interpretations of factual data. Many students find it almost impossible to perceive (i.e., admit as evidence) facts which to a teacher are conclusive and above dispute.

The teacher of social studies who says, "My students will have to learn some facts before they can do any thinking in this course," is revealing a poor understanding of perception. It is nearer to the truth to say that students must do a great deal of thinking before they can acquire a fact. Even professional historians now seem to agree that there are no facts without interpretation.

In a given situation, the perceptions of two or more individuals, although never the same, may approach a common meaning, and on this basis they are able to get along. Sometimes at crucial moments individual perceptions diverge so that an impassable gulf is created between perceived worlds; communication fails, and rational behavior disappears. This is particularly likely to occur in closed areas.

One may come to doubt his own perceptions. When this happens, he does not know what to believe. If a situation is unclear—that is, in any way puzzling or confusing—a person tries to make sense out of it. Let us imagine a boy who is trying to learn how to fly-cast. He takes his rod to his backyard and begins to practice. He finds that every time he pitches his backcast forward, his line, leader, and fly strike him on the back of the neck or head. Sometimes they wrap around his neck. He keeps trying, rather aimlessly varying stance and arm motion. Nothing seems to work, and he becomes more and more puzzled as to a solution. Suddenly, he realizes that on the swing he is pointing the tip of the rod inward. He begins to concentrate on keeping it vertical. His next cast is a success. He has learned that one must swing his rod in a vertical arc if he is to control his cast.

Discovery of a possible solution to a problem is what field theorists mean by a hypothetical insight. It is a sensed course of action with reference to a goal and a confronting situation. It is a sensed or imagined "way through" or "answer." This meaning for insight is not the one most commonly employed by laymen. We often hear it said that someone is a man of "insight—perhaps of "great insight." This usage assumes that insight is "wisdom." A person of insight, in this sense, is one who knows a lot and knows it well. His solutions to problems are the correct ones. In contrast, our use of the term does not imply wisdom or its absence. An insight may be correct or incorrect, and the aim of democratic education is to improve insights by submitting them to thoughtful examination. The boy in our illustration had a correct insight, and therefore added to his store of knowledge. Moreover, he had a simple and direct test of his insight which enabled him easily to ascertain its correctness. Many of our "solutions" to problems, insightful though they be, often turn out to be wrong, that is, not solutions at all. These bad insights will be cast aside by rational persons.

Learning how to fly-cast involves mastery of a motor skill. Ordinarily, teachers of social studies, unless they become embroiled in the perplexities of driver training, are not concerned with the teaching of this type of motor skill. Student perplexities more commonly revolve around concepts, beliefs, and values. In this kind of problem solving it is usually not easy for the learner to distinguish between good insights and poor ones.

INSIGHT IN THE SOCIAL STUDIES

Many insights are "caught" before words come to express them, and sometimes an insight is never given verbal expression. It remains a sense of pattern, particularly when learning is primarily motor as in the case of the boy learning to fly-cast. A person may improve his golf swing by getting the "feel" of it without necessarily being able to describe just how he has changed his procedure.

Much of students' experience in the social studies is as vicarious as words can make it. If a student's social insight is to be tested, then it must be "put into words"; it cannot always be tested by direct action.

Insights put into words are called *hypotheses*. A hypothesis is the statement of a proposed solution to a problem. Implicit in it is an if-then relationship. All hypotheses may be regarded as insights. Those that pass the test of evidence are said to be true insights. They add to one's store of knowledge.

A teacher of social studies may set the stage for development of insight by asking a question that identifies a discrepancy in belief. He may ask: "Why do some of the people who believe in free enterprise support fair-trade laws?" This question will not make sense to any student who lacks an understanding of the concepts, free enterprise and fair-trade laws. If this understanding is lacking, the teacher will have to explain the concepts in one way or another. Once a student understands the concepts, he will be as perplexed by the inconsistency as his teacher wants him to be. The student will wonder why people who want competition seek to destroy it. His learning goal is to understand why persons who claim allegiance to free enteprise (defined as a system of free, competitive pricing) support retail price maintenance, and indeed, many other forms of price-fixing.

He cannot solve this rather complex problem without recourse to a number of previously verified insights. In order to keep our illustration simple, let us examine only one of the dozens of possible hypotheses which might be adduced to explain the apparent contradiction. Suppose the student thinks of this explanation: *Retail-price-maintenance laws do not effectively prevent free pricing.* How did he get this idea? Let us assume that it is original to him. Even so, there must be a particular background on which to draw; otherwise, he would not be able to imagine such an explanation. Perhaps he has had experiences with merchants in which they have evaded legal price maintenance by granting generous trade-in allowances. He has generalized from these experiences, assuming that it is a rule of doing business to grant such price concessions. Perhaps he has also had experiences with mail-order houses whose products were not fair-traded but yet were generally available. To him, merchants are persons who evade fair-trade laws or persons whose merchandise is not covered by fair-trade legislation. We see, therefore, how it was possible for him to achieve the above insight. Whether it is a good insight or not depends on two things. Does it have the support of all relevant evidence, and is it pertinent to the discrepancy he wishes to explain? These two questions can become one: Will his idea, if it turns out to be true, explain or remove the contradiction?

Education has been defined by John Dewey and others as the reconstruction of experience. The foregoing illustration shows how this may occur. If the student, upon testing his insight, decides it is a poor one, his conception of what merchants do will change. If he finds support for his insight, his present conception of merchants will be fortified and perhaps expanded—merchants will be *persons who prevent fair-trade laws from stifling competition.*

TESTING AN INSIGHT

There is a tendency to generalize insights. When a person has an insight, he is likely to assume that it will work in similar situations in the future. Suppose, for example, that in studying a particular situation I hypothesize, "Jerry became a shoplifter because he felt unwanted by his parents." If this hypothesis stands the test in Jerry's case, then I am likely to reason further, "Boys who feel unwanted at home may become thieves." Of course, this generalization is *suggested*, not *warranted*, by the single case. Before generalizations become reliable, it is usually necessary that they rest upon a number of specific cases, all suggesting the same conclusion. Moreover, human events are likely to have multiple causes. Not all thievery can be attributed to parental rejection.

Dependable generalizations are usually products of considerable experience. Further, they tend to change and develop with the course of experience, evolving continuously in the direction of greater usefulness as analytical tools and guides to action.

Tested generalizations have the character of *rules*, *principles*, or *laws*, and are assumed to be valid in any future situations similar to those in which they were tested. It helps to promote the testing of generalizations to cast them in the form of if-then statements. Ordinarily, generalizations are made as simple declarative sentences. For example, the declaration, "An increase in the quantity of money is likely to produce a rise in prices" could also be phrased as, "If the quantity of money in circulation is increased, then, prices are likely to rise." An if-then statement suggests the operations to be performed, and therefore throws emphasis upon experimental tests.

There are two basic ways in which a learner may test an insight. First, he may check it against the results of experience. An insight may be considered supported if it harmonizes all the relevant data known to the learner. There are inherent difficulties in this sort of test, stemming from the fact that each person is unique and therefore interprets previous experience differently. What one person construes as harmonizing support for an insight may be thought by another to cast doubt upon it. Tests based wholly upon referring a hypothesis to "remembered facts" are highly subjective, and not always easily communicable from one person to another. The influence of individual prejudice is reduced when this kind of subjective test is performed by an entire class in the social studies.

An experimental test is more significant. The aim of an experimental test is to see whether, when an insight is acted upon, the predicated results occur. The if-then relationship implied by an insight sets the course of action. Since the pattern of action and its consequences may be described and similar courses of action tried by other persons, an experimental test is often easily communicable to others. This is not to say that we may not communicate our procedure when we refer a hypothesis to the previous facts of experience, but only that experimental tests, by and large, are more objectively communicable. An experimental test constitutes an operational definition of insight. It is the method preferred by science today, although scientific workers commonly use both historical and experimental tests, checking the results of one against the other.

In a social-studies classroom both tests are used when an idea is tested through use of any data that students can recall from experience, plus any additional data they may acquire from research activities.

If a given insight successfully deduces the data of past experience and predicts future outcomes, that insight is true and we have dependable knowledge.

It may be useful at this point to distinguish between intelligence and wisdom. Intelligence refers to acting with foresight, or with regard to the future. An intelligent act is designed to achieve a given end. Wisdom, on the other hand, stems from possession of a store of tested insights. As the product of experience, it represents achievement. The insights of a wise individual are more likely than those of the unwise to have the predicted results. A person may be intelligent and unwise; but he could not be wise and unintelligent; although someone with only moderate intelligence, might in time acquire a good deal of wisdom.

All that we have said about insights and the testing of them should be accompanied by two warnings. To act with foresight involves an act of faith. This is so because generalizations are never true in an absolutistic sense. When we act upon a tested insight, the probability is *high* that a given consequence will follow. But we wish to emphasize the probability character of any generalization. Even in the most exact sciences, laws are now regarded only as probabilities.

The second warning has to do with the nature of experimental tests in the social studies. It should not be assumed that we refer only to controlled experimentation as practiced in the physical sciences. Nagel, in arguing for the possibility of a social science, has developed the concept of controlled *investigation* as a meaning for experiment. Controlled investigations, in his judgment, can produce knowledge that is as reliable as that acquired from controlled experiments. An exact science such as astronomy relies upon controlled investigation as a research technique. One does not run controlled experiments with the universe.[2]

The Continuity of Learning

The first learning of an infant, although we know it to be insightful, involves considerable fumbling. As learning progresses, the amount of fumbling decreases. As a child's store of tested insights increases, the comprehensibility of his world also increases. By the time of adulthood, problems are often solved quickly and smoothly by drawing upon tested insights.

Learning is to be regarded, then, as a chain affair—one insight leading to another, the latter leading to still another, and so on, *ad infinitum*. The idea of learning as continuity suggests that social-studies teachers who wish students to gain insights must build on the insights they already possess. Students can learn that their existing beliefs and knowledges are inadequate as means for attaining worthwhile ends, and ways in which

[2] Ernest Nagel, *The Structure of Science*, Harcourt, Brace & World, 1961, pp. 450–459.

their attitudes, beliefs, and knowledges may be confused, mutually contradictory, or poorly grounded. They are thereby motivated to re-examine their cognitive structures, in which process they will presumably enlarge and refine their background.

It is necessary to emphasize how important it is for teachers to move learners to ever-higher levels of insight. A single act of thought may begin with reconsideration of a particular belief or item of knowledge; it may end with affirmation or rejection or modification of this same belief or knowledge. But in the learning process, additional data are evaluated; new facts come to the attention of the learner. His store of tested beliefs expands. He "knows more" in the sense both of possessing additional quantities of material, factual and conceptual, and of gaining greater depth of understanding. Bayles has this same idea in mind when he says that teaching should begin with a child's *world of insight* and should seek progressive expansion of that world in the direction of encompassing a child's *world of effect*. The world of effect is that part of his environment which impinges upon him. It includes not only the local environment but also certain aspects of world and national scenes. It includes social forces of which he is not in the least aware. It takes in all aspects of the environment which he needs to understand in order to live with maximum intelligence. In contrast, his world of insight is limited to what he is able to perceive and understand at a given level of intellectual development. It is probable that no one ever achieves a world of insight that completely encompasses his world of effect.[3]

Unfortunately, social-studies teachers in the past have often disregarded a child's world of insight and have begun his education with study of a world of effect which to him was remote if not entirely incomprehensible. In so doing, they have used materials which the students felt to be completely unrelated, or but insignificantly related, to their current beliefs, values, attitudes, and habits. Such teachers may refer to all classroom discussion as the "pooling of student ignorance." It is not to be wondered that their teaching has often been inconsequential.

INSIGHTS AS TOOLS OF TRANSFER

A theory of transfer is implicit in the theory of learning which we are advancing. Viewed historically, the theory of transfer most compatible with our theory of learning is that of Charles H. Judd. Judd asserted that transfer is a function of generalization. If a student generalizes a learning experience by subsuming it under a rule or principle, then, carrying it over to future and somewhat different situations is possible. Judd's con-

---

[3] Ernest E. Bayles, *Theory and Practice of Teaching*, Harper & Row, 1950, p. 119.

ception is now regarded by some as inadequate because he neglected the role of insight and purpose in learning. He assumed that, if a confronting situation is favorable, transfer is automatic. Yet there is no reason to suppose that transfer will occur unless a student has sufficient insight to see how he may serve his goal by applying some known principle.[4]

Let us imagine a situation identical in all significant respects with earlier situations in which a rule or principle was discovered and tested. For example, a student has learned that if a merchant stages a succession of going-out-of-business sales, there is good reason to suspect that his "sale-priced" items are not real bargains. Any time in the future that this student finds a merchant who conducts several such sales, he will, without particular reflection, apply the rule he has learned and govern his behavior accordingly. Of course, if such a procedure is to be wise, the student should ascertain beyond question that the circumstances are essentially the same as those under which he validated the rule. If this requires investigation, then, we cannot refer to the situation as nonreflective.

Fortunately, many types of situations occur repeatedly in essentially similar form. The meaning of such situations has become sufficiently stabilized to be taken for granted; we say that the situation and its meaning occur simultaneously. For instance, a motorist enters a busy thoroughfare from a side road. This situation means "danger," and it calls forth without protracted reflection the rule "Stop, look both ways before proceeding," together with appropriate action. It is relatively standardized situations of this sort which make habits possible. A habit is nothing more than skillfully executed application of a rule (often involving motor behavior) in a situation wherein invocation of the rule will help a person achieve a goal. Habits are not to be regarded as automatic or blindly and compulsively repetitive. They are precise adjustments to specific situations; they are products of tested insight. If a changed situation requires revised insight, adjustments which have never been made before, actions change accordingly. In this sense, a habit does not always represent an action that has been performed before. Habits at any given time are functions of a psychological field and are thus rooted in the requirements of the present.

A disposition to reflect may be a habit. (The habit of thinking reflectively is undoubtedly the most valuable habit which students can be helped to develop.) Given a situation in which reflection provides the quickest and easiest way to achieve a goal, one who has previously gained insights as to the role and method of reflection will reflect without stopping to debate whether he should. If a goal can be reached successfully without reflection, he will not stop to reflect; he will reach the goal in the easiest and most direct way which he senses or sees.

[4] Bayles, *ibid.*, pp. 96–98.

Application without modification of tested insights in order to reach a goal is the part of wisdom, provided this is actually the easiest way to reach the goal. If, however, the confronting situation is dissimilar at crucial points from the situations in which an insight was originally tested and found good, it is highly unwise to apply that insight. Because situations are seldom alike in all important respects, even the best of tested insights must be adjusted as they are applied to a particular situation. Insights undergo continuous test and modification, if a person has the habit of coming at life reflectively. We learn in order to continue learning.

The Role of Facts in Learning

We have noted that insight leads to generalization. Unless generalization occurs, insight can have little transfer value. Learning which cannot function in making a person's behavior wiser is futile. Teaching, if it is not to be a waste of effort, must lead to generalization.

Discrete or single insights or items of information do not by themselves have meaning or usefulness. It can mean little to a student to memorize a statement such as "Aaron Burr killed Alexander Hamilton in a duel," unless its connection with some *general principle* or *rule* is made explicit. A fact can function in thought (reflection) only when it comes to have the character of evidence—that is, the quality of supporting or casting doubt upon some general idea. The most important aim of social-studies education in a democracy is to help students acquire a store of tested social theory, or body of principles, relevant to contemporary social issues and beliefs.

Assertions that cannot be made to function as evidence in supporting some insight or its implied general rule are *arbitrary statements* or *arbitrary associations*. Philosophers and other students of inquiry have called them insignificant facts as distinguished from data that are significant for purposes of theory building. They lack the character of data or evidence. This means that they must remain largely isolated, set apart, and discontinuous from a learner's world of action and belief.

There is no question, of course, but that arbitrary statements can be learned. We know that students do learn them, often great numbers of them. If it serves the purposes of a student to memorize arbitrary, nontransferable associations, he can do so—provided that they make some sense to him. Even nonsense syllables can be memorized. Experiments show, however, that such syllables cannot be memorized unless the learner sees or imposes upon them some kind of pattern. Likewise, a sentence such as, "Robespierre was an important figure in the French Revolution," may be committed to memory by a student who understands, however vaguely, the meaning of some of the words and has a nebulous sense of Robespierre as a man in a revolution.

It is probable that even learning of this kind produces change in insights, but not in the insights which teachers hope to communicate. It is sometimes claimed that arbitrary associations may gain significance after they are memorized. But their immediate significance is likely to lie in their being seen as instruments by which to "pass tests," "win diplomas," or gain some other goal unrelated to the literal content of the statements themselves. Students may even form the insight that schools are places where significant questions and beliefs are meticulously avoided. When individual teachers ask significant questions, these students have to reconsider their conception of a school.

The claim that students may later discover in memorized statements connotations not seen at the time of memorization, makes relevant a discussion of the *background misconception*. Teachers commonly assume that students must acquire background information before they can be expected to think or to test their insights. They conceive of the mind as a kind of container, into which discrete facts may be poured to be stored. When needed at some later time as grounds for generalization, these facts may be sorted quickly and appropriate ones extracted for use in thinking. In short, it is assumed that one may learn facts at one time, and generalize from them at another. It is doubtful that any pedagogical claim is less tenable than this one.

Facts memorized solely for future use, in isolation from their use in present thinking, are seldom retained for very long, and their transfer value is close to nil. When they serve their immediate purpose of securing teacher approval, they are quickly forgotten. The fact that forgotten facts can be relearned in less time than it took to learn them for the first time is a relevant observation only if we intend to keep students in school situations forever.

The social-studies curriculum, as it is now constituted, largely consists of factual content that is irrelevant to any generalizations that students might bring with them to school. Much textbook space is devoted to descriptive matter consisting largely of detached or isolated facts. If the facts occasionally bear upon generalizations of any sort, the generalizations are likely to encompass matters which are difficult, if not impossible, to relate to attitudes and beliefs held by the students. Particularly, it is uncommon to find factual data or generalizations that throw any light on the meanings of student beliefs, values, and concepts in the closed areas.

Fortunately, many students do a great deal of thinking without teacher stimulation or guidance. Many students can and do incorporate facts into their thinking, when they see relevance, and in ways not understood by their teachers. Students learn in some situations in spite of textbooks and teachers, and the mental processes by which they learn are quite different from those which their teachers assume to occur.

To summarize, there is only one role which facts can play in meaningful learning: to function as evidence. If they do not, they may perhaps be memorized and retained for a while, but their meaning and future usefulness will be slight.

READING AND THE LEARNING PROCESS

We have described learning as a process by which a person in an unclear confronting situation seeks interpretations of the situation which will enable him to cope with it. A learning experience involves the kind of interaction between a person and his environment which transforms both. The environment changes in its meaning as the learner acquires new rules by which to respond to it.

John Dewey on occasion claimed that learning as insight arose from problematic situations. He defined such situations in these terms: "Unless there is something doubtful, the situation is read off at a glance; it is taken in on sight; i.e., there is merely perception, recognition, not judgment. . . . But if it suggests, however vaguely, different meanings, rival possible interpretations, there is some *point at issue*, some *matter at stake*. Doubt takes the form of . . . controversy within the mind. Different sides compete for a conclusion in their favor. . . . Every judgment proceeds from some such situation." [5]

Does this theory imply that students do not learn from reading unless what they read supplies ideas or data useful for understanding some problem? Suppose that a group of students reads that twenty-seven babies starved to death in their city during the past year. Have they learned anything? The information is new to them, and it will be seen as useful information by anyone for whom understanding his community is a learning goal. There are many items of information not in our possession, and for which we feel no particular need. But as soon as any of these items are brought to our attention we see instantly their relevance to a generalized need to be better informed. A great deal of information is no doubt acquired in just this way. How long it is retained must depend upon something more crucial, however, than a need to be informed. The existence of this generalized need does not imply, however, that any or all information is welcome. Students who read widely, for example, are not alike in respect to what they acquire or retain. It is even possible for a student to read many pages of information without retaining anything at all. Very likely he retains only information that impresses him; and he is probably impressed most by information that supports or refutes one of his more firmly held convictions.

[5] John Dewey, *How We Think*, Heath, 1933, p. 121.

As we have stated before, a field theory of learning is concerned with the *meaning* of facts, and individuals can vary widely in their perceptions and interpretations. Some students may even perceive as a fact what others reject as ungrounded opinion. Is it a fact that twenty-seven babies starved to death last year? Or is this an opinion circulated by those who want to cast our community in a bad light? Were these deaths preventable? Or inevitable? What can be done toward reducing the incidence of infant deaths? Can anything be done? Should anything be done? Would policies for reducing infant deaths have other consequences, some of which might be worse than infant deaths? Obviously, the total meaning of any item of information is open to dispute. It is the task of a social-studies class to select the most valid meanings for the facts confronting them.

It is important to the teaching of social understanding that a teacher know how a student responds to a given fact, whether that fact is encountered in a reading assignment, or in some other form. Does the student accept as fact only that information that supports what he already believes? How does he react to a fact that conflicts with his convictions? Does he reject its truth, or wonder about the adequacy of his beliefs?

If a teacher can use information to create and resolve problems, the information that is learned will usually be better understood, longer remembered, and more functional in students' lives. Provided that problems are not so intense and formidable as to produce neurotic responses, the more keenly a problem is felt the more highly motivated students will be, and the better the quality of learning that takes place.

The learning "problems" commonly presented in social-studies textbooks, courses of study, unit plans, and workbooks are problems only to the person preparing the material, if to him. It is not unusual to read a list of "problems" such as the following:

To learn about the public utility companies of your community.
To see how many articles devoted to farming and rural life appear in the local newspaper.
To find out how many ways there are to send money from one city to another.
To find out what instructions are given to Boy Scouts for the protection of forests.
To learn more facts about life insurance.
To determine the advantages and disadvantages of good roads.[6]

It is unlikely that any of these would actually be a problem for students. A problem is personal and intimate, and cannot be transferred easily and directly from one person to another simply by saying that it

[6] These "problems" come from an actual list brought to the authors' attention.

exists. Each problem "belongs" to someone. This is not to say that many persons may not share the same problem; they often do. But each person in the group must feel the problem to be of significance to him personally as well as to others; otherwise, no problem exists for him. Problems vary in intensity, of course—some create but a mild tickle; others cause an impelling itch.

The most impelling problems appear only when a student feels that a currently held belief is somehow in jeopardy. The tendency in education to label the most nonproblematic activities and projects "problems" stems from the associationist tradition in psychology, and evidences a misunderstanding of what a problem is. Problem solving was never well understood by the older associationist psychologists.

The intensity of felt problems rises sharply as beliefs and attitudes of students become involved. *The most effectual learning emerges from situations where cherished beliefs or attitudes are felt to be at stake.* In such situations the principle of continuity of learning is always operative. It is this type of situation which the authors recommend as most desirable for learning in the social studies, and it is toward achievement and exploitation of this type of situation that most of the rest of this book is directed. The recommended chronological progress of this pedagogy may be diagramed as follows, and this schematization, since it portrays learning typical of the most effectual teaching in the social studies, will be assumed throughout the book:

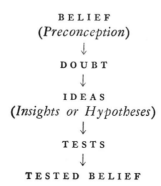

BELIEF
(*Preconception*)
↓
DOUBT
↓
IDEAS
(*Insights or Hypotheses*)
↓
TESTS
↓
TESTED BELIEF

Conflict and Consistency

It is essential, at this point, to show the bearing of intrapersonal conflicts on the type of learning situation we are proposing. An *intra*personal conflict, as defined in Chapter 1, is a sensed incompatibility of outlook which places an individual in disagreement with himself. A person may feel a problem without experiencing intrapersonal conflict, as when he is merely puzzled or doubtful. But the appearance of conflict is normally regarded as a problem for persons experiencing it. There seems to be a drive toward harmony in human nature, once disharmony is recognized as such. Awareness of inconsistency or of inner conflict makes a person feel uncomfortable; it thus creates its own learning goal.[7]

That the urge for consistency does not appear more often may be explained by the fact that much inconsistency has not been discovered to be such by inconsistent persons. Myrdal has provided an explanation of why this is so. According to him, valuations exist at differing levels of generality. Our central beliefs and values, which include what Myrdal labels the American Creed, represent the more general valuation. For example, many Americans tend to value equality—but at a high level of abstraction. On the other hand, some of the same persons practice racial discrimination and segregation. But their beliefs concerning segregation are on a more specific, or less general, level. This explains why Americans so often profess high ideals but regularly violate them in practice. Specific practices often remain intellectually unrelated to ideals. Stereotypes, conventions, and compartmentalizations help us to ignore these inconsistencies. Myrdal maintains, however, that the spread of knowledge, changed material conditions, changed technology, and growing interdependence of society are exposing such inconsistencies to more and more persons. As inconsistencies are revealed, people tend to seek new equilibriums in their valuations. Myrdal believes that these new equilibriums normally embrace the more general, or abstract, valuations.[8]

But not always. Some people, when faced with intrapersonal conflict involving an ideal and a specific behavior, resolve the conflict by rejecting the ideal. One who favors equality and segregation and who comes to see them as inconsistent may reject equality. We assume that democratic-reflective study of such issues is more likely than unreflective procedure to resolve them in the direction of fuller commitment to democratic ideals. Our position advocates reflective reconstruction of beliefs as a means of clarifying and preserving the central ideals of democracy; it is in a large sense, therefore, a "conservative" outlook. It is conservative in a further sense: awareness of inconsistency without opportunity for reflective resolution theoretically might eventuate in accumulation of unmanageable and frustrating conflicts, which in turn might produce

[7] Max Wertheimer, *Productive Thinking*, Harper & Row, 1945, pp. 198–200. Also see Leon Festinger, *A Theory of Cognitive Dissonance*, Stanford University Press, 1957.

[8] Gunnar Myrdal, *et al.*, *An American Dilemma: The Negro Problem and Modern Democracy*, Harper & Row, 1944, vol. I, pp. 75-77; vol II, pp. 1031-1034.

violent social disturbances. Myrdal, for example, sees reflective resolution of conflict as an antidote to revolutionary impulses.

Our position has significant implications for the problem of mental health, as noted in Chapter 1. When individuals hold mutually contradictory beliefs and attitudes, neurotic conditions may result. A reflectively oriented social-studies curriculum which focuses on a study of the pervasive ideological or moral issues of the culture should have the effect of preventing absorption of unrecognized conflicts and should also give students basic habits helpful in resolving conflicts which are recognized. Although we do not maintain that social-studies teachers should try to play the role of psychiatrists, we feel strongly that reflective study of closed areas in our schools would have a "preventive-hygiene" effect and over the long run would reduce our many national schizophrenias.

We feel these generalizations to be warranted: (1) The learning problems capable of producing maximum motivation, maximum learning, and maximum transfer grow out of awareness of intrapersonal conflict, whether in the closed areas or elsewhere. (2) Reflective study of such conflict, more than any other type of study, holds promise of improving the mental health of individuals, of producing commitment to democratic ideals, and of leading to orderly and peaceful social change.

Questions which ask students to explain what, in terms of their present concepts, is unexplainable may create problematic situations. Until mechanical teaching and learning have discouraged them, youngsters have an abundance of natural curiosity. We have known relatively immature youngsters to become highly interested in trying to answer questions such as, If millions of persons in India are starving, how may we explain their refusal to kill cattle for food? and, How may we explain the fact that in some places Eskimos have wastefully destroyed the natural resources on which their own lives depend? Of course, such questions will not produce thought if the principle of continuity of learning is violated; there must be, in the background of students, belief or knowledge which can provide a basis for hypothesization.

Even junior-high-school students can have their interest in ideological questions developed. We may promote such interest by raising questions about matters of belief. For example, it is common in the United States to require study of the Federal Constitution in the seventh or eighth grade, as part of either civics or American history. Teachers have difficulty making study of the Constitution meaningful at this grade level. Learning is often mechanical and lifeless.

But suppose a teacher opens discussion of the First Amendment with a description of attempts to have comic books censored, or of present policies with regard to television or movie censorship, or perhaps of restrictions placed upon freedom of students to study controversial topics.

Then suppose he asks, "Do you feel that comic-book censorship violates the First Amendment?" or "Are restrictions on the freedom of students to study certain topics unconstitutional?" or, in the case of the Fifth Amendment, "What is meant by the expression, Fifth-Amendment Communist?" Even among junior-high-school students, approaches of this type are likely to generate interest in conflicts in beliefs and attitudes.

For students of junior and senior high school we recommend that, in as far as possible, social-studies learning be approached through the medium of mutually contradictory beliefs, attitudes, and values. With ingenuity of teaching, probably all socially important issues confronting Americans may be approached through reflective analysis of the beliefs and attitudes students have acquired from out-of-school environments. It is generally possible to help students expand their *world of insight* to encompass more nearly their *world of effect* through the study of ideological questions.

DISCUSSION QUESTIONS AND EXERCISES

1. How should a teacher proceed with a student who cannot perceive the "facts" in a closed area? Can such perceptual failures be remedied by good teaching?
2. What does it mean for teaching to say that students do not agree on what the facts *mean?*
3. Do you agree with the idea that facts are useless unless they are seen as relevant to the testing of a hypothesis?
4. How is it possible for a person to hold contradictory or inconsistent beliefs without knowing that he does? By what techniques can a person conceal from himself such confusion?
5. Should a teacher awaken latent but unrecognized conflicts?
6. Is it necessary that students learn facts before they can be expected to think?
7. Can students learn facts without thinking? Can students learn facts from thinking? How do your answers to these questions affect your conception of student background, and how background may be enriched or deepened?
8. What is a problem? Can we have problems without having doubt? Is it possible for teachers to create doubt? Can they stimulate thinking without creating doubt?

REFERENCES

BAYLES, ERNEST E., "The Idea of Learning as Development of Insight," *Educational Theory*, April, 1952.

An excellent article on learning based upon field theory. Also available as a Bobbs-Merrill reprint.

Bigge, Morris, "A Relativistic Approach to the Learning Aspect of Educational Psychology," *Educational Theory*, July, 1954.

Explores relationships between field theory and pragmatism of Boyd Bode.

Bigge, Morris, and Maurice P. Hunt, *Psychological Foundations of Education*, New York, Harper & Row, 1962.

A textbook in educational psychology that is oriented toward field theory Contains an excellent critique of Skinner's operant conditioning.

"Current Research in Social Studies," *Bulletin of the School of Education*, Indiana University, March, 1964.

Research studies of reflective teaching, with suggestions as to how research in social studies education might be improved.

Hilgard, Ernest R., and Gordon H. Bower, *Theories of Learning*, 3rd ed., New York, Appleton-Century-Crofts, 1966.

Standard textbook on learning theory. Still one of the best.

Hill, Winfred R., *Learning: A Survey of Psychological Interpretations*, San Francisco, Chandler, 1963.

A good review of various learning theories.

"Indiana Experiments in Inquiry: Social Studies," *Bulletin of the School of Education, Indiana University*, May, 1963.

Contains research reports on effects of reflective teaching in American and world history. Based upon dissertations by Byron Massialas and C. Benjamin Cox.

Indiana Social Studies Quarterly, Muncie, Indiana, Ball State Teachers College, Autumn, 1961.

Entire issue devoted to reflective thinking as teaching method in the social studies.

Lewin, Kurt, *Field Theory in Social Science*, New York, Harper & Row, 1951.

Contains some of Lewin's most technical and sophisticated papers. An excellent reference on field theory for advanced students.

Lewin, Kurt, *Resolving Social Conflicts*, New York, Harper & Row, 1948.

This book reports some of Lewin's research on group conflicts. Reports the kind of research findings that support field theory.

Murphy, Gardner, *Historical Introduction to Modern Psychology*, New York, Harcourt, Brace & World, 1946.

Traces the history of various learning theories. Concludes that there are essentially only two conceptions of learning, despite many recent attempts to develop "new" theories.

PART II

Method and the Social Studies

CHAPTER 3

Reflective Thought as Teaching Method

THE DEVELOPMENT of improved insight in students depends on whether teachers can induce students to think reflectively. Most teachers say that they want their students to think, and hopefully they mean reflective thinking. Only a few are able to implement the wish. No doubt there are many reasons for this discrepancy between aim and accomplishment. Teachers have other objectives which they allow to compete with that of thinking, and by the time these are accommodated no time is left for thinking. Many teachers do not understand reflection well enough to promote it, and in our view this is the main reason why it is usually absent from classrooms. If teachers understood reflection, that is, knew what it is and what conditions give rise to it, they would be able not only to promote it, but to relate its use to other objectives. These objectives then would not compete with thinking. There are few objectives in the social studies, or in any other school subject, that cannot be achieved by use of reflection as a teaching method.[1]

Reflective Thought Defined

The oldest and still the best discussion of reflective thought is to be found in John Dewey's *How We Think*, a book first published in 1909, and still used as a basic reference in philosophy courses. Early in this book Dewey states clearly his meaning for reflective thought. "*Active, persistent, and careful consideration of any belief or supposed form of knowledge in the light of the grounds that support it and the further conclusions to which it tends* constitutes reflective thought." [2] Dewey then clarifies this meaning of thinking by comparing it with three other meanings found in common usage.

One meaning people have for thinking is the "uncontrolled coursing of

[1] An excellent reference which describes the use of reflection as a teaching method in a variety of subjects and grade levels is Ernest E. Bayles, *The Theory and Practice of Teaching*, Harper & Row, 1950. Another good reference is William H. Burton, Roland B. Kimball, and Richard L. Wing, *Education for Effective Thinking*, Appleton-Century-Crofts, 1960.

[2] John Dewey, *How We Think*, Heath, 1933, p. 9. Italics in original.

ideas through our heads." A teacher never has to stimulate deliberately this kind of thinking. Reverie, or daydreaming, or building castles in the air is a common occurrence. As Dewey puts it: ". . . In this sense, silly folk and dullards *think*. The story is told of a man in slight repute for intelligence, who, desiring to be chosen selectman in his New England town, addressed a knot of neighbors in this wise: 'I hear you don't believe I know enough to hold office. I wish you to understand that I am thinking about something or other most of the time.' " [3] Everyone has something on his mind every moment. Teachers do not have reverie in mind when they express the wish that their students would do more thinking.

Another common meaning for thinking refers to things "not sensed or directly perceived." It is not always possible, or particularly significant, to distinguish this kind of thinking from the free flow of ideas associated with reverie. The imaginative stories we invent and narrate exemplify this kind of thinking.

A third meaning for thinking makes it synonymous with believing. As when a man says, "I think Mary is unhappy." This meaning differs from the other two in that everyone recognizes its contact with reality. But it confuses product with process. Thinking leads to belief, but many of our beliefs have not been acquired or tested by thinking. Many of our beliefs, observes Dewey, have been "picked up from others" and we accept them only because they happen to be current, not because we have "examined into the matter." Our minds have taken no active part in "reaching and framing" such beliefs.

THE NATURE OF PREJUDICE

Two men may hold that there are no inferior races. One man can produce no evidence for his belief. Perhaps he comes from a "liberal" family in which this belief prevails. We say that his belief, although true, is ungrounded. The other man may be able to define his terms, state his assumptions, declare his values, and marshal his evidence. His belief, although the same as the other man's, is different. In addition to being true it is grounded. It is intelligently held. It belongs to the man; and the man is not possessed by it. We refer to the first man's belief as a prejudice even though it reflects a favorable view of Negroes. In Dewey's words, it was not reached "as the result of personal mental activity, such as observing, collecting, and examining evidence. Even when they happen to be correct, their correctness is a matter of accident as far as the person who entertains them is concerned." [4]

Teachers who are concerned only with correctness of belief can

[3] Dewey, *ibid.*, p. 4
[4] Dewey, *ibid.*, p. 7.

purvey as much prejudice as they seek to destroy. It is not uncommon in the physical sciences for teachers to expose and correct misconceptions. Teachers of social studies may take an identical approach to students' social prejudices. The trouble with this procedure in either area is that it may simply substitute one set of beliefs for another. Students may be wrong in many of their beliefs. A teacher may be correct in most of his. But if his beliefs crowd aside and take the place of students' beliefs without any reflective activity on their part, the new beliefs are not likely to be any better grounded than the ones that were displaced. They therefore function as prejudice.

Equally bad, if not worse, is a situation in which a teacher with prejudiced beliefs is at work. He may try to "correct" students' beliefs that are more correct than his, although not necessarily any better grounded. Or he may reinforce those incorrect students' beliefs with which he happens to agree. In either case, a reduction of prejudice, if we define prejudice as ungrounded belief no matter how correct it may be, fails to take place. Because schools prize recitations in which many "right answers" are regurgitated, and because teachers in such schools commonly view themselves as unprejudiced authorities on prejudice, it is not surprising to find that public-high-school graduates are seldom able to defend or fully justify their beliefs.

Reflective Thought and Scientific Method

Reflective thought, then, is thought controlled by an end. Its basis is grounded and tested belief. Its purpose is not reverie or storytelling— although both contain elements of reflection, and either may develop into a full-fledged example of reflection. As many see it, there is no essential difference between reflection and the scientific method of inquiry. But there may be reflection that uses criteria other than scientific ones, as a person's way of arriving reflectively at a definition of democracy, or the "proof" of a geometrical theorem from basic premises.[5] Moreover, the term *scientific* carries a meaning for some people which is less suited to our purposes than does the term *reflective*. "Science" implies white-gowned technicians, microscopes and telescopes, chemical tables, cyclotrons, and computers. It suggests precise measurement, use of mathematics, controlled experimentation, and a large amount of esoteric wizardry. "Reflection," on the other hand, refers to the essential but non-gadgetlike features of science, and to an attitude of mind and a generalized set of mental operations with which to approach all problems, whether social or physical in nature.

[5] This is not to deny that such reflection *is* logical.

Any act of thought, depending on how complete it is, progresses from belief, to doubt, to idea, to testing of idea, to verified belief or conclusion. This process is outlined below.

Recognition and Definition of a Problem. A problem is usually an outgrowth of a sensed discrepancy in data or beliefs. Because students vary somewhat in their perceptual fields they do not always agree in their definition of a problem. Teachers find it difficult to get a problem defined so that it is the same problem for everyone in the class. They find it even more difficult to create a problem. To *feel* that a problem exists, students must come to realize that one or more of their beliefs is inadequate. Everyone holds tenaciously to his beliefs, and resists any challenge that would create real doubt as to their meaning or truth. The *subject-matter switch,* to be discussed in Chapter 8, is one of the more effective techniques for shaking strongly held beliefs and for getting a problem created.

Formulation of Hypotheses. A hypothesis is any idea which, if true, would explain a given discrepancy in data or belief. "Thinking up" a hypothesis puts strain on the imagination and knowledge of students. The more unimaginative a group of students is, the less practice they have had in reflection, the skimpier their knowledge, the more assistance they require from a teacher. A no-hypothesis situation is quite common in classrooms. Another difficulty at this stage is to get hypotheses stated in a form that permits evidence to go to work. This is more than a problem of form. Substantively speaking, certain kinds of knowledge are beyond a reflective test. When these kinds of knowledge function as sources of hypotheses, the results are untestable ideas. The difference between testable and untestable ideas, and what to do about the difference, will be discussed in some detail in Chapter 6.

Elaboration of Logical Implications of Hypotheses. At this stage, a problem solver asks: If my hypothesis is to be rated true, what else would have to be so? The first step toward testing a hypothesis is to deduce any statements contained within it. Every hypothesis, and indeed every declarative sentence, implies or predicts further ideas. If someone says, "I think it is raining," he is implying wet streets.[6] The prediction, wet streets, is checked by observation. To discover dry streets would force one to give up his hypothesis or find a reason why streets might be dry during a rain. On the other hand, wet streets would not prove that it is raining; one could settle upon rain as an explanation only when one's observations have ruled out other possible explanations. Hypotheses of an if-then nature are valuable as guides to direct the search for evidence.

Testing of Hypotheses. A hypothesis is tested by throwing against it

[6] This example is taken from H. Gordon Hullfish and Philip G. Smith, *Reflective Thinking: The Method of Education,* Dodd, Mead, 1961, p. 68.

whatever pertinent knowledge the problem-solving group possesses or is able to acquire. It is usually inefficient for a group to try to "solve" a problem by discussion alone. Discussion will enable members of a group to pool their knowledge accumulated from past experience, and sometimes this collective accumulated knowledge is complete enough to warrant reaching a conclusion. When it is not, then the group must seek additional data from such sources as observation, experimentation, library study, and consultation with authorities.

Drawing of a Conclusion. This stage involves acceptance, rejection, or modification of a hypothesis in light of evidence used in testing it.

The purposes of reflection will be defeated by a teacher who regards the above five steps as mechanical procedures to be followed in a certain order. The unit plan that assigns the first week to problem identification, the second to formulation of a hypothesis, and so on through the list is too rigid to permit genuine reflection. Any act of thought will have its discursive moments, and even its phases of reverie. Thinking can not be put on a schedule, and there will be much backing and filling in any problem-solving experience. We shall have more to say on this point when we distinguish between authentic and pseudoproblem-solving.

The Reflective Classroom

We have said that a teacher whose only concern is with "right answers" or "correct belief" may discourage reflection and thereby the improved insights of grounded belief. Dewey had in mind such danger when he issued this warning:

The operation of the teacher's own mental habit tends, unless carefully watched and guided, to make the child a student of the teacher's peculiarities rather than of the subjects that he is supposed to study. His chief concern is to accommodate himself to what the teacher expects of him, rather than to devote himself energetically to the problems of subject matter. "Is this right?" comes to mean "Will this answer or this process satisfy the teacher?" instead of meaning "Does it satisfy the inherent conditions of the problem?" It would be folly to deny the legitimacy or the value of the study of human nature that children carry on in school, but it is equally undesirable that their chief intellectual problem should be to produce the answer approved by the teacher, and that their standard of success should be successful adaptation to the requirements of another person.[7]

This is important prescription and it is sometimes interpreted to mean that a reflective classroom does not seek right answers. No interpretation

[7] Dewey, *op. cit.,* p. 61.

could be more wrong. Ignorant teachers cannot function as effectively as knowledgeable ones. A teacher of thinking will not accept every answer as right. Neither will he dismiss a wrong answer peremptorily, and thus fail to capitalize on its learning value. It is a teacher's treatment of an answer, whether it be right or wrong, that determines whether a student engages in reflection. Through a line of questioning a teacher and his students can ascertain whether an "answer" is understood so well that they can provide a ground for it. The following anecdote describes a teacher's approach to a wrong answer when reflective thought is a matter of teacher concern. In this anecdote, the student who was wrong eventually achieved a correct response; in addition, he learned the basis of his correctness:

A student, for example, once offered the suggestion that "vapor condenses when the temperature rises." The answer was given honestly, and the teacher, instead of saying, "No, that is wrong, you tell us, George" (and George and several others were waving hands to indicate they knew the answer to be wrong), initiated a line of questioning to compel the student to "do battle" for his answer. The teacher pointed out that when a person wearing eyeglasses steps into a warm room on cold days the glasses steam over. He then asked if the suggestion accounted for this fact. The student proceeded to show that the air within the roof was warm and that, therefore, a rise in temperature was the cause. When questioned about the sweat on an ice pitcher in the summer, the hoarfrost on a man's mustache in the winter, the dampness of refrigerator pipes in warm weather, the steam on windowpanes in the winter, and the regular phenomenon of frost, the student demonstrated, to his own satisfaction in each case, that a rise in temperature was the cause. Warm air surrounded the pitcher; the man's breath was warmer than the air he breathed; warm air completely surrounded the refrigerator pipes; the air within the room was warm, and, hence, that air closest to the windowpanes condensed; the warmth of the earth caused the regular coating of frost on nights when cold air hovered over the ground.

The student was eagerly matching wits with the teacher; and, as the process continued, the rest of the class visibly took sides, although not overtly participating. The teacher, it is clear, kept bringing varying facts to bear on the suggestion, knowing that in each instance the student would weave his web stronger by explaining them in the light of his hypothesis. Obviously, it was up to the teacher (or to the class, had he turned to them) to furnish a crucial case, a specific instance, in which the hypothesis would not stand up. Unless this could be done, the student must be conceded to have a plausible answer to the problem of condensation. Finally, therefore, the teacher described the case of steam escaping from a boiling kettle, and, as before, the student continued with his hypothesis, though with less assurance. When the teacher started to ask why clouds were overhead if his were the right explanation, the student suddenly shouted, "Vapor condenses when there is a lowering of temperature." He then quickly reviewed, under the direction of the teacher, all of the incidents he had misinterpreted to show that in each case the cause had been a lowering of temperature.[8]

In the above example, how did the teacher produce thought? A principle or hypothesis was supplied by a student. It could have come from the teacher or a textbook. This principle was tested against a number of cases, each familiar to most students. Only when the hypothesis failed to explain one of the cases was it revised. Teacher and student then reviewed all the cases, showing that a new hypothesis accounted for them.

Some teachers make elaborate plans called units in which provision for problem-solving experiences is included. This science teacher may or may not have had such plans. We make no brief for or against the planning of units. But this anecdote illustrates the fact that any teacher may promote reflection within a standard recitation provided he is alert enough to know what to do with a student answer that conflicts with established knowledge.

There are teachers who regard it as a waste of time to help a student discover a better insight. Thinking takes time, and many teachers prefer to tell a student that he is wrong and offer reasons why. Such teachers would rather save time than promote thought.

Reflective thought is also possible in the social studies, even though principles may not be as well established, in every case, as they are in natural science. The following example illustrates a teacher's successful attempt to get reflection, starting with a factual statement in a textbook. The particular statement chosen by this teacher was as prosaic as most standard social studies content:

Let us suppose a world history course in which students have encountered . . . the statement . . . "Alexander crossed the Hellespont with 35,000 men and began the series of conquests that quickly made him master of Darius' empire."

In the actual course of events, this statement would be "believed" in the limited sense of "not doubted," but nobody would be likely to care much one way or the other about it, except on the off chance that an examination might call for its regurgitation. . . .

Suppose, however, that the teacher raises the question, "Could that sentence be a misprint? Surely it doesn't sound reasonable that 35,000 troops could conquer a land containing many millions of people."

That much is enough to get the flow of hypotheses started. "Maybe there weren't so many people in those days." Investigation will bear this out, but not in sufficient degree to explain Alexander's conquests. "Maybe his army increased as he went along." Investigation supports this also—at least, a student can readily find out that Alexander trained some 30,000 of his conquered sub-

[8] Hullfish and Smith, op. cit., pp. 198-199.

jects in Macedonian military techniques,—but again the explanation is quantitatively inadequate. "Maybe the people had no weapons." But Macedonian weapons were not particularly complicated, as the student can readily discover. Vast numbers of peoples armed with only equipment for hunting, farm implements, clubs, and stones could make a fair showing against a small army. However, a new question could be introduced by the teacher, namely, "Why didn't Darius see to it that every household contained the simple weapons of his day?" . . .

Sooner or later, someone will discover that the ordinary inhabitant of an Asiatic empire never took part in wars at all—that he apparently cared not at all who ruled over him. By the time a student has found out why, and has come to compare the passive helplessness of the natives of Persia with the vigorous self-defense against Persia carried on by the Greek cities a century and a half earlier, and perhaps to wonder what had enabled Alexander to conquer those same Greek cities, the comparison with the present scene will have become painfully obvious. . . .[9]

A teacher of social studies, then, may treat even the most meaningless of factual content in a way that shifts student attention to ideas in propositional form. The fact, that "Alexander crossed the Hellespont with 35,000 men and began a series of conquests," leads into a consideration of the idea that "People will not fight to maintain a government in which they believe they have no stake." It is this shift from facts to suggested ideas and the testing of those ideas with facts that characterize a reflective classroom. This kind of classroom can exist in history and the social studies as well as in science.

The Conflict Between Knowledge and Student Belief

Clearly, a teacher who favors thinking will also favor the "right answers" to which thinking leads. It is necessary for this teacher to settle in his own mind what constitutes a desirable relationship between his knowledge and student beliefs. This relationship, presumably, should not do violence to the process of thinking or the pedagogical conditions that give rise to it.

There are actually three variables involved here—knowledge, teacher belief, and student belief. Teachers as well as students may believe much that is not so. And students as well as teachers may believe much that is

[9] Alan F. Griffin, *A Philosophical Approach to the Subject-Matter Preparation of Teachers of History*, Unpublished doctoral dissertation, Ohio State University, 1942, pp. 179-181.

so. Whenever there is a clash between teacher belief and student belief, an objective observer will want to know whose knowledge is pitted against whose ignorance. Let us not forget that a reflective classroom defines knowledge as grounded belief. Without ground a correct belief does not qualify as knowledge.

A conflict between what students believe and what social scientists and historians know is a common occurrence in social studies classrooms. Sometimes this interpersonal conflict passes unnoticed because a teacher, as well as his students, does not have the relevant knowledge. Or, even more commonly, a teacher with the knowledge fails to see its relevance to the beliefs students have just expressed. In both cases, an opportunity to promote reflection has been missed, and ignorance has been preserved.

Some teachers, although aware of the conflict, may fail to promote reflection because their valuing of student opinion has been placed in opposition to their valuing of knowledge and thinking. These teachers lean over backwards to avoid imposing their beliefs (knowledge) upon students, because they hold to the belief that teachers have no right to change what students believe.[10] They are reluctant to play God, or to claim that their beliefs are better than any others.

They may also believe that it is undemocratic for a teacher to try to substitute his beliefs for those held by students. They quote the democratic ideology incompletely when they say that "every one is entitled to his own opinion." This understanding of democracy is sometimes accompanied by a belief that history and the social sciences are lacking in firmly established knowledge. Such teachers stand in awe of mathematics and physical sciences. An unfavorable comparison is made between physical sciences and social, leading to extreme tolerance of everyday opinions, which are taken to be no worse than the "theories" and "hypotheses" of social scientists.

High-school students are quick to take advantage of this extreme tolerance. They begin to act as if their rough-hewn opinions had considerable merit. The social-studies classroom becomes a place where one does not have to be prepared. Discussion takes the place of scholarship. Students talk back, or argue with the teacher. Any student who has not been cowed or drugged by the public-school bureaucracy will argue with a teacher over acceptance of any idea that conflicts with his common-sense convictions.

This argumentative stance contrasts starkly with the attitude commonly taken by the same students in a mathematics or physics class,

---

[10] Many of these same teachers will not hesitate to try to change the way students behave!

where they are humble, and receptive to the teacher's knowledge. There is usually an eagerness to learn what the physics teacher knows, rather than a tendency to doubt his sanity, as is the case when a teacher offers socialism or free love as an hypothesis.

The student belief that a teacher does not know very much may be particularly prevalent in a history course where the subject matter lacks a technical vocabulary. Nothing can awe a student quite as effectively as the special vocabulary of mathematics or physics. Physics, moreover, can point to a variety of inventions and other technological achievements as proof that physicists really know something, whereas a history teacher can only talk vaguely about social understanding. The students will not know, of course, that *good* physicists never point to invention as proof that their pudding is worth the eating.

The tendency of students in the social studies to talk back can be converted by the teacher into an advantage. From such argumentation he may at least acquaint himself with what students believe—information useful to any teacher who wants students to think reflectively about their beliefs. In order to promote reflection, however, he will find it necessary to go beyond the mere airing of opinions. He will want to create in as many students as possible some kind of intrapersonal conflict in place of the interpersonal conflict that pits student against student, or students against teacher. To do this he must have confidence in his knowledge. Such confidence can be achieved by a teacher as he learns to distinguish between his knowledge and his prejudice. Even the best-prepared teacher will have some ungrounded beliefs in his possession. Unless he is aware of this and can make the distinction, a teacher can be permissive or restrictive in his attitude toward student beliefs, but he cannot be a teacher of thinking.

The problems of student resistance to knowledge and a teacher's tendency to be permissive without submitting student beliefs to a reflective test can exist in science as well as social studies. It is possible for the content of a natural science to conflict with a student prejudice. There is no doubt that students of biology who *understand* the concept of evolution often simply refuse to *believe* it. Some teachers are satisfied with this understanding, and do not press for belief. Many of these students perform well on national scholarship examinations. The "knowledge" that enables them to pass examinations is kept in a separate compartment where it cannot play havoc with their fundamentalist religious views.

Any teacher who would help students to formulate a philosophy of life consisting of beliefs and understandings that hang together and make internal sense will try to break down compartmentalizations of all kinds, and will not settle for a state of affairs in which what a student learns has nothing to do with what he really and truly believes.

THE PSEUDO-REFLECTIVE TEACHER

Any skepticism that students bring to a social-studies classroom can have a healthy effect upon their intellectual and moral development. Teachers often wish that their students were more critical of ideas than they actually are. Teachers committed to reflection want this criticism to be directed at ideas, not at sources of ideas. They do not want students to accept—or reject—any idea simply because it originates with a teacher or some other authority. Unfortunately, not all teachers are able to live up to this commitment; those that fail may be called pseudo-reflective teachers.

A common reason for this failure is that it is always difficult for a teacher to question a student answer that his knowledge or prejudice tells him is correct. The most common practice is for a teacher to question an answer only when he finds something wrong with it. This practice not only means that students are able to make correct responses without understanding; it also means that students are failing to learn to use thinking as a way of getting and testing answers. The following anecdote is a good illustration of a kind of teaching that treats "right" answers one way, and "wrong" answers another:

The writer vividly recalls observing a teacher who avowed as her sole aim the development of independent thinking among her pupils. The class had embarked upon the discussion of such current events as happened to be treated in the weekly paper to which they subscribed for this purpose. The lead story was on the then-current coal strike. A boy in the class delivered himself of the idea, "If miners would be sensible with their money, instead of throwing it all away on whiskey, they'd find that their wages were more than they need."

The teacher moved in fast. Under a barrage of well-placed questions, the lad admitted that (1) he had no idea how much a miner was paid; (2) he had no firsthand knowledge of the personal habits of miners; (3) his sole source for the view he had announced was a muttered reaction of his father's at the breakfast table; (4) he doubted that his father had any actual information on either of the relevant points; (5) he recognized that one ought not to make such a drastic or sweeping generalization unless he had facts to back it up. So far, so good.

The next reaction came from a girl who remarked with deep feeling that whenever men strike they lose money, and that this fact so disturbs wives as to upset their home life very seriously. "So," she concluded, "I think that whenever men strike they must be in the right, or they wouldn't do a thing that's going to be so unpleasant for them." The writer's eyes were on the teacher as he waited for this avowed foe of the facile generalization to swing into action.

All that the teacher did, however, was to beam and announce solemnly, "Helen, that's what I call a very nice insight." [11]

Students who happen to agree with this teacher will not learn much. Those who disagree may learn a great deal, at least about thinking. What is needed in this classroom, and indeed in any classroom that takes reflection seriously, is a set of criteria by which to determine when an answer is right. Teacher approval of an answer, even when that approval is based upon sound knowledge, is an inadequate criterion if we want students to base their answers upon thinking.

The criteria are to be found in the following rules or axioms which are applied when a person decides reflectively in favor of one idea over another:

1. Whenever one belief or conclusion is accepted in preference to another, it is presumed that reasons exist for its acceptance. The grounds for acceptance may be scant, but so long as they are better than the grounds any competing belief can offer, they justify its acceptance.

2. Conclusions are always made provisionally. All knowledge is assumed to be relative, in the sense that no question is closed to reexamination provided that a reason to reexamine develops. This does not mean that one may not establish laws or principles which are assumed to be valid indefinitely. Such laws are not absolutes so long as there is willingness to reopen the question of their validity, whenever there is reason to doubt their adequacy.

3. Conclusions are consistent with each other. Contradictory beliefs can never be true at the same time. This does not mean that one may not switch from one belief to another which is incompatible with it. Changing one's mind is not an example of inconsistency; a person is inconsistent only when he holds two opposites at once. He can hold opposites without knowing that he does, through the practice of compartmentalization. A person should not switch from one belief to another unless new evidence or new insight makes this change necessary. Finally, he should not confuse contrariety with contradiction; one belief may be inconsistent with another without being its exact opposite.

4. All pertinent evidence known to the investigator is scrutinized before conclusions are drawn. Obviously, pertinent evidence which is unknown to an investigator cannot be utilized. If the "investigator" is a high-school social-studies class, the burden of seeing to it that pertinent evidence is not overlooked rests heavily upon the teacher. Hence, the necessity that teachers be knowledgeable, and able to keep prejudices out of the investigation. An investigator looks at all pertinent facts known

[11] Alan F. Griffin, "The Teacher as Citizen," *Educational Leadership,* October, 1952, p. 7.

and available to him, no matter how unpalatable some of them may seem. There is never a slanting, ignoring, or distortion of data to prove a point. Taboos and ungovernable prejudices do not mix with a reflective approach.

5. The authority for a scientific conclusion is to be found in perceivable phenomena, which suggests observation and experiment. This is sometimes construed to rule out mystical experience. Whether mystical experience is always hallucinatory, or whether it may represent for a small portion of our people contact or involvement with an "otherworldly" realm, is a matter of some dispute. A reflective person does not like arbitrarily to rule out any kind of evidence. He prefers the idea of openness in which anything is possible. But without better evidence than is now available he will remain skeptical of mystical claims. This means that one tends at present to accept the old logical-positivist view that the ultimate authority for any conclusion is to be found in natural phenomena. Evidence which is purported to come from a world other than the "here and now" is viewed with suspicion.

6. All operations must be performed openly and in a fashion which will enable others to repeat the same procedures. Each act of reflection must be able to supply its own recipe, so to speak. Stated in another way, the methods of an investigator must be subject to operational description. The term *publicly verifiable* best describes the method of reflection, and its data.[12]

A teacher who understands these criteria can communicate them to students as a better basis than teacher authority for determining the adequacy of an idea. Of course, they will not want to accept these criteria simply because a teacher has recommended them. These criteria can be compared with alternative conceptions of truth, and in doing so the adequacy of the scientific method becomes an object of student inquiry. Whether science can answer all our questions, or whether there are methods that can answer a question that science cannot answer becomes the heart of such inquiry. It is here that revelation, intuition, extrasensory perception, and even simple religious faith become issues.

Pseudo Problem-Solving

Reflective teaching is problem-centered teaching. Those who advocate a problem-solving method sometimes encounter stiff opposition. But just as common is the kind of assent that says, "But I have been doing that for

[12] For an excellent discussion of these rules, particularly the rule of public verifiability, see Max C. Otto, "Scientific Humanism," *Antioch Review*, December, 1943.

years." One gets the same kind of assent when he advocates a unit approach. A closer look at this assent suggests that many of our problem-solving practices omit *problems* and *reflection*. Much teaching is *pseudo* problem-centered, and should be clearly labeled as such. What is commonly labeled problem-centered teaching takes the form of organizing a block of instruction around what a textbook writer, curriculum expert, teachers' curriculum committee, classroom teacher, or someone else has decided is a problem. There is something self-defeating about putting a problem in a textbook. The fact that students have read a chapter entitled, *The Farm Problem*, does not mean that they have a problem, unless it is the problem of understanding what the chapter says—or, what is more likely the case, the problem of figuring out what the teacher wants them to note as important in the chapter.

A problem, as we define it, is *felt* by someone. It *belongs* to someone. Many of the problems that are covered in a problems course are not felt as problems by most students. In fact, many teachers do not feel these problems as problems. To feel a problem is to be aroused psychologically to the point where one wants to learn enough about it to do something about it. This feeling has two components, *doubt* and *concern*.[18] These components are both intellectual and emotional in their content. Any attempt to create a problem without arousing students emotionally can only result in a pseudo problem. When students are disturbed, upset, and perhaps even angry, they are closer to having a problem than will ever be the case in classes that are free from the clash of ideas.

We have authentic rather than pseudo problems in classrooms when students sense inadequacies or incompatibilities in their beliefs, concepts, or values. We have said that this may disturb or upset students. It may even make some of them angry. Whether they are too disturbed or too angry to reflect will depend upon classroom climate; a problem to be discussed in some detail in Chapter 9. A classroom in which students have not been upset to some degree can never be problem centered, for students will not have the doubt and concern associated with feeling a problem. Sometimes a teacher can create the necessary doubt by presenting data sharply relevant to and in conflict with a belief held by a substantial number of students. This technique will work if students see the data as data, and see its relevance to something that they believe.

Another technique that sometimes works is to develop in students through questions a recognition that one of their deeply cherished beliefs

[18] Some writers object to the term doubt. They believe that doubt leads to cynicism, skepticism, nonbelief. They may have in mind religious doubt, and have offered as alternatives such terms as perplexity, puzzlement, wonder, and uncertainty. We make no brief for one term over another as long as the concept is communicated. Much of this word picking boils down to what Sidney Harris has called antics with semantics.

is in conflict with another of their deeply cherished beliefs. This technique is especially effective as it places conflict within students, and not between students and teacher. This is where the conflict must exist for a problem to be felt. Unless students feel uncertain and inadequate in some respect, they will not feel a problem. Students will feel frustrated, however, if in addition to feeling a problem they feel that there is no hope of solving the problem.

Some teachers avoid the big social problems, and have students work on some school problem that is amenable to pupil manipulation—for example, developing a form of student government that has a genuine voice in running a school. Teachers argue that students are interested in such problems but are not interested in unemployment, war, poverty, and prejudice as problems. We deny that this is the case. Students can be terribly bored by the immediate problem, and deeply interested in the large social problems, or vice versa. It all depends on whether either is felt as a problem, and this depends on whether student convictions have come to be doubted. If a student doubts the meaning or truth of one of his convictions, he is almost certain to be concerned. But problems that merely puzzle him, whether they be immediate or remote, may not create any concern in him at all.

Elizabeth Berry, in a discussion of some of the problems of teaching English, has described the difference between pseudo and authentic problem-solving. Her comment is relevant to social studies as well as English. She offers as an example of pseudo problem-solving the English teacher who conducted a unit on "The Role of the Newspaper in the World Today." The teacher began by announcing to the students that they were going to study a unit on newspapers. She spent most of the time on the first day telling them why such a unit of study was important to them. On the second day the class, under teacher leadership, developed a list of objectives. Their objectives paraphrased the arguments made by the teacher on the first day. Then the teacher announced some activities which if pursued would lead to the achievement of agreed-upon objectives. The activities were taken up and completed in systematic fashion. For each activity the teacher supplied materials and prescriptions in profusion. Newspapers were read, news items were discussed, letters were written to editors, and articles were prepared for the school newspaper. A local reporter spoke to the class, and proved so delightful that the class had no doubts as to the importance of the press. The letters written to editors were first graded, and then presumably mailed. Some time was even given to vocabulary drill in order that students might increase their understanding of news reports and editorials. The unreflective nature of the entire enterprise is revealed by the fact that at no time did the teacher question the accuracy of a news report. She conveyed instead the impression that anything in print is probably so. In the concluding evaluation, the students agreed that they "had learned how to read a newspaper," and "recognized the importance of reading, and expected to confirm their interest by making a daily reading of the newspaper a part of their lives." The last act of the teacher in this unit was to announce that "it was time to move on to another unit, which would be a study of *Macbeth*." [14]

Berry taught the same unit quite differently. Because she wanted students to become critical readers as well as improve their language skills, she addressed the unit to the student belief that anything in print is true. She began by making available reprints of reports on the same subject from three different newspapers. The three articles were read and discussed separately, one at a time on successive days. At the end of the third day the students were genuinely puzzled, and spent most of the fourth day wrangling over the truth. Out of this discussion came a definition of a problem that was not announced or imposed by the teacher. Next, the teacher planned with the group some activities that might enable them to answer the questions involved in their problem. These activities were of the sort that make students active as researchers and problem solvers. The unit took them not only to the library but into the community. They studied not only newspapers and newsmagazines, but semantics and the press as a social institution. One student stumbled on the technique of comparing an original article with the condensed version in *Reader's Digest*. Many of their activities resembled those carried out by the first teacher, but the spirit in which they were performed was different because the students were confused and concerned over the question of what to believe in a newspaper, and how to determine what to believe.[15]

In this chapter we have defined reflective thought, we have set forth its stages, and we have illustrated it with examples. We have also set down some methodological rules by which to determine whether one answer is better than another. We have finally warned against the pitfalls of mechanical and false problem-solving. Despite this warning many teachers will miss the message, and thereby misinterpret and misapply our theory. Perhaps, one more thing needs to be said. *A teacher who wants students to reflect upon what they believe will fail to achieve this objective if he is unwilling to reflect upon his own beliefs.* When we ask students to think, we ask them to entertain alternatives to what they already believe. If a student differs with a teacher in some belief, he is

---

[14] Elizabeth Berry, "The Unit Process," *The Educational Forum*, March, 1963, p. 364.
[15] *Ibid.*, pp. 364–366.

asked to consider the teacher's belief as an alternative to his own. He may even be asked to consider more than one alternative. In effect, he is asked to treat his belief and the teacher's belief as hypotheses, with no prereflective edge given to either. *We cannot ask students to reflect upon alternatives without asking ourselves to do the same.* To follow any other course of action will suggest to reflective students that teachers advocate reflection for others, but not for themselves.

DISCUSSION QUESTIONS AND EXERCISES

1. A student cannot think about every idea he reads, hears, or holds. There isn't that much time or motivation in anyone's life. Most teachers only ask for thinking when they encounter an "incorrect" belief in a student. What are the consequences of this teacher habit? What are the consequences of a teacher's failure to question an "incorrect" belief? What beliefs should a teacher question?
2. Does a person think reflectively when he: (a) writes a short story or poem, (b) draws a picture, (c) constructs a chart or graph, (d) reads a map, (e) debates a proposition, (f) studies a school assignment?
3. What is the difference between authentic and pseudo problems?
4. On what basis can a reflective teacher determine whether a student answer is wrong?
5. How can a reflective teacher keep his prejudices under control?
6. How can a reflective teacher free students from dependence upon teacher approval? Is this possible under a grading system?
7. Should a reflective teacher ever express his opinions to his students?

REFERENCES

BAYLES, ERNEST E., *Democratic Educational Theory*, New York, Harper & Row, 1960.

Chapter 12 contains an excellent discussion of reflective teaching.

BAYLES, ERNEST E., *Theory and Practice of Teaching*, New York, Harper & Row, 1950.

Entire book is devoted to a discussion of reflective thought as a teaching method for exploring inconsistent beliefs.

BURTON, WILLIAM H., ROLAND B. KIMBALL, and RICHARD L. WING, *Education for Effective Thinking*, New York, Appleton-Century-Crofts, 1960.

A textbook on the nature of reflective thinking. Thinking is discussed as a teaching method. Appendix contains some interesting unit outlines in various subject fields.

DEWEY, JOHN, *How We Think*, Boston, Heath, 1909, 1933.

Probably the best book ever written on reflective thought as a method of teaching.

HULLFISH, H. GORDON, and PHILIP G. SMITH, *Reflective Thinking: The Method of Education*, New York, Dodd, Mead, 1961.

Based upon Dewey's concept of reflective thought. An advanced and difficult but profound book.

CHAPTER 4

How to Teach a Concept

WHEN WE discussed on pages 76 and 77 the methodological rules by which to tell correct from incorrect answers, we may have seemed to imply that all content consists of generalizations or singular statements that can be tested by citing evidence. Actually, there are several kinds of content, each represented by a different kind of statement, or sentence. Any teacher glancing at the pages of his textbook can identify at least four kinds of statements—concepts, generalizations, singular statements (sometimes called "the facts"), and value statements. *Concepts* define some feature of a situation. *Generalizations* explain a total situation or summarize a large body of data. *Values* function either as justification for a course of action or as a basis for rating objects, events, persons, or situations. *Singular statements* are identical with the arbitrary associations discussed in Chapter 1. These latter have little value to the thinking process except as they are given some kind of order in the construction of concept or generalization. Concepts, on the other hand, are the basis of all thinking and knowing. (Teachers sometimes say that thinking is impossible without facts. It is more to the point to say that thinking is impossible without concepts.)

It is not unusual for a methods textbook to treat the teaching of concepts and generalizations as if they composed a single instructional task possessed of a single internal logic. It is our argument that the logic of a concept differs from the logic of a generalization, and that both differ from the logic of valuation. One cannot teach a concept with the same strategy that is appropriate to teaching a generalization, even though a concept may be viewed as a certain kind of generalization. Likewise, one cannot teach values in exactly the same way one would teach descriptive concepts or generalizations. In this chapter, we will discuss the problems associated with attempts to teach concepts. In Chapter 5, we will discuss problems associated with teaching generalizations; and in Chapter 6, we will discuss the problem of values.

Distinctions Between Concepts and Other Statements

The distinctions made between concepts, generalizations, and values correspond to the distinctions drawn by philosophers between analytic, synthetic, and valuative assertions.

FACTS

The most naive mistake a teacher can make with concepts is to confuse them with facts. In one study, an attempt was made to rate according to relative importance 938 "concepts" in United States history. Nearly every alleged concept in the list is a factual statement such as "Christopher Columbus, attempting to reach Asia by sailing west across the Atlantic, discovered America in 1492." This statement, taken as a whole, is not a concept or a generalization. It is what most philosophers would call a singular statement, or a fact. Concepts are not facts. There is a difference between teaching facts and teaching concepts. We use facts in teaching concepts but it is possible to "teach" many facts without teaching a single concept.

GENERALIZATIONS

Another confusion arises when concepts are defined as generalizations. Such expressions as "people migrate when they are hungry," or "generals are babes in politics," or "bad money drives out good," or "the welfare state undermines individual initiative" are often labelled concepts. Actually, they are generalizations. We look upon generalizations as lawlike statements which express a relationship among concepts. The generalization, "deficit financing contributes to inflation under conditions of full employment," is a lawlike statement expressing a relationship between the concept "deficit financing," and the concepts, "inflation" and "full employment": i.e., "If the national government practices deficit financing under conditions of full employment, then inflation of a certain kind is likely to result."

CONCEPTS

These distinctions suggest that a concept "defines." The verbal expression of a concept is a definition. Some concepts, however, are almost never expressed verbally. Bruner comes closest to our meaning when he defines a concept as a category.[1] He would have us think of a concept as

[1] Jerome Bruner, *et al., A Study of Thinking,* Wiley, 1956, p. 1.

a basket into which we put those objects that belong together because of the attributes they are said to share under a given system of classification. A category includes within it a range of discriminably different items which are treated as if they are the same. For example, many discriminably different wars are placed together in a category called civil war. This is done in accordance with certain criteria. Bruner calls these criteria the defining attributes of a category. A particular war can be classified as a civil war only by first defining civil war according to its attributes, and then showing that the war in question has those attributes.

Bruner has said that "to categorize is to render discriminably different things equivalent, to group the objects and events around us into classes, and to respond to them in terms of their class membership rather than their uniqueness." [2] All social science has classification as its basis.

Concepts as Inventions

We are accustomed to the view that science is devoted to making discoveries, to finding out what the world and universe are really like. More accurately, science invents concepts, which are creative ways of structuring our perception of reality. Without the invention of concepts, science could not make its "discoveries." Even discovery is an invention, in the sense that we never know whether a discovered truth will survive all future tests and is therefore truly a part of reality.

The artificial nature of concepts, as well as the necessity of their invention, is illustrated by Bruner in the following way: It has been estimated that there are more than seven million discriminable colors. A person "perceives" most of these in a lifetime. But if asked to give names to different colors one is forced to give the same name to many different colors. No one has a vocabulary of seven million color-words. A typical person may have no more than a dozen colors in his vocabulary; and seven million colors can be forced into a dozen categories only by pretending that quite different colors are the same.

We simplify our environment and the signals from it by imposing an order or pattern that includes a manageable number of categories. For purposes of everyday living, no more is required. Without a manageable number of categories, the formation of insight would be very unlikely, if not impossible. Teachers, on guard against oversimplification, are not always aware that simplification is necessary to intelligent behavior. Without simplification, our environment would be intolerably complex and practically meaningless. It is, of course, possible to carry simplifica-

[2] *Ibid.*

tion too far. We all have heard of the old-time doctor who was able to fit all sickness into two categories: "If you can see it, put iodine on it. If you can't, give the patient a dose of salts." This doctor oversimplified medical diagnosis, as many of his dead patients would testify if they could.

The theoretical power of a concept is proportionate to the number of testable and tested insights derivable from it. That is, the strength of a concept depends upon the number of established relationships between it and other concepts. Bruner says the same thing when he asserts that "the test of the invention is the predictive benefits that result from the use of invented categories." [3]

Kinds of Concepts

Concepts have been classified in three ways—according to their nature, their use, and their certainty. Bruner has suggested that, classified according to their nature, there are three kinds of concepts: the conjuctive, the disjunctive, and the relational. Teaching strategy should be affected by the kind of concept involved.

CONJUNCTIVE AND DISJUNCTIVE CONCEPTS

A conjunctive concept is defined by the joint presence of several attributes. Most of the research on the teaching of concepts has dealt with this kind of concept. A good example of a conjunctive concept is *social class* when it is defined according to a person's occupation, source of income, neighborhood, and type of housing.

A disjunctive concept is defined by alternate attributes. A good example of a disjunctive concept is *citizen*. A citizen may be defined as a person who was born in this country, or whose parents were born in this country, or who has passed certain examinations. Another example would be a *strike* in baseball. A strike is a pitch within a certain zone, or a pitch that the batter misses when he swings, or a pitch that the batter hits outside the foul lines when the count on him is less than two strikes.

Note that a conjunctive concept connects attributes with "and"; a disjunctive concept separates them with "or." We typically learn a conjunctive concept by looking for elements that are common to several examples of the concept. The "old mathematics" taught the concept of triangle by confronting the student with an array of triangles, each one very different from the others, and asking him to determine what all the triangles had in common. This is good teaching strategy if triangle is a conjunctive concept.

[3] *Ibid.,* p. 7.

It would be a mistake to try to teach a disjunctive concept in this way. Imagine an American trying to teach an Englishman an understanding of the antics on a baseball field. He might start with an attempt to teach the concept, strike. After each strike, he might say to his English friend, "That was a strike!" If the Englishman then tried to invent a concept of strike based upon an attribute or set of attributes common to all strikes, he would fail and likely feel that baseball was too complicated to understand. This kind of frustration will be created in a student when a teacher tries to teach a disjunctive concept as if it were conjunctive.

For example: A standard dictionary meaning of imperialism reads, "the policy of extending the rule or authority of an empire or nation over foreign countries, or of acquiring and holding colonies and dependencies." According to this definition, imperialism is a disjunctive concept. One could have, then, instances of imperialism that would lack a common meaning. Some teachers handle this problem by talking about different kinds of imperialism. Students will nevertheless wonder whether the different kinds have anything in common because they generally assume that all concepts are conjunctive.

We do not know how many concepts in social science are disjunctive. There are probably a great many, as this is characteristic of infant sciences. Bruner cites dermatology as an example: The large number of sensitivity tests necessary in order to identify an allergy indicates that medical science has not been able to find a substance common to all allergy-producing agents. The possibility that there is no such substance will not deter scientists from looking for it. Any science that possesses disjunctive concepts will strive to reduce them to conjunctive ones, and it is easy to see why. If a concept is defined by the presence of attributes a, b, and c, it is then possible to infer much from little. From a knowledge of the presence of any one of the three attributes we can infer the remaining two, provided that we know the class membership of the object before us. We cannot do this with a disjunctive concept.

RELATIONAL CONCEPTS

Although scientists prefer conjunctive to disjunctive concepts, they have an even stronger preference for relational concepts. This kind of concept is defined by a relationship among attributes. The numerical laws of physics is one example. Density is defined as mass divided by volume. If we know the values for two of the attributes, we can compute the other. Bruner has used as an example, income-tax bracket, defined as a relationship between level of income and number of dependents.

It is easy to confuse the relational concept with generalizations. Our earlier statement that there is a testable relationship between deficit financing, inflation, and full employment is not a relational concept but a generalization. An example of a relational concept would be full employment defined as a relationship between number employed as a percent of the labor force, length of work week, and per capita productivity expressed in constant dollars. The difference between a relational concept and a generalization is best seen in the way that each is developed and grounded. A concept structures the facts, while a generalization is based upon the facts. As we said before, the difference between concepts and generalizations reflects the philosophical distinction between analytic and synthetic content.

Concepts as Analytic

Synthetic content, sometimes called contingent statements, includes those assertions whose truth depends upon the evidence. A contingent statement is any assertion about which it can be said, "It could be true, but it might be false." The fact that it could be false makes its truth contingent upon evidence. Analytic content consists of definitions and axioms. These are the formal and necessary truths in any field of knowledge. Analytic statements can never be shown to be false. A self-evident statement such as "a person cannot be in two places at once," is a good example of analytic content.[4]

The axioms of Aristotelian logic also exemplify analytic content. Mathematics is entirely analytic, although its content can be applied to the empirical world. Definitions and axioms are beyond the reach of empirical test. As Hullfish and Smith have put it, they remain true, come what may in experience. This does not mean that we do not change our concepts on the basis of our experience with them. When a theory becomes useless, intelligent men discard it.

The term analytic can be misleading. To say that a statement is analytic rather then synthetic is not to say that it arises from analysis, from taking things apart, or that it results from a process different from synthesis. Both analytic and synthetic statements can be analyzed. We can provide a warrant for either kind of statement—the difference in how each is grounded has great bearing on how we teach.

Classroom Procedures for Teaching Concepts

The statement that "bachelors are unmarried males" expresses a concept. How would a teacher proceed if his students doubted its "truth"? If they

[4] For an excellent discussion of analytic and synthetic statements, how they differ, and how each may be grounded, see H. Gordon Hullfish and Philip G. Smith, *Reflective Thinking: The Method of Education*, Dodd, Mead, 1961, chaps. 5 and 6.

doubted the truth of a synthetic statement such as "married males live longer than unmarried," recourse to evidence would be the only appropriate procedure. But doubt or dispute over the meaning of bachelorhood could not be resolved in this way. No teacher would be foolish enough to suggest "Let's make a survey of our local community and find whether any of our bachelors are married." Yet many teachers do make the mistake of trying to "test" a concept with evidence when its analytic character is not so obvious. This mistake is easily made by teachers who do not know the difference between a definition and a proposition.

How should a teacher treat any analytic statement, if it is a definition, and his purposes are reflective? What activities would he suggest to his students? What questions would he ask? And what would be the point of his questions and suggested activities?

In general, we can say that he would want to guide the class toward answers to such questions as, Can the statement be made more clear and precise in its meaning? Is the assigned meaning customary or unusual? Is the definition too broad or too narrow? He might also be interested in a comparative study of different meanings for the same term, and the practical results of such difference. He might keep in mind as a guide that, as Hullfish and Smith have said, the concepts of science are more explicit, precise, rigorous, abstract, general, and systematic than those of common sense.[5]

EXTENSIONAL AND INTENSIONAL MEANINGS

It contributes to the clarity of a definition, or concept, to distinguish between its *extensional* and *intensional* meanings. A precise definition states the meaning of a concept in terms of its characteristics. This gives the intensional meaning of a concept, and is what Bruner means by concept attainment, learning the properties of a category. When we can do no better than to offer examples as definition, we limit ourselves to extensional meaning. The Beardsleys have expressed the difference this way: "The extension of a word is the set of things to which it is applied, according to a rule; the intension is the set of characteristics that things must have in order for the word to apply correctly to them. The extension of 'city' is London, Paris, New York, Berlin, Tokyo, Moscow, Nairobi, etc. The intension of 'city' is (roughly) the characteristic of being a politically independent area of high population density and large population total."[6] Obviously, city is a conjunctive concept by this definition.

If students cannot agree on whether a given community is a city, they

[5] *Ibid.*, p. 73.
[6] Monroe C. and Elizabeth L. Beardsley, *Philosophical Thinking: An Introduction*, Harcourt, Brace, & World, 1965, p. 24.

can resolve their differences only if someone can state an intensional meaning of city which is acceptable to everyone. Some agreement must be reached on the characteristics common to all cities, assuming that city is a conjunctive concept. Then it must be decided whether the community in dispute has those characteristics. The reflective task is to determine a meaning for city, and to then decide whether the community in question is properly designated city or noncity. In order to do this, what "facts" are needed? Is it a fact that we customarily label a community a city only if it has certain characteristics? What are the characteristics we customarily associate with a city? And is it a fact that community X has those characteristics?

In a culture with language and other symbolization as advanced as ours, a person is at a serious disadvantage when he cannot express the intensional meanings of concepts. More importantly, theory building is seriously handicapped when intensional meanings are unclear. It is impossible to deal with questions of causation without resort to theories, and it is equally impossible to build theories when basic concepts are fuzzy. We cannot settle for a scholarship that can merely cite examples.

On the other hand, we may suspect that a student who can give a verbal definition of a concept but cannot recognize or supply examples does not understand the concept. Ideally, we want students to be able to define a concept intensionally, and then be able to illustrate it with concrete examples, indicating for each example why it qualifies as an instance of the concept.

PERSONAL AND OFFICIAL MEANINGS

In addition to classifying definitions as intensional and extensional, it is useful to deal with their personal and official character. Official definitions are those set forth by law, scholarship, religion, or some other authority. If we want to know what is meant by disease, we turn to the medical profession for an official meaning. The legal profession defines tort and contract for us. The Supreme Court has defined racial segregation as equivalent to racial discrimination and has applied this definition to interpretation of the Fourteenth Amendment. In some communities, considerable trouble has resulted from conflict between this official Supreme Court definition and personal definition.

Teachers should avoid the mistake of accepting any personally held definition as just as good as another. Students should acquire official definitions in place of personal ones whenever scholarship demands that they do so. They should learn what *economists* mean by labor force, rather than have their own versions. Technical or specialized vocabularies have been developed to overcome certain theoretical difficulties. A teacher who wants his students to be creative and critical, as well as knowledgeable, will permit and encourage them to consider whether certain official definitions might advantageously undergo some recasting. For example, why are the services performed by housewives not counted as part of the gross national product? Should we redefine GNP so that such services would be counted? Questions like these make it possible for an intellectual discipline to grow and develop along new lines. Students of disciplines grow and develop in the same way.

The superiority of official definitions over most personal definitions does not mean that a teacher should have no interest in students' personal definitions. Asking for personal definitions is a practice that helps a teacher acquaint himself with the backgrounds of students. A social-studies teacher might ask each of his students to write a paper on "What Democracy Means To Me." Each student might very well produce a somewhat different conception, although they would no doubt share some meanings. The teacher would be derelict in professional performance if he failed to treat reflectively the opinions that had been aired. Even the term democracy has its official aspects. There is a rich literature in philosophy and political science upon which students can draw as they sift and compare various conceptions of democracy. There is surely enough authority available to enable them to deal with the idea, sometimes expressed by opponents of legislative reapportionment, that minority rights include the right to rule.

Values and Definitions

The preference for one meaning over another often depends upon a person's values. Whether we prefer an official meaning made available to us by a scientific authority may depend on whether our purposes are scientific. The work of a scientist, be he physicist or economist, is to make it possible to explain, predict, and control. Definitions usually reflect classification systems that facilitate this by making it possible to deduce the largest amounts of information from a given amount. Shifts from Ptolemy to Copernicus, or from Newton to Einstein, or from Smith to Keynes represent changes in systems that enhanced the capacity of a science to do its job in the simplest possible way. Why do biologists, for example, want students to learn to use a classification system under which whales and porpoises are perceived as mammals, and not as fish? Is this preference merely a quirk of scholarship intended as an irritation to laggard students? Kuhn has suggested a different explanation:

After various classification systems are tried, that one is considered best which contains the largest amount of information for the purpose of the scientists. It is the most efficient system for handling the kinds of information the scientists want, or more precisely, the system which permits the largest amounts of information to be deduced from a given amount of information. For example, the biologist is distressed if someone refers to whales and porpoises as fish, insisting adamantly that they *are* mammals, not fish. We will accept his assertion that they *are* mammals under his system of classification, and go beyond to inquire why biologists prefer a classification system which thus categorizes them. They could, after all, put all water-dwelling animals in one group and all land-dwelling ones in another, with appropriate but non-overlapping subdivisions of each. In such a system the whale and porpoise could never fall into the same category with any land animals, as they now do.

We will now try to see why a system which classifies whales and porpoises as mammals, which are overwhelmingly land animals, provides more information than a system which classifies them as water animals. Under the existing system, if we possess a specimen of a thing called a fish, we know without looking further that we will find a particular kind of circulatory, nervous, excretory, and other systems, and that we will also find gills for the breathing of water. Suppose instead that the term "fish" were broadened to include whales and porpoises, because they look like fish and live in the water. Then even if we knew that we had a fish in front of us, this fact would not tell us whether the specimen has lungs or gills, or what kind of other internal systems it would show. Another well-known conspicuous example is the classification of bats as mammals instead of birds.[7]

The student who asserts that whales are *called* mammals because they *are* mammals is confusing analytic and contingent content. Children mistakenly believe that the names of things mirror the nature of things. Vigotsky, upon asking children whether we could switch names so that a cow would be called ink, and ink cow, received as a reply, "No, because ink is to write with, and cows give milk." [8]

Although definitions should be the results of reflective inquiry, sometimes opposition to or support of a social policy becomes a dominant purpose, and definitions are thereby affected. At the turn of this century, for example, a certain group opposed voluntary health insurance as an instance of socialized medicine. Some years later, the same group began to advocate voluntary health insurance as an alternative to socialized medicine! In 1900, voluntary health insurance was part of the extensional meaning of socialized medicine. Later it was not. How did this rather radical shift in the extensional meaning of a term come about? Americans

[7] Alfred Kuhn, *The Study of Society: A Unified Approach*, Dorsey Press, 1963, pp. 32–33.
[8] L. S. Vigotsky, "Thought and Speech,' *Psychiatry*, 2:36, 1939, quoted by Kuhn, *loc. cit.*, p. 33.

in general have a negative attitude toward socialized medicine. Therefore, if they can be convinced that x is an instance of socialized medicine, they are likely to oppose x without any other knowledge of x. When voluntary health insurance was viewed as a threat to the profits of organized medicine, it was a strategic move to label such insurance with a bad name. Later, after organized medicine had made peace with voluntary health insurance, compulsory insurance became the enemy and was given the same bad name. A teacher could ask students to produce an intensional definition of socialized medicine for either era, and then to compare the attributes of any kind of insurance, voluntary or compulsory, with the attributes of socialized medicine. This is proper procedure for teaching any concept reflectively.

The tendency of some to call this country a republic rather than a democracy poses a similar problem. A policy such as a minimum-wage law may be advocated in the name of democracy, only to be met with the comment, "But America is a republic, not a democracy." How can a teacher expose this comment to reflective criteria, and so avoid any temptation to indoctrinate his own point of view? If he takes an extensional approach, he might point out that Red China and the Soviet Union are usually cited by political scientists as republics. Are these countries democracies? Is this country a republic? Is it a democracy? Can any country be both a republic and a democracy? Why do Red China and the United States oppose one another, if both are republics? Are the differences between us at all political? This line of questioning moves gradually into the problem of intensional definitions of republic and democracy. Students will learn from this line of questioning that some republics are more democratic than others, and that growth toward democracy does not undermine our republican form of government.

The procedure of defining a category intensionally, and sorting examples according to whether they belong in or out of the category, rather than using meanings that relate to narrowly conceived social purposes, is the proper way to attack any problem that involves conflicting meanings.

A somewhat different approach is to be recommended with problems that involve the truth or falsity of contingent statements. The assertion, to use one example, that socialized medicine leads to a loss of professional freedom among physicians is not an analytic claim as much as a contingent one. It is the kind of claim that should be tested against the evidence, provided that evidence is available. This claim does, however, have its analytic elements. That is, we could not test its truth without first establishing the meaning of "socialized medicine" and "professional freedom." A reflective teacher seeks to have students deal with both the analytic and contingent elements of an idea.

Testing the Analytic

Our discussion thus far would seem to indicate that the only test of a concept, or any other analytic expression, is a logical one. Bruner has expressed their logical nature when he refers to concepts as a "network of inferences that are or may be set into play by an act of categorization." [9] He puts it more clearly perhaps when he says: "We see an object that is red, shiny, and roundish and infer that it is an apple; we are than enabled to infer further that 'if it is an apple, it is also edible, juicy, will rot if left unrefrigerated, etc.' . . ." [10] This pattern of inference, of course, is appropriate only to a conjunctive concept. The network of inference would be quite different for disjunctive or relational concepts.

The use of logic in testing analytic content is best exemplified in a school subject such as geometry. In plane geometry, one proves a theorem by demonstrating that a certain conclusion follows from certain definitions and axioms. A proof can be wrong only if one errs in his logic. Students who know the nature of geometry, in addition to knowing geometry, are aware of its built-in logic. Because logic is built into the subject, it was once believed that study of geometry would develop a person's logical powers. This proved to be erroneous. Perhaps it would have been less erroneous had teachers made their students aware of the analytic nature of mathematics and of how logic is used in putting mathematical concepts to a test. It is this kind of teaching that some people may have in mind when they refer to making students aware of the structure of a discipline.

In addition to a logical test, the analytic may be examined on a practical basis. That is, how useful is a given analytic system for the achievement of certain human purposes? Hullfish and Smith have pointed to this test as a way of making analytic content responsive to experience in much the same way that the synthetic regularly responds. The nature of this test is revealed whenever we attempt to use analytic content to achieve some end. Although it is true that analytic content is invented, rather than discovered, and therefore does not mirror reality, it can be applied to reality. We apply the analytic content of Euclidean geometry to reality when we lay out a baseball diamond. Another kind of geometry, with different conceptions, is required to put a man on Mars. Whether Euclidean geometry and its concepts is good geometry depends upon our purposes.

Entire conceptual systems and theories may be rejected when it becomes apparent that they no longer serve important human purposes.

[9] Bruner, *op. cit.*, p. 244.
[10] *Ibid.*

Consider for a moment the fate of the full-employment theory in classical economics. According to this classical theory propounded by Adam Smith, an economy could be in equilibrium only if employment were full. If the supply of labor exceeded the demand for labor, the surplus labor (unemployment) would drive down wages. This would then cause some reduction in the labor supply and some increase in labor demand with the result that the supply and demand would come into balance. At equilibrium, there would be no unemployment. No one would be looking for work without being able to find it. This neat and automatic adjustment could best take place without government interference. In the 1930's, this theory failed completely as a basis for explaining or implementing economic growth and full employment. It was Keynes, with new concepts, who explained the failure and offered a remedy. His basic conclusion was that an economy such as ours could be in equilibrum at a point short of full employment, and that it could remain in such equilibrium unless government took action.

Stereotypes and Concepts

There is a special kind of concept called a stereotype. Here, the category implies several traits, but the traits do not imply the category. A stereotype is different from a scientific concept in the same way that a one-way street is different from a two-way one. Compare the stereotype that some people have for Negro with a scientific concept such as mammal. The stereotype holds that all Negroes are lazy, stupid, and untrustworthy. People who accept this stereotype will reason that *anyone* who is a Negro is lazy, stupid, and untrustworthy. They will not, however, reason than anyone who is lazy, stupid, and untrustworthy is a Negro. They reason from the category to traits, but never from traits to category. Hence, stereotypy is always a one-way street.

It is quite otherwise with a scientific concept. If we know that a whale is a mammal, we infer certain traits. If we know that an animal has these traits, we infer that it is a mammal. We reason from category to traits, *or* from traits to category. Unless we can travel both ways on a street it is not marked as scientific concept.[11]

An objection to the foregoing treatment of concepts and stereotypes is that stupidity, laziness, and unreliability are not defining attributes of the category, Negro. The defining attributes are the physical traits with which we identify persons as Negro. Beliefs about the moral and intellectual character of Negroes constitute the stereotype, but not the cate-

---

[11] Again, we refer only to conjunctive concepts.

gory. It is nevertheless true that part of the meaning of this category is to be found in its stereotype.

Inductive vs. Reflective Teaching

Within any generalized model for teaching concepts, different kinds of teaching are possible. Inductive teaching, sometimes called "the method of discovery," has become one of the most popular of so-called new methods. It is usually urged as a more effective kind of teaching than the expository type followed by most teachers. The method of discovery, now typical of many of the new experimental curriculums, first came to everyone's attention when Max Beberman, with a financial assist from the Carnegie Corporation, proceeded to revolutionize the teaching of high-school mathematics.[12] It received additional publicity from Bruner's now-famous essay.[13] (The fact that Pestalozzi, and others more ancient than he, discovered discovery centuries before Bruner is not generally acknowledged by those who are modern-day enthusiasts of inductive teaching.)

This method of teaching is now a central emphasis in many of the curriculum projects in the social studies; and, although the method enjoys increasing popularity, many of its advocates are not clear as to what is meant by inductive teaching. Whether inductive teaching is the same as reflective teaching is one of the confusions.

One of the clearest definitions of inductive teaching has been presented by Henderson, an intelligent and mild-mannered advocate of the method.[14] He has also indicated what he believes to be its strengths and weaknesses. In his definition, he sets forth four steps or phases.

First, the teacher selects a concept or generalization that he wants students to learn.

Second, the teacher selects, or has his students select, instances of the concept or generalization. In the social studies this might well mean that the teacher who wants his students to learn the concept of revolution would put before them descriptions of several cases of revolution. Each revolution would have its unique features, but there would hopefully be some properties that all the examples would have in common, and which would constitute the meaning of revolution.

[12] Max Beberman, *An Emerging Program of Secondary School Mathematics,* in Robert W. Heath, ed., *New Curricula,* Harper & Row, 1964, pp. 9–34.

[13] Jerome S. Bruner, "The Act of Discovery," *Harvard Educational Review, 31*: 21–32, 1961.

[14] Kenneth B. Henderson, "Anent the Discovery Method," *Mathematics Teacher,* April, 1957, pp. 287–291.

Third, the teacher guides the students' thinking so that their attention is focused upon relevant detail. He does this through questions and prescriptions. He is concerned at this stage that students look for common features of revolutions. He wants students to learn what distinguishes revolution from nonrevolution.

Fourth, the teacher actually educes the concept to the point where students can put it into words, or some other kind of symbolization. If he encounters difficulty at this stage, he may repeat stages two and three, using different and perhaps simpler questions and prescriptions.

There are some teachers, and these are among the more effectives ones, who ask students to apply the newly acquired concept to situations similar to the ones from which the concept was acquired. A teacher might ask, for example, whether a revolution is now taking place in Vietnam. This is called the application stage.

Advocates of inductive method believe that it increases student interest, and that a student is more likely to retain that which he discovers. These may be valid claims, but Henderson points out that it is unfair to expository teaching to compare good examples of inductive teaching with poor examples of expository teaching. Either kind of teaching can be done well or poorly. It is poor expository teaching to make no effort to relate one's teaching to students' background. It is poor inductive teaching to give students psychological clues—as happens when the smile of a teacher indicates to a class that its guessing is "getting warm." Because the discovery method encourages students to hypothesize (make guesses) they are alert to any sign that they are making more accurate guesses. They should measure progress by logical criteria, not by signs of teacher approval. Studies that compare inductive teaching with expository teaching have been rare, and the few we have are not conclusive in their findings.

Henderson has indicated that there is a danger that students who experience only the inductive method will get the erroneous idea that all content is synthetic in nature. Because this method engages them in inductive thinking, its exclusive use in a subject such as mathematics may lead them to believe that mathematics is the same kind of science as physics. If they are to learn that mathematics is an exercise in postulational thinking, their teacher must develop for them the difference between analytic and synthetic truth. The same obligation falls upon a social-studies teacher who wishes to teach a difference between concepts and generalizations. To carry out this obligation a teacher may find that expository teaching is a useful device.

Inductive teaching elicits from students inductive thinking. To the extent that it omits any emphasis upon deductive thinking it is not fully reflective. There is no doubt however that reflection has discovery as one of its aspects. A review of reflective teaching in science class as reported on pages 70 and 71 points up the role of discovery. Sometimes inductive teaching gives inordinate attention to a search for supporting cases, and almost no attention to the possibility of negative ones. A variant of this emphasis upon positive cases is having the students reach the conclusion a teacher wants them to reach. Bruner, an advocate of inductive teaching, has issued this warning:

> Much of the problem in leading a child to effective cognitive activity is to free him from the immediate control of environmental rewards and punishments. That is to say, learning that starts in response to the rewards of parental or teacher approval or the avoidance of failure can too readily develop a pattern in which the child is seeking cues as to how to conform to what is expected of him. We know from studies of children who tend to be early overachievers in school that they are likely to be seekers after the "right way to do it" and that their capacity for transforming their learning into viable thought structures tends to be lower than children merely achieving at levels predicted by intelligence tests. Our tests on such children show them to be lower in analytic ability than those who are not conspicuous in overachievement. As we shall see later, they develop rote abilities and depend upon being able to "give back" what is expected rather than to make it something that relates to the rest of their cognitive life. As Maimonides would say, their learning is not their own.[15]

Bruner directed his comment to those who conduct recitations, or engage in other acts of expository teaching. But the same pupil sensitivity to teacher approval can develop under inductive teaching. If the teacher gives away the answer through facial expressions or tone of voice, a kind of rote learning can occur in students. Compliance to teacher authority can develop if a teacher refuses to entertain any meaning for a concept other than the one he has selected in advance for students to learn. With empirical generalizations, a teacher may focus student search upon positive cases rather than emphasize a search for exceptional or negative cases. Any of these practices can mean that inductive teaching fails to be inductive, and fails in its intended purposes.

Inductive teaching, even when it succeeds in becoming an exemplification of inductive thinking, is not the same as reflective teaching. Reflective teaching has both inductive and deductive elements. The method of discovery is probably most effective for testing empirical generalizations, provided that due attention is given to a search for negative cases. It is probably least appropriate for the teaching of con-

[15] Bruner, "The Act of Discovery," in Richard C. Anderson and David P. Ausubel, eds., *Readings in Cognitive Psychology*, Holt, Rinehart, & Winston, 1965, pp. 612–613.

cepts; not because it is ineffective, but because it misrepresents concepts by peddling them as empirical truths. If we are to teach the nature of concepts, then we are forced into some kind of deductive (expository) teaching. Expository teaching, if it is well executed, can avoid the pitfall of rote learning. The claim that expository teaching can result only in rote learning, and that only the method of discovery can produce genuine insight is probably not a valid observation. If teaching is reflective, it probably makes use of some combination of inductive and expository teaching.

When Is a Concept Learned?

The answer to this question depends partly upon a teacher's expectations and demands. It is evident in the literature of education and psychology that mastery of any concept may take place at several levels. Broudy has discussed nine degrees of mastery.[16] The least mastery is demonstrated by a student who responds to the question, "What is a tariff?" with the textbook answer, "A tax on imports." The greatest degree of mastery, according to Broudy, is offered by the student who can use a concept such as tariff as one of the elements in a social theory.

Henderson has identified six levels of concept attainment.[17] He agrees with Broudy that the least mastery is exhibited by the student who can repeat textbook content verbatim. His second level is represented by the student who can give a definition in his own words. At the third level the student can give examples. The next level in attainment is found in a student who can apply his concept to new problems for which he may have been told by the teacher that the concept is relevant. The fifth level is one at which a student can see the relevance of a concept to a problem without any help from the teacher or any other second party. The sixth, and highest, level of mastery is to be found in a student who can prove his concept as well as apply it. Henderson doubts that the method of discovery can achieve this sixth level of understanding. He has no empirical evidence for this claim, but bases it upon logical grounds.

LEVELS OF CONCEPT ATTAINMENT

If we accept Bruner's notion of concept as category, it is convenient to think of four levels of concept learning: recognition, classification, definition, and generalization.

[16] Harry S. Broudy, *Mastery*, in B. Othanel Smith and Robert H. Ennis, ed., *Language and Concepts in Education*, Rand McNally, 1961, pp. 72–85.
[17] Henderson, *op. cit.*, pp. 290–291.

Recognition. If a student gives meaning to a term in context, at least to the extent that he feels no perplexity such as might turn him to a dictionary, we say that he is able to handle the term on a recognition level. When this student meets a concept such as "big business" or "competition" in his reading assignment, he is able to read on without stopping. He has seen these terms in this context before, and they give him no trouble. He thinks that he knows what they mean, and indeed he may. But his teacher is not always sure, and few of us would settle for this level of attainment. There is too much to suggest that recognition alone does not represent what most of us mean by conceptual learning. Everyone at one time or another has fallen into the pitfall of easy familiarity. Sometimes a teacher quickly learns how little a student understands a certain concept by placing it in another context or frame of reference.

Classification. If we ask a student to give examples of big business or competition, we are trying to move him to a second level of attainment, i.e., classification, sometimes called identification and sorting. Let us suppose that we give a student a list of events and ask him to pick out the ones that are instances of competition. In this sorting assignment, he is asked to identify those events and only those events that belong in the category, competition. He has been asked to group events into classes, and to respond to them in terms of their class membership rather than their uniqueness. This concern with the generality of events, not their isolated particularity, is essential to any successful attempt to teach concepts in the social studies.

Definition. Even though students may know a concept well enough to sort instances into and out of it, they may not know the concept well enough to express verbally the basis of their sorting. A student might recognize examples of competition but be unable to put into words the criteria upon which membership in the category is based. He is like a small child who never confuses an apple with a grape but cannot verbally indicate their differences. Unfortunately, we have teachers addicted to the expression "merely verbal," who flinch at any notion that verbal knowledge is superior to knowledge manifested by behavior. Verbalism, they say, is bad, and the real purpose of education is to change behavior.

This kind of argument, if carried far enough, denies the importance of man's conceptual superiority over other living organisms—a superiority based in no small part upon possession of a culture, a major ingredient of which is language. The highly evolved symbolic systems of physics and mathematics are in a certain sense merely verbal, and it is difficult to imagine what we would teach in social studies if we rejected verbal content. The very instances we ask students to identify and sort will in most cases be verbal instances. Perhaps in our condemnation of "merely verbal" learning we should have in mind the student who can only memorize and repeat verbatim the contents of textbooks. The capacity to indicate verbally the basis for behavioral sorting of objects or events we take as evidence for a third level of concept attainment—i.e., definition.

Generalization or Theorization. Once students can see the basis for sorting instances into or out of a category, their understanding of that category is enhanced as they come to see its role within a total conceptual system. Conceptual systems consist of relationships among concepts. A part of the meaning of any concept is to be found in its relationship to another concept or concepts. The teacher who seeks this level of concept attainment may ask his students not only to relate one concept to another, but to look for empirical evidence on the validity of any hypothesized relationship. In the teaching of economic understanding, for example, the teacher will foster a study of possible relationships between such concepts as economic growth, economic stability, and economic security. This study could include studies of policy statements issued by business, labor, government, and agriculture; each of which may suggest somewhat different relationships between growth, stability, and security. An examination of policy statements to determine whether they would achieve their stated consequences would constitute the heart of such inquiry. This kind of inquiry requires students to use economic theory as a basis for examining probable consequences of specific policy proposals. This fourth level of concept attainment moves one from considerations definitional to matters propositional.

Although this chapter has focused on concepts as analytic statements, definitional and categorial in nature, this fourth level of concept attainment makes clear that the testing of synthetic statements constitutes part of the import of any concept.

In this chapter, then, we have distinguished between concepts and generalizations, and have suggested that each calls for a somewhat different kind of treatment. The classroom procedures that help students learn concepts are different in crucial respects from those that help students use evidence in the examination of generalizations. At the same time, concepts and generalizations are not unrelated to each other. Without concepts, it is impossible to make generalizations.

Much of the meaning of any concept is to be found in linkages between it and other concepts. It may be useful to think of a concept as having both broad and narrow meaning. When we think of a bachelor as an unmarried male, we are dealing with the narrow meaning of a concept. When we include all the beliefs that people hold about bachelors, and all the attitudes that are taken toward them, we are dealing with the broader meaning of this particular concept.

We cannot effectively teach a concept without taking up its broad meaning. First, however, it is desirable to make sure that students are clear as to its narrow meaning. It is in this sense important that we use a strategy in teaching concepts that is different from a strategy for teaching generalizations.

DISCUSSION QUESTIONS AND EXERCISES

1. How is a concept different from a fact? From a generalization?
2. Is a generalization ever a fact?
3. How do we teach a conjunctive concept?
4. On what basis can a teacher conclude that a concept has been learned?
5. If there is dispute in a classroom over the proper meaning for a concept, how should the teacher handle the dispute? Does every concept have a proper meaning?
6. Compare inductive teaching with expository. With reflective teaching, is one clearly superior to the others?

REFERENCES

BEARDSLEY, MONROE C., and ELIZABETH L., *Philosophical Thinking: An Intro-duction*, New York, Harcourt, Brace & World, 1965.

> Excellent material on the differences between analytic and synthetic content. Contains a good discussion on the nature of science.

BROUDY, HARRY S., B. OTHANEL SMITH, and JOE R. BURNETT, *Democracy and Excellence in American Secondary Education*, Chicago, Rand McNally, 1964.

> Some excellent analysis of the teaching of concepts can be found in Chapters VIII and IX.

BRUNER, JEROME, et al., *A Study of Thinking*, New York, Wiley, 1956.

> An important study in the learning of concepts. Has some rich material on the nature of concepts, their function and kinds. Bruner is one of the leading cognitive psychologists.

HULLFISH, H. GORDON, and PHILIP G. SMITH, *Reflective Thinking: The Method of Education*, New York, Dodd, Mead, 1961.

> Read Chapters 5 and 6 for an understanding of how to ground analytic and synthetic content. The distinction between form and function is basic. It is possible for a statement that is synthetic in form to function in thought as an

analytic statement. In such a case, attempts to run a synthetic test usually fail to produce thought.

SMITH, B. OTHANEL, and ROBERT ENNIS, eds., *Language and Concepts in Education*, Chicago, Rand McNally, 1961.

A most important book on education. Basic articles on concepts of education and teaching are included.

CHAPTER 5

Teaching Generalizations

STATEMENTS that perform a synthetic function are of two kinds, one singular, the other general. The statement that "Brown lives in Illinois" is an example of the synthetic singular. Such statements are usually designated by teachers as "facts." When teachers claim that such facts must be learned before thinking is possible, they exhibit a misunderstanding of the thinking process.

The synthetic general is exemplified by a statement such as "People who live in cities commit more crime than people who live in small towns and rural areas." The synthetic general is just as factual as the synthetic singular, and any generalization that happens to be true can be designated a fact. Many teachers are eager to teach those facts that are represented by the synthetic singular, but hesitate to teach generalizations as represented by the synthetic general.

In this chapter, we shall use the term *fact* when we wish to refer to the synthetic singular, and the term *generalization* when we wish to refer to the synthetic general. Readers should keep in mind, however, that any generalization that has been tested and found to be true qualifies as a fact. A true generalization is a more meaningful fact than any synthetic-singular statement could ever hope to be, because it covers more territory—refers to more cases.

Brodbeck has said that facts are trivial unless they are connected with other facts. A generalization connects facts with each other. The fact that a student's IQ is 110 means very little. But, if there is a generalization that relates IQ to school achievement, we can hazard a prediction about the student's likelihood of success in college. Without generalizations, prediction or explanation is impossible. Significant facts are those that tell us whether a certain generalization is probably true. Teachers who want facts to have meaning, and who want students to learn explanations of events and to acquire some capacity to predict events, will necessarily emphasize the teaching of generalizations.[1]

As indicated in Chapter 4, facts may be given another kind of order through invention and use of concepts. Without concepts and general-

[1] May Brodbeck *Logic and Scientific Method in Research on Teaching*, in N.L. Gage, ed., *Handbook of Research on Teaching*, Rand McNally, 1963.

izations, facts exist in a state of disarray. When teachers think about organization of content, they should think about the concepts and generalizations they want to teach. A student cannot understand conflicts in the closed areas or disharmonies in personal belief until he learns relevant concepts and generalizations.

Evidence and Generalizations

Students will find that many of their beliefs take the form of generalizations. They will also encounter generalizations in their reading assignments. Any generalization becomes a hypothesis when someone doubts its truth. A hypothesis is tested by determining how well it explains propositions deduced from it and how well it anticipates new data. If one wishes to discover whether men are more intelligent than women, one deduces if-then propositions, such as "If men are more intelligent than women, then, they should make higher average scores on intelligence tests." These deduced propositions are then tested with factual data, which either support or cast doubt on the hypothesis. What is the nature of the factual data used in this testing?

Facts, as we use the term, are not objects or processes; they are statements which represent tested insights. Facts have a creative aspect; they never mean exactly the same to any two individuals. However, if they are acquired reflectively and state matters which are relatively simple to investigate, they may have approximately the same meaning for large numbers of individuals. One aim of education is to accomplish this commonness of meaning.

Factual evidence, then, consists of statements that have a high probability of being true and are relevant to determining the truth of a hypothesis. In connection with the IQ hypothesis above, the following statement would be pertinent evidence: "The average IQ score of a representative sample of women is 103; the average score of men, 99." This statement is likely to have approximately similar meanings for most people who understand what is involved in intelligence testing. To serve adequately as evidence in problem solving, factual statements must have the same general qualities as hypotheses; they must by their nature be verifiable. They are cast in declarative-sentence form, with meanings phrased as unambiguously as possible.

It is important to understand that hypothetical and factual statements are interchangeable. *Hypotheses* become *facts* as they are tested reflectively and *fact judgments revert to hypotheses* whenever there is good reason to doubt their truth. However, the relationship between hypotheses and facts is more complex than this. Sometimes a statement that cannot be adequately verified is made to function as evidence because, at that time, there is *somewhat* more warrant for accepting it than for accepting the hypothesis it is being used to test. In other words, in a given problem, we may use statements of which we are *more sure* to test statements of which we are *less sure*. This may not appear to be a satisfactory situation, but it is the best we can do, given the nature of scientific truth getting, and the exigencies of daily living. Although a person who tries to live reflectively usually withholds action until he has had a chance to think about it, he cannot wait until "all the data are in." It is never possible to know when the data are all in; yet in social affairs, action is always necessary. A decision not to act is a decision, and even a form of action. If a person acts in terms of the best evaluation he can make of currently obtainable data, he behaves wisely. Reasons for pursuing one line of behavior may be only slightly better than those for pursuing another. If we are reflective, we follow the behavior which commands the most support.

WHERE WE GET DATA

Students in social-studies classes may make use of factual data drawn from several sources: (1) remembered experience, (2) observation and experimentation, and (3) authorities.

Data from remembered experience usually come from students themselves. That is, for every problem studied, students will have a background on which to draw. Evidence a group of students can recall from their own experiences may, of itself, be sufficient to solve some problems. In such cases, students pool information and interpret remembered facts in accordance with requirements of the problem. Many problems involving school, home, and community affairs are handled in this manner.

Students may find it useful to examine the remembered experience of others—teachers, adults in general, parents, specialists. To this end they may solicit information through polls or interviews, or invite resource persons into the classroom. Another source of remembered experience is documents—books, magazines, pamphlets, and newspapers. Remembered data is sometimes called historical data.

A word of warning on the use of remembered data is appropriate at this point. Although personal experience is often a valuable source of evidence, it is necessary to make certain that what is adduced from experience is dependable evidence. It is not uncommon for persons to romanticize, falsify, and misinterpret their own experiences, despite the best of intentions. Before personal experience is admissible as evidence it requires rigorous interpretation. Teachers must be prepared to ask, "Did it really happen that way?" "Is this your personal interpretation, and would others regard it the way you do?" and "How conclusive is an experience of this sort?" Even documentary evidence must undergo careful scrutiny before it can be treated as valid data.

The second broad class of data, facts procured through current observation or experiment, represents "new" data, contemporary rather than historical. The use of research, in the sense of creating new data, is not now common in social-studies classes. However, students sometimes conduct community surveys of one sort or another, or pursue other limited types of research. Social-studies teachers need grounding in the research techniques of the social sciences in order to make greater use of contemporary data.

Whether data are drawn from remembered experience or from contemporary research, much of the time students of the social studies will have to rely to some degree on the opinions of authorities. It is essential, therefore, that we examine the role of authorities in the social sciences. Most of the time, we use facts verified by someone else, taking his word for it that the statements are actually true. Even if one had the time and opportunity to investigate directly all of the problems in which he is interested, he would still have to rely heavily on the observations or experiments of others.

In the case of questions which have been settled to the satisfaction of most investigators, we may accept the facts disclosed with a great deal of confidence. Though never to be taken as finally conclusive, consensus of competent investigators is one of our best indications of truth. However, many issues in the realm of social affairs have not been settled in such a definitive way. The most respected authorities are likely to disagree among themselves as to which insights are most reliable in such areas as economics, politics, sex, religion, and race.

Some of the problems involved in using expert opinion in the social sciences are well illustrated within the field of economics. This field is split into a number of "schools of thought"—neoclassicists, institutionalists, socialists, underconsumptionists, and Keynesians, to name a few—and the opinions of members of one school may differ drastically from those of members of another. To the great confusion of the unsophisticated, these differences of opinion may occur in connection with fundamental issues. Nevertheless, there are many propositions in economics on the truth or falsity of which most economists agree. It is well to note that some of the differences among economists reflect differences in values, not in knowledge and understanding.

Before a class places reliance on the pronouncements of any supposed authority, it should ask and try to answer questions such as these:

1. Is he recognized as an authority by other experts in the field in which he speaks?

2. Is he in substantial agreement with other authorities in his field?
3. Does he base his opinion on evidence gained from the reflective method?
4. Is his own social and economic status unrelated to the disputed issue? (i.e., does he have any personal reasons for being biased?)
5. Is he likely to be free from bias on other counts—e.g., is he free from marked religious, racial, class or other prejudices? [2]

Unfortunately, pseudo authorities are very common in our society. There is no question on which most newspaper columnists and radio and television commentators are not willing and eager to make confident pronouncements. Many politicians, preachers, professors, and business men seem equally disposed to make dogmatic assertions about social issues. These individuals let their publicly expressed opinions range freely over the fields of economics, history, political science, sociology, psychology, anthropology, and philosophy even though most of them have but little, if any, specialized training in these fields. Often they have axes to grind—as when a power-company executive gives the "inside story" of the TVA, or a labor leader "describes" the economic effects of various wage policies. Both teachers and students must be on guard against pseudo authorities.

It is always a mistake to judge the truth of an idea according to its source. A very sound idea may come from an inexpert source; and sparks of truth may appear even as axes are ground. The ultimate test of a hypothesis is evidence, not origin.

It is necessary to use great care in interpreting responsible experts. One of the most common errors in interpretation is using a quotation out of context. The meaning of a sentence or paragraph can usually be fully understood only in relation to what has gone before, or what comes after. As Beardsley points out, "You can make the Bible say, 'There is no God,' if, in quoting, you omit the first part of the sentence. . . ." [3]

HOW TO USE DATA AS EVIDENCE

The testing process applied to a hypothesis cannot be understood apart from its general aim, which is not to reach certainty—i.e., not to achieve absolute or ultimate truth—but to find either corroborating or damaging cases. Whether such cases are corroborating or damaging, we learn something. We learn whether to believe our hypothesis.

A hypothesis is supported when facts *implied* by it correspond to facts

[2] For a more thorough treatment of the role of authorities in investigation see Anatol Rapoport, *Science and Goals of Man*, Harper & Row, 1950, chap. 5.
[3] Monroe C. Beardsley, *Thinking Straight: A Guide for Readers and Writers*, Prentice-Hall, 1950, p. 35.

acquired by observation, or from memory or reliable authorities. By the implied facts of a hypothesis we mean those statements which must be true if a hypothesis is to be taken as true. An example of hypothesis testing by direct observation may clarify what we mean: Suppose a school janitor enters a classroom after teacher and students have gone for the day. He finds one of the windows broken. He remembers boys playing baseball in the adjoining field shortly after school. The idea (hypothesis) suggests itself to him that a pitched or batted ball smashed through the window. Now what does it mean to say that a hypothesis such as this implies some facts that may or may not correspond with observed facts? If the window had been struck by any kind of flying object *from the outside*—a general statement of the janitor's original hypothesis—most of the broken glass should be found *inside the room*. If observation reveals that most of the broken glass is located within the room, the hypothesis has been corroborated. Finding most of the broken glass outside the room would damage the hypothesis.[4]

It takes less evidence to reject or modify a hypothesis than to confirm it. If any observed fact contradicts any fact implied by a hypothesis, truth of the hypothesis must be seriously questioned. Finding most of the broken glass outside the room is damaging enough to force the janitor to reject or rephrase his hypothesis. On the other hand, finding most of the broken glass inside the room, although confirming the hypothesis, does not clinch the case for it. The janitor will want to make additional tests by looking for other examples of correspondence between implied and observed facts. Finding a baseball in one corner of the room would constitute additional corroboration.

In the course of his investigation, the janitor may exhaust his supply of observed facts, and be forced to turn to facts available to him only indirectly. That is, he begins to interview other people—students, teachers, other janitors—in an effort to find whether any of them have observed a fact which confirms or refutes his hypothesis. Most problem solving eventually makes use of such indirect knowledge.

Suppose all the available facts support more than one hypothesis. Suppose that most of the broken glass is outside the room and that no baseball has been found. These observations would support the idea that the window was broken by a blow from within the room. But the same evidence could be interpreted to mean that the window was broken by a batted ball from the outside, and that the guilty person entered the room, swept up most of the debris, and deposited it outside the window, in order to leave the impression that the window had been broken from the inside.

[4] Boyd H. Bode, *Fundamentals of Education*, Macmillan, 1926, p. 110.

Note that the facts as to the present location of broken glass confirm equally either hypothesis. In most cases, further investigation would turn up additional facts which would refute one of the hypotheses, and thus make it possible for an investigator to settle upon the other. But what if this is not the case? Can an investigator express a preference for one hypothesis over another when the facts support both? There is a principle in scientific inquiry called the rule of simplicity. One can validly prefer the simpler of two hypotheses, the one that calls for the fewest assumptions. We shall have more to say about this rule later.

What are we to conclude about any hypothesis for which the data are contradictory? If we find in one community that there is a strong positive correlation between education and income, in another community a strong negative correlation, and in still another no significant correlation at all, we must discard any hypothesis that relates or associates these two variables. A hypothesis is useful, i.e., serves its purpose, only when it brings order to obtainable and pertinent data. Ideally, a hypothesis should explain data that would otherwise lack order. The data should all point in the same direction. There should be no data which we do not understand because they do not "fit" our ideas. In short, hypotheses, if they are to have maximum reliability, should harmonize all the pertinent facts. As long as a hypothesis fails to explain or harmonize all the data available and pertinent, we should continue the search for a better one. At any given time we make use of the most adequate hypothesis we can achieve, but we continually reconstruct it as we gain new insight.

Ideally, we accept a hypothesis only if it has no exceptions. Such an exceptionless hypothesis is, in modern usage, called a law. A law has a descriptive-explanatory function. Sometimes we cannot achieve this ideal. Hypotheses which do not order all the data may be phrased to allow for exceptions. The use of terms such as "usually" or "probably" or "possibly" allow for exceptions, as does the word, "tendency." The use of such terms, if not carefully watched, can conceal the fact that the hypothesizer knows less than he is willing to admit.

On the other hand, the use of accommodating terms need not lead to an underevaluation of our knowledge: Not every child who is exposed to measles acquires the disease, but most children who acquire the disease have been exposed to those who have it. Although we cannot predict the percentage of exposed children who will acquire measles, we do have knowledge sufficient to recognize possible results of exposure and to prevent exposed children from contracting the disease. It is perhaps saying a great deal to say that exposed children, unless treated, *tend* to get measles. Social-studies teachers can be at least as unabashed as practitioners of medical science.

A hypothesis stated in such a way as to allow for exceptions is often a good "explainer," if not always a good "predictor." For example, to borrow once again from medicine, syphilis and paresis are known to be associated—although the correlation is not as high as some people assume. Paresis without syphilis is not usual, but syphilis without paresis is common. To put it another way, if a person has paresis, it makes sense to explore syphilis as a cause. But most syphilitics, even if untreated, never acquire paresis. It is risky then to predict that a person with syphilis will become paretic unless he seeks treatment. But it is easy to explain paresis by reference to syphilis. In the social studies, our explainers are often better than our predictors. Yet it is not impossible, and is becoming more and more common, for social scientists to predict accurately the consequences of a social policy.

Rules of Reflection

In order to teach generalizations, it is necessary to distinguish between good generalizations and poor ones. In practice, this distinction is more complex than simple application of the criteria offered on pages 76 and 77. Effective use of the reflective method depends, in part, on an understanding of the methodological principles upon which these criteria are based. First among these is, of course, the problem of sampling; then there are the principles of repetition, simplicity, adequacy, harmony, and continuous control to be considered. Each of these will be discussed in the following sections.

THE PROBLEM OF SAMPLING

Indirectly acquired knowledge is sometimes used in the formulation and testing of hypotheses simply because the personal observations of the problem solver are inadequate. One kind of indirect knowledge consists of relevant generalizations. Our school janitor, for example, applied a general knowledge about broken windows to a particular problem.

Social-studies students frequently do not have relevant first-hand knowledge. Their knowledge of war, unemployment, and poverty is likely to be indirect. At the same time, students do possess some generalizations relevant to some problems. Many of these generalizations may be false; others, though true, are ungrounded. A part of the teaching process will involve the student in a reexamination of these insights. This, in turn, will require him to use general knowledge from the various social sciences as evidence (provided that he can accept it as such) in testing his ideas.

In addition to making use of generalizations known to them and to their teacher, students may formulate and test hypothetical generaliza-

tions not yet a part of their present knowledge. To say that these generalizations are hypothetical means that they are hypothetical to any student,
or group of students, who are not sure of their truth, albeit their truth is
known to social scientists or teachers of social studies.

A hypothetical generalization is like any other hypothesis in that its
verifiability depends upon its content and phraseology, and how it
functions in thought. The methodological considerations for any hypothesis also hold for a hypothetical generalization. But another dimension has
been added. As if, for example, the janitor of the just-discussed episode
had wished to explain, not how a particular window was broken, but why
windows in general break, and thus add to his general knowledge about
windows. The janitor's original hypothesis arose from the methodological
considerations of (1) an ordering of all relevant data with (2) the simplest possible hypothesis. But an additional consideration applies whenever a hypothesis takes a general form: the *representativeness* of any
sample upon which a general conclusion is based. This criterion is as vital
to the students toying with a hypothetical generalization as it is to the
social scientist who is reaching for a new generalization.

Use of a sample is involved in any generalization that a social-studies
class might formulate and test. It makes no real difference whether the
class uses data already in its possession or whether it seeks additional data
from social-scientific studies. Both sets of data are based upon some
samples of a larger population. The student who states a generalization—
about, for example, juvenile delinquency—arising from his own experience may doubt its truth when his teacher asks, "How many juvenile
delinquents have you known, and were they typical delinquents?" The
student who reports the findings of a scholarly investigation in sociology
can be challenged with "Did the investigator study all delinquents?" and,
since no investigator ever does this, "Was his sample large enough, or,
more importantly, representative enough to permit us to conclude
anything about all delinquents?"

Since sampling technique is fundamental to investigation in the social
sciences, we shall examine it in more detail. One way of choosing cases
for study is to use *random selection.* For example, suppose we have on
cards the names of all people in a city, one name to a card. We shuffle the
cards thoroughly and—as in a lottery—draw out the number of names
required to make up our samples. The more heterogeneous the master
group, the larger the sample must be if it is to be truly representative. If
the master group is absolutely homogeneous—i.e., if all individuals are
identical—then only one case constitutes an adequate sample. If the
master group is relatively heterogeneous, we may draw items from it at
regular intervals. That is, instead of shuffling, we arrange the master
group according to some predetermined pattern (depending on what we

want to find out) and then pull, say, every tenth card, or interview every fifth family.

Proportional selection involves first examining all cases and noting the composition of the whole with respect to all significant factors. To illustrate: Suppose we want to conduct a poll of voting intentions in Precinct 20. We must first decide which factors are important in causing people to vote as they do, such as age, economic status, and party affiliation. Then we must determine just what proportion of voters are in each age group, in each economic class, and in each party. The sample is then deliberately chosen so that it will have the same distribution of ages, class, and party membership as the total population of the precinct.

Proportional selection is good sampling technique whenever it is possible to determine accurately the relevant typicalities of the master group. When these are known, increasing the size of the sample does not always increase its representativeness. A sample of a thousand cases may accurately represent a total population of millions.

There are no rules of thumb as to how large a sample must be to be representative, but there is an empirical test which shows well enough whether a sample is adequate: Select several samples by the same method and compare them as to results. If they differ very much, they are not representative.

An understanding of sampling technique will be of use to social-studies students undertaking community surveys or any other type of investigation which requires sampling procedures. More often, it will be of value in helping teacher and students to judge the validity of conclusions proffered by authorities. For the most part, social-studies students are "research consumers" rather than "research producers"; and critical use of the research of others depends on ability to appraise its reliability. An understanding of sampling technique helps students guard against overgeneralization in any situation where reflection is in process. Students (and sometimes teachers) often make sweeping generalizations from only one or two cases—even when dealing with items as heterogeneous as human beings. An elementary knowledge of sampling should help them evaluate the worth of a generalization based on one or a few cases.

Although increasing the size of a sample has no effect on the representativeness of a sample known to be representative, it does affect our confidence in any generalization suggested by data drawn from the sample. A discussion of the rule of repetition will make this point clear.

THE RULE OF REPETITION

Let us suppose that we have a representative sample of all voters in a rural Iowa county. As we study the voting habits revealed by the sample data we look for relationships among variables. (All generalizations express relationships among variables.) Our study might reveal that people in the sample who dislike price-support legislation are more likely to vote Republican than Democratic. The variables, voting Republican and disliking price-support legislation, are seen as related. We express the relationship as follows: "In such-and-such county in the State of Iowa, people who dislike price-support legislation tend to vote Republican." If anyone questions whether the voters in the study were typical of the voters in that county, we point to evidence on the representativeness of the voter sample.

There is another possible objection to our study. Someone might argue that the discovered relationship was a matter of coincidence and that a study based upon all voters in the county would show the relationship to be different. In answer to this argument, we have recourse to what has been called the *law of repetition*. This rule, which is used by all scientific investigators, states simply that:

When two things (events, characteristics) are observed to be repeatedly associated with each other (simultaneously or in succession) in a regular way (that is, the percentage of cases in which they are associated is constant), count on the association to continue, with a degree of confidence that increases with each case observed.[5]

In a representative sample of 50 cases, we might find that 60 percent of the Republican voters as against 25 percent of the Democratic voters had a negative attitude toward price-support legislation. A suspicion that this relationship was coincidental would be allayed if we found essentially the same relationship in a much larger sample. The more cases upon which a generalization is based, the more confident we are that the relationship will hold for future cases. If increasing the size of the sample results in a significant change in the character or size of the originally discovered relationship, we are left with two possibilities. Either the original sample was not as representative as we thought it was, or the original relationship was a matter of coincidence. The law of repetition cannot be applied unless one is confident that his sample is representative.

The fact that each additional supporting case strengthens a generalization, and the further fact that we never exhaust our supply of cases—what about Republicans and Democrats not yet born—means that an empirical generalization never achieves the status of final and absolute truth. (See discussion later in this chapter on the principle of continuous control.) We are willing to generalize about the future whenever we have a

[5] Monroe C. and Elizabeth L. Beardsley, *Philosophical Thinking: An Introduction*, Harcourt, Brace & World, 1965, p. 198.

generalization we think time is not likely to destroy. This kind or degree of confidence depends upon how long, or more accurately for how many cases, the generalization has worked.

Generalizations that rest upon scanty evidence are regarded as *trial generalizations*. These retain the status of hypotheses. As additional supporting cases become available, we gain confidence in these generalizations, and in time they may come to be regarded as highly reliable tools. But no generalization ever loses its trial character; it is always tentative, if it is empirical, in the sense that it is always subject to the test of further experience. Even the best grounded of generalizations have evolved from experience; and, since there is no end to experience, one cannot be totally sure that the future will not force a change in presently held insights. If we are sure that the sun will rise tomorrow, it is only because we have had thus far only supporting cases.

THE RULE OF SIMPLICITY

Earlier, we indicated that there is a preference for the simpler of two hypotheses when the data support both. This preference is based upon the *rule of simplicity*.

When two incompatible alternative hypotheses explain the same facts, and neither can be eliminated by available evidence, then, other things being equal, choose the simpler of the two hypotheses.[6]

This rule is also sometimes called the principle of parsimony. The history of science is replete with examples of its use. The mention of one is sufficiently illustrative: The ellipses of Kepler explain certain data more simply than do Ptolemy's epicycles, or Copernicus' complicated circles. In expressing a preference for simplicity the danger to avoid is oversimplification. We must be certain that the more simple hypothesis actually explains a situation without doing violence to its inherent complexities. We never prefer a simple explanation simply because it is simple. It must also be correct.

A careful reading of the rule of simplicity reveals that the alternative hypotheses must be incompatible. That is, acceptance of one forces rejection of the other. If it is possible to believe both hypotheses, or if each explains a different set of facts, the rule does not apply and ought not to be invoked.

Sometimes the word "simplicity" is used in reference to that which is understood;—we describe a situation we understand by calling it simple, while labeling as complex anything we don't understand. Ths is not the meaning of simplicity used in the rule of simplicity. Rather the rule

[6] *Ibid.*, p. 202.

refers to an explanation that employs the fewest possible number of concepts or variables.

THE RULE OF CONTINUOUS CONTROL

This principle is intended to alert investigators against the pitfall of absolute truth. Man may search for absolute truth, if he is unscientific, but he can never know whether he has discovered it. Scientists believe in endless inquiry for the same reason they do not believe in ultimate or absolute truth. Any belief—singular or general—about matters of fact is open to modification or rejection some time in the future regardless of how firm its support in the present.

The principle of continuous control observes a difference between warrant and correctness. When we say that we have warrant for believing something, we mean that we rest our belief upon evidence known to us. On the basis of known evidence we say that a given belief is correct. Further experience with this belief may reveal evidence not known to us in the past which reveals its incorrectness to us now. This means that our past warrant was not as good as we thought it was. Warrant is always a matter of evidence, and correctness is always a matter of warrant. Since no one can ever prove that he has all the evidence, it is risky to assume that beliefs which today are taken to be warranted will always enjoy that status in the future. Any warranted belief may turn out later to be incorrect and any unwarranted belief may develop later into a correct belief, provided that we keep ourselves open to new evidence. It is this openness to the voice of experience that the principle of continuous control would have us observe.[7]

THE RULE OF HARMONY

This principle emphasizes the importance of consistency. Generalizations should be consistent with each other, and with the data.

The rule of harmony asserts that a hypothesis is true if it brings order (harmony) to data that otherwise would not hang together and make sense. Take the following situation from everyday life:

A high school senior with a wide acquaintance is hurrying to school. She passes a dozen people she knows and mumbles a casual greeting to each. Suddenly her attention is caught. She turns and peers intently after the receding shape of Annabelle, who did not answer. Is this, perhaps, not Annabelle at all, but a total stranger? No, there is that hideous purple sweater. It is Annabelle. . . . Is Annabelle distracted, troubled, preoccupied? Has she perhaps quar-

[7] For the best discussion of the principle of continuous control see H. Gordon Hullfish and Philip Smith, *Reflective Thinking: The Method of Education,* Dodd, Mead, 1961, pp. 65-67.

reled with Joe? Or—wait a minute—could Helen have told Annabelle what I said about her the other day? [8]

In this example, absence of harmony is indicated by Annabelle's failure to respond to a greeting. This is the problem to be explained. The hypothesis that the person was not Annabelle but someone else was dismissed because the datum, hideous purple sweater, did not fit. The hypothesis that Annabelle was preoccupied will do if there are no data that fail to fit, and if it removes or explains the original disharmony. The same test applies to the hypothesis that Annabelle has fallen heir to some gossip. In order for either hypothesis to be satisfactory it must harmonize all known and relevant data. The extent of the data to be harmonized brings us to consideration of another rule or principle.

THE RULE OF ADEQUACY

This principle asserts that a conclusion should be consistent with all the data that are relevant. A hypothesis that harmonizes some of the relevant data, but not all of it, is unsatisfactory. That is, it fails to pass the test of the rule of adequacy. The words *all* and *relevant* need to be examined with some care before this rule can be understood.

Obviously, no teacher, student, or group of students ever knows all the data. Much data has not yet been discovered (hence, the relevance of the principle of continuous control), but much that is known is not known to a particular investigator or group of investigators. Bayles has said that a student or teacher observes the rule of adequacy if either is "inclined always to consider all data available and to obtain all data possible." [9] The rule is violated "if a pupil is inclined to ignore certain data or to terminate his quests for data while more are still obtainable." [10] Relevant data are any data which affect the truth status of a hypothesis.

Suppose that a person claims that Negroes are less intelligent than whites. In support of this statement he cites data which indicate that the average IQ of southern whites is greater than the average IQ of southern Negroes. In order to remove region as a factor, he may also cite data that northern whites have an average IQ greater than that of northern Negroes. If someone then observes that northern Negroes have an average IQ greater than southern whites, the claim of racial superiority is rendered dubious. We need a new hypothesis, another explanation. Data which indicate a cultural bias in intelligence tests may suggest that all the

[8] *Critical Thinking in Current Affairs Discussion,* Junior Town Meeting League, 356 Washington Street, Middletown, Connecticut, Wesleyan University, 1956, p. 5. The author of this passage is unknown, but it very probably was Alan F. Griffin.
[9] Ernest E. Bayles, *The Theory and Practice of Teaching,* Harper & Row, 1950, p. 123.
[10] *Ibid.*

above differences in average IQ may be explained by a hypothesis that relates IQ not to race but to learning opportunities. This hypothesis is acceptable because it harmonizes all relevant data available to us, and so far as we know, there are no obtainable data in conflict with it. That is, the hypothesis passes the tests of adequacy and harmony.

The application of the rules of repetition, simplicity, adequacy, harmony, and continuous control to the study and teaching of generalizations should result in improved insight, provided also that adequate attention has been accorded the sampling problem. An insight is likely to prove successful as a plan of action (or a generalization to live by) to the extent that it produces expected or intended consequences. Tested insights are useful as guides to action in proportion as they encompass and add consistency to as many data as possible. The critical test of a person's insights is whether they provide him with a set of beliefs about himself in relation to his social and physical environment which are extensive in scope, dependable in action, and compatible with one another.

DISCUSSION QUESTIONS AND EXERCISES

1. List five ideas or hypotheses. Indicate for each the implied data that would have to be actual data if the hypothesis is to be judged true.
2. Jesus was said to have been conceived immaculately. According to Christian history, this event has not been duplicated before or since the birth of Jesus. Does this mean that the belief that Jesus was the Son of God is a trial generalization? Be careful and thoughtful in your answer.
3. Do teachers have to choose between teaching facts and teaching generalizations?
4. What relationship, if any, do you see between the material in this chapter on teaching generalizations and the material in the preceding chapter on teaching concepts?
5. Do we use facts or generalizations or both in teaching and testing generalizations?
6. Describe a problem-solving activity in which the rules of adequacy and harmony were violated.
7. Does the rule or principle of continuous control mean that all religious beliefs are unreliable?
8. Should all human belief be scientific?

REFERENCES

BARZUN, JACQUES, and HENRY F. GRAFF, *The Modern Researcher*, New York, Harcourt, Brace & World, 1957.

Parts I and II have some helpful hints for the researcher, particularly for those who work in the field of history.

BRONOWSKI, J., *The Common Sense of Science*, New York, Vintage Books, 1960.

This book has become something of a classic in philosophy of science. A good book for those who mistakenly believe that science is largely concerned with the invention of gadgets.

BURTT, E. A., *The Metaphysical Foundations of Modern Science*, Garden City, N. Y., Anchor Books, 1954.

The sections on Copernicus, Galileo, and Newton may clarify the rule of simplicity and some of the other rules of scientific method.

CAMPBELL, NORMAN, *What is Science?*, New York, Dover Publications, 1952.

Some very interesting material on the laws of science and their discovery.

CONANT, JAMES B., *Modern Science and Modern Man*, Garden City, N. Y., Anchor Books, 1954.

Relationship of science to technology, human conduct, and spiritual values.

LERNER, DANIEL, ed., *The Human Meaning of the Social Sciences*, New York, Meridian Books, 1959.

Part III deals with issues in social inquiry.

OBLER, PAUL C., and HERMAN A. ESRIN, eds., *The New Scientist*, Garden City, N. Y., Anchor Books, 1962.

A remarkable collection of essays on the methods and values of science.

CHAPTER 6

Value Analysis and Value Clarification

A THEORY of teaching provides for the instructional treatment of different kinds of content. We have indicated what is involved in the reflective treatment of concepts and generalizations. Another kind of content consists of the values held by people. In this chapter, we shall consider the bearing of reflective thought upon values. Can they be tested, and is it possible to say in any reflective sense that some values are better than others? Does the world of scholarship have anything relevant to say about the valuing activities of man? If the response to these questions were entirely negative, reflective teaching of conceptual and factual content would be well nigh meaningless. We know that much of our perception is screened by our purposes and values. If it is not possible for reflection to change our values, then it is surely the case that "objective" perception is impossible. To say that reflection cannot justify any value is to say that reflection cannot even justify itself.

The import of the value problem is not limited to questions of pedagogy. In the opinion of many observers, the present stage of western civilization, including those nonwestern cultures subjected to westernizing influences, is one of great moral uncertainty and confusion. Value conflicts are numerous and destructive. And the confusion is so great that many people appear to have no values at all, or endorse so many conflicting values they resemble the general who would ride his horse in all directions at once.

The United States is a particularly striking example of this value confusion. We want to preserve our cherished civil liberties; yet the exercise of these liberties, particularly if it takes the form of "untimely debate," is viewed as a form of subversion bordering upon treason. We would like to retain a free-enterprise system; we also value certain economic ends which only government seems able to achieve. We want to practice economy in government; we also want our government to contain Communism in all parts of the world. We want to extend democracy to everyone; but we want to exclude from our company, and particularly from our marriages and neighborhoods, those whom we perceive as non-Caucasian in their racial ancestry. We want to give everyone maximum opportunity for mental health and good adjustment, yet continue to honor our tradition of sexual repression—which value is being continually undermined by the fact that we vigorously support sexual titillation as a major commercial enterprise. These are illustrative moral problems, and do not in any sense constitute a complete list. However, the list is complete enough to threaten the sanity of every priest, prostitute, pundit, and politician in the land.

Our moral problems are so challenging as to make technical problems minor by comparison. In fact, few of the social problems we seem unable to solve are rooted in technical deficiencies. In the United States, for example, we can eliminate poverty, slums, and unemployment any time we choose to do so. We have all the technical resources for achieving these goals. That we have not solved these problems simply means that we do not value doing so. Nor do we value not doing so. Moral paralysis is one consequence of value confusion.

Progress toward solution of moral problems would occur more rapidly if public education included a reflective study of value alternatives. Instead, we find that our schools ambivalently float between two traditions. One of these earnestly attempts moral education and character development by engaging in heavy-handed moralizing. The other, stemming from a certain version of logical positivism, treats all value judgment as a cognitively empty enterprise. Neither tradition nourishes the intellectual development of young people.

Moralism in the Schools

Moralism assumes that morality in young people is largely a matter of their learning the difference between right and wrong. A good person is simply one who does the right thing. It is good for people to be honest, loyal, kind, cooperative, and independent. It is bad for them to be dishonest, disloyal, unkind, uncooperative, and dependent.

Schools go about the development of desired traits in a variety of ways, one of which is the teaching of precepts. This practice has been criticized as largely verbal, and therefore ineffective. But few are the schools that do not use it in some way. Under it, adages and other wise sayings abound. "Honesty is the best policy," or "A stitch in time saves nine," may be communicated in the curriculum in many ways, devious or direct.

Another common practice among moralists is the setting of good examples. This is believed to be more effective than the verbalisms of precepts. Teachers are expected to behave, when before pupils, in exemplary fashion. The crude language that pupils hear at home is out of place in the classroom. Pupils receive the impression that teachers who use foul language in school are more sinful than businessmen who charge high interest rates, fix prices, engage in fraudulent advertising, or sell cancer-inducing cigarettes. Until the labor shortages of World War II, married women were not permitted to teach in most public schools, possibly on the assumption that virgins could set better examples.

Because teachers are as human as parents, and therefore not always able to project an image of purity, moralists sometimes draw their examples from legendary sources. Stories of a legendary nature, in which protagonists exemplify a purity no twentieth-century teacher could ever achieve, are a regular part of the curriculum. The prevalence of stories about great men and their sterling traits is particularly noticeable in elementary grades and junior high school. High-school students are often too cynical or reality bound to take such tales seriously. One youth commented on the story about Washington and the cherry tree by observing that "the old boy went far in politics considering the handicap with which he started"[1] (and thus revealed his stereotype about politicians).

The use of patriotic ritual is another device practiced by our moralists. Singing the national anthem and pledging allegiance to the flag are opening exercises at many a school function. Whether it is moral to be patriotic, or whether democratic patriotism is different from other kinds of national allegiance, or whether one can be loyal to both God and Country as the Eisenhower version of allegiance to the flag implies, are questions seldom raised by those who use legend and ritual as their approach to character education.

Probably, the most sophisticated and modern form of moralism is environmentalism. It is now recognized by most moralists, particularly those who pride themselves on being "modern" and "progressive," that environment has much to do with what people become. Under the slogan, "values are caught, not taught," students are ostensibly surrounded by "good" influences. In order that students may learn democratic values, it is believed necessary that they learn in democratic classrooms. Democratic behavior is said to be absorbed from classrooms that are democratic. Parents act on the same principle when they surround their children with "good" books, "good" music, and "good" art. It is expected that children will absorb "good" taste from their surroundings. The notion that one can learn democratic values only as one chooses reflectively from alternatives is not entertained by most environmentalists.[2]

When the environmentalism practiced by moralists works, young people are inducted into democratic behavior without learning concep-

---

[1] This comment was reported by the late Boyd H. Bode.

[2] This "résumé" of moral education is a paraphrase of one to be found in Harry S. Broudy, B. Othanel Smith, and Joe R. Burnett, *Democracy and Excellence in American Secondary Education*, Rand McNally, 1964.

tually what democracy means. Such students cannot cope with criticisms of democracy, and when democracy conflicts with undemocratic alternatives they cannot make rational choices. They also have difficulty in applying democratic attitudes to new situations. The problem of adapting democratic values to the new realities of urban America is a source of continuing frustration to them.

All such attempts to teach children to distinguish between right and wrong—using precepts, setting examples, telling stories, ritualizing, and environmentalizing—share a tendency to preach and exhort. All are linked into a system of rewards and punishments which reinforce "good" behavior. An associationist psychology of learning is consistent with these practices. Under this approach, objectives in moral education depend entirely upon societal preference. What society defines as the good life becomes the life that children are taught to live. In a society that has moral uncertainty and flux as a defining trait, this approach is worse than useless. It provides young people with bundles of conflicting values, without arming them with a reflective method by which to remove conflict from their outlooks.

The indoctrinative practices of moralism lead to hypocrisy in adults and cynicism in youth, as the former teach the latter values that adults no longer practice except in faint-hearted ways. A way out would be for society to teach its youth how to examine reflectively the value conflicts that characterize society. We cringe at doing this, because we fear that many of our institutions would not survive this kind of examination.

THE NATURE OF VALUE CONFLICT

One of the most serious deficiencies in the moralistic approach is its conception of value conflict. Conflict is seen as competition between good values and bad. The idea of conflict between good values and *good* is foreign to moralism.

Moralists probably overestimate the difficulty involved in teaching children to distinguish good from bad behavior. Most children learn the cultural attitudes toward good and bad at a comparatively early age. Most children want to be good, to do the right thing, just as do most adults. But neither children nor adults find it easy always to be good. Several difficulties arise. Those who want to be honest are not always able to perceive what honesty means in particular situations. This is a difficulty in both application of a principle and analysis of a concept. Another difficulty arises from the contradictory prescriptions of our kind of culture. And finally, there is the kind of conflict between good and good that can arise even in a stable and well-integrated culture. For example, a culture may agree to foster a valuing of honesty and kindness but fail to teach its children how to make a choice when these values conflict.

Should one always tell the truth, or should one sometimes withhold part of the truth in order to be kind? And how does one decide?

A moralist who has no reflective sense will teach children always to be honest and kind. Obviously one can be honest in many situations without being unkind, just as in a host of circumstances one can be kind without being dishonest. But let us suppose that Mr. and Mrs. Brown and their small son, Johnny, have been invited to dinner by the Joneses. Mrs. Jones asks Johnny how he likes the soup. Johnny, if he is honest, will say that it is the worst he has ever tasted. This answer is anything but kind, and is very likely a response that none of the adults want him to make. If Johnny has been taught always to be honest, and always to be kind, he is likely to be tongue tied. Should he be honest, or kind? And how is he to decide, when reflective analysis of value alternatives has not been part of his education? If Johnny has been taught to be sophisticated as well as honest and kind, he might murmur something trite and unintelligible, hoping all the while that he would not be offered a second serving. But, whether to be honest, kind, or sophisticated is still a problem to be solved reflectively.

This is not a problem that can be solved through a fixed hierarchy of values—higher values invariably being preferable to lower ones. Any value hierarchy would have to be flexible enough to permit values to move up or down a scale according to qualifying circumstances. Without flexibility in the hierarchical ordering of values, wise or intelligent behavior would be impossible. Perhaps it is intelligent behavior or wisdom that we most need to develop through our programs in moral education. If so, the kind of moralism that asks us merely to choose good over evil will not do.

Adults, also, experience difficulty in making choices among conflicting values. The story is told of a secretary who sought advice from the editor of a lovelorn column in a local newspaper. The secretary wrote that she was working for a man for whom she had developed strong feelings of loyalty. He had raised her salary several times, provided liberal vacations, furnished good working conditions, and even helped to finance the medical care of her aged mother. The secretary learned that her employer had made false income-tax returns. She wanted to know whether she should be loyal to this man and keep her mouth shut, or whether she should be honest and report his crime to the tax authorities. In this situation, it would have been no help at all to advise that a moral person is always both loyal and honest.

We have the same kind of conflict at the national level, e.g., the decision between a policy that prevents inflation and one that fosters fuller employment. Bankers may fear inflation more than unemployment, and wage earners may have a different ordering of values. What is best for the general welfare? Full employment or price stability? To say that we should always support full employment and price stability may not be a discerning answer in all circumstances.

How does one proceed when he has a conflict between honesty and loyalty and his moral training has uncritically inculcated an absolute valuing of both? The usual procedure is for a person to decide in some way what to do, then rationalize his decision. His moral training has made moral responsibility impossible, and rationalization and self-deception a necessity. Furthermore, a culture such as ours, rich in clichés, makes irresponsibility easy to practice. A person who puts off making an important decision can offer as his excuse a reluctance to "jump from the frying pan into the fire." On the other hand, any tendency to make a decision in haste and without appropriate deliberation can be rationalized with the observation that "he who hesitates is lost." One can play with proverbs, but morality is a most serious business. To say that "appearances are deceiving" may be a wise saying, but so is the claim that "a man is known by the company he keeps." When "wisdom" conflicts, what does the good man do?

Confused and self-contradictory thinking will exist in the area of values as long as we teach that moral problems are limited to choices between good and evil, with no recognition of competing "goods." The felt moral problems of our culture, and probably of all cultures no matter how integrated they may be in their core values, arise when people find it desirable to satisfy two cherished but incompatible ends. To an outsider not caught up in the agony of choice, morality may appear to be ability to distinguish between good and evil. For a person making a choice, moral decision usually requires distinguishing between two or more "goods." When at least two desired courses of action come into mutual conflict, moral choice becomes necessary. Yet even textbooks on social problems read as if good opposed evil in our world. We are asked by such books whether urban renewal is a good thing, not whether urban renewal conflicts with other "goods."

In recent years, this country has been worried over what economists have called the balance-of-payments problem. In order to avoid continued loss of gold to other countries, we have been tempted to follow policies that bring about a more favorable trade balance; often these have been policies that encourage unemployment in excess of 4 percent. Full employment and a more favorable balance of trade are both viewed by many Americans as desirable goals. When desired goals conflict with one another, wise men will always search for a policy that preserves both goals. Failing to find such a policy, they must then decide which goal is the more important. In this connection, John Maynard Keynes once proposed a policy that would have made it possible for countries such as the United States and the United Kingdom to pursue policies of full employment without worry as to balance of payments. It took reflection, not moralism, for Keynes to work out this policy. The fact that the policy was never adopted only proves that reflective solutions to problems are not always politically popular.

THE MORAL PROBLEMS OF YOUTH

That typical moral problems of youth involve choices among competing goods is supported by a study of beliefs and behavior in sixteen-year-old boys and girls.[3] Havighurst and Taba report that the adolescent peer culture places great value on social participation, group loyalty, and individual achievement and responsibility. The group studied also accepted the traditional middle-class values of a midwestern community —respectability, thrift, responsibility, self-reliance, and good manners. Adults could hardly find fault with the predominant values of youth in this community. High-school students seemed committed to the ends most revered in our society.

The study also clearly revealed the kinds of moral conflicts created by the American culture. Loyalty to one's friends is a universally respected value. And this was one of the most cherished values of the sixteen-year-olds, among whom loyalty to the group seemed to require following the pattern of behavior generally practiced in the group: i.e., mind your own business, don't criticize your friends, and don't let anyone else criticize them. Therefore, group members felt obligated to protect those peer-group members who violated traditional moral standards. Thus, they were caught in a conflict between two loyalties—one to the peer culture and one to the adults of the community who were trying to enforce the conventional mores. Two good ends were at stake, not a good end and a bad one.

Since these sixteen-year-olds had never been taught the nature of moral choice—the analysis of value conflicts—it is hardly surprising that a great deal of confusion and self-deception was evident among them. Test results showed that when they were confronted with a value conflict they tended to choose courses of action that violated the abstract principles in which they believed. Not more than one-third of those examined seemed able to apply their abstract beliefs about morality to concrete situations. The reputation of a student, for good or bad, seemed to have little to do with his understanding of moral principles or his ability to apply it in specific situations. Reputation seemed to be based on adoption and consistent application of certain overt behavioral forms, which included cooperation with teachers, regular church attendance, and verbal (and

[3] Robert J. Havighurst and Hilda Taba, *Adolescent Character and Personality*, Wiley, 1949.

vocal) espousal of traditional middle-class moral standards. Students who seemed most confused, and most likely to follow expedient courses of action, were those with social ambitions.

Although the Havighurst-Taba study is now many years old, times have not changed enough to invalidate its findings. In 1966, a news magazine reported the results of a poll taken by Louis Harris and Associates, Inc. Interviews with a representative sample of thirteen- to seventeen-year-olds revealed that 96 percent believed in God. But such practices as copying one another's homework, plagiarizing from critical essays, carrying crib notes to class, and stealing examination questions from faculty offices were the fashion, according to teachers' and administrators' reports, and by students' own admissions. Allen Barton, who studied students at 99 colleges, concluded that half his sample cheated, and that cheating would be more prevalent in high school.[4]

Another study, dealing with college students, found that most of them disapproved of cheating, but that cheating was considered all right if everyone else was doing it. The tendency to practice cheating if others were doing it was strongest among religious students. Irreligious students were least likely to succumb to conformity.[5]

Jacob, in his study of college students and their values, reported that 66 percent would not report a cheater if he were a personal friend, but only 16 percent would fail to do so if he were not a friend. The same students would undercut friendship in favor of honesty if there was evidence that the college authorities knew about the cheating incident. In such circumstances only 27 percent (compared with 66 percent in other circumstances) would fail to report a friend. There was a strong undercurrent of opportunism functioning in lieu of strong moral commitments.[6]

Logical Positivism

We said at the beginning of this chapter that the schools are caught between two intellectually sterile approaches to moral education, moralism and positivism. Neither approach values reflective study of value alternatives, as we see it. Having completed our discussion of moralism, we turn next to positivism, a philosophy that continues to dominate much of the thinking in social science.

Positivism claims or assumes that only *judgments of fact* are verifiable.

[4] Newsweek, March 21, 1966, pp. 59–60.

[5] Rose K. Goldsen, et al., *What College Students Think*, Van Nostrand, 1960. This study also revealed that religious students had stronger racial prejudices. (Charles Y. Glock and Rodney Stark, [*Christian Beliefs and Anti-Semitism*, Harper & Row, 1966] link belief in Christianity to expressions of anti-Semitism.)

[6] Philip E. Jacob, *Changing Values in College*, Harper & Row, 1957.

All *judgments of value* are unverifiable. Properly defined, these terms no doubt have some pedagogical value, but positivists have oversimplified their use.

According to positivists, judgments of fact are statements about present or past reality. They describe relationships among things; they are objective, and have assumed referents in nature. The ground or warrant for any judgment of fact lies in observations or experiments. Judgments of fact, to use an earlier expression, are testable only with public evidence. Any investigator can verify another man's judgment of fact by repeating his observations or experiments. Examples of judgments of fact in the social studies include generalizations (such as, women on the average live longer than men) and singular statements (such as, the price of corn is $1.10 a bushel).

A judgment of fact, it follows, may or may not be true. Its distinctive quality depends, not on its being true, but on the supposition that its truth can be checked objectively. For example, the statement "bigamy is legal in South Carolina" is a judgment of fact but untrue. After it has been checked and confirmed, a *judgment* of fact becomes a *fact*. It appears, then, that judgments of fact are equivalent to the contingent-synthetic statements discussed in Chapter 4.

Whether a statement is a judgment of fact hinges, not on whether it can be verified at the time it is made, but on the type of subject matter with which it deals. Although mankind does not now have the evidence to verify it, a proposition like "some form of animal life exists on the planet Mars" is a judgment of fact. And so is a proposition like "the adoption of socialism in a country leads eventually to loss of political freedom," which deals with objective, cause-and-effect relationships, and is thus theoretically verifiable.

The term *judgment of value* (or value judgment) refers to a statement whose subject matter, according to logical positivists, is not subject to the test of observation or experiment. A value judgment is thought unsusceptible to verification, not because evidence is lacking but because its subject matter deals with feelings and preferences. All such judgments, it is held, express personal preference or taste.

Value judgments are usually identified by the presence of one or more value terms. A value term denotes the quality of a preference which the utterer intends to express. In the sentence "Marilyn is a beautiful woman," the value term is *beautiful*. Commonly encountered value terms are *good* and *bad*, *right* and *wrong*, *naughty* and *nice*, *decent* and *indecent*, *moral* and *immoral*.

A student who dismisses the comment of a teacher, or other student, with the expression, "But that's a value judgment," is being positivistic. Any statement that can be classified as a value judgment is typically regarded by students as one they need not commit to memory. Such statements are not treated as items of knowledge or information, except by teachers who cannot tell a value judgment from a judgment of fact.

Another example of value judgment is any statement containing the words *should* or *ought*. These statements are called *policy statements*. Examples are: "The government should not spend more money than it receives as tax revenue," or "Women ought to wear higher necklines than they do." Translated, these read, "It is good for government to spend no more than it receives as tax revenue," or "It is good for women to wear higher necklines." Before we classify as a value judgment any statement that contains the words *should* or *ought*, we must pay careful attention to context. Sometimes such words refer simply to possibility and not to moral judgments, as in the expression, "I should be able to make the 6:30 train."

RELATIONSHIP OF FACTS TO VALUES

It is to the credit of logical positivism that it sensitizes people to the difference between values and facts, and to that extent fosters objectivity. As a tradition, it is preferable to the moralistic emphasis upon preaching and exhortation. But its oversimplifications lead to ethical neutralism, and it overlooks or underplays the impact that facts and values have upon each other. It is hard to deny that some values are better than others, yet this denial is implicit in logical positivism. We also recognize that factual developments have valuational meaning. A typical college textbook in American history, for example, relates the invention of the automobile (a factual achievement) to certain changes in sexual mores. It is also true that changes in values can affect the nature and direction of scholarly pursuits. The desire to avoid the mass unemployment of the 1930s has no doubt had some effect on the research activities of professional economists, and this in turn has had an effect upon the emergent content of economics.

Philip Smith has observed that the early conflict between science and religion was resolved on the basis of a truce. Science was given the job of seeking truth; religion reserved to itself the task of morality. One consequence was that science devoted itself to seeking new truths, whereas religion pursued the discovery or maintenance of eternal values.[7] This truce broke down, however, because the new truths of science inevitably had value consequences. Consider the effect on traditional morality of the development of effective contraceptives.

Logical positivists have always been aware of the relationship between facts and values, but apparently have not always sensed its methodological implications. If other scientific discoveries (i.e., facts) can effect value

---

[7] Philip G. Smith, *Philosophy of Education*, Harper & Row, 1965, p. 162.

change and if value change can affect our scientific activities and the findings that arise from those activities, perhaps the simple wall between fact and value, built by logical positivism, is resting upon a shaky foundation.

Concepts, Descriptive and Valuative

Careful analysis suggests that the distinction commonly made between judgments of fact and judgments of value is misleading in the extreme. The usual distinction conveys the notion that judgments of fact are divorced from acts of evaluation; that they are merely true or false descriptions of a physical reality outside an observer—objective, exact, and dependable; and that judgments of value refer to nothing existent or substantial. That is, fact judgments refer to what is "real," value judgments to what is "unreal." If this were the case, value judgments would have no place in inquiry. It is also misleading to suppose that any such hard-and-fast distinction can be made between statements. We saw earlier how difficult it is even to distinguish between relational concepts and empirical generalizations.

In one sense, all statements are evaluative. If one person says to another, "You are a thief," he is employing a judgment of fact, but also expressing disapproval (a judgment of value). Even relatively neutral statements may reflect acts of valuation. Suppose a person says, "Marilyn wears a size 4 shoe." This is a judgment of fact. But why was it said? Clearly, the speaker attaches importance to knowledge of Marilyn's shoe size. That he has chosen to focus attention on this particular judgment of fact indicates a valuation. It seems likely that all thought involves the making of valuations—continuous selection of what is important in relation to one's ends.

Even though values permeate descriptions, it is believed that judgments of fact are verifiable. Why, then, the insistence that value judgments are always unverifiable? Let us take the statement, "Mexicans are good agricultural workers." The presence of the term *good* suggests that a value judgment has been made. But, if we intend the statement to describe Mexican workers as workers, "good" would imply qualities such as skill, willingness to work, and reliability. If our intention is to describe the morality of Mexican workers, then "good" would imply qualities that define moral. In either case, the implied qualities can be defined intensionally or extensionally in terms of behavior, traits, or examples; and, thus, on the basis of factual data, the statement can be verified. Anyone who accepts our definitions can obtain the same factual data—therefore, our value judgment is subject to public verification.

Any statement whose truth can be tested by scientific means, any statement which may be shown through public tests to be true or false, may function as a hypothesis in reflection. The testability of any proposition depends, not on the presence of particular types of words, but on whether the concepts in the proposition can be defined meaningfully (that is, according to defining criteria) in a way that is clear, if not acceptable to all investigators.

The confirmability of any statement depends upon the definitiveness of its concepts. Its (public) verifiability depends upon whether there is general agreement on the meaning of its concepts. When all investigators agree on the attributes or properties implied by a value concept, then there is good possibility of agreement as to the truth of a tested proposition containing that concept. These properties should, of course, whenever possible, be stated in measurable, observable, or operational terms.

Obviously, some value terms are more difficult to define than others. Consider the phrase, "This pie is delicious." "Delicious" may refer to a group of highly subjective judgments, the grounds for which are hard to communicate. On the other hand, deliciousness may be defined in terms of certain qualities—sweetness, tartness, juiciness, or tenderness; in which case, it is possible to consider the statement more objectively. Properties stated as poetry or metaphysics pose far greater obstacles to reflection than does any valuative concept.

Rather than trying to classify statements by means of rigid distinction between fact judgments and value judgments, it is more realistic to think of statements as falling on a continuum, at one extreme of which are those having a common meaning, and at the other those expressing highly individualized and subjective preferences without shared or collective meanings. It should be remembered, however, that a statement at the preferential end of the continuum can be shifted toward the opposite end by reflection upon the problem of definition. Whether a given statement falls toward one end or the other of the continuum depends on the meaning shared by those engaged in investigation. We express our manner of describing and classifying statements as follows:

Fact-Value Continuum

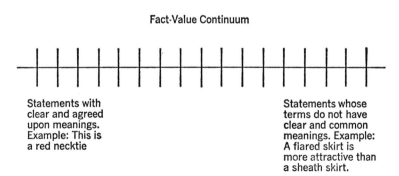

Statements with clear and agreed upon meanings. Example: This is a red necktie

Statements whose terms do not have clear and common meanings. Example: A flared skirt is more attractive than a sheath skirt.

Statements that fall toward the right end of the scale generally contain value terms with highly subjective meanings—*attractive* would probably present serious difficulties in definition. Used as hypotheses or as "factual evidence," such statements create unmanageable problems in investigation. But these problems can be solved. For example, the statement that some women have physical features which make it unwise, if not impossible, for them to wear a sheath skirt, is testable enough; and such women are probably more attractive to most people when attired in a flared skirt.

In Chapter 4, it was suggested that the teaching of descriptive concepts, at least those that are used for classificatory purposes, involves a procedure that sets forth their defining attributes, thus making the intensional meaning of a concept as clear and specific as possible. In the game of baseball, we said, a strike is defined as (1) a pitch within a certain zone, (2) a pitch that a batter misses when he swings, or (3) one that he bats into foul territory with a count on him of less than two strikes. Sometimes an argument will develop during a baseball game over whether a given event is a strike. Players may surround the umpire and argue against his decision. Everyone agrees on the definition of a strike; the only point at issue is whether a certain pitch matched the attributes of a strike. This is a factual matter, a judgment of fact. All decisions of a baseball umpire are judgments of fact to the extent that rules and definitions are agreed upon in advance by players on both sides. Arguments may develop over application or interpretation, and these can become so acute as to result in the ejection of a player from a game. But how much more vociferous and unmanageable the conflict would become if there were no prior agreement on definitions and rules—i.e., on what the game means. If umpires had to make up rules as the game was played, it might be impossible to play a game at all.

Logically, value concepts pose no problems not posed by descriptive concepts. If we could define our moral terminology, judgments of fact would tell us whether a person was engaged in a moral or an immoral course of action. These judgments are now labeled value judgments *only* because our value concepts do not have the same meaning for most people. This lack of agreement on what concepts mean—or their defining attributes—prevails in the value realm of modern life. It is misleading to assume that such agreement is impossible. Barriers to agreement in the moral realm are indeed great, but no more insurmountable than they are in other realms of scholarship.

Science is a realm of scholarship, and we are told that science can ascertain the truth but cannot define our ends or set forth the meaning of virtue. It would be more to the point to say that *no one can ascertain truth unless he first defines truth.* The biology teacher who lists evidence to support his claim of truth for a theory of evolution may encounter opposition from someone who claims to possess a higher truth. This "higher truth" is often said to have divine origin and is not defined as that which can be verified in nature under experimental conditions. Revealed truth is not experimental truth. To accept a theory of evolution as true expresses a preference for experimental truth.

Is the conflict over the meaning of truth an irreconcilable or unsolvable matter? Evidently not, since the conflict steadily wanes as scientific evidence increases. More and more, people have come to embrace the experimental meaning of truth. Revealed truth still has its devotees, particularly when it does not conflict with experimental truth, but these become fewer in number with each succeeding generation. Most of those few who still doubt the truth of the evolution theory, do so because they lack familiarity with the evidence, not because they prefer nonexperimental truth.

There is also conflict over the meaning of morality. There are those who contend that whether a moral principle is good depends upon the consequences of acting upon it. A consequences test is an experimental test. On the other hand, there are those who believe certain moral principles to be inviolable and eternal regardless of the consequences of acting upon them; just as there are those who, preferring revealed truth to experimental truth, hold to belief in some absolute, unchanging truths regardless of scientific evidence. Needless to say, those who base their morality upon eternal principles are as absolutistic as those who define truth as fixed and unchanging.

The basis for absolutism is not always religious, it may be political or economic. Any philosophy can offer absolutes, and only certain versions of pragmatism lack absolutes of the kind we have been discussing.

Value Analysis: A Teaching Model

Analysis of value concepts, as we have seen, logically resembles analysis of descriptive concepts. What we know about the testing of analytic statements, as reported in Chapter 4, applies to valuative content. But much more than concept analysis is involved in the testing of value judgments.

Many value judgments take the form of policy decisions. We ought to increase government spending, or we ought to cut taxes, or we ought to recognize the government of an unfriendly power, are examples. A policy decision requires in addition to concept analysis a consideration of consequences. This consideration of consequences has three phases, (1) an

attempt to anticipate or project consequences (2) an appraisal of consequences in terms of their goodness or badness by application of criteria,
and (3) a justification of the criteria used to appraise consequences.

An outline of the teaching procedures for dealing with both conceptual
and empirical aspects of valuation would run as follows.

I. What is the nature of the object, event, or policy to be evaluated?
This question plainly poses a task in concept analysis. If the students
are trying to evaluate the welfare state, they should define this object
as precisely and clearly as possible.
   A. How is the welfare state to be defined intensionally and extensionally? By what criteria is it to be defined intensionally?
   B. If students disagree over criteria, and therefore in their definition
of welfare state, how is this disagreement to be treated? Must
they agree? Can they agree to disagree? Are there criteria by
which welfare state ought to be defined? On what basis can we
select among different sets of criteria?
II. The consequences problem.
   A. What consequences can be expected or anticipated from the policy in question? Is it true, as some have claimed, that the growth
of the welfare state destroys individual incentive? How does one
get evidence for answering this kind of question?
   B. If students disagree in their projection of consequences, how is
this difference to be treated? Can evidence produce agreement?
What is the difference between a disagreement over criteria and
a disagreement over evidence?
III. Appraisal of consequences.
   A. Are the projected consequences desirable or not?
   B. By what criteria are the consequences to be appraised? How do
different criteria affect one's appraisal of consequences?
IV. Justification of criteria.
   A. Can criteria for appraising consequences be justified? How?
   B. If students disagree on criteria, and therefore in their appraisal
of consequences, how can this difference be treated? What re-
lationship ought to exist between one's criteria and one's basic
philosophy of life?
   C. Are students consistent in their use of criteria?

The entire problem outlined above has been called the problem of
justification. If we cannot justify a definition or a policy, we are morally
paralyzed. We have many social-science experts in government and
industry who will serve any purpose that is proposed by their employer,
but who are reluctant to participate in the formulation and justification of

purposes. Their reluctance is rooted in a belief that purposes cannot be determined by either science or scholarship.

APPLICATION OF THE MODEL

Let us suppose that a teacher wants his class to understand and evaluate a policy of collective bargaining. He may start by asking the class whether collective bargaining has had beneficial effects for the country as a whole. Students are likely to diverge in their responses. Some will answer in the affirmative; some in the negative. Many will no doubt answer that some of the effects have been desirable, but that other effects have been undesirable. Up to this point, questions have been for the purpose of focussing student attention upon the policy to be evaluated. The teacher's next questions will be intended to enlist students in a quest for more knowledge. He will proceed upon the reasonable assumption that evaluation of any policy depends in part upon how much we know about that policy.

Two kinds of knowledge are reflected in the above outline. We discussed these in Chapter 4. One kind is analytic, the other synthetic. If we ask students, What is collective bargaining? we are asking for definition, which, as indicated earlier, is an analytic form of knowledge. At the stage of concept analysis, then, the teacher asks for examples of collective bargaining (hence, deals with extensional meaning) and for the defining attributes of collective bargaining (its intensional meaning). The teacher also wants his students to have a knowledge of the effects of collective bargaining. This kind of knowledge is empirical, that is, synthetic or contingent, and is involved when the teacher asks questions about consequences. These two kinds of knowledge are equally essential to evaluation of policy, but they should not be confused with one another.

At the stage of concept analysis, the teacher concentrates on definition. He does not ask for the causes of collective bargaining, as would be the case if he asked his class why we have more unions today than in 1800. Nor when concept analysis is the task at hand, does he ask the class to discuss the effects or consequences of collective bargaining. A history of collective bargaining is also inappropriate, unless there is something in that history that throws light on the meaning of collective bargaining. The method of comparison and contrast is one of the most effective teaching methods at this stage. Students may not be able to pin down the essence of collective bargaining except as they contrast it with individual bargaining. No matter how many examples of collective bargaining students may be able to supply, the teacher will not be satisfied until they can state its intensional meaning.

When a concept is undergoing analysis, students will frequently con-

sult a dictionary, or a glossary of terms in a textbook. Specialized diction-
aries as well as a general, unabridged dictionary will prove useful. Even
when these resources are used, students may not always agree on what a
concept means. If the occasion warrants, the teacher will refer to an official definition as an authority. Regardless of the occasion, the teacher will
be alert to instances in which definitions possess internal inconsistencies.
For example, the teacher will not ignore the inconsistency revealed by
students who define welfare legislation as legislation that advances the
welfare of some groups at the expense of other groups, but who fail to see
protective tariffs as examples of welfare legislation.

Once a class achieves some clarity as to the intensional meaning of
collective bargaining, it is ready to concentrate on the question of
consequences. Some consideration of consequences has no doubt been
present during the concentration on concept analysis. For example,
during the stage of concept analysis, the teacher may have asked such
questions as: Could we have collective bargaining without unions?
Without a closed shop? Without the right to strike and picket? These are
empirical questions because they ask how unions, closed shops, strikes,
and picketing affect collective bargaining. A part of the meaning of
collective bargaining is to be found in its relationship to other concepts.
Some foray into empiricism, then, always accompanies concept analysis.

The stage at which the search for consequences is concentrated is simply
one wherein emphasis on empirical questions is more deliberate and organized than in other stages. It is at this stage that the teacher hammers
hard at the whole question of where a given policy leads. History has
recorded many experiences with collective bargaining and ultimately, the
empirical question of consequences can be answered only by turning to
experience as recorded in history.

If, at this stage, students cannot agree on consequences, the teacher will
confront them with evidence. Since their disagreement is over judgments
of fact, an appeal to evidence is a logical step. Only by testing various and
conflicting judgments of fact can students decide on the truth about consequences.

Probably, the students who dislike collective bargaining will predict
dire consequences, while those who favor it will predict desirable consequences. In this respect, students tend toward tunnel vision. That is to
say, they predict only a very narrow range of consequences. A teacher
can try to combat this lack of objectivity by directing attention to any
and all evidence of more or less incontrovertible nature. This kind of
evidence is not always easy for students to find, or to recognize when
someone else finds it for them. Students are prone to believe that evidence
on consequences is unobtainable in the social sciences, and that all claims
as to consequences are conjecture and opinion. They have yet to learn

that a generalization about the effect of unions upon wages is a testable statement. They have also to learn that often there is a range of possible predictions, and that one must choose that which has the most support, regardless of how sparse that support may be.

If the evidence is convincing enough, students may agree on the consequences of collective bargaining. Whether they agree or not, the next step in valuing is to appraise consequences as desirable or undesirable.[8] Let us suppose that students agree that collective bargaining results in real wages higher than those available from individual bargaining. Is this good? The answer depends upon what criteria are used. If students differ in their criteria, they will differ in their answers to the question of good. It is important to note that the criteria used to evaluate consequences are not the same criteria as are used to define a policy. Definitional criteria set forth the essential meaning of a policy, but appraisal criteria assume certain valued ends.

Some students may argue that the higher *real* wages resulting from collective bargaining are too high. By "too high" they may mean that wage earners achieve gains that are greater than gains in labor productivity. Those who reason this way may be assuming that wages set by individual bargaining are more likely to reflect labor's actual contribution to production. This amounts to saying that the wages set by a free market are more just than those established by the cooperative efforts of workers.

Students who disagree with this reasoning may argue that wages set by a free market are not always living wages. In their rejection of a free market, they advocate collective bargaining. They may also assume that employers are in a position to exploit workers, that is, pay them less than the value of their contribution to the productive process.

We see then that the students using a free market as their basic criterion evaluate the consequences of collective bargaining differently from those students who reject this criterion. This difference over a criterion, therefore, amounts to a difference in opinion over the nature of the consequences. One group is saying that a free market pays people what they have earned, in a productive sense, whereas the other group argues that this is not always the case.

At this point, the teacher may want the two groups to consider together whether a free market is always preferable to one in which buyers and sellers enter into collusion against one another. But before doing so, he may want to test both sides as to the consistency and constancy of their respective devotions. To find whether the advocates of a free

---

[8] It simplifies matters if students evaluate the same consequences, and for this reason the teacher always tries to get as much agreement as possible on the likely consequences of a policy.

market are consistent in their advocacy, he may ask them such questions as: Do you favor tariffs? Do you favor trust busting? Do you believe in subsidies of any kind? Is it right to support farm prices by restricting production? These questions are intended to find out whether the advocates of a free market are consistent in their advocacy.

To students who believe in collective bargaining, he can address the same questions, hoping to find whether they consistently reject the free market. Although teachers may differ over whether they have a right to teach their students to value the free market, or indeed to teach students their own values, *there can be no doubt that logic alone demands that we help students to realize the value and meaning of consistency.* Students can be consistent in their valuing, without necessarily agreeing with a teacher.

We are left with one question. Can students justify whatever criterion or criteria they use in evaluation of consequences? In the case we have been considering, this means literally: Can those who use the criterion, free market, justify their preference for markets that are free over ones that are not? Or can those who prefer a nonfree market justify their preference?

Most economists would argue that a free market results in the most efficient allocation of scarce resources. If efficiency is one's sole criterion, there is no question as to the superiority of a free market over any market in which buyers or sellers are able to combine. The same economists will grant that few of our markets are really free. Evidently, men have had objectives other than efficiency, and many of our public policies have been formulated to combat some of the effects of free competition.

A free market is a neat theoretical model which is never completely achieved in practice. To have a free market, it would be necessary for each participant in it to be fully informed on alternatives. For example, each individual, before making a wage contract with any employer, would make certain there was not some other employer in that market willing and able to pay a higher wage for the same kind and amount of work. If there were, he would, if rational, sell his services to that employer. It would likewise be necessary for each person and each resource to be mobile enough to go where its services were in greatest demand. Above all, each person in a free market must behave rationally in an economic sense, if the market is to remain free. These three assumptions seldom operate with full force, and consequently our markets are seldom entirely free.

Even though our markets are not entirely free, they could be more free than they are. When one questions the monopolistic practices embodied in unions and collective bargaining, he is asking for greater freedom in the labor market. But, as he reaches in this direction, he may be asked why we should not restore freedom in other markets. Should we eliminate the practice of having the government deliver mail at less than the cost of providing the service? Should we repeal all tariffs on imported goods? Should we eliminate all advertising that fosters product differentiation? Should we eliminate public schools and state universities, and restrict education to those who can afford to pay its cost? Should magazines and newspapers pay postage rates that cover the cost of delivery rather than receive, as they do at present, an indirect subsidy in the form of an uneconomically low postage rate? What about monopolies that seem to result from advanced technology and mass production? Should they be busted by the government, and can this be done without destroying our technology? These are fair and reflection-promoting questions. In order to oppose collective bargaining while supporting other exceptions to free competition, one must develop justifiable criteria for doing so. One can do this if he can develop a rationale for a mixed type of economy, in which there is some planning and some competition.

Different Meanings of Valuing

Our teaching model for values attempts three achievements: (1) intensional definition of value concepts (2) instrumental use of values, and (3) intrinsic worth of values. The question of whether value concepts may be intensionally defined and thus serve as elements in testable hypotheses is not the same as the question whether, apart from their instrumental use, values can be shown to be intrinsically worthwhile. Smith has treated these differences with remarkable clarity by distinguishing three meanings for the expression "X is good."

$$X \text{ is good}$$

$$\text{because} \begin{cases} 1. \ X \text{ leads to } Y \\ 2. \ \text{The goodness of } X \text{ is entailed by } S \\ 3. \ \text{I like } X \end{cases} \text{ and }$$

that is sufficient reason for valuing X [9]

The view that X is good because it leads to Y illustrates the treatment of X as an instrumental value. We did as much with collective bargaining when we discussed its consequences. This treatment has a strength and a weakness. Its strength is that people sometimes support or oppose a value without knowledge of consequences. Once such knowledge of consequences is acquired, people may change in their valuing of collective bargaining. If those who oppose collective bargaining learn that its

[9] Smith, *op. cit.*, p. 189.

abolition would likely result in widespread unemployment and a lower standard of living for almost everyone, they might come to approve collective bargaining. The weakness in the instrumental treatment of values, however, is that, although one may learn that X leads to Y, he may not be certain that Y is worthwhile. Instrumentalists then suggest that one look into the further consequences of Y. Does it lead to Z, and is Z worthwhile? Instrumentalists often assume that value perplexities can be resolved at some point on a means-end continuum.

The expression that X is good because it is entailed by S can be translated to mean: I like X because I believe in democracy. If X stands for collective bargaining, and S stands for democracy, then, this defense of X simply means that those who believe in democracy must also believe in collective bargaining. This approach amounts to a logical test of X. We deduce a valuing of X from a valuing of democracy. In contrast, the instrumental testing of X is an empirical one. Both tests are necessary in a fully reflective classroom experience.

Logical and empirical tests can be combined into a single test. One could say that X is good because it leads to Y, which is entailed by S. Whether X leads to Y can be settled by recourse to evidence. Whether Y is entailed by S is an exercise in pure logic. If there is doubt whether S is worthwhile, one can apply a similar test to S. But where does all this reflection end? Is inquiry endless? Does it ever have a termination?

Consideration of what it means to say that X is good because I like X is helpful on this point. Smith observes quite accurately that this is the most troublesome question we face in the value realm. The traditional view has been that "likes" and "dislikes" are private feelings not subject to public test. Two qualifications of this traditional view seem to make sense. First, people don't always like what they say they like, or believe they like. This inner discrepancy can exist when people do not pay adequate attention to the Socratic dictum, "Know thyself." Teachers of social studies would do well to pay more attention than they traditionally have to the kinds of educational methods that give students practice in self-examination. This emphasis is plainly present in our values model. Teachers may recurrently ask questions along this line: "I notice that many of us say that we like classical music. Why don't we ever listen to any? Do we really like it?"

One can investigate publicly whether his likes are in harmony with one another. A person may observe a pretty girl and say to himself, "I like that." But a moment later he may also find himself saying, "But, if I do anything about it, that would be adultery." How do I feel about adultery? Do I like it? Would its commission produce in me feelings of anxiety and guilt?" We have said that this self-examination can be done publicly. That is, harmonies and disharmonies in likes and dislikes can be subjects of class discussion. "If we like X can we also like Y?" Bayles, more than anyone else has made this kind of teaching a central emphasis in education, and has developed a rationale for its implementation.[10] Smith says the same thing when he suggests that we look at the expression, "I like X" in terms of whether this preference is in harmony with our basic character.

That a given value judgment is in harmony with one's basic character does not mean it is a judgment that everyone ought to make. Value judgments are relativistic, as are all scientifically made judgments of fact. A judgment of fact is true *relative* to the chosen definition of truth; judgment of value is right *relative* to what a person is, or wants to be. Judgments of both fact and value can be made reflectively, if we recognize the values of relativism as opposed to the values of absolutism.

A scientific or reflective methodology cannot provide absolute or perfect warrant for any value judgment. But neither can it provide this kind of warrant for a judgment of fact. Whether a person tends toward absolutism or relativism may have more to do with his basic character than any other factor. Value education that centers upon selfhood and its development will necessarily include study of comparative philosophies, for this is the kind of value education that places the value problem *within* persons, not between them. If two people disagree in their value judgments, they may be able to compromise. But it is hard to compromise if one has not come to terms with himself. A person adrift never knows whether compromise is necessary or even possible.

The role of a democratic teacher in all this is not to strive to make students agree with him on all value judgments. A value judgment that is in harmony with my basic character may not be in harmony with yours, and your basic character may be as good as mine. A democratic teacher will offer to students every inducement and encouragement to accept the values implicit within reflective method. He cannot dodge this choice. But within this method a wide range of value judgments and basic characters are possible. In expressing a preference for this method over other ways of knowing, the teacher is declaring himself an adherent to democratic teaching. Ultimately, every student has to decide whether his basic character is to be democratic-reflective in its central values. Such a decision is highly personal, but teachers of social studies can help students to make it reflectively.

We want students to be consistent in their values, but we also want them to justify values by recourse to criteria derived from a philosophy

[10] Ernest E. Bayles, *The Theory and Practice of Teaching*, Harper & Row, 1950. Also his more recent *Democratic Educational Theory*, Harper & Row, 1960.

to which they subscribe. Whether they choose to subscribe to a democratic philosophy is their decision to make—probably the most important decision in their lives.

DISCUSSION QUESTIONS AND EXERCISES

1. Can we have social unity if we cannot agree on values? Does a commitment to reflective method imply that some values are better than others? If everyone does his own thinking in the moral realm will we have agreement on values?
2. If people do not agree on the meaning of "good," can they agree in their value judgments? Do they have to agree on values in order to cooperate? Does democracy require that individuals agree in their values?
3. Can we have a society based upon common purposes if individuals fail to agree on ultimate values?
4. Could inductive teaching be applied to values? What would be the consequences of teaching values inductively?
5. Most teachers reward good pupil behavior, and punish bad. Is this practice consistent with a reflective approach to moral education? Is this practice necessary to good discipline?
6. Can we teach concepts and facts without teaching values?
7. How would you teach an understanding of a value conflict?
8. What are the functions of criteria within valuing? Can criteria, defining or appraising, be justified? How?

REFERENCES

BROUDY, HARRY S., B. OTHANEL SMITH, and JOE R. BURNETT, *Democracy and Excellence in American Secondary Education*, Chicago, Rand McNally, 1964.

   Contains an excellent discussion of similarity between descriptive and valuative concepts.

FLEW, ANTONY, ed., *Logic and Language, First and Second Series*, Garden City, N. Y., Anchor Books, 1965.

   This interesting collection includes a paper by J. O. Urmson entitled "On Grading" which is excellent for its discussion of the use of criteria in valuing.

HULLFISH, H. GORDON, and PHILIP G. SMITH, *Reflective Thinking: The Method of Education*, New York, Dodd, Mead, 1961.

   Chapter 7 discusses the problem of achieving warrant for value judgments. Should be read in conjunction with Chapters 5 and 6 on analytic and synthetic functions.

HUNT, MAURICE P., and LAWRENCE E. METCALF, *Teaching High School Social Studies*, New York, Harper & Row, 1955.

Chapter 5 discusses values and reflection.

MYRDAL, GUNNAR, and ARNOLD ROSE, *An American Dilemma: The Negro Problem and Modern Democracy*, New York, Harper & Row, 1962.

Appendices 1 and 2 are brilliant for their discussion of the relationship between facts and values.

NAGEL, ERNEST, *The Structure of Science*, New York, Harcourt, Brace & World, 1961.

Chapter 13 has a good discussion of the problem of bias in the social sciences.

OLIVER, DONALD W., and JAMES P. SHAVER, *Teaching Public Issues in the High School*, Boston, Houghton Mifflin, 1966.

A report on a successful attempt to teach students to examine value conflicts embedded in questions of public policy.

RATHS, LOUIS E., MORRILL HARMIN, and SIDNEY B. SIMON, *Values and Teaching*, Columbus, Ohio, Merrill, 1966.

An excellent book on value education at all grade levels and in all subjects. Part I develops a theory of value clarification that emphasizes uncoerced choice.

SMITH, PHILIP, G., *Philosophy of Education*, New York, Harper & Row, 1964, 1965.

Chapter 7 has a discussion of the value problem.

CHAPTER 7

Teaching History Reflectively

MORE SECONDARY students are enrolled in history than in any social study. Junior-high-school students usually are required to study United States history, often in eighth grade; senior-high-school students take it in eleventh or twelfth grade. In most high schools world history is an elective in ninth or tenth grade, and there is now some sentiment in favor of making it a two-year course. Large urban high schools frequently offer as electives Latin American and European history. Several states require students to take a course in the history of their state.

Students also study United States history in elementary school along with some geography. Consequently, high-school graduates typically have had three exposures to United States history, and much of the literature on the social-studies curriculum has struggled with problems of duplication and repetition. Any suggestion that one of these exposures might well be omitted from the curriculum receives strong opposition, particularly from veterans' organizations that view history as an opportunity to teach patriotism.

Despite the amount of instructional time devoted to history there is general dissatisfaction with the results. In theory, learning in history should be the same as learning in any other social study. Students would be expected to cast and test hypotheses, using data from experience and experiment as a basis for achievement of tested insights. History handled in this way would present no special problems in teaching. Unfortunately, many historians do not agree with this conception of history, with the result that the dominant approach in the secondary school largely promotes the learning of arbitrary associations, and generalizations cast in the past-tense rather than the present.

Is History a Social Science?

Historians cannot agree on whether history is a social science or one of the humanities. This disagreement acquires significance when one notes that how a subject is conceived has some effect on how it is taught. To determine whether history is a social science requires some definition of social science.

The social sciences are those fields of inquiry—presumably "scientific"—which deal with the social behavior of man. The aim of a social scientist is to gain such insights into human behavior as will make possible its prediction or explanation in specified situations. It is *laws* (however tentative) of human behavior which social scientists are seeking.

History, it is often contended, is not a true social science. Both historians and social scientists can be found to support this view. Stuart Chase, after polling a great many social scientists, concluded that history should be regarded as an accessory discipline. "History," he said, "deals with events which have gone into limbo . . . and can never hope to measure living phenomena or use the full scientific method." [1] Robert Lynd, a sociologist, has said, "There probably never was another era when 'the appeal to history' uncorrected by multiple new variants in the situation meant less." [2]

The aim of reflective thought, as we have noted repeatedly, is to achieve warranted present-tense generalizations cast in the form of if-then propositions. These are of the nature of rules or principles. Their role is to predict and explain, and, applied in problematic situations, to suggest new hypotheses. Learning such generalizations makes transfer of training possible. The aim of all scientific inquiry is to achieve tested generalizations of this sort. This is what theory building is all about; and ultimately science is theory building and nothing else.

To the extent that historians generalize, all but a few do so in the past tense. Gottschalk, in a solid and famous study, has identified six kinds of historians. These can be classified according to their attitude toward building present-tense generalizations.

First, there is the historian who would not knowingly make any kind of generalization. If he occasionally generalizes, it is only because the flesh is weak. Once he becomes aware that he has made a generalization he begins to work on its elimination. This kind of historian hopes to have it proclaimed at his last rites, "He died, bereft of generalizations." Gottschalk labels this kind of history "the school of the unique." [3] Only compilers of documents and chroniclers are genuinely representative of this school.

A second kind of historian belongs to the "school of the strictly limited generalization." Members of this school make generalizations "knowingly

---

[1] Stuart Chase, *The Proper Study of Mankind,* Harper & Row, 1948, p. 48.
[2] Robert S. Lynd, *Knowledge for What?* Princeton University Press, 1948, p. 131.
[3] Louis Gottschalk, "Categories of Historiographical Generalization," in Louis Gottschalk, ed., *Generalization in the Writing of History,* University of Chicago Press, 1963, p. 113.

but intend to limit their generalizations strictly to exposition of the historical subject matter under investigation and of that subject matter only in its own setting." [4] These are the purely narrative-descriptive historians, and their generalizations are necessarily in the past tense.

A third group, called by Gottschalk the interpretative historians, "make a deliberate effort to go beyond the historical subject matter in hand in order to indicate its interrelationships with antecedent, concurrent, and subsequent events" and in doing so "risk broad interpretative syntheses but still limit their interpretations to interrelated trends." [5] Weber's thesis that the Protestant ethic contributed to the rise of capitalism, or Beard's claim that the American Constitution reflected a desire for stability on the part of certain vested interests are examples of interpretative history. Gottschalk properly observes that any synthesis of this kind can be generalized further. When this is done with Weber, we get a present-tense generalization to the effect that "a certain kind of religion is associated with a certain kind of economic system." Most historians are reluctant to make this kind of extended generalization, and consequently refuse to behave as social scientists.

A fourth kind of historian belongs to "the school of generalization on the basis of comparisons." The comparative historians "draw parallels and analogies" between "the subject matter at hand" and "other times or places" whether or not otherwise interrelated.[6] Comparative historians usually cast their generalizations in the past tense, but it would require only a tiny step for them to become genuine generalists. Like the interpretative historians, their generalizations are suggestive of the present-tense generalizations of the social scientist.

The fifth category in Gottschalk's taxonomy identifies as a school the nomothetic historians. He calls this group the "school of generalizations that have validity for prediction and control." He describes these men as "those who venture propositions about past trends or analogies in such general or abstract terms as to leave the implications, if they do not indeed state explicitly, that their propositions may well be extrapolated to events in the future." [7] A teacher who would teach history for reflective purposes will necessarily treat the historical content of schoolbooks with the same methods used at the research level by nomothetic historians—historians who search the past for regularities. These are the only historians who define history as a social science. Their generalizations are necessarily in the present tense.

[4] *Ibid.*
[5] *Ibid.*
[6] *Ibid.*
[7] *Ibid.*

Finally, Gottschalk mentions the "school of cosmic philosophies of history." They "propound philosophies that are intended to provide a cosmic understanding of the course of human events past and to come."[8] Cosmic philosophers are usually guilty of special pleading. They reason from a priori principles and ignore or distort data that conflict with their principles.

Other historians sometimes reject the nomothetic historians along with the cosmic philosophers. They regard the erroneous generalizations of cosmic philosophers as a natural consequence of any attempt to discover historical laws. The baby is emptied with the bath. The essentially *unscientific* character of the cosmic philosophers is confused with the essentially *scientific* character of the nomothetic historian.

Gottschalk does not identify by name present-day historians who could be designated nomothetic. He does argue that many historians tend to engage in nomothetic reasearch, knowingly or not, and offers the following as samples of generalizations with a predictive and explanatory cast:

1. A politically satisfied populace might well accept an administration less than perfect whereas a politically dissatisfied one could always find fault with even the most laudable intentions. (From Arthur G. Haas, "Metternich, Reorganization and Nationality, 1813–1818," Ph.D. dissertation, University of Chicago, 1961)

2. . . . . wherever a European state which is not now free may gain or regain political freedom, there the parliamentary system is sure to be established. (R. K. Gooch, *Parliamentary Government in France: Revolutionary Origins, 1789–1791*, Cornell University Press, 1961, p. 37)

3. And history is witness again and again that size and prestige have no fixed correlation. Indeed, its first lesson is that true prestige has always been the product not so much of genuine power as of genuine excellence. (Barbara Ward, "The Highest Resolve—True Prestige," *New York Times Magazine*, January 1, 1961, p. 37)

4. It seems far more probable [than an explanation in racial terms—Celtic and Germanic] that geographical factors determined the kind of settlement the peasants of medieval Europe made. (Jerome Blum, *The European Peasantry from the Fifteenth to the Nineteenth Century*, Service Center for Teachers of History, 1960, p. 3)

5. The religious art of all peoples and periods has always been the expression in visual form of their belief in unseen supernatural powers governing their lives and destinies. (Benjamin Rowland, "Religious Art East and West," in the papers submitted for the Second Conference of the Frank L. Weil Institute for Studies in Religion and the Humanities, Cincinnati, 1961)

6. But the driving force behind the innovations in outlook and methods of

---

[8] *Ibid.*

these European scientists [of the seventeenth century] came in no small degree
from the immense confidence they possessed in the powers of the mind to find
truths concerning the universe which was then almost universally believed by
learned Europeans to be the creation of God, as Christ had revealed Him.
(J. U. Nef, "Can There Be a New Christian View of History?" in the papers
submitted for the Second Conference of the Frank L. Weil Institute for
Studies in Religion and the Humanities, Cincinnati, 1961) [9]

These six generalizations are not of the same kind. The kind of generalization, truly nomothetic in nature, that social scientists typically seek is
best represented by 1, 3, and 5. The second generalization in the list has a
nomothetic element but falls short of being genuinely nomothetic because
it is limited to Europe. Conceivably, there is a nomothetic insight concealed within it awaiting only a specification of general conditions favorable to the rise of parliamentary government. The last generalization in
the list is more typical of what historians like to produce as an observation. It is cast in the past tense and makes no claim to universal validity.
One wonders why Gottschalk offers it as having predictive-explanatory
power. Perhaps the following comment constitutes his reason: "All of
them, however, are intended to have universal validity, for, to recast a
point already made, even when they deal with agricultural institutions or
religious art of the past, they lay down general factors by which institutions or art may be affected (and understood) in the future." [10]

Most historians when they generalize at all prefer past-tense generalizations, e.g., "Large corporations were able to exert an unhealthy
influence in politics," or "The tariff enabled American manufacturers to
raise their prices above what competitive conditions would have made
possible at the time." Instead of saying that "Soldiers who make war on
primitive peoples are more likely to win if they adopt some of the
practices of the enemy" they prefer to say that "Unless American soldiers
fought like Indians, the redmen usually defeated them." Historians who
pride themselves on being scientific, in the sense of getting the facts
straight, scrupulously avoid theorizing. They argue that history can
continue to be scientific only if it avoids theoretical generalizations.

*Such an argument misconstrues the nature of science. The purpose of
science is to construct ever-better theories, and thus increase its power to
predict and explain. Mere description, no matter how accurate, is not a
science. History as a field of inquiry can qualify as a social science only
insofar as historians work at the development of theoretical generalizations.*

Past-tense generalizations do not qualify as theoretical generalizations.

[9] *Ibid.*, p. 127.
[10] *Ibid.*, p. 128.

Past-tense generalizations may imply theoretical ones, but the latter are always *timeless* in quality—they refer to past, present, and future. It helps students to understand history if implied generalizations are put before them and submitted to the test of data. Many of the generalizations made by nomothetic historians, or implied by descriptive historians, have something wrong with them, and the purpose of reflective tests is to expose faulty generalizations whether stated or implied. This is what we mean by making history clear.

It is doubtful that students can remember and use historical data unless it is incorporated in sound present-tense generalizations. Present beliefs can be tested with data, some of which comes from memory. History can extend a student's memory back into the past, so that he may experience events and their meaning even though they occurred prior to his lifetime. One's memory may include specific bits of information, such as the color of Uncle Abner's nose; but the most useable content in anyone's memory consists of lessons learned from experience. Historical experience can become part of one's present experience if it confirms or disconfirms the lessons of one's remembered experience. How we teach history has much to do with how far back our memory will be able to go.

Perhaps the role of historical data, as well as the instructional task of history teachers, may be made clearer by analyzing briefly the role of experience in learning. It is not past events per se which affect present behavior but, as Kurt Lewin has said the "psychological past." Present behavior is affected by past experience *if* such experience has made the present look different from what it otherwise would. It is the *contemporary* meaning of objects which determines our behavior toward them. The past is crucially important, but only as it affects our thinking about the present. An event in one's past is insignificant unless it entered into one's experience at the time he encountered it and changed the way he now sees his environment. In short, it is the insights one gains, and the enhancement of wisdom which comes from them, that afford a measure of the value of experience.

One may say that what is important in life is the "living past" but this living past is not necessarily limited to the past we have lived. Many past events the occurrence of which preceded our existence can become part of our living past as they are integrally incorporated in our present outlook. One might look into his past and find meaning in some event which had little meaning when it occurred. In the same way one may find meaning in something that occurred centuries before one was born.

Obviously, a great amount of the history of the human race does bear on possible present-tense generalizations (that is, present outlooks), including those which serve the natural interests of students. It is only necessary that the potential relevance of historical data to such generalizations be shown. For example, historical data can support or cast doubt upon many rules or principles of human behavior. Ancient history may be as productive of fruitful content as modern; world history may be as useful as American. Probably certain events of the fourth century B.C. are more relevant to several large issues today than most of the "news" reported in current-events classes. The task of a teacher of history is to bring history into the experience of youngsters; and this may be done only as youngsters are helped to use historical facts as data in the purposeful testing of ideas.

Historians who avoid the development of theoretical generalizations and teachers of history who discourage students from drawing lessons from history have some well-grounded fears behind their avoidance. History lends itself to rationalization. History, like Christianity, has been used to prove almost anything. This has led some to conclude that it can prove nothing at all. It is hard to follow the logic of those who argue that the misuse of history proves it has no use. We feel that it has use, but that its usefulness depends upon a willingness to take the risks of rationalization and hope that mistakes in generalization will deter no one from using past experience as a source of hypotheses for refining present outlooks.

The historian may find himself behind the eight ball as he tries to do this. There probably are not many generalizations about human behavior (social theory) which can be supported dependably with historical evidence alone. At the same time, a social theory that ignored relevant past experience would be a very poor theory. It is the test of relevance that is crucial. The total field or ground against which human behavior occurred in 1855 could be very different from the environment a hundred years later. Whatever social theory is suggested by history needs to be verified against evidence of the present. Contemporary observation and experimentation, as provided by nonhistorical social sciences, is needed as a final test. Contemporary history, if conceived as a social science, can also contribute to this test. That there is a difference between the methodologies of history and social science has been suggested by Lewin:

> To determine the properties of a present situation . . . one can follow two different procedures: One may base one's statement on conclusions from history . . . , or one may use diagnostic *tests of the present.*
>
> To use a simple example: I wish to know whether the floor of the attic is sufficiently strong to carry a certain weight. I might try to gain this knowledge by finding out what material was used when the house was built ten years ago. As I get reliable reports that good material has been used, and that the architect was a dependable man, I might conclude that the load probably would be safe. If I can find the original blueprints, I might be able to do some exact figuring and feel still more safe.

Of course, there is always a chance that the workmen have actually not followed the blueprints, or that insects have weakened the woodwork, or that some rebuilding has been done during the last ten years. Therefore, I might decide to avoid these uncertain conclusions from past data and to determine the present strength of the floor by testing its strength now. Such a diagnostic test will not yield data which are absolutely certain; how reliable they are depends upon the quality of the available test and the carefulness of testing. However, the value of a present test is, from the point of view of methodology, superior to that of [a historical test.][11]

Lewin goes on to suggest that two steps must logically be included in any historical test: (1) An investigator must determine what the past situation was—often no easy feat; and (2) he must show that nothing unknown has interfered in the meantime—that the theoretical generalization derived from the analysis of historical events is as true today as in the time that suggested it. The latter task is usually even more hazardous than the first.

This is not meant to suggest that a historical approach has no value. Rather it is intended to show the difficulties involved in giving the field of history stature as a social science. Admittedly, there are obstacles to be faced by the nonhistorical social sciences as well; but they are of another sort. As a school subject capable of helping students acquire tested social theory, history may be less useful than other social studies, unless it is regarded primarily as a source of hypotheses and data to be checked against data from nonhistorical social sciences. As a source of hypotheses, rather than proofs, it may be richly rewarding—if taught with that purpose in mind.

Using Springboards in History

History can be a source of data as well as hypotheses. Every human problem, when subjected to scientific study, requires a look at history—the history of man's struggle with that problem. Apparently all scientific fields find it necessary to make use of both historical and contemporary data. Without experience—which, in a broad sense, is history—human behavior could never be intelligent. Historical knowledge is absolutely essential.

We are not talking here about the content of conventional school textbooks in history. We are talking, rather, about carefully selected historical data—facts which are relevant to the problems we wish to study. These problems are not those of the past but consist of the present contradictions and confusions in the minds of individuals—the problems of

[11] Kurt Lewin, *Field Theory in Social Science*, Harper & Row, 1951, pp. 48–50.

today. Historical knowledge as it bears on such problems is indispensable; historical knowledge which is irrelevant is pointless. Nor can we assume the "background fallacy" which holds that most persons can memorize and retain historical knowledge outside of problematic situations and at some later time employ it in problem solving.

High-school students who study history can increase their understanding of the present only to the extent to which they can be led to hypothesize about the present meaning of past events. Hypotheses may be suggested by a passage in a history text or by content from nonhistorical social sciences which can be brought to bear on the meaning of a passage in a history text. We call these passages *springboards*. The testing of such hypotheses would utilize data from both history and the nonhistorical social sciences.

Springboards are of three kinds. One kind is a descriptive passage in a history textbook. A teacher asks questions which encourage students to interpret the passage in terms of its contemporary significance. The questioning seeks to relate the passage evidentially to a live issue of the present or to some currently held social theory or belief which in turn may be related to a live issue. In any case, study of the implications of the passage should lead students to formulate one or more generalizations of potential future usefulness. The following descriptive passage and its treatment is offered as an example.

Spain forbade English traders to enter Spanish waters. But the treasure ships from America were a great temptation to the skillful sailors of England. Attacks upon foreign commerce in distant waters were regarded as piracy rather than war and English sea captains did not hesitate to seize any Spanish ship which was not well defended. John Hawkins and Francis Drake were only two of the many who sold slaves in Spanish colonies, sold goods in violation of Spanish laws, and captured Spanish ships.[12]

The following questions could lead students to think about this passage:

1. Were Hawkins and Drake guilty of violating the laws of Spain? What did the Spanish think of Hawkins and Drake? Were their deeds criminal by modern standards?
2. Did the British regard Hawkins and Drake as lawbreakers and thieves? What did the British people think of these men? Were they regarded as heroes or criminals?
3. Are persons who are regarded as criminals by one country sometimes regarded as heroes by another? Can you think of any modern examples? Is it common or uncommon to use different standards in judg-

[12] Dwight L. Dumond, *et al., History of the United States*, Heath. 1048. p. 12.

ing a person of one's own nationality and a person of another nationality?

In answering these questions the teacher would have students consider such generalizations as:"A person may be called a criminal by one nation and a hero by another," or "People of any nationality are likely to use a double standard in judging themselves and foreigners." Some students, perhaps, will have been doing the latter without being aware of it; study of data and the idea may thus appear as a challenge and motivate them to serious reflection.

A second kind of springboard begins with a theoretical idea, not a piece of description. Such ideas can be found in school textbooks, albeit rarely. The following were found in books actually used in high-school history courses:

> The business of the United States is business. [Expressive of a philosophy attributed to Harding, Coolidge, and Hoover]
> Inflation injures everybody.
> A protective tariff creates prosperity.
> Riches may bring evil as well as good. Too much wealth may lead to waste and neglect.
> Paper money is not real money.

Such generalizations may seem outrageous to some students. This may provoke them to try to find out what is wrong with them. Even acceptable generalizations may serve as springboards into student thinking, if a teacher asks provocative questions.

When theoretical passages such as the above are taken from a textbook they may be handled by raising questions designed to inquire into their validity. Students may question the assertion that lack of business confidence causes business recessions and depressions, for example, when they learn that the worst depression in American history began under a political administration in which business was given every reason to have confidence. The noting of this fact may stimulate a search for other explanations of business declines, including nonpsychological theories of the business cycle. Effective learning will have occurred when students gain some grasp of theoretical explanations of the business cycle which can be applied to contemporary business fluctuations. If the generalization encountered in the text is about past behaviors or situations (a past-tense generalization), questioning should be designed, first, to explore whether the statement has continuing validity, and if it is agreed that it has, to determine its accuracy.

A third kind of springboard comprises facts or ideas which seem mutually contradictory. Textbook writers do contradict themselves with surprising frequency. In a study of the economics content of selected high-school textbooks no less than twenty-one instances were uncovered in which, if one takes literally what was said, authors appeared flatly to contradict themselves.[13] Because such contradictions may resemble disharmonies in personal outlooks of students they are especially provocative of reflective thought. Here are a few examples:

Money can never be created, but over 90 percent of American business is done with "checkbook money."

Business is almost always conducted in an enlightened, strictly honest way; but consumers in the United States had better beware or they will surely be taken advantage of.

A capitalist economy is inherently peaceful, but most major wars have resulted from competition for markets and sources of raw materials between capitalist nations.

Because human nature is what it is, business cycles are inevitable; but there are no business cycles under communism.

Economic affairs are governed by natural laws which are beyond the power of men to influence, but the best way to cure a poorly functioning economy is for each individual to apply the Ten Commandments in his economic life.

A reflective method of teaching history uses textbook passages as springboards for problem-solving discussion. It is the steady, persistent, and varied use of this technique which makes the school subject of history an accessory in the building of social theory. Of course, the amount of accurate social theory now available to social scientists is limited by the immaturity of their own subject fields, and the most effective teaching techniques will not enable high-school students to theorize more effectively and more richly than social scientists have been able to do. But it is necessary for high-school students themselves to theorize if they are to understand and use theoretical generalizations. The springboard technique can lead to such theorizing.

SPRINGBOARDS AND ATOMIZATION

It might be charged that the development of springboards, as proposed here, will atomize history; that if teachers select successive focal points which may be several pages apart in a textbook students will acquire fragments of historical knowledge without awareness of continuity or relationship in historical events. Quite the contrary can be the case. A skillful teacher with a clearly formulated philosophy of education can use the springboard technique to unify history into some form other than the chronological narrative. At the beginning of a course, springboards may

[13] Maurice P. Hunt, *The Teaching of Economics in the American High School,* unpublished doctoral dissertation, Ohio State University, 1948, pp. 247–249.

be single passages, but as the course progresses the generalizations formulated will tie the passages which first suggested them to other passages. By the end of a course, students may be able to identify twenty or thirty events (as described in the textbook) which support or question a single generalization. In other words, all these events are seen as having the same meaning. *Because they are seen as data supporting or refuting a single generalization, they possess unity.* Furthermore, groups of events supporting single generalizations tend to fall together under increasingly more inclusive generalizations, until large parts of man's history are seen as illustrating certain general ideas.

There are many generalizations which can be illustrated time and again from United States history; once they are understood they unify many items of descriptive content. The following are examples of such social theory:

1. People tend to cling to many customs and beliefs long after the causes which gave rise to them have disappeared.
2. From generation to generation, people to some degree change their moral standards and their fundamental beliefs about many matters.
3. Americans tend to accept technological innovations more readily than they accept social or ideological innovations.
4. Technological innovations tend to produce social tensions which can be eased only by appropriate social innovations.
5. People commonly violate in behavior ideals to which they verbally subscribe.
6. To some degree, political parties represent economic interests and groupings.
7. War is a stimulus to certain kinds of economic expansion and overall prosperity.

GUARDING AGAINST OVERGENERALIZATION

Many, and perhaps most, theoretical generalizations suggested by events in history cannot readily be tested with any degree of finality by high-school students. It is very easy to create a generalization, to find two or three events which seem to support it, and then to conclude that it is accurate, a suitable guide to behavior. The cure for this superficiality is not to be found in instruction which discourages any attempt to generalize. Unless generalization occurs, no transferable learning has taken place and instruction has been futile. Furthermore, bright students in any class, and even the not-so-bright, will make some generalizations—often superficial ones—no matter how hard a teacher tries to avoid theorization.

If a teacher deliberately entices his students to generalize, he can then watch for overgeneralization and teach his students how to distinguish between good and poor generalizations. One aim of high-school teaching of social studies (including history) should be an increased capacity to generalize. Moreover, students can be taught to regard every conclusion as a starting point for additional inquiry. Although many student conclusions deserve considerable suspicion and reexamination, these weakly grounded principles are often better guides to action than the prejudices which typically govern much of American life. It should also be remembered that students learn as much from rejecting or modifying a generalization as they learn from acceptance of one. This is a point lost from the sight of those teachers who avidly seek to promote learning of "right" answers.

Perhaps the chief weakness against which to guard is a teacher's tendency to rationalize—to help students find historical support for the teacher's beliefs. If he knows that he has a preference for a particular interpretation of history, a teacher should consciously strive to create doubt in his students concerning the validity of such an interpretation when it is presented by a textbook author or other authority. Enough doubt to get alternatives considered would appear to be the guiding principle for a teacher who would protect students against teacher rationalization.

CURRENT EVENTS AND HISTORY

The current-events movement is a product of the belief that proper content of social studies education is not limited to what has been discovered about the past; it should include, in addition, facts which are in the process of emerging. It is now customary in many classes for a teacher to suspend textbook study for one class period a week and have discussion and reports on the news.

Although the current-events movement has introduced fresh content into the curriculum, it is open to criticism. It tends to focus on the trivial and to emphasize reporting of news rather than analysis and interpretation. Also it generally fails to link study of current events with the remainder of a course. When this occurs in a history course, the current significance of past events may be slighted, and the historical roots of current developments may be missed.

Teachers have ignored an obvious cure. To be understood, any social issue must be studied in the light of historical as well as current data. Some contemporary issues do not have deep historical roots. Others do, but standard history textbooks may omit consideration of them; and other relevant instructional materials are not always available. Consequently, a teacher must select issues which can be studied *profitably* in history classes through materials which are available (sometimes only a textook).

The following propositions are a brief sample (meant only to be illustrative) of the hundreds potentially suitable for study in a history class. Each proposition is controversial in some of its aspects and, with its converse, reflects an issue which might exist in some American community. One cannot determine outside a particular teaching situation whether students could be made to feel some of these issues as problems. Nevertheless, they are likely to be appropriate to many high-school history classes. No attempt is made to list types of evidence which a typical history textbook might conceivably provide; probably an adequate analysis of some of the listed propositions would require evidence from additional sources.

1. In order for a nation to make economic progress, it must be willing to increase the size of its national debt.
2. A capitalist nation makes its greatest economic progress when taxes and controls imposed on business are kept at a minimum.
3. New machines create more jobs than they destroy.
4. The immigration of foreigners into the United States causes unemployment among native-born workers.
5. The adoption of a socialist economy inevitably leads to a loss of political freedom.
6. Professional soldiers seldom make successful Presidents of the United States.
7. Businessmen in the United States usually support freedom and democracy as well as free enterprise.
8. The mixing of races through intermarriage produces inferior and degenerate offspring.
9. Atheists tend to be maladjusted and often immoral.
10. The nonwhite races are inferior to whites in business and financial acumen.
11. The class structure in America represents a natural ranking based upon innate mental, moral, and physiological differences.
12. There are no social classes in America.

Issues such as these are likely to appear in current events as explicit or hidden sources of social conflict. Their examination can increase students' understanding of news reports.

Historical Content—Its Analysis

Historical writing, including that found in high-school textbooks, abounds with concepts, generalizations, and values—as well as descriptive facts and chronological narrative. All that has been said in previous chapters about the teaching of such content applies to the teaching of history. Some pointed and illustrated comment is nevertheless in order.

CONCEPTS AND HISTORICAL DESCRIPTION

It is true that much of the history that teachers assign students is sheerly descriptive and places no great strain on their mental capacities. But some of this descriptive material cannot be understood unless concepts are taken apart and put back together again. A discussion of "normalcy" in a typical high-school history text suggests the problem.

In their domestic policies the administration of Harding and Coolidge made it apparent that "normalcy" meant a general retreat from government regulation of business. Although the federal government actively aided business men by levying protective tariffs and by protecting American investments in Latin-American countries, its overall policy was one of laissez faire.

A possible approach to the clarification of this passage would be a straightforward explication of the concept of laissez faire. This concept embodies a body of belief about the functions of government. One who believes in laissez faire believes that the functions of government ought to be limited to: (1) enforcement of those contracts freely entered into, (2) provision for the national defense, and (3) maintenance of domestic law and order. This conception of government serves as a defining attribute for the category "classical liberal."

The above quoted text passage left the concept, laissez faire, undefined. This is often the case in schoolbooks, for space does not permit careful definition of every term. The writer of a text may simply assume that students understand a term, or that the teacher will take time to explicate the more basic concepts. More often than not the key concepts in an assignment require considerable explication.

A student cannot understand "normalcy" as a departure from laissez faire unless he understands both terms well enough to compare and contrast them. The text helps him a bit with "normalcy." It says in effect that the criteria were at least two, a reduction in governmental regulation of business; and an increase in the subsidy of domestic industry and the military protection of overseas investment, particularly those in Latin America. If a teacher makes this meaning of normalcy clear, and if he develops the meaning of laissez faire with equal clarity, his students will appreciate that normalcy was not a return to laissez faire except in a half-hearted sense. To accept the text's statement that Harding and Coolidge had an overall policy of laissez faire, they would have to evaluate certain departures from that policy—in the form of subsidies and Latin American intervention—as fickle notions of the moment scarcely typical of the period called "normalcy."

A teacher can, if he desires, push the analysis further. He can review with his students Wilson's New Freedom and show that the meaning of this term is different from both normalcy and laissez faire. He can also anticipate study of the New Deal by developing briefly its concern with relief, recovery, and reform. A treatment of these alternatives can help to sharpen the meanings of normalcy and laissez faire. Some students may begin to sense at this point that major power groups and social classes in America have never preferred laissez faire to easy street, and that an understanding of history may be increased by recourse to such concepts as social stratification, class struggle, and the role of economic interests in politics.

A teacher may test his students' understanding of normalcy by asking them to sort a list of policy instances, indicating in each case on what basis the policy instance is to be classified as an example consistent or not with the doctrine of normalcy. The teacher's treatment of normalcy and other concepts should have made clear to students the properties or attributes by which membership in a class (category) is determined. Some procedure such as we have outlined is necessary to teaching any concept defined as a category (see Chapter 4).

CONCEPTS AND HISTORICAL EXPLANATION

In the above explication of normalcy and laissez faire no reasons were explored as to why governmental policies have always departed to some degree from the doctrines of laissez-faire, sometimes to the advantage of labor and agriculture, sometimes to the advantage of business and industry. Today it is difficult to find a group that is not in some way, direct or indirect, the beneficiary of government aid. To make explanations of any kind moves inquiry into the realm of social theory and conceptual systems. The most effective teaching of history or the social sciences is bound to take us in this direction, and indeed textual materials in every-day use require us to do so.

In the same text from which we took the comment on normalcy we read:

During the war, industry had begun to spread into the South and West, so there was increased sentiment for protection in these agricultural areas.

At another point a few pages later it says:

Andrew Mellon, Secretary of the Treasury from 1921 to 1932, believed that heavy taxes on excess profits, inheritances, and large incomes "penalized success" and discouraged the investment of capital in productive business enterprise.

And still later we read:

> In spite of strong objection from President Coolidge this law (Immigration Quota Law of 1924) excluded Japanese entirely. The unfortunate result was to increase the effectiveness of Anti-American propaganda put out by militarists.

In each of these quoted passages, concepts are used for explanatory rather than merely descriptive purposes. The first statement offers an explanation for a certain development in public opinion. The second relates taxation policies to incentives to invest, and the third suggests a relationship between the effectiveness of propaganda and a policy followed by a nation against whom the propaganda is directed.

A teacher can approach any such suggested explanation by reducing it to a syllogism. If we do this with the first of our examples, we get a syllogism that runs somewhat as follows:

Major Premise. If an agricultural region begins to acquire industries, an initial result is an increased public sentiment favorable to protective tariffs.

Minor Premises. During World War I new industries began to develop in southern and western United States, two regions traditionally agricultural.

Conclusion. During World War I the sentiment in favor of protective tariffs increased in its vigor and incidence within southern and western United States.

It would make for dull and exorbitantly logical writing if the author of a text put each of his explanatory passages in a syllogistic form. But a teacher who reduces an explanatory passage to this form can more easily teach the nature of an explanation (an important concept in itself) and also help his students to determine whether a particular explanation is adequate. In the above example, the teacher would involve his students in several phases of inquiry. First, he would explore with them the meaning of each premise, making sure that his students would know what they were talking about. This phase would obviously call for the precise definition of any concept in either premise the meaning of which was not clear to all students. Second, he would ask students to test each premise empirically. This phase is concerned with the truth of each premise, and involves the students in all problems connected with the testing of synthetic statements—matters which were discussed in Chapter 4. Questions such as the following might be raised in connection with testing the major premise:

1. Do agricultural regions always change toward a more favorable opinion of tariffs as they undergo industrialization?

2. Can you think of any exceptions?
3. Does sentiment in an agricultural region ever become more protectionist without the stimulus of industrialization?
4. Do people always base their opinions upon economic interest?

The reader can easily formulate for himself some of the questions related to an empirical testing of the minor premise in our example.

The final phase would be directed toward determining whether the conclusion in the syllogism follows logically from the premises. This phase makes it possible for students to learn a simple principle in logic: If the premises in an argument are true, and if the conclusion can be deduced from those premises, then, the conclusion has to be true. If a conclusion can be false, even though the premises are true, we are forced to the view that the conclusion does not follow from the premises.

CONCEPTS AND NORMATIVE JUDGMENTS

In addition to description and explanation, textbooks include moral judgments. In descriptions of events and personalities, writers often allow values to intrude. The reader is not always sure whether a person or institution has been described or evaluated. In a "description" of the Harding administration one text had this to say:

> But too many jobs went to incompetent or dishonest personal friends. Corruption was even more widespread and on a larger scale than under Grant. The head of the Veterans Bureau, for instance, arranged fraudulent contracts which cost the taxpayers an estimated 200 million dollars. The Secretary of the Interior eventually went to prison for secretly leasing to private interests oil lands reserved for the navy at Elk Hills, California and Teapot Dome, Wyoming, in return for bribes totalling over $300,000.

A great deal of evidence on the Harding administration's hanky panky is included in the above passage. But a reflective reader may wonder how much is accurate description, how much is condemnation. Do words such as "incompetent," "dishonest," "corruption," "fraudulent," and "secretly" function as descriptive or valuative concepts? Can a concept both describe and evaluate?

At another point in the same text we read:

> Coolidge had many of the virtues associated with rural, small town America. He was intensely conservative, cautious, and given to few words. In his occasional public speeches he preached the old-fashioned virtues of honesty, thrift, and hard work.

Concepts such as honesty, thrift, and hard work are often used as normative concepts to express approval of the objects to which they are attached. At the same time, they may be said to describe an object. When these terms are encountered in a school assignment, a teacher will ask students for the meaning of honesty, and then help them determine whether this meaning was held by the writer of the text. It makes little difference whether honesty is used in a descriptive or normative sense. The logical procedure is the same. What are the attributes of honest behavior, and can Mr. Smith be said to be honest because his behavior manifests these attributes? Although normative concepts are logically no more difficult to analyze than descriptive concepts, psychological difficulties can arise when persons are not willing or able to operationalize their meaning for a normative concept.

Another problem in normative thinking is the ability to justify our value judgments. We justify such judgments by giving reasons for them. In the passage about Coolidge, we are told that thrift, honesty, and hard work are old-fashioned virtues. What does the author mean by this? Does he mean that the practice of such virtues is no longer appropriate to an urban, industrial society? Or does he mean that a certain meaning for each of these terms is no longer appropriate? If this is what he means, what meaning would be appropriate? What is the meaning that is said to be inappropriate? What would be the consequences of practicing thrift in the city? Would the same consequences result from practicing thrift in a small town? In the countryside? What is behind the author's claim that certain values refer to small town virtues? Does he mean that virtue is not everywhere the same?

Regardless of the specific questions asked by a teacher they must fall within a generalized model for analyzing value judgments. If we are to develop a reasonable view toward a proposed policy, we must ask what that policy would create as consequences, and develop criteria for judging whether those consequences are desirable. A study of thrift as a policy would take this line:

1. What is thrift? What do we mean by it?
2. What would be the consequences of thrift?
3. Are such consequences to be judged good or bad?
4. By what criteria are the consequences to be judged?
5. What justification is there for our criteria?

The reflective study of policies and values was discussed in some detail in Chapter 6, but a little repetition is in order here. The first phase, which explores the meaning of thrift, is obviously an exercise in concept analysis, and all that has been said so far about the teaching of concepts would apply to this phase. The second phase, which projects the consequences of thrift, would obviously deal with the testing of synthetic statements. The third and fourth phases are concerned with the application of values to the appraisal of consequences. The fifth and final phase relates values to philosophical systems. A democrat would justify values that a Communist or other totalitarian would not.

A reflective approach to values is not value free. It is, rather, dominated by all the values implicit in a reflective methodology; and these values can be justified only by reference to some philosophical system.

In conclusion, the problems of teaching history reflectively are no different from the problems of teaching any other social study reflectively. Its content is replete with facts, values, concepts, generalizations, and theories. Historical data shares with remembered data a role within reflective process, and this is a process that can make historical content more clear and understandable to its students.

Whether history is a social science, whether it possesses laws, whether there are lessons to be learned, whether regularities can be identified, whether we should study the past to understand the present, are issues the resolution of which helps a teacher to decide whether to teach history reflectively. It should be noted further that regardless of whether history has laws, it does make use of laws from social sciences; and a reflective teaching of history helps students to decide whether its generalizations qualify as laws. It appears, then, that there is no good reason why historical knowledge should not be treated in classrooms as we would treat any kind of knowledge that contains its analytic, synthetic, and valuational elements.

DISCUSSION QUESTIONS AND EXERCISES

1. Much is made of the difference between historical data and contemporary data. Is this a useful distinction? When does the past end and the present begin? Is everything past as soon as it happens?
2. Define a social science. Can history be a social science?
3. Why do some historians oppose generalizations? Why do some prefer past-tense generalizations?
4. How is a nomothetic historian different from a cosmic philosopher of history? Could you distinguish between a nomothetic historian and a social scientist?
5. How does the study of present-tense generalizations solve the problem of relating past events to present ones?
6. Does the claim that certain events led up to later events "explain" why the later events occurred? How is this type of explanation different from or similar to the syllogistic type? How can a history teacher avoid the *post hoc, propter hoc* fallacy?
7. How can a teacher of history avoid bias and rationalization? Is this possible? Can it be minimized?

8. Can history be used to prove anything?

9. Are history and social science different in their concepts of truth?

REFERENCES

GARDINER, PATRICK, ed., *Theories of History*, Glencoe, Ill., Free Press, 1959.

> An excellent collection of articles on the nature of history. Part II is entirely devoted to the problem of explanation. It contains a famous article by Carl Hempel which sets forth the syllogistic model characteristic of the natural sciences, and suggests its use in history. This position is criticized by Scriven, Dray, and others.

GOTTSCHALK, LOUIS, ed., *Generalization in the Writing of History*, Chicago, University of Chicago Press, 1963.

> A collection of papers on the problem of generalization. An article by Gottschalk classifies historians as to type. An article by Potter examines the role of data and assumptions in historical study.

METCALF, LAWRENCE E., "The Reflective Teacher," *Phi Delta Kappan*, October, 1962.

MEYERHOF, HANS, ed., *The Philosophy of History in Our Time*, Garden City, N.Y., Anchor Books, 1959.

> Interesting articles on the nature of history by such figures as Dewey, Collingwood, Becker, Beard, Toynbee. Pirenne, White, and many others.

NAGEL, ERNEST, *The Structure of Science*, New York, Harcourt, Brace, & World, 1961.

> See Chapters 1 and 2 for the difference between science and common sense in their handling of explanations. See Chapters 13, 14, and 15 for discussion of problems of explanation in history and social science.

PALMER, JOHN, "Explanation and the Teaching of History," *Educational Theory*, October, 1962, pp. 205–217.

> Two views of history and explanation are presented. The implications for teaching and teacher education are then developed. Palmer compares the syllogistic view of explanation with the idealism of Collingwood.

PART III
Technical Problems

CHAPTER 8

Techniques for Stimulating Reflection

THE LITERATURE of education seldom makes a distinction between method and technique, and often uses the terms interchangeably. In this book, method refers to a basic mode of teaching. Methodological questions are questions of epistemology. Technique, on the other hand, refers to the particular way in which a method is applied. Reflection is the method advocated in this book. By what techniques can this method be implemented? In this chapter, we are concerned to show how techniques can be made to increase the amount and quality of reflection among pupils. It is not our purpose so much to show *which* techniques are to be used as *how* techniques are to be used. Reflective teaching is less a matter of selecting a particular technique than of knowing how to use any of a variety of techniques so as to promote reflection. There are discussions and discussions; only certain kinds of discussions involve thinking.

Importance of a Basic Philosophy

It is usually unsound to divorce theory from practice. Technique for technique's sake is pointless, even dangerous. There is nothing in a technique per se to give its user a sense of direction, or to provide him with a guiding theory or philosophy.

There is growing realization that a technician lacks the qualities of a professional if his training has given insufficient attention to questions of theory. And in many professional fields there is increasing emphasis on the priority of theory over technique. Rogers has commented on the training of counselors: "Our concern has shifted from counselor technique to counselor attitude and philosophy, with a new recognition of the importance of technique on a more sophisticated level. . . . We have proven in our own experience Kurt Lewin's oft-quoted statement that 'Nothing is so practical as a good theory.' "[1] He has also said that once a counselor achieves an orientation that stresses the worth of each person, he does not have much difficulty in learning the client-centered tech-

---

[1] Carl Rogers, *Client-Centered Therapy*, Houghton Mifflin, 1951, pp. 14–15.

niques that are needed to implement this attitude. And, furthermore, that if one tried to use client-centered techniques without having the proper philosophy, he would fail to achieve their purpose.

The position taken by Rogers does not decry the teaching of technique. Rather, it views full mastery of technique as contributory to the clarification of theory. Teachers who have read and discussed a reflective theory of teaching will increase their understanding of the theory as they try out and evaluate techniques for its implementation. An ideal situation is undoubtedly one in which prospective teachers receive abundant philosophical and theoretical training while simultaneously receiving instruction in the practical implementation of specific theories. A methods course would require that they study techniques so as to define operationally one or more theories of teaching.

Elements of Reflective Procedure

In this section we will use the term *belief* in a broad sense. It may refer to concepts, attitudes, or values as well as the testable propositions that take the form of singular statements or generalizations.

If teaching is to be reflective, each teaching technique should be fashioned to help and encourage students to move through one or more of the steps involved in an act of reflective thought. The pattern of reflection is not rigid. The steps of an act of thought are to be regarded as phases which are indispensable but not necessarily followed in 1–2–3 order or given equal emphasis. In short, the act of thought has a fluid character. It includes hesitation, repetition, forward jumps, and doubling back. However this may be, thought is necessarily structured, and an effectual teacher will be aware of how each of his actions contributes to one or more of its necessary aspects.

Probably the most fruitful way of approaching the problem of selecting and using techniques is to consider the matters for which a teacher is responsible. The specific responsibilities of teachers in fostering reflective learning we take to be as follows.

ACKNOWLEDGMENT OF STUDENT BELIEFS

Teachers must familiarize themselves with present knowledge, understandings, and beliefs of students. One often hears the injunction, "Teachers should start where pupils are," which reflects the principle of continuity of learning. Unfortunately, teachers neglect this principle; particularly do they ignore points of conflict and confusion *in the beliefs of students*. According to the theory underlying this book, student beliefs are raw materials—starting points—for reflective learning. Therefore, teachers need the most comprehensive and accurate picture they can obtain of their students' beliefs. They may get this picture by studying the students—observing their behavior and listening to what they say—or by student interviews. Other techniques for bringing beliefs to the surface are the permissive type of discussion, written assignments, and paper-and-pencil tests. If all these techniques are used and the results cross checked, a more accurate picture is likely to be gained than if only one or two are used.

Studies of student beliefs indicate that students are strongly influenced by community ideology. Therefore, teachers can make promising inferences about student beliefs by studying the belief pattern of the community. This pattern is revealed in editorials and letters to the editor in local newspapers; speeches by community members; church sermons; and the give and take at union meetings, service-club meetings, and community forums. Most teachers follow these sources regularly, but seldom as deliberate observers and students of community ideology.[2]

A teacher may also study national or regional public-opinion polls dealing with issues of general significance, and the platforms, programs, and public pronouncements of national and regional organizations (e.g., political parties, labor unions, veterans' and patriotic associations, and businessmen's organizations).

Teachers may find it useful to compile a written record of the beliefs they have encountered among their students. Each statement of belief could be put on a card and the cards filed under general categories. Such a file would show conflicts, inconsistencies, and points of confusion in belief. It is usually wise not to associate particular beliefs with particular students.

SELECTING BELIEFS FOR STUDY

Next, it is the teacher's responsibility to select a belief for study. In traditional classrooms, selection of content is usually thought to be a prerogative of teachers (or, more often, textbook writers). If the reflective method is to work, teachers, although still arbiters of content, must learn to select beliefs for study with careful regard to present development and background of students. They must take cognizance of what can be made problematic to most of their students.

[2] Each year literally hundreds of books are published which document in some detail various aspects of the belief patterns that characterize American culture. These studies, usually made by teams of social scientists—including psychologists, sociologists, and anthropologists—are among our most reliable sources of data from which to infer the beliefs of high-school students. Not a few of the studies focus directly upon high-school students. Some of the oldest studies are among the best. The studies of Middletown made by the Lynds more than thirty years ago are still a good source of what people believe in the Midwest.

It should be clear that selection of the beliefs to be examined indirectly determines the content to which students are to be exposed. If certain beliefs about races and other minority groups are to be examined, it follows that certain content from sociology and anthropology becomes relevant. One cannot examine any belief without drawing upon relevant content. What is relevant depends upon what beliefs are examined.

No matter how motivated and efficient a teacher, no student can reflect upon the meaning and truth of everything he believes. No student stays in school, or even lives long enough, for that to be possible. One person put it well when he said that a child of ten believes more stuff than he will ever understand. Since students cannot examine everything they believe, it is crucially important that they be encouraged to examine their important rather than their trivial beliefs. A teacher faces the same question when he tries to decide what content in a history course to emphasize. Either decision requires criteria by which to select important over unimportant content. We recommend the following criteria:

1. The belief selected should be capable of being related to some important social issue, or should serve as a stepping stone to later examination of beliefs related to critical social issues.

2. Priority should go to beliefs related to sharply controversial issues, to beliefs held on the level of sheer prejudice, to beliefs which reflect confusion and uncertainty, and to mutually contradictory pairs of beliefs (conflicts) held by students or community adults, or suggested in text materials. In other words, curricula should be planned in terms of *issues to be studied* rather than of competencies—knowledges, skills, and attitudes—to be achieved.

3. The belief selected should be held by a substantial portion of students in either its positive or its negative form, or both, or in a related form. It does not matter whether students accept or reject it, so long as they have some feeling about it.

4. The belief selected should be one which, in the judgment of the teacher, will lend itself to fruitful study—that is, a belief which the teacher is prepared to handle and one for which a worthwhile amount of understandable factual data is available to students.

CREATING A PROBLEM

Having selected the belief to be studied, it is then encumbent upon the teacher to make certain that the students *feel* that a problem exists. Failure here automatically destroys whatever opportunity may have existed to stimulate sustained and energetic reflection. As suggested previously, a student may feel a problem when his background is incapable of interpreting or explaining a situation that confronts him. Problems are characterized by the generation of tension. The most urgent problems will result when students become aware of evidence which questions some cherished belief.

Many of the problems treated by a reflectively oriented teacher should be those of which students are aware, however confusedly, before classroom study is undertaken. This will inevitably be the case whenever a classroom situation is sufficiently permissive to allow students to select for themselves the conflicts or confusions in belief to be studied.

Sometimes treatment of a problem involves nothing more than clarification, i.e., helping students better understand problems that they already feel. Clarification comes through talking to others about the problem and through learning to describe the problem clearly (perhaps with the help of others). For example, if a student feels conflict but is not able to describe it intelligibly either to himself or to others, obviously the nature of the conflict is unclear to him. By delving into it he may become able to describe it in such a way that it can become a subject of further study. Even though a student feels that he understands a given problem very well, it is usually possible to help him understand it still better.

However, the obligations of social-studies teachers have not been fulfilled by clarification and study only of problems already felt. There are latent or potential problems in the background of every individual. That is, all of us at some time espouse beliefs which are mutually contradictory or incompatible with our behavior. We do so without awareness of conflict because we have not as yet been confronted with any situation which has thrown the discrepancies into relief. Whenever an inconsistency becomes evident to us, a problem is felt.

A teacher has a responsibility to expose as many latent or potential conflicts as possible. This involves not merely clarifying problems, but also "creating" them—in the sense that, where previously there was no awareness of conflict or feeling of discomfort, a teacher deliberately tries to bring a conflict to light and to make students feel uncomfortable enough to try to resolve the conflict reflectively. In short, one of the teacher's jobs is to get students into "an intellectual jam." If it seems fairly certain that a specific problem will develop later, perhaps in a situation wherein a person will have not have sympathetic or professional help, the sensible course would seem to be to expose it earlier, when it can be dealt with wisely. This position is rejected by those who believe that it is better to let sleeping dogs lie—an argument that denies validity to the idea of preventive therapy generally accepted in fields of medicine, mental hygiene, and social work.

How should teachers "create" problems for students? One way is to confront them with highly convincing negative evidence. Such evidence should be forceful—that is, easily understood, factual, and patently decisive. Quoted opinions are usually not the most forceful kind of evidence; nor are high-order generalizations if introduced by themselves. Concrete evidence is called for—evidence which can be translated into quantitative terms ("The facts and figures," as we sometimes say). As a rule, evidence introduced into a teaching situation for the express purpose of creating a problem for students is deliberately simplified by the teacher in order as clearly as possible to negate or confirm the belief in question.

Another way to create a problem is to shake a cherished belief by helping students see ways in which their behavior or other beliefs contradict it. Awareness of inconsistency, similar to that produced when a student is presented with new evidence from an outside source, may thus be developed. The basic technique used in exposing inconsistency and confusion in belief is that of asking questions. Teachers ask many questions, but they do not always ask probing questions, nor do they always stay with an issue long enough to bring to light students' thought processes.

Often a contradiction in belief patterns can be exposed by a questioning device known as the *subject-matter switch*. A subject-matter switch is performed when we generalize, or reduce to principle, a particular belief, then demonstrate how another belief is incompatible with the principle and, consequently, with the first belief. For example, a student may express the belief that "Welfare payments should be kept low; otherwise recipients would never look for jobs, and people not yet on welfare might seek to become recipients." This is a popular belief with those who believe that poor people should not be coddled or given large handouts. A teacher who hears a student express this belief and notes that many in the class indicate assent then seeks agreement with the idea that "Poverty is the best incentive a man can have for working," or the related idea that "getting something for nothing" undermines one's initiative and character. If students generally agree to either of these principles, the teacher then places the principle in another context (i.e., gives it a different subject matter) with a question like, "If this is true, then, would it not be well to prevent inheritance of wealth by the rich?" Students who also believe that "Any limitation on accumulation of property would destroy incentive," are placed in a position which forces them to revise one or more of their beliefs. If it is wrong for people on welfare to receive something for nothing, should rich parents be allowed to leave their wealth to adult sons and daughters who might otherwise have to earn their own living?

DEVELOPING HYPOTHESES

As soon as doubt and a desire to reduce it begin to motivate students, the next responsibility of the teacher is to guide them in the development of alternatives to the belief or beliefs which have come to seem inadequate.

This step is called the casting, clarifying, and defining of hypotheses. Alternatives to the idea in question may emerge from students' own thinking or may be suggested by the teacher. A teacher may suggest hypotheses by saying, "Here are some possible solutions which have been suggested by others." Or, "Here are some ideas which have occurred to persons who have studied this issue."

Once ideas for examination are before a class, they must be rephrased where necessary to clarify meaning. By question and discussion, a teacher encourages students to remove as much ambiguity as possible.

If the problem originated in a conflict over the meaning of a concept, a great deal of attention will be directed at alternative meanings and the logic of definition, as discussed in Chapter 4. If the problem concerns the examination of alternate theories and generalizations, it will be necessary to make certain that hypotheses are testable. Testability depends in part on whether key concepts are clear.

If the problem originated in a conflict of values, the class will arrive at statements suitable for hypotheses only as concepts are defined and values given instrumental or logical treatment. A question such as, "Why do people hold this belief?" may bring out judgments of fact which can be tested. (A review of the material in Chapter 6 on the logic of values may be useful at this point.)

Clarifying and defining hypotheses is often a lengthy procedure, but it is necessary if thought is to go forward at all. One of the most common reasons why discussions deteriorate is that a group tries to discuss a proposition which defies examination because of certain built-in vaguenesses or ambiguities.

TESTING HYPOTHESES

The next task is to encourage students to test the hypotheses that have been developed. Testing consists first of deducing consequences from hypotheses, then finding out whether the deduced consequences actually follow. The purpose of testing is not to prove hypotheses true or false in any final sense, but to demonstrate their relative accuracy or inaccuracy as predictive tools. It should be noted that tentative affirmation is often possible and that definitive proof of the inadequacy of a belief is very common in classrooms. As noted previously, the best test of any hypothesis is the scientific one—whether it harmonizes all available and obtainable data.

While it is his function to acquaint students with the nature of hypothesis testing, a teacher should not devise or employ tests that cause students to feel obligated to accept his personal selection and interpretation of evidence. Neither should he allow students to become dependent upon him for all data and interpretations of data. Permissiveness must now prevail if the interests of reflection are to be served. Permissiveness does not mean, however, that students are to be "turned loose" to disregard the criteria of relevance and representativeness, which, under reflective procedure, are the only defensible criteria for selection of data. It is essential that a teacher help students to understand the proper bases for selection of data, and to see that they avoid violating these bases. A teacher must exercise special care to prevent the student search for evidence from degenerating into a search for positive (supporting) or negative (damaging) cases only. The search must be for all cases obtainable and pertinent, be they pro or con.

If the pooled experience of students can provide all obtainable pertinent evidence, the testing of hypotheses may be completed through class discussion alone. Otherwise, testing operations will require not only discussions but also research of some sort—perusal of documentary materials, trips, surveys, and polls.

CHECKING CONCLUSIONS

The final step of reflective problem solving is drawing conclusions. A teacher is obligated to help students understand the generalized rules by which decisions are made and to check all decisions offered against these rules.

If the decision involves problems of definition, students must observe rules different from those that are operative in the testing of propositions. Value problems also have rules to be observed as decisions are made. In order to decide among values, we have to observe the rules that govern definitions and the testing of propositions, plus the logical rules that tell us whether one value decision is consistent with another.

If there is general classroom agreement as to the rules of reflection, failure to reach consensus should be infrequent. It is assumed, however, that conclusions reached by students will be their own. If a teacher does his best to help them understand the requirements of reflection, and his best to help them check their conclusions against these requirements, he can do no more. In the final analysis, the environment of conclusion making must be permissive, not in the sense that the teacher does not participate, but in the sense that he does not use his authority to dominate decisions. The study itself must determine the conclusion—not the prefixed beliefs of anyone, teacher or student.

We have already treated the scientific criterion for judging conclusions when the idea under test is a general proposition. To restate briefly, hypotheses are accepted or rejected on the basis of whether they explain all available and obtainable data. That is to say, a conclusion will be considered satisfactory only if it represents a resolution of some discrepancy which takes into account all available data and from which can be logically deduced new data. These data can then be sought and will, if found, serve as further verification.

If the foregoing principle is understood by students, they can then evaluate a teacher's proposals just as a teacher who understands the principle can evaluate theirs. In short, we can have a give-and-take situation in which each person (including the teacher) is free and obligated to make proposals and criticize proposals made by others. In such an environment, when students and teachers find it desirable to reexamine previously accepted conclusions, it is not inappropriate for a teacher to acquaint students with the conclusions reached by social scientists, historians, and other experts.

Techniques for Promoting Reflection

It has been suggested that a given technique may be judged by whether it contributes at some point to one or more of the steps of a complete act of thought. If it does, then, is it possible to identify any technique as better than others for producing reflection? And is it possible to recognize techniques that have special value in furthering a particular step in an act of thought? The answers seem to be that, although reflection does not depend on any single technique, some techniques are more likely than others to encourage reflection; and some are more applicable than others to a given stage in thought. Those who use the method of reflection must never forget, however, that the significance of any technique *is not the technique per se but how it is used*—and how it is used depends upon the purposes and theory of the teacher.

In the sections to follow, various techniques will be discussed with respect to their potential usefulness in stimulating reflection, and with reference to the manner in which they must be used if they are to produce a maximum of reflection.

Techniques may be classified as either *directed* or *undirected*. Directed techniques are those which place teachers in a central position in the teaching-learning process. They require a maximum of activity and responsibility on the part of teachers and a minimum on the part of students. Undirected techniques require a minimum of activity and responsibility from teachers and a maximum from students. This classification is one of convenience; obviously, techniques may be placed on a continuum ranging from relatively directed to relatively undirected. Most fall somewhere between the two extremes.

Techniques may also be regarded as *authoritarian* or *permissive*. This is a useful distinction but not suitable for general classification. Probably any of the techniques we are about to describe may be used in either authoritarian or permissive fashion. Authoritarianism and permissivism are not functions of a technique per se but of how it is used. When used for authoritarian ends, techniques serve to impress a teacher's thought processes on the minds of students, allowing him to dominate a group intellectually. Permissive techniques, on the other hand, encourage intellectual independence among students. They stimulate reflection and free the mind. Directed techniques may be permissive. Undirected techniques, on the other hand, might conceivably serve authoritarian ends, as when students ostensibly are allowed great freedom in selecting learning projects but, in their reading, are given materials which are slanted to support a teacher's personal convictions.

INVESTIGATORY TECHNIQUES OF TEACHERS

The job of teachers, outside of actual classroom teaching situations, has generally been thought to consist of reading to "keep up," making lesson plans, devising and scoring tests, making study guides, and supervising extracurricular activities. Under a reflective approach to teaching, although a teacher may do all these things, he must do more if he is to succeed.

Just as a psychiatrist needs to know all he can about the mental processes of a patient, so a teacher needs to know all he can about the mental processes of his students. This would be true even if he planned to use relatively undirected learning situations in which students function largely as free and independent agents. Reasons for the need to be familiar with the belief patterns of students have already been discussed.

One of the functions of a teacher, as we have seen, is to assist in hypothesis testing by acquainting students with publications and other community resources from which pertinent data may be drawn. This involves something more than just "keeping up," in the usual sense. Many routine publications in a field—new texts and reference books, research monographs, professional journals—contain some data pertinent to the belief conflicts of students. In addition, a teacher needs to read widely in popular and semipopular periodicals and newspapers—with the intent of procuring information on and ideas of a sort useful in testing beliefs. Taking notes is an essential part of this activity; so is development of clipping files.

In this process, a teacher must guard against selecting data which support only his own point of view. Investigation of the sort we are discussing here is similar in nature to the investigation a scientist might conduct in order to test a hypothesis, except that the hypotheses which a teacher has in mind are suggested by student conflicts, and data collected will be simple enough for students to understand. We do not imply that students should not be encouraged to find their own sources of data. But, when concerned with problems for which there are no local sources of information, students are completely thwarted unless they use their teachers as resources.

TRANSMITTING OR TELLING TECHNIQUES

These include any means by which a teacher directly transmits ideas or information to his group. He may "tell" them through lectures and demonstrations, or by reading to them. Audio-visual presentations also may be classified under this general heading. Opaque projectors, transparencies, and film strips have become popular telling techniques in recent years.

First, let us consider the lecture. Lectures have been in disrepute among professors of education, many of whom lecture for hours each semester on the evils of the lecture system. To the extent that lectures are condoned at all, it is urged that they remain infrequent, short, informal, and interesting. Yet, if instruction is approached with the aim of promoting reflection, the criterion for judging a lecture is not its frequency, its length, its informality, or even whether it is entertaining. The test is whether it does, in fact, stimulate or contribute to reflection.

It is true that the attention span of typical high-school students is not very great, and that they are not capable of being stimulated by a lecture for as long a length of time as college students or adults. This finding may have little relevance, however, once teachers enter the closed areas. When the issues are vital to them, their attention span lengthens. A rule of thumb for lectures in high school might be to limit them to 15 or 20 minutes in length. If they do not produce thought, this is much too long; if they do, it may be too short. Any attempt to dress up a lecture with various kinds of provocative audiovisual material can make a longer lecture a reasonable risk.

There are two stages in reflection where lecturing (or telling) may be highly fruitful. One is at the point where a teacher is trying to help students clarify or feel a problem (he may need to present negative evidence, which is often best done through telling), or where he wishes to describe some situation in which values are in conflict (in the hope that students will feel involved because of analogous situations in their own lives).

Telling may also be appropriate in formulating or testing hypotheses. When a teacher has access to evidence not available to students, he may wish to give facts from his own experience, or from his reading. He may wish to review books, articles, or monographs which would be too difficult for his students to read. Or he may wish to present a guest speaker, or play a radio talk he has recorded. The day will soon arrive when inexpensive equipment will make it possible for a teacher to record on videotape a television program which can then be played back in class the next day.

The most deadening kind of lecture is one which gives students "the answers." Under the reflective approach, this is not a function of teachers or of group leaders. Lectures should raise problems or communicate pertinent evidence; they should always leave students with "something to think about."

Another category of transmitting or telling techniques is audiovisual presentations. Audiovisual materials include models, specimens, exhibits, field trips, motion pictures, still pictures, radio programs, television programs, recordings, charts, graphs, and maps. It is usually assumed that these materials bring more reality and concreteness to experience than can written or spoken words. Their use, however, leaves much to be desired. They may be used as an end in themselves, as when a film arrives and the principal announces an assembly to "look at pictures." Presented thus, films are often irrelevant to anything classes are doing, and are shown without preparation or follow-up. Much of this nonsense may be cured as schools begin to acquire with Federal funds their own supply of audiovisual teaching materials. Past practice has been to show a film on loan whenever it happened to be available. In the future, it may be possible to show a film when it is needed by borrowing it from a local film library. Teachers will plan to buy and store films for use when appropriate.

Most textbooks on audiovisual education, as well as most courses taught on the subject, stress the necessity of a film's "fitting in"—that is, being related to content in the unit under study. Emphasis is also placed on preparatory activities, by both teacher and students, and on follow-up activities, including evaluation. All these procedures are frequently described as mechanical procedures. Taken in themselves, there is nothing about them to produce reflection. Students who are studying China may see a film on the life of a Chinese peasant. But does it contain anything to challenge beliefs which students now hold, to raise questions, or to communicate evidence pertinent to a problem confronting students? If not, it may be a pleasant interlude in a student's day but it is scarcely of educational worth. Again, suppose a teacher conducts an elaborate preparation, including study questions and preliminary discussions. Whether reflection results depends on why and how it is done. Presumably, a teacher who understands what value conflicts are real to students could introduce a movie before it is shown, so that its *evidential* quality will be clear. He might try through discussion to identify controversial beliefs to which a film is relevant. Or, in follow-up activities, questions might be raised as to what general ideas the film suggests and whether it tends to support or negate them.

Bruner has made this comment on a particular film and human dilemmas in general:

> I took a group of fourteen-year-olds to see Peter Ustinov's *Billy Budd* on film. The intensity of the discussion of moral philosophy on the way home convinced me that we have overlooked one of our most powerful allies in keeping alive our engagement in history, in the range of human life, in philosophy. Drama, the novel, history rendered with epic aids of its patron goddess Clio, are all built on the paradox of human choice, on the resolution of alternatives. They are in the best sense studies in the causes and consequences of choice. It is in their gripping quality, their nearness to life, that we can, I would urge, best make personal the dilemmas of the culture, its aspirations, its conflicts, its terrors.[3]

Unfortunately, the content of most audiovisual aids now available is unsuited to reflective learning of the sort most needed in high-school social studies. But the teacher who makes a careful search can locate a sufficient amount that bears upon controversial issues. Some of this may even touch upon the closed areas, and do so with a minimum of propaganda. The paucity of this kind of material suggests that teachers may sometimes do better by producing their own material. They can record radio programs, or have students do so. They can take pictures of slum areas, picket lines, government power dams, and civil-rights demonstrations.

One of the authors had occasion to participate a few years ago in a graduate seminar on living conditions of migrant agricultural labor in the San Joaquin Valley of California. One of the participants was able to get from the files of a local newspaper a series of photographs showing dilapidated shacks, filthy privies, and hungry-eyed children. These pictures had more impact on the group than any amount of telling could have had. Only an actual trip to a labor camp would have been more effective. Beliefs that were challenged by this evidence include notions such as these:

No one ever goes hungry in the United States.

People get what they deserve.

The lower classes are usually happier than anybody else.

Another type of transmitting-telling technique is the demonstration, conducted by teacher or students. The authors have seen the following examples in classrooms:

[3] Jerome S. Bruner, *Toward a Theory of Instruction*, Harvard University Press, 1966, p. 162.

How Galileo demonstrated the behavior of falling bodies. [Had a bearing on the meaning of scientific method, the contrast between experimental and authoritarian methods of getting truth.]

How the Chinese eat with chopsticks. [Had a bearing on culture differences, "The American way is the only efficient or sensible way," etc.]

The position in which a cotton picker works, and the hand movements necessary in manual cotton picking. [Had an evidential bearing on an argument class had had as to whether agricultural labor is "hard work," whether it requires a high degree of skill, whether it is underpaid, etc.]

Arithmetical processes with and without the use of zero. [To support idea that Moslems made fundamental contributions to Western culture, which in turn has evidential bearing on ethnocentric belief that "Everything which is good in modern life is a product of Christian-Hebraic culture."]

THE USE OF QUESTIONING

Historically, questioning has been one of the most popular means of instruction in the social studies. As traditionally used, it is a part of text-book-recitation technique. Students are assigned material to read in a textbook and are then asked questions about it. Teachers may ask questions in class, put questions on the blackboard, mimeograph and distribute sheets of questions, or ask students to answer questions appearing in a textbook or workbook. As Horn suggests, question-and-answer recitation is common "even where instruction is labeled to indicate other patterns of teaching." [4]

Question-and-answer recitation has been subjected to abundant criticism. Schutte, for example, says "If a pure question and answer method —and nothing else—is used in the classroom, we probably might as well dispense with the teacher. Someone could work out a series of questions and have them mimeographed. A janitor could distribute them to the pupils at the beginning of the period and later gather the answers, which could then be scored by someone else." [5] The modern emphasis on teaching machines would also dispense with the janitor.

As commonly used, question-and-answer technique is ineffective in promoting reflection. It usually requires the recall of more-or-less unrelated factual materials. This is education in the associationist tradition. The technique may help students to memorize answers, but it is not consistent with the needs of reflection and conceptualization.

However, questioning does have a necessary role in the stimulation and guidance of reflection. Questions may be used to inaugurate and push forward each step of an act of thought. Questioning is a natural technique

[4] Ernest Horn, *Methods of Instruction in the Social Studies*, Scribner, 1938, p. 338.
[5] T. H. Schutte, *Teaching the Social Studies on the Secondary Level*, Prentice-Hall, 1942, p. 336.

for clarifying and creating problems. With questions like the following a teacher may help students to probe present concepts, beliefs, and values.

"Why do you say that?"
"Do you agree or disagree and why?"
"If you believe such-and-such, then how can you believe so-and-so?"
"Is such-and-such behavior [or belief] consistent with so-and-so behavior or belief?]"
"What would you do in a case like this?"
"How do you explain this fact?"
"Why do you believe that?"
"Why would you do that?"
"Why do you think that so many people in our community believe so-and-so?"
"If you did that, what might the results be?"
"Can you define that clearly, and give us some examples?"
"What does this statement mean?"
"What other way could you say it?"
"Can you give an example or illustration of this?"
"How would you define this word?"
"How could we prove or disprove a statement like this?"
"How can we get facts which will answer this?"
"How reliable are such data?"
"What do these facts mean?"
"What can we conclude from a study of these data?"
"Which consequences do you prefer?"

Questions such as these are intended to elicit thinking, not the recall of a date, a name, a town, or a battle. They are probably the only kinds of questions with which teachers should bother.

The quality of the questions used by teachers can be improved by a study of educational objectives and attempts to formulate questions that serve some of these objectives. Bloom has classified certain objectives in thinking, and Sanders has designed questions for each objective. Bloom has stated that comprehension, application, analysis, synthesis, and evaluation constitute cognitive objectives that involve thought as well as recall.[6] Sanders has made some modifications in this classification but basically does not depart from it. His study indicates to teachers how they can formulate questions that engage students in probing experiences.[7]

[6] Benjamin S. Bloom, ed., *Taxonomy of Educational Objectives, Cognitive Domain*, Longmans, Green, 1956.
[7] Norris M. Sanders, *Classroom Questions, What Kinds?* Harper & Row, 1966.

TEACHER-LED DISCUSSION

Very often what teachers label "discussion" is nothing more than question-and-answer recitation, perhaps of the most routine variety. Discussion can be a form of group inquiry, in which questions are freely raised and answered. Discussion may range in degree of control from that in which a teacher closely dominates to that in which a teacher plays a minimum role.

In the literature of teaching methods, discussion is usually treated as a largely mechanical process. "Tricks" which may be used by a teacher to keep a class orderly during discussion are usually described. Also considered important are the amount of control to be exercised by a teacher, procedural rules, and physical conditions of the classroom. Although these are important points, focusing upon them evades the main issue, which is whether discussion is getting anywhere. Unless a causal connection exists between what occurs in discussion and the steps of an act of thought, discussion is probably producing confusion (or killing time) rather than instigating reflection. At any given point during its course, a discussion should be clarifying or exposing a problem, suggesting and refining hypotheses, or testing hypotheses.

Discussion would improve if teachers were more alert to its logical, if hidden, difficulties. Passmore has an excellent discussion of discussion, and how its logic may be improved.[8]

UNDIRECTED DISCUSSION

This is a "bull session" type of discussion among the students during which the teacher keeps largely in the background (see page 207). Students may raise or clarify problems during undirected discussion. Its informality encourages a free exchange of ideas and participation of even the backward students. Often, however, instead of using undirected discussion as a basic technique of reflection, teachers do not *use* it at all. They simply allow it to occur, possibly for want of something better. Whether such discussion can be a medium for organized investigation of problems depends on the maturity and size of the class, and its understanding of techniques of group inquiry. In most cases, undirected discussion is not a good tool for implementing a complete act of thought.

PROJECT AND ACTIVITY TECHNIQUE

Student "projects" or "activities" are learning experiences carried on more or less independently by students. A project may be undertaken by an individual or by a committee. It usually involves some kind of as-

[8] John Passmore, *Talking Things Over*, Melbourne University Press, 1963.

sembly and manipulation of materials requiring actual physical movement and leading to an outcome which is "practical" in the sense that there is something visible to show for it. Because projects involve physical activity they are often regarded as being necessarily "progressive" and therefore desirable. Examples of projects are:

Keeping a notebook
Making a map
Drawing a picture or cartoon
Building a model
Writing an essay
Making a book report
Making a survey of some community problem
Taking an opinion poll
Writing and producing a short play
Making collections and preparing exhibits
Giving a report on a current event
Doing exercises in a workbook
Making diagrams, charts, graphs, tables
Making a series of lantern slides
Writing a letter to a congressman

Projects may be highly directed. When a teacher assigns projects and tells students exactly how to perform them, the technique is fully teacher dominated. But a project *can* be relatively undirected, more so than any technique except discussion. A project that grows out of a student's own thinking and is freely planned and executed by him is undirected. Projects of one sort or another represent the basic investigatory technique of students.

As projects commonly operate, it is doubtful whether they produce much reflection. Project work is popular because of its "progressive" flavor and also perhaps because it is an effective way of keeping students occupied with little effort from a teacher. One often sees notebooks, workbooks, scrapbooks, gaily colored posters, maps, and exhibits which although carefully prepared by students, are meaningless if judged from the viewpoint of reflective learning. Unless a teacher has a clear sense of purpose, projects easily degenerate into busywork.

Even when used with conscious purpose, projects are probably often meant as an *aid* to memorization of cut-and-dried content. That is, they reflect an associationist conception of learning. It is erroneously assumed that if a student combines bodily activity with the act of memorization, he will be able to memorize faster and retain the material longer.

To function as an instrument of reflection, projects must at all times be regarded as an investigatory technique. Through projects, students read, search for relevant radio and TV programs, study the community, or talk with people, for the purpose of locating data useful in solving a problem.

Project technique, more than most others, enables a teacher to gear learning situations to individual differences, particularly if projects are conducted within a permissive framework. For example, a class may be divided into committees roughly in accordance with ability. Groups of brighter students may conduct investigations which would be beyond the capacity of duller students. They might read and report on mature books and articles, or study radio and TV programs which handle their materials on an adult level. Special knowledge may be a basis for projects, as when two or three students with a knowledge of photography are assigned to take pictures of something which the entire class cannot visit. Project assignments may also reflect opportunity, as when the only student in a class who has visited the TVA region reports his experiences.

Projects are often an excellent means of presenting evidence to a group. Perhaps committees or individuals have gathered data which they feel will be useful to the rest of the group. They may report these data through use of charts, graphs, diagrams or posters, or through written or oral reports, or through displays or collections (as of photographs).

DISCUSSION QUESTIONS AND EXERCISES

1. Comment on the following statement: "There are many methods of teaching, each of which is valuable in its place." Do you agree or disagree? What assumptions about the meaning of method are implied?

2. List the techniques of teaching which you remember having experienced as a student. What were the commonly used techniques of your (a) elementary, (b) secondary, and (c) college education? Which techniques were most effective in inducing you to reflect? Which were least effective?

3. React to the following statement, made by a high-school principal: "I try to hire teachers on the basis of personality. A teacher who is pleasant and cooperative, and who gets along well with students and colleagues, is bound to be a success." What is the role of a teacher's personality? Is it more important than mastery of a theory of teaching?

4. Review the general nature of a subject-matter switch. Devise as many subject-matter switches as you can, confining them to subject matter in areas of cultural conflict.

5. Compare springboard with subject-matter switch as techniques. Could a springboard ever lead into a subject-matter switch?

6. Prepare a dozen or so questions (for discussion or study) about issues with which you think members of the class are familiar. Make them as thought provoking as you can. Discuss with the class their potential effectiveness.

REFERENCES

AUER, J. JEFFERY, and HENRY LEE EWBANK, *Handbook for Discussion Leaders*, New York, Harper & Row, 1954.

A helpful reference on various kinds of discussion, including panels, forums, debates, and lecture forums.

BODE, BOYD H., *Fundamentals of Education*, New York, Macmillan, 1926.

Treats philosophical ideas fundamental to a method of teaching.

PASSMORE, JOHN, *Talking Things Over*, Victoria, Australia, Melbourne University Press, 1963.

An excellent, short, paperback on the logic and dynamics of discussion.

SANDERS, NORRIS M., *Classroom Questions, What Kinds?* New York, Harper & Row, 1966.

Supplies a teacher with innumerable questions. Organized around Bloom's taxonomy of cognitive objectives.

WAGNER, RUSSELL H., and CARROLL C. ARNOLD, *Handbook of Group Discussion*, Boston, Houghton Mifflin, 1965.

Another interesting reference on problems of discussion.

WOODRUFF, ASAHEL D., *Basic Concepts of Teaching*, San Francisco, Chandler Publishing, 1961.

Part III discusses the planning of teaching. Must be used with care and caution, but some useful hints can be found.

CHAPTER 9

Climate Making as a Part of Method

A TEACHER'S success in inducing reflective learning in connection with critical social issues hinges on how open-minded students can become. The chief aim of the present chapter is to explore ways in which learners can be made receptive to points of view that are more scientific than the common run.

For this purpose we shall draw rather heavily from experience in fields outside formal education. Specifically, we shall survey briefly some findings from psychiatry which bear on the problem of reducing emotional blocks to learning. We shall also examine the area of study known as "democratic group leadership" in an attempt to see what an understanding of the dynamics of democratic adult groups may reveal concerning classroom practice. It should be noted at the outset that we make no attempt to apply directly to classroom practice the procedures which have been developed for use in therapeutic or normal adult groups. Many of these procedures are inapplicable in school classes. However, experience in these fields does suggest important clues for making learning in the social studies more reflective, functional, and permanent.

Resolution of Conflict from a Psychoanalytic Point of View

Psychotherapists differ in their interpretation of causes of emotional conflict. Freudians attribute conflict to a combination of instinctive drives and early childhood experiences. Non-Freudians are more inclined to emphasize a patient's present environment as a source of conflict. Therapists likewise differ in their approach to treatment, one group assuming that therapy should expose and help a patient reinterpret early experiences in life, and another that therapy should focus on changing a patient's contemporary life situation. Another source of disagreement is in the question of how directive a counselor should be during counseling sessions. Still another issue relates to whether, in treating certain forms of mental illness, individual or group therapy is the more valuable. Because they are particulary pertinent to the problem of the present chapter, we shall explore briefly the last two of the issues mentioned.

DIRECTIVE VERSUS NONDIRECTIVE THERAPY

In the language of psychotherapy, the issue posed here is between directive and nondirective (or patient-centered) therapy. What is probably the first attempt at careful description and defense of a nondirective approach to therapy was made by Rogers.[1]

We can best describe nondirective therapy through comparisons and contrasts. Rogers suggests that virtually all historical approaches to psychotherapy place a therapist in an authoritarian position with reference to a patient. These approaches assume that a counselor can and should determine a socially accepted goal for a patient and help him rearrange his personality structure or his life situation so that he can achieve this goal. A patient may be told what to believe and do by subtle and indirect methods, but told he is nevertheless.

Nondirective therapy avoids substituting a therapist's purposes for a patient's. A warm and permissive atmosphere is created in which a patient feels perfectly free to talk about his problems. The counselor accepts, recognizes, and clarifies feelings expressed by the patient, who talks his way through his problems, moving successively from a phase of "blowing off steam" to a phase of better self-understanding and heightened capacity for reflective handling of his own problems. Although nondirective therapy places more emphasis upon emotional adjustment than do some approaches, it is assumed that an *outcome of therapy will be reflectively achieved insight*. The responsibility for this outcome is placed squarely on patients; whatever decisions they make are theirs alone.

We shall confine ourselves to one further point: In contrast to Freudian approaches to the theory of neurosis, nondirective therapy assumes that, rather than being largely internal and psychic, conflicts have a large cultural component. That is, they are mostly a result of one's present relationship with his environment: they grow from "some new cultural demand which opposes individual need."[2] This appears to be saying much the same as is said elsewhere in the present book: Most emotional conflicts are a result of a person's internalizing, or incorporating within the self, discrepancies of his surrounding culture (i.e., conflicting beliefs and behaviors).

A nondirective approach to psychotherapy has important implications for teaching. Although a teacher should not be "nondirective" in the sense described by Rogers, the idea of encouraging individuals (including students) to formulate their own purposes and solve their own problems in the presence of an adult who, rather than dictating, merely gives

---

[1] Carl Rogers, *Counseling and Psychotherapy*, Houghton Mifflin, 1942.
[2] *Ibid.*, p. 54.

encouragement, has broad significance for group management in a democratic society. Limitations of the Rogerian outlook for school use will be treated later in the chapter.

INDIVIDUAL AND GROUP COUNSELING AND BEHAVIORAL CHANGE

Psychological counseling which acquaints a patient with "the facts" concerning his situation may fail to produce logically implied changes in behavior. For example, Rogers says, "It has come to be recognized that we do not change the client's behavior very effectively simply by giving him an intellectual picture of its patterning, no matter how accurate." [3] Change in knowledge leads to the adoption of new values. But if a situation rewards old values, they will continue to dominate the new. When this is the case, behavior reflects the old values and remains unchanged.

One reason a counselor may not succeed in bringing about significant changes in behavior is that the behavior of every individual is firmly rooted in the persons with whom he associates. That is, actions of a patient are largely controlled by groups to which he belongs and can be changed only as behavior of the groups themselves changes.[4]

One of the basic drives of human life is for security. The chief means of achieving security is through membership in a group. When a person feels that he has a place in a group, that he "fits in," that he is wanted, he feels secure. As Lewin points out, "The social climate in which a child lives is for the child as important as the air it breathes. The group to which a child belongs is the ground on which he stands. His relation to the group and his status in it are the most important factors for his feeling of security or insecurity." [5] One achieves membership in a group by conforming, at least to a degree, to the mores of the group. To be accepted in a group of thieves, one must act like a thief; to be accepted in a group of saints, one must act like a saint.

This is not to say that an individual is completely subject to group control. He may develop beliefs and values which are novel to a group and may get them accepted by others in the group. With widening acceptance, the new beliefs and values become effective in controlling group behavior. The extent to which an individual can project his own unique personality into group life, and change a group thereby, depends on the situation (e.g., whether the group is itself democratic and the extent to which the larger culture outside the group is hostile or friendly to the changes) and on his own capacity for persuasion. A modern sociologist is

---

[3] *Ibid.*, p. 27.

[4] As used in the present chapter, *group* is taken to mean two or more persons *in psychological interaction* with each other. Related terms are *in-group, primary group,* and *face-to-face group.*

[5] Kurt Lewin, *Resolving Social Conflicts,* Harper & Row, 1948, p. 82.

likely to regard the process of interaction itself as the basic social datum; every group is constantly shaping individuals in it and simultaneously is being shaped by them.

Even though interaction is always present, we cannot imagine large changes occurring in individuals out of relationship to their primary group associations. A psychotherapist is constantly aware of the fact that there is little he can do to help a patient reorganize his personality *as an individual*. Such reorganization as may occur must fit exigencies posed by the patient's associations—the various needs and pressures, often highly subtle and complex, which grow out of the fact of group membership itself. This is particularly the case where values are concerned, and even more particularly, values in closed areas.

During World War II, experiments in group psychotherapy were undertaken out of necessity. There were not enough therapists or facilities for individual counseling. The results of counseling with groups of patients were often gratifying. Now, in certain situations, group therapy is seen as having advantages over individual therapy.[6] The reason appears to lie in the previously mentioned supposition that it is easier for an individual to change his values and behavior if other persons with whom he is in intimate contact are also changing.

There is disagreement as to whether in group therapy the therapeutic effect comes primarily from the relationship of each member to the therapist or from relationships of members to each other, but the latter interpretation seems to be growing in popularity. In some instances a patient can express himself more freely in a small face-to-free group than in individual relationship to a counselor, perhaps because he feels less alone, the group gives him courage, and other members have established precedents for speaking frankly. Through the give-and-take of free discussion some persons may come to see their own problems better than through individual counseling situations. As one writer suggests, "Patients can accept censure, suggestions, interpretation and guidance from each other with less disturbance and hostility than from the therapist." [7]

A group situation may also stimulate one to deal openly and creatively with his own conflicts. Foulkes summarizes this possible therapeutic effect of a group: ". . . Lectures, exhortations, sympathy, pity, advice, medicaments, explanations, encouragement, all can help a little but they can not move the patient out of his fortress of entanglement. In the long run, they can only help him to entrench himself deeper in it. . . . If he is, however, brought into a situation, which he himself is continuously helping to create, to shape, he is forced to come out into the open with

---

[6] See Leon Gorlow *et al.*, *The Nature of Nondirective Group Psychotherapy*, Teachers College, Columbia University, 1952, p. 8.

[7] S. R. Slavson, quoted in *ibid.*, p. 10.

his own reactions and their contradictions." [8] Whether a patient benefits more from group than from individual therapy depends in large part on the nature of his illness. Group therapy is regarded as of limited usefulness for the mentally unbalanced and probably for extreme neurotics. The nearer a patient is to normality, the more effective group therapy is likely to be. Its greatest value may be, as Hobbs points out, "in the neglected field of therapy for the normal person with debilitating situational conflicts. . . ." [9]

What is the significance to classroom teachers of clinical experience in individual and group psychotherapy? The hypothesis is suggested that a wide range of personally felt problems may be handled successfully among normal persons, including adolescent youth, with resultant permanent changes in outlook and behavior, if they are encouraged to air problems freely in the give-and-take atmosphere of a face-to-face group. Although this general idea is not new, modern psychiatric practice offers clues as to the most effectual managerial techniques for such learning situations.

The Democratic Group-Leadership Movement

Related to the development of group psychotherapy is the democratic group-leadership movement. This movement embraces a body of experiments and practices with normal adult and youth groups. Its aim is to translate a democratic philosophy into action on a group level and to compare the learning and behavioral results of democratic groups with those of nondemocratic groups. An understanding of the dynamics of groups is valuable to a social-studies teacher. In the concluding section of the chapter, we shall make applications, and also show why, because of differences in aims and competence of most adult groups involved in experimentation, certain aspects of the management of adult groups are not transferable to classroom situations.

The democratic group-leadership movement is rooted in a democratic social-political philosophy dating in the United States from the Jeffersonian period, and from earlier than that in Europe. The modern concept of group work seems to combine our traditional democratic philosophy with an understanding of group psychology which in human affairs is relatively recent.

In a large sense, the democratic group-leadership movement is a coun-

---

[8] S. H. Foulkes, *Introduction to Group-Analytic Psychotherapy*, William Heinemann Medical Books, Ltd., 1948, p. 70.

[9] Nicholas Hobbs, "Group-Centered Psychotherapy," chap. 7 in Carl Rogers, *Client-Centered Therapy*, Houghton Mifflin, 1951.

terpart, for normal groups, of group psychotherapy for abnormal. Although there is disagreement as to just how directive a leader can be and still remain "democratic," democratic group leadership appears to be an application of some of the principles of nondirective group therapy. It is to be expected, therefore, that among the contributors to our understanding of group process we find the names of numerous psychiatrists and psychologists. As Haiman points out, modern methods of group leadership "find their origin in the work of Sigmund Freud and follow the patterns of the psychiatric tradition which has flowered since his time." [10] Because there are significant relationships between the concepts of psychiatric medicine and of leadership of normal groups, psychiatrists have transplanted their philosophy and methods to normal group situations.

New concepts have developed as to how a democratic group functions and the role of a leader in it. It has become clear also that the idea of a democratic group, as developed in the democratic group-leadership movement, is very similar to the idea of a therapeutic group, as developed in the field of group psychotherapy.

THE NATURE OF A DEMOCRATIC GROUP

A democratic group is self-governing. But it must provide for situations where disagreement occurs. Ideally, democratic decisions are by consensus—that is, mutually agreeable decisions reached through discussion and compromise. Then, by common consent action is taken. If consensus is not possible, a democratic group votes. Each person has an equal vote, and a majority vote wins. Votes are taken to facilitate action, not to enforce belief.

Successful and permanent operation of democracy seems to require that a group maintain certain conditions which, although not a part of the central idea of democracy, contribute to its functioning. For example, if participation is to be full and free, a group must establish an accepting atmosphere—an atmosphere in which every member is considered important and has his opinions guaranteed a hearing. Participation implies reasonable freedom of communication, and freedom of speech and thought. If any single individual or minority group gains disproportionate control over agencies of communication and opinion, the society has lost equality of participation in decision making.

It would also seem that, if a democratic society is to survive over time, a majority of its members must learn to make reflective decisions where socially important questions are involved. A democratic society assumes competence on the part of its members; any different assumption would

[10] Franklin S. Haiman, *Group Leadership and Democratic Action*, Houghton Mifflin, 1951, p. 39. This reference is one of the best general treatments of the subject and the following pages draw heavily from it.

lead to distrust and rejection of the principle of equal participation. We assume that without wise leadership no society can solve its problems and endure. In a democracy, wise leadership is a function of wise citizenship. If a democracy is to survive, then its members must take steps to insure that the principle of reflection is employed as widely as possible in making choices of group concern. Among other things, this means that a democracy should always be in the process of reducing the number and extent of its closed areas.

THE ROLE OF DEMOCRATIC LEADERSHIP

Behavior of a group is influenced significantly by its leaders. Particularly if a group is immature, its overall emotional and intellectual climate and its direction and extent of growth depend largely on the conduct of its leadership. As a group matures, it becomes less dependent on particular leaders. It develops capacity to produce leaders from its own ranks and reject and select leaders according to need.

The role of democratic leadership is *to help a group realize its own potentialities for growth.* Such a statement becomes meaningful only when "growth" is defined. One attempt at definition seeks to specify a number of "dimensions" of group growth,[11] including the following:

1. Progress toward fuller intercommunication among members. This includes growing acceptance and understanding by members of mechanics of language, with particular reference to meaning.
2. Progress toward viewing objectively the functioning of the group. This includes ability of all members to make and accept interpretations about member and group functioning and ability to collect and use pertinent information about itself.
3. Progress toward developing shared responsibilities. This includes growth toward a sharing of leadership functions, participation in setting goals, and cooperation in achievement of goals.
4. Progress toward developing group cohesion. Cohesion should be adequate to permit assimilation of new ideas without group disintegration, assimiliation of new members in a way to strengthen rather than disrupt the group, holding to long-range goals when a situation requires, and making constructive use of internal conflicts.
5. Progress toward developing ability to inform itself, to think straight, and to make creative decisions about problems. This includes learning to make full use of the contribution potential of all members, to discover and utilize appropriate resource materials and persons, and to detect and correct fallacies in group thinking.

[11] National Training Laboratory in Group Development, *Report of the Second Summer Laboratory,* Washington, D.C., Department of Adult Education, 1948, pp. 113–114.

What specific functions does a democratic leader perform if a group is to move in these directions? He may execute or administer, serve as judge or arbiter, be an advocate (or shaper of opinion), or render expert advice. He may also play the role of discussion leader. Although a discussion leader may on occasion assume any of the above roles, his function is distinctively different from and more inclusive than any of them. He helps a group to achieve self-growth. Or, as one writer puts it, he tries to "release the creative talents of the members of a group, help them solve their own problems, and reach their own decisions." [12] Functions and techniques of discussion leadership are treated in detail in Chapter 10.

Classroom Teachers as Democratic Leaders and Climate Makers

In order to understand the task of teachers as it relates to the problem of creating open-mindedness and willingness to change beliefs and behaviors, we need to examine in detail how emotional blocking can prevent such changes. Only as a teacher understands the process of blocking and the manner in which it manifests itself can he take steps for its removal.

FAILURE OF PERCEPTION AS A CAUSE OF "CLOSED MINDS"

In just what way does blocking interfere with reflection? It might be supposed that, no matter how strong one's emotional attachment to a belief, if he is confronted with facts which seem clearly to question it, then question it he must. Any other course would appear highly unreasonable. Yet a normally intelligent and perfectly sane person may appear blind to evidence which others find thoroughly convincing.

Such behavior is not to be interpreted as willful irrationality. We agree with Wertheimer when he says that human beings have a "willingness to face problems straight, a readiness to follow them up courageously and sincerely, a desire for improvement, in contrast with arbitrary, wilful, or slavish attitudes." [13] What occurs, as a result of emotional blocking, apparently, is *failure of perception, which is not understood by the person involved and which without help he cannot prevent or overcome.*

What is failure of perception? Answering this question raises complex technical as well as philosophical issues. At any given moment of consciousness a person has a "perceptual field." It is that part of his physical and psychological environment of which through his senses he is directly aware.

[12] Haiman, *op. cit.,* p. 71.
[13] Max Wertheimer, *Productive Thinking,* Harper & Row, 1945, p. 198.

There is disagreement as to whether a person can perceive directly with his senses the physical, social, and psychological surroundings which are assumed to exist. Philosophical realists assume that he can. The position taken in this book is essentially that of field theory, which maintains that a person takes the data of sense experience and *imposes on them* pattern, order, and meaning. This imposed pattern is what we mean by insight. Insights are dependent not only on the nature of the environment, or confronting situation, but also on the influence of past experience and one's purposes at the time. Thus, in a given situation we cannot expect the insights of any two persons to be identical. Nor can we assume that for an individual any reality exists except the insights which he has achieved.

The literature of psychotherapy defines failure of perception as "loss of contact with reality." The goal of therapy is the reestablishment of accurate perception, or the reestablishment of contact with reality. What does this terminology mean? In the present book, when we say that perception is accurate, or that a person is in touch with reality we mean that his beliefs are accurate guides to action. That is, they have been or can be verified experimentally or experientially. They are consistent with the verified data of past experience (*facts* as we use the term here) or they produce the consequences which a person anticipates when he acts on them. This is what we expect of any scientific theory.

When we say that a person is suffering from a failure of perception, we mean either that his beliefs are inconsistent with one another or that deductions made from them do not check with the data of observation. Now it is true that a person who is out of touch with reality may deduce consequences from a proposition and make observations to see if the anticipated events occur. But he is likely to make faulty deductions and faulty observations; that is, he is likely to claim the occurrence of events which a disinterested public cannot detect, or deny the occurrence of events which, to others, clearly happen.

Ideally, perception brings events of one's physical, social and psychological environment into a person's consciousness with a minimum of distortion. But in normal life, it is probable that most persons frequently perceive events which others do not and fail to perceive those which others do, or exaggerate, or minimize the significance of events which they see. Rationalization is a matter of creating or disregarding facts in order to support a foregone conclusion. Most of the time it is quite unconscious; in fact, when we become conscious that we are reading into a field what we want to see there instead of what might enable us to make more accurate predictions, we tend to become uncomfortable.

A person is especially likely to experience a failure of perception when he is under heavy emotional pressure. If he feels insecure or frightened, particularly with respect to the integrity of his own personality, he tries to read into the perceptual field whatever immediately appears most likely to restore his security. In other words, if he feels that a cherished belief is under attack, he will read the facts of perception in such a way as to protect and preserve the belief.

Failures in perception are most likely to occur in the closed areas of belief and value. Here a person simply *does not see facts as data*. To him they remain as an insignificant—and perhaps entirely undifferentiated —part of his perceptual field, bearing no relevance to the issue under consideration. Consequently the facts do not change his thinking or behavior. We can hardly expect a person to incorporate data into his thinking when he remains unaware of their presence or significance. As Lewin says, "Since action is ruled by perception, a change in conduct presupposes that new facts and values are perceived." [14] Simply telling a person that data are there is often futile. If his perception does not permit him to see them, we must approach the problem in such a way as to remove the distorting factors.

We have not yet distinguished clearly the role of perceptual failure in blocking changes in behavior. Failure of perception may prevent changes in insight. But very often changes in insight appear to occur, without the changes in values (and their corresponding behaviors) which we would expect to result. When this is the case, other competing insights remain which furnish warrant for the old values. In short, we assume that all values and related behaviors issue logically from insights, and the former will not change unless the latter change also. But a person may hold to competing and contradictory insights (with corresponding contradictory values and attraction toward contradictory behaviors). In this case, the insights, attitudes, and behaviors which seem most attractive at the time remain dominant.

With the foregoing interpretation we may explain a phenomenon which was noted earlier in the chapter: namely, that a person may appear to accept a new set of facts, opposed to what he has heretofore accepted, without *observable* changes in behavior. If we understand that an individual in such situations is dominated by one of two competing cognitive structures and corresponding behavioral sets, then it is clear that he is a victim of inconsistency, either recognized or unrecognized. Failure of perception in this case is a failure to recognize the inconsistency.

Once a person is aware of inconsistency, we assume that he will take steps to change one of the two competing outlooks (and its corresponding behavioral pull). If he has a strong emotional need, however, to follow his old (and, to disinterested observers, perhaps less wise) pattern

[14] Lewin, *op. cit.*, p. 63.

of behavior, he is likely to try to minimize the conflict, to try to live with it, or to escape through some neurotic response. However this may be, it should be apparent that failure to adjust overt behavior to what seems to be a change in insight is a problem of inconsistency and pedagogically must be treated so. In a democratic school, such incompatibilities are studied reflectively.

What are the conditions under which perception achieves maximum accuracy? How can we set the stage so that a person will most easily adopt new outlooks or see his inconsistencies?

Insofar as experimental evidence allows an answer, it appears that the first requirement is a *nonthreatening* emotional atmosphere. What are the specific conditions of a nonthreatening climate? A *threat*, as the term is used here, is anything said or done by others which *appears to a learner* to jeopardize his present beliefs. It is the equivalent of an anticipated attack on the self. A normal individual wants to maintain a feeling of consistency and adequacy in his beliefs and values, which feeling is what we mean when we refer to integration or integrity of personality. A person's knowledge and values may be shot through with inconsistency and confusion, but if the person is not aware of this, he may continue to feel integrated. If he does feel that someone is trying to destroy his integrity of self, he is likely to resist. Rogers describes this problem very well: "Experience which, if assimilated, would involve a change in the organization of self tends to be resisted through denial or distortion of symbolization. The structure and organization of self appears to become more rigid under threat; to relax its boundaries when completely free from threat. Experience which is perceived as inconsistent with the self can only be assimilated if the current organization of the self is relaxed and expanded to include it." [15]

For a climate to seem nonthreatening, it is necessary for a subject to feel that no one is trying to judge him. He needs to feel completely accepted. He is particularly likely to resist criticism if it comes from someone he regards as having arbitrary power and authority over him. He needs to feel complete freedom to express his opinions without danger of censure, no matter how ill formed or unorthodox they may be.

The type of climate in which a person feels so secure that he dares entertain evidence contrary to his present knowledge and values seems best achieved in a small, face-to-face group in which warmth and permissiveness have been deliberately cultivated. Some techniques which a teacher may use in creating such a situation, and in leading a class to change its view and behavior, will be discussed in the following section and further illustrated in Chapter 10.

[15] Carl Rogers, *Client-Centered Therapy*, Houghton Mifflin, 1951, p. 390.

CLASSROOM TECHNIQUES FOR ASSISTING COGNITIVE
AND BEHAVIORAL CHANGE

Reducing Threat and Promoting Open-Mindedness. We have suggested that a student feels threat to his ego if he regards his beliefs as under fire. The intensity of threat depends on its source, its power, and the valuation placed on beliefs which are in jeopardy. Unless threat can be largely eliminated, a student is not likely to entertain evidence contrary to present beliefs or, when facts warrant, to change his mind. Several techniques are available for keeping a sense of threat to a minimum.

One rule is that a teacher should treat student opinions with respect. This does not necessarily mean that a teacher expresses approval; but he avoids ridicule or sarcasm, or any expressions which might be so interpreted by students. He does not cast aspersions on the intelligence or motives of students who render serious opinions. Opinions offered in good faith are taken for what they are—the best insights which students have been able to achieve up to then.

On occasion, as during relatively undirected discussion preceding serious study of an issue, it may be advisable for a teacher to give students plenty of opportunity to express the very beliefs which he hopes later to bring under question. It may even help for a teacher to express considerable sympathy with these ideas—for the time being to "go along." Lewin, for example, recommends that a group leader may get farther by letting members of a group freely express the very values which he hopes to change because "a feeling of complete freedom and a heightened group identification are frequently more important at a particular stage of reeducation than learning not to break specific rules." [16]

When a teacher wishes to challenge an opinion expressed by a student, he should do it in such a way that conflict is internalized. That is, the student is made to feel the conflict within his own personality. He may not feel a problem, or at least not the problem which the learning situation demands, if he sees the conflict merely as a contest between him and someone else. For this reason a teacher should not argue with a student. Arguments between students also are usually fruitless. When a teacher desires to contest the opinion of a student, he may best handle it something like this: "You have an opinion, and I think I understand and appreciate your reasons. But there are contrary opinions which are widely held in this country. I wonder if there is any merit in a point of view such as . . . ?" The student is thus asked to entertain, not an opinion of the teacher or a classmate, but simply an opinion which "some persons" hold. When a group is presented with a problem to discuss, be-

[16] Lewin, *op. cit.*, p. 68.

liefs and behaviors contrary to those accepted by group members are more likely to be seriously entertained and later adopted if the problem is discussed with reference to persons other than themselves, at least in early phases of discussion.

Another means of inducing students to internalize conflict is to arrange the learning situation so that facts "speak for themselves." Other things being equal, facts—especially if impersonal, sharply relevant, and simple enough to be easily grasped—are more likely than expressions of opinion to break through an emotional barrier. This is particularly true if the facts are coming to a student in life situations. It may then only be necessary to remind a student of their relevance and their bearing on a problem. For example, a trip to a slum may speak eloquently against the notion that everyone is adequately housed, or the witnessing of a congressional investigation over TV may show quite convincingly that traditional American principles of fair play are not always employed. Lewin has suggested that "An individual will believe facts he himself has discovered in the same way he believes in himself or in his group." [17]

In most instances it probably pays to minimize, or at least not encourage, expressions of personal opinion in social-studies classrooms. Issues may be handled as issues and propositions discussed on their merits. The learning enterprise should focus on raising questions about what will come of acting in accordance with a given proposition or hypothesis. An opinion may be converted to a proposition by saying, "Here is an opinion which is before the class. Let us take it as a proposition to be tested. If it is true, what consequences may we deduce from it?" If propositions are relevant to beliefs of students, then students often make their own connections. Even though beliefs are not studied directly, significant revisions may come. It is necessary, of course, that students do see connections; if emotional blocking prevents this, steps must be taken to expand perception. Perhaps only mentioning the connections will be enough; perhaps patient effort will be needed further to reduce emotional barriers.

Encouraging Group Decision. A student is more likely to drop prejudices, revise his moral values, or make almost any other type of significant change if he is a member of a group *which is making the same change together.* Assuming that a teacher does all he can to produce a non-threatening climate, what can be done to form a class into a true in-group, a "team," so to speak, and help them, as a team, to change basic outlooks?

Although significant learning may occur in discussion groups formed of strangers, learning in areas of strong prejudice (such as in the closed

[17] *Ibid.*

areas) seems more likely to occur in groups characterized by friendships and some degree of mutual intimacy. There may be sound pedagogical advantages in helping students become well acquainted with each other, whether simply through classroom informality or by deliberately fostering out-of-school contacts.

Cliques, self-contained groupings based on religious or social class affiliations, racial groupings, or associations based on academic achievement may develop within any school and be reflected in a single classroom. Such groupings may entirely omit certain students, who in turn become social isolates. With development of subgroups of this sort, especially if chauvinistic attitudes are involved, a class may become badly split and team spirit difficult to achieve. If observation or use of sociometric devices suggests to a teacher that an unhealthy social situation exists in his classroom, he should take steps to alleviate it.

In establishing group feeling, there are possible advantages to be gained from group study and group projects. When this sort of thing is attempted, it is usually necessary to divide a class into small groups and to see that the same students do not always work together. A committee system can ordinarily be made to work fairly well for gathering information. Whether it can be made to function in reflective evaluation of data and the productive solution of problems depends on the maturity of students and their familiarity with the rules of reflection. Generally, a teacher must be central to reflective deliberation if it is to be productive.

Encouragement of full and free communication among members will heighten the cohesiveness of a group. If students understand each other, they will almost inevitably work together better as a group. A teacher should urge and help students to state opinions and propositions meaningfully. He should discourage use of emotive language, particularly when students are inclined to direct personal jibes at each other. He should make certain that every member has a chance to be heard and is correctly interpreted.

A teacher's personality may contribute much to group spirit. A teacher can add warmth to a classroom by smiling frequently and keeping a weather eye open for jokes which will appeal to students. He should cultivate a friendly interest in everybody and demonstrate it by expressions of concern over student problems and a knowledge of affairs in which students are involved.

Although important, these suggestions concerning the development of "groupness" are peripheral to the problem. In a given learning situation, group spirit probably hinges primarily on whether all members of a class feel personally involved in the problem under study. If motivation to study a problem is high, a common interest exists which transcends lack of acquaintance, clique interests, or personal antagonisms. In the final analysis, whether group spirit is achieved at the point where it is needed —where a problem is to be studied and beliefs are to be changed— depends largely on a teacher's skill in focusing effort on a common goal.

No matter how great their internal rapport, groups do not change beliefs automatically. As we have observed, the most effectual situation for producing group change appears to be a democratically led discussion. For purposes of the present analysis, probably the most important aspect of discussion (or other modes of study) designed to change basic attitudes is that it have the quality of freely permitting self-learning. (This should not be taken to mean absence of directedness.) We have already noted, in our discussion of threatening situations, that students resist outside pressure to change opinions. As Lewin has indicated, the object in achieving change is not to apply pressure from outside but to remove counterforces within the individual.[18] Although a teacher can and usually must help in the removal of these counterforces, students must perform the actual removal. If they can independently explore a problem, feeling no authoritarian pressure from above to explore it in a particular way or emerge with particular conclusions, they are much more likely than otherwise to undergo real and permanent changes in cognitive and behavioral patterns. They need to be encouraged to use investigatory techniques of their own, to explore by themselves provocative readings, trips, interviews, radio and TV programs, and the like. A teacher's role here is to suggest possible directions of exploration and to help students evaluate facts which are exposed.

For maximum change, permissive discussion of problems should culminate in group decisions. That is, in addition to discussing and studying a problem, students as a group should consider what conclusions are warranted, what these conclusions mean to them, and what if anything they intend to do about them. Students need to communicate their views to each other, so that intentions of each are known to all. If it is evident to individuals that most members of a group have revised their outlooks and expect to change their behavior in stated ways, then members who are reluctant to change because of long-standing attachment to certain beliefs may find change easier. This should not be interpreted to mean that a group or its leader should pressure individual members to accept conformity. We are referring to changes which individuals see the logic of making but find difficult because of opposing forces. The opposing forces

---

[18] Kurt Lewin, "Group Decision and Social Change," in Theodore M. Newcomb and Eugene L. Hartley, eds., *Readings in Social Psychology*, Holt, Rinehart & Winston, 1947, p. 342.

are often social pressures exerted by peer culture, community mores, or parental dictates. These may be combatted more successfully if a student feels that others intend to combat them with him.

Ideally, group decision should represent consensus. Proposed changes in belief normally should be kept within the bounds of what is possible for all. If a group is in agreement on the rules of reflective methodology, if it confines its learning operations to the testing of propositions, and if the threat-removing techniques employed by a teacher are sufficient so that without serious inhibitions all students are able to examine pertinent facts, then at least some degree of consensus is likely. This point of view assumes that for many problems there will, at a given time, be a "best" answer, in the sense that one hypothesis, more than any other, will adequately harmonize data deduced from it. This is a denial of the common belief that "every problem has two sides" and the further implication that "one opinion is as good as another." Of course, if consensus based on reflection is impossible, no attempt should be made by a teacher to force it.

A TEACHER'S ROLE IN A DEMOCRATIC CLASSROOM

Within a democratic framework there is room for disagreement as to the amount of centralized direction which is required. A democratic group is distinctively different from a laissez-faire or authoritarian group. It would seem as unreasonable to try to establish these as completely hard-and-fast categories as any other differentiated concepts. A democratic group might, under certain circumstances, operate with a minimum of centralized leadership and appear to approach the laissez-faire extreme. On the other hand, it might delegate to particular persons positions of such authority as to appear to approach the authoritarian norm. (The former extreme might be illustrated in a small adult study group, the latter in a democratic nation which, during a war, grants extraordinary powers to its executive branch.)

We would place a nondirective discussion group, as defined by Rogers and others, near the laissez-faire end of our scale. We would hesitate, however, to place such a group outside the democratic framework. Although under certain circumstances it may resemble anarchy (which is not necessarily the same as chaos), a nondirective group may also produce firm leadership from within its own ranks and formulate and pursue purposes with dispatch and efficiency. When nondirection is employed with an immature group, however, such an outcome is doubtful.

We would place an ordinary classroom, as dominated by a textbook-recitation procedure and arbitrary decision making by a teacher, near the authoritarian end of the scale. This is not to suggest that, if a teacher has certain types of authority over students, a teaching-learning situation necessarily violates democratic practice. We shall try to show how such authority may be compatible with democracy. Many classrooms, however, gravitate in structure and pattern of leadership toward the concept of an authoritarian group, as defined in experiments by Lippitt and White.[19]

It is not enough simply to say that in a classroom a democratic pattern is preferable. Democracy in a classroom and democracy in adult discussion or psychotherapeutic groups ordinarily take different forms. In examining the form of democracy in a classroom the following points are pertinent:

1. Although it gives us valuable clues with respect to the dynamics of emotion, experience with therapeutic groups is not fully applicable in classrooms. A typical group of students is composed chiefly of normal persons. The cognitive structure of an ordinary student is often inadequate in the sense that it is a poor guide to behavior—owing to erroneous, incomplete, and contradictory concepts. But concepts of a typical student are certainly not so inaccurate as to be largely unusable, as is the case with insane persons or incapacitated neurotics. Conflicts may be troublesome for ordinary high-school and college students and emotional disturbance may become conspicuous at times, but we do not expect to find many deep neuroses. Basically, then, persons with whom a teacher deals are different from those with whom a professional therapist deals.

This difference, between normality and abnormality, immediately suggests some differences in the job of a leader. Emotional blocking which might prevent reflection is probably much easier to remove in a normal group than in an abnormal group. A psychotherapist working with abnormals must usually use extreme and time-consuming methods in order to relieve repression to a point where insights can become reliable predictive tools. Furthermore, a private counseling session or a small discussion group of disturbed adults led by a psychiatrist represents a situation where more drastic means for relieving inhibition may be used. The mores of our culture do not tolerate in school classrooms the freedom of expression which can be permitted in a true therapeutic group. Whenever catharsis requires that a person talk freely about deep personal issues which would seem shocking or embarrassing to others, the case is one not for a teacher but for a trained therapist. One major difference, then, between a social-studies class and a therapeutic group is that the former will be less free to delve deeply into personal problems, less free to tolerate extreme and shocking expressions of opinion.

[19] Ronald Lippitt and R. K. White, "An Experimental Study of Leadership and Group Life," in *Readings in Social Psychology, op. cit.,* pp. 315–333.

Thus it is both possible and desirable in a classroom to place more emphasis on intellectual experience and less upon catharsis than is done in a therapeutic group. It seems preferable to think of the expression of emotion—of catharsis—as a *tool* for achieving conceptualization rather than as an end in itself. What we want in a social-studies classroom is an increase in amount and an improvement in quality of thinking. Emotional release is to be encouraged only as it helps to achieve reflection.

In the literature of client-centered psychotherapy we find the opinion that, if a patient is placed in a nonthreatening, accepting climate and allowed to talk freely about his problems, he will by himself gain more adequate insights. In a social-studies classroom, however, a good psychological climate and free discussion are not usually enough to produce accurate insight *because of the difference in learning goals and type of problems discussed.* In a social-studies classroom many of the problems treated involve complex social issues and much of the complicated and extensive evidence required to work with them successfully is unknown to students. Although relatively undirected discussion may be desirable to get issues into the open, to expose data from the prior experience of pupils, and to reduce repression, it is not enough. If students do not know what a tariff is, for example, such discussion will not make them more intelligent about tariff issues. A teacher must be in charge to lead discussion, inject criticism, suggest research, and in general head the learning enterprise.

2. How far can we go in applying to a social-studies classroom principles of democratic leadership as developed through experiences of the democratic group-leadership movement? First, a classroom can and should be fully as democratic as any adult group. There are impelling reasons: School may be the only part of a child's environment where he has a chance to experience by living it the meaning of democracy. All too often he experiences authoritarian practices in home, church, and part-time employment. Not that a person must necessarily be able to live democratically in order to learn to appreciate democracy; it is conceivable that while in a concentration camp a person could learn to appreciate democracy deeply. But a child is more likely to understand and value democracy through direct experience with it than in any other way.

Once having stated the necessity for democracy in classrooms, we must make certain qualifications. In a democratic society, every member has an equal share in determining the goals and behavioral rules of the society, an equal share in deciding which freedoms and restraints are to apply. But this democratic principle applies only to the larger group (i.e., the entire society), which may limit the jurisdiction of its own subgroupings in any way it pleases. For example, jurisdiction over certain matters is left to adults, under the assumption that children are not competent to decide some things. Within the limits of their jurisdiction, students should have the same right of equal participation in decision making as adults.

Let us explore further the question of jurisdiction. Adults have seen fit in various ways to limit the overt behavior of children. For example, children are not permitted to destroy property, to flout community mores, or to loaf through school (when it can be helped). The adult community holds teachers responsible for seeing that the actions of children conform to these rules. In this sense a teacher is a representative, or agent, of the larger community. Although a democratic teacher will encourage his students to discuss problems of behavior, independently formulate rules which are reasonably compatible with those of the larger community, and obey them voluntarily, he must retain the right to overrule students if necessary. On some questions a teacher's vote must remain a majority vote. But only where matters of action or overt behavior are concerned. It is presumed that in a democratic school, freedom of thought among students is not restricted; students have exactly the same freedom as adult groups. However, even this statement requires qualification.

We have assumed that, if a democratic society is to govern itself wisely, the principle of reflection will be a necessary adjunct of democratic life. We have assumed further that, if a democratic society is to live into the future, the principle of reflection must be extended into all problem areas which seriously threaten democracy. Now not all adult members of a democratic society will agree that these needs exist. Many persons may reject reflection and the critical study of certain areas of controversy. But probably a majority of adult Americans do uphold the principle of reflection and the necessity of free and critical thought in all areas of general social concern. If this is the case, then teachers may be regarded as agents of the larger community in acquainting students with the rules of accurate thinking and in encouraging them to think seriously about the most troublesome issues. Even when a local community objects to such practices, a teacher's responsibility to the larger group would seem to obligate him, insofar as he is able, to select methodology and content which are reflective and socially important.

Students in a self-governing classroom might select learning experiences capable of making effective citizens of them; but again they might not. Whether or not students want to think, a teacher must be an instigator of thought. If they want to, the job is easier; if they don't, a teacher has to arouse the desire to think. Whether or not students want to study critical social issues, a teacher must see that, to the best of their ability, they do.

The obligations of leaders in adult democratic groups are no different from the obligations of teachers. But, because of their greater competence, all members of an adult group are to some degree presumably capable of assuming leadership roles. Although in given cases they may not be, members of adult groups are often somewhat acquainted with reflective problem solving and in a position to decide wisely which problems they should pursue. Student groups, on the other hand, are less mature, less cognizant of the meaning of reflection, less aware of troublesome issues in the culture. By and large, therefore, teachers must play a more dominant role than leaders of adult groups.

DISCUSSION QUESTIONS AND EXERCISES

1. Do you know persons who have made noticeable shifts in their fundamental beliefs as a result of classroom experiences? Can you identify changes which you yourself have made? Under what circumstances have you observed such shifts?
2. Does a democratic culture, more than any other, provide conditions which make for open-mindedness and mental flexibility? If so, is this an asset or a liability?
3. Have you known of situations where students reexamined and perhaps revised basic beliefs under the direction of a tyrannical teacher? If so, does such behavior contradict the hypotheses advanced in this chapter? Could a teacher be autocratic and permissive at the same time?
4. If a democratic group is the most effective instrument for promoting change in basic outlooks, how do you explain the drastic changes in outlook achieved by Hitler, using methods of propaganda and coercion?
5. Could many of the guidance functions now performed by counselors be performed better in group situations? Does the key responsibility for guidance fall on classroom teachers? What is meant by the expression, "Education is guidance"?
6. Does a search for consensus in a group imply a totalitarian outlook? Can consensus ever be achieved without putting pressure on individuals to conform? Is majority vote a more democratic practice than seeking consensus?

REFERENCES

BODE, BOYD, *Progressive Education at the Crossroads*, Chicago, Newson, 1938.

A stimulating discussion of the need for directed learning. Forcefully rejects laissez faire in education in favor of a directed, but democratic, pattern.

CANTOR, NATHANIEL, *The Dynamics of Learning*, Chicago, Foster and Stewart, 1946.

One of the most provocative treatments of how a teacher or group leader may reduce resistance to new insights among group members. Also useful is Cantor's *Learning Through Discussion,* Human Relations for Industry, 1951.

LEWIN, KURT, *Resolving Social Conflicts,* New York, Harper & Row, 1948.

Interesting papers on theory and research of group change.

ROGERS, CARL, *Client-Centered Therapy,* Boston, Houghton Mifflin, 1951.

A basic text in nondirective counseling. Some of its principles can be adapted to classroom teaching.

WILES, KIMBALL, *Teaching for Better Schools,* Englewood Cliffs, N.J., Prentice-Hall, 1952.

Application of group dynamics to specific classroom teaching situations.

CHAPTER 10

Discussion as a Tool of Reflective Learning

Types and Values of Discussion

DISCUSSIONS, like techniques in general, may be classified as *directed* or *undirected*, depending on how much responsibility a teacher takes for guidance. Or they may be *authoritarian* or *permissive*, depending on the degree to which a teacher tries to stamp the group with his own thought processes. It is assumed here that a teacher will always try to maintain at least minimal permissiveness, as suggested and described in Chapter 9. For our purposes, the most useful classification is that based on degree of directedness, and the present chapter will be devoted to explanation and illustration of undirected and directed discussions as tools of conceptual learning.

Since the aim assumed for discussion is reflective learning and since this kind of learning in the social studies emerges from situations which appear to students to be problematic, the chief interest of the present chapter wiill be on *problem-solving discussion*, which in the main is necessarily directed discussion. First, however, we shall consider undirected discussion since, although this form is not likely to lead to much reflection, it can play a significant preparatory role in the learning process.

UNDIRECTED DISCUSSION

Undirected discussion is informal and loosely organized exchange of views in which no systematic attempt is made to reach conclusions—or, in fact, to follow any predetermined direction. In order to get students to talk freely, the teacher deliberately imposes as few restraints as possible. Undirected discussion is similar to an out-of-class bull session.

Such discussion may serve very worthwhile purposes. It requires a student to formulate his own opinions and to watch how they fare in a give-and-take situation. It requires him to listen to the opinions of others. All of this should help an individual student to become more aware of what he believes, and to identify common points of dispute and agreement within the group. It may make him more tolerant of divergent or unorthodox views. Undirected discussion also serves a climate-making function in that it "warms up" a class by making students feel at ease and encouraging backward students to talk. It may also—and this is most important—help a teacher to identify the real problems of students, or to discover unexamined beliefs (prejudices) which can later be brought under question in such a way as to create problems. Undirected discussion may therefore be of great value in helping a teacher plan and lead more organized discussion later.

By and large, classroom discussions tend to be relatively undirected in the sense that no organizational pattern is evident. They are likely to wander, and seldom produce grounded conclusions. Prevalence of this sort of discussion probably results from the fact that, although at times it is difficult to control, little planning is required on the part of teachers or students. Since few teachers understand the potential values of undirected discussion, the largely undirected discussions they conduct may serve no good purpose at all.

But even when used deliberately and purposefully, undirected discussion has conspicuous limitations. It may expose students' problems, but it can do little toward solving problems which require methodical examination of evidence. It may prepare the soil for reflection, but it is hardly capable in itself of supporting sustained reflection. It may create a situation which encourages participation, but it is not designed to lead to continuously constructive effort. The all-but-exclusive emphasis in schoolrooms on relatively undirected discussion or variations of it has led to the charge that typical classroom discussion is a mere "pooling of ignorance." A teacher must know when to permit undirected discussion and when to discourage it.

PROBLEM-SOLVING DISCUSSION

Problem-solving discussion is perhaps indicated when a class needs to reach a decision, form a policy, establish a program, or take some other step in the face of difficulty more or less common to the whole group. It is distinguished from undirected discussion in being a disciplined, sharply pointed form of group thinking. It always has the purpose of moving thought forward. Unless students emerge with increased understanding of issues they confront, it fails to advance its purpose.

The essential task of problem-solving discussion is reflective testing of a hypothesis under the established rules of scientific method. A problem-solving group selects a hypothesis for testing, defines it, determines what kind of evidence is needed to test it, seeks and examines evidence, and comes to some conclusion. Discussion may be led by one person or by all or several members of a group sharing the functions of leadership. These functions include establishing climatic and other conditions for group reflection and helping the group move through the steps of a complete act of thought—or as far in this direction as possible.

Although when writing about the subject one may establish neat classifications, it is much more difficult in practice to lead discussion so that it will appear to an observer to fit into one of the established categories. The terms *undirected* and *problem solving*, as applied to discussions, are relative. Undirected discussion tends spontaneously at various points to develop some of the structure of a problem-solving discussion. And the latter at times may appear undirected. Thus, many discussions fall somewhere between the two types, or alternate from one to the other.

Participants in a problem-solving discussion are limited in the extent and nature of the techniques of inquiry which they can use. For example, they can only mentally perform experiments during discussion proper. They can examine the results of observations and experiments made by others, however, and can plan to do individual or group research during recesses in discussion, deferring decisions until further evidence is before them.

Besides learning the attitudes and skills of reflective method, students may also be expected to gain control of substantial quantities of factual data relevant to problems which concern them. There is reason to believe that factual content acquired in this way is remembered longer, and applied more readily and meaningfully, than that learned through recitation or individual study. Students will also, it is hoped, develop disposition and ability to work closely with others in solving problems of group interest, and move nearer to agreement on basic issues or at least understand better the source of their differences. Achievement of these aims naturally presupposes reasonable skill on the part of a teacher in directing discussion and in encouraging development of discussion skills in students.

Although they may be more apparent than real, problem-solving discussion has certain limitations. Just as serious reflection in an individual may lead into blind alleys and have its periods of frustration and despair, so may cooperative reflection also experience periods of retreat and bewilderment. Discussion may therefore appear to be a time-consuming technique. However, if well led, it is probably one of the most efficient techniques for producing conceptualization. And if we are interested in results which are permanent and functional, discussion is probably one of the most efficient means of teaching informational content.

Discussion gives best results in small groups. To secure the benefits of discusssion in very large groups (say, 100 or more) special techniques are required: the panel, round table, or symposium. In most instances, teachers work with groups of forty or less and need not make use of large-group techniques unless they have special reasons for doing so.

The physical requirements of a small-group discussion are simple and can be met in most classrooms. In an ideal situation, students sit around a large table or draw their chairs into a circle. The teacher is at a focal point, but not separated from students by platform, desk, or speaker's stand. If this arrangement is not possible, students may be seated with reasonable compactness near the front of a classroom and the teacher may sit, stand, or move slowly around the room. The purpose of physical arrangement is to promote an informal, friendly atmosphere—one in which all that is said may be readily heard and in which the "total" person speaking may be easily observed.

Some Responsibilities of Leadership

As suggested in Chapter 9, the modern view is that a teacher does not have a monopoly on tasks of leadership. There are certain leadership functions which must be performed if a discussion is to remain for long on a problem-solving level, and it does not matter who performs them, so long as they are performed satisfactorily. It is a teacher's responsibility to see that they are carried out but not necessarily to monopolize their performance. Probably the more widely the functions of leadership are distributed the better. This should not be taken to mean that a discussion profits from an absence of direction; it means only that furnishing directedness may often be the cooperative task of several persons. Obviously, a group consisting of young students or students who have had little experience in problem-solving discussion will require more direction from a teacher than other groups.

The remainder of this section deals with a number of the functions of leadership and, wherever it seems profitable, illustrates the conduct of these functions by means of verbatim excerpts from classroom discussions. These transcripts are not supposed to represent perfection in leadership technique; they are meant to be suggestive only.

ESTABLISHING PROCEDURAL RULES

If possible, rules of procedure should be made democratically. That is class members should be encouraged to initiate and help enforce their own rules. A classroom situation naturally determines the rules. In general, large classes call for stricter application of rules than do smaller groups, and students who are accustomed to discussion can operate under more lenient rules than novices. Procedural rules should never be regarded as ends, but rather as tools. They should be freely modified as a situation demands. Some commonly observed rules follow:

1. Before he speaks, each student gains recognition from the teacher. At times, of course, it may be stifling to require every pupil to first ad-

dress the teacher; but unless this rule is followed noisy confusion often develops.

2. Students speak one at a time. In spite of a teacher's best effort, during a heated discusssion students will break this and the preceding rule. But a group should learn to accept the rule as the best means of respecting the right of each to be fairly heard.

3. Students gain recognition by raising a hand. Also, as soon as a student is given the floor, all hands go down. The student who is talking deserves the best possible conditions in which to make his point; a roomful of waving arms is a discourtesy.

4. When more than one student wants the floor, a teacher gives preference to a student who has not yet spoken; or if all have spoken, to the student who in the past has said least.

5. A teacher spreads discussion around as much as possible. Any time they show the slightest inclination to speak, he encourages students who are usually silent to talk. He expresses appreciation for the contributions, no matter how feeble, of timid students. He is always careful not to give the appearance of favoring one student, or one group of students, over the rest.

6. A teacher may establish a time limit for individual comments, or a limit on the number of times a single student is allowed to speak. This rule may be needed to prevent a few from monopolizing discussion.

7. The teacher makes sure that students remain impersonal in their remarks. Statements such as "That is just stupid . . ." or "Coming from you, I'm not surprised," have no place in discussion.

ESTABLISHING AND MAINTAINING A WARMLY PERMISSIVE EMOTIONAL CLIMATE

For good psychological reasons, it is essential that a teacher manage discussion so that students feel relaxed, in a good mood, and free from threat. A distinctive function of discussion is that, properly conducted, it is one of the best tools for inducing permanent changes in beliefs and values. But, as suggested in Chapter 9, most persons find it possible to change their fundamental thought habits only in a permissive emotional climate. Discussion excerpts below illustrate some of the points made previously.

In the following two examples the teacher tries to insure that students feel their views are respected.

RUTH: Well—I don't really know much about this subject—maybe I'd better just keep still—
TEACHER: I'm sure we would all like to hear your opinion.
RUTH: I don't think it's fair that we should be partial to industry over agri-

culture in our tariff rates. That is, industry enjoys a high degree of protection. It wouldn't be fair to lower the tariff on farm goods and keep it on—say—autos.

TEACHER: A good point, a very good point. Your idea is that if we were going to lower tariffs, we ought to lower them equally on agricultural and industrial products.

HAROLD: Well, you know what people always say—it's even in the textbooks—kids should honor and respect their parents. In a way, I believe that but I think parents ought to honor and respect kids, too, and not do some of the things they do.

TEACHER: That sounds like a perfectly reasonable point to me.

HAROLD: Yeah, but as soon as a guy like me says that some parents deserve to be hated and disobeyed—then people start thinking there is something wrong with you.

TEACHER: I should think that generally when a boy or girl hates his parents he has some reason—maybe a pretty good one.

Often a teacher needs to introduce opinions contrary to those his students hold. Such opinions should be presented not as personal viewpoints but as positions which are held by some persons, as outlooks common in our society. The following examples illustrate how one teacher tried to introduce fresh opinons and facts without generating resistance among students.

TEACHER: You have suggested several possible policies that the government might follow with respect to taxation—but no one has suggested that taxes ought generally to be raised.

JOHN: Who would want taxes raised, anyway?

TEACHER: Maybe it's an idea we ought to explore.

RALPH: Do you think taxes ought to be raised? Or are you kidding somebody?

TEACHER: I wasn't advocating raising taxes. I simply mean that there are some persons who do and that there is a definite school of thought along that line. I thought you might be interested in the line of reasoning of a person who favors higher taxes.

JACK: Well, I don't see why the Western states shouldn't have control of the public land within their boundaries. Local people ought to know how to use it better than a bunch of Washington bureaucrats.

JOE: I never could figure out how the federal government could legally hold title to millions of acres of land in the West anyhow.

MARY: Isn't the whole idea of public lands—well, like socialism in some way?

TEACHER: I think for the moment it might be better to avoid trying to pin labels on it. Wouldn't it be better first to get some of the arguments, pro and con, out into the open?

JOE: My dad's a cattleman and all I've been hearing for years is arguments. And they all add up to one thing.

TEACHER: Would you be willing to grant that there is an argument on the other side—in favor of the present system of federal control?

JACK: Someone must believe it, or things would change.

TEACHER: I'm no expert on this and right now I wouldn't express an opinion one way or another. But there is a line of reasoning which you read fairly often, and unless you know what it is you can't defend your own view intelligently. Some persons who prefer federal ownership and control of public lands do so because they question the competence of most state governments to exercise control wisely. Is there anyone who will volunteer to read a magazine article which came out recently on this subject?

In a permissive classroom, students themselves always carry a large measure of responsibility for their own thinking. That is, they make their own decisions and expect to be asked to defend them. The following excerpts illustrate how a teacher may encourage students to think for themselves.

KAREN: (to teacher) Well, offhand, as things are right now, wouldn't you say there is a need for military preparedness?

TEACHER: I'd rather not try to answer that. Class, Karen is raising a question about our need for military preparedness. How about it? What do the rest of you think?

CHARLES: On this election I'm caught right in the middle. Dad's for the Democratic candidate and mother's for the Republican.

TEACHER: And whom are you supporting?

CHARLES: I just can't decide—I think a person ought to vote for the man, not the party. Which do you think is the better man?

TEACHER: Even if I wanted to try to help you decide, I couldn't until you told us what you mean by "better"—what is it you want in a President?

CHARLES: Well, that's not easy. You make a problem out of it. I suppose honesty might be one thing.

TEACHER: Okay. Why don't you make a list of the qualities you think the candidate should have and then try to see which man fits best?

CHARLES: If I make a list, then will you give me your opinion as to which candidate I ought to support?

TEACHER: I'm afraid not. You will have to decide. But I can help you find what biographical material there is on each candidate.

Just as a student has a right to be heard, he also has a right not to talk if he doesn't want to. Many teachers have found that it is better not to ask questions of designated students, particularly if a question is one which delves deeply into touchy areas of belief. One point of view is that if students want to talk they will volunteer and if they do not want to talk—but are required to—they will give minimal answers. That is, the answers will be sufficiently ambiguous or noncommittal to prevent the student's being exposed to later attack. The teacher is aware of this problem in the following illustrations.

HAROLD: (who has been showing signs of interest but seems reluctant to talk) There are some things—like in connection with the family problems we've been talking about—that you can't tell people.
TEACHER: That's true. If you have a specific case in mind, then use your own judgment about whether you want to mention it.
HAROLD: Well, it fits in but it's sort of personal.
TEACHER: Okay, use your own judgment—you are among friends, you know.

TEACHER: I want to ask several people in the class their opinions of the statement which is written on the board. But I want to repeat that no one needs to feel obligated to answer just in order to seem cooperative. Some of you may not want to say anything at all, and some may want to wait a while until some of the others have had their say. In other words, I'm not interested in putting someone on a spot. James, your name is the one I pulled out of the hat first, so to speak. What is your opinion, if you care to give one?
JAMES: I don't think I have any.
TEACHER: That's all right—maybe you'll get one later and if you do, feel free to express it. How about you, Helen?
HELEN: Well, I'm no expert on taxation—
TEACHER: (laughing) None of us here is. You're among equals.
HELEN: Well, I'll try.

Humor and good will are indispensable in helping to create a permissive atmosphere. A student is helped to be himself by such displays of warmth. He is helped to eliminate tensions and hostilities. The exchange below modified the tone of a discussion which had lacked warmth:

MELVIN: (following an explanation of some of the details of a plan for Universal Military Training) Some of the things usually associated with the military would be eliminated. In fact, many additional safeguards as to health and morals and the effects of military association would be eliminated or reduced under the type of plan they have in mind.
TEACHER: You mean that they would try to keep the young men away from women, liquor, gambling, and that sort of thing? (laughter)
MELVIN: Well, yes, I'm only quoting. They even have it figured out how many chaplains they would need and plan to locate training centers away from communities which have an—ah—unsavory reputation. (laughter)
TEACHER: I don't think the young men will want to go. (laughter)

FACILITATING COMMUNICATION

Students must be helped to make themselves understood. Sometimes this requires only that a class be asked to be more attentive to what a student is saying or that a contributor be asked to speak louder. More often it involves problems of semantics, of clarification of intended meaning. We will consider three aspects of communication.

Insuring That Individuals Are Heard. Whenever a teacher suspects that some in a class have not heard a statement, he should ask the contributor to repeat it in a louder tone of voice, or he himself should repeat it. Sometimes it is well to investigate how much is being heard by asking, "Did everyone hear what was just said?" Sometimes a teacher can induce shy students to talk louder by standing on the far side of the room from them.

Helping to Reduce Ambiguity. Probably the major cause of faulty communication is ambiguity. This in turn stems from inadequate language skills or a haziness of thought processes. One means of counteracting muddiness is to ask for examples or illustrations.

JANICE: Well, there are all these cases of creeping socialism, as it has been called. Trying to reduce everyone to a common level of wealth, or maybe poverty. That's what I'm talking about—

TEACHER: Can you give an example of creeping socialism?

JANICE: Well, there must be lots of examples—the TVA has been cited—I don't really know—

TEACHER: Do you have in mind activities of the federal government—or state and local governments?

JANICE: I think the threat must come mostly from the federal government.

TEACHER: Then is the TVA as good an example as you can think of? If so, can you tell the class something about the TVA—what sort of organization it is?

Sometimes a student uses an unintended word or phrase which confuses his entire statement. Questioning designed to draw a student out further, to get him to rephrase or repeat, may help, as in this illustration:

GEORGE: I remember one argument of one senator about the excess profits tax—that it should be spread out and cut down—I remember he said, I think—from 20 to 10 or 5 percent and apply it to all industries, instead of 20 percent on some products and none on others.

TEACHER: I don't exactly understand that because the maximum rate under the present excess profits tax is a lot higher than that, and it applies impartially to all firms earning over a certain level of profit.

GEORGE: Well, this senator, as I recall, wanted it spread out more to correspond to our national heritage of taxation—taxes for all instead of the few, or something—I don't remember. I'm pretty balled up myself. Taxation, in his opinion, should cover food to some extent. I remember his mentioning bread, milk, or something that should have a 5 percent excise tax—

TEACHER: Oh, are you talking about excise taxes?

GEORGE: Yes, excise.

TEACHER: You had us a little confused there—I understood you to say excess profits—

GEORGE: I guess that was a mistake—I meant excise.

Sometimes the easiest means of reducing ambiguity is for a teacher to repeat in clearer language what a student is trying to say, if he can infer what the student is driving at.

GEORGE: One reason I'm opposed to Universal Military Training is because of the effect it would have on the minds of the young men of the country —the army has an outlook which is—well, okay maybe for the army, but to build it up in everybody—

RALPH: I question whether UMT would give everyone who went through it a military outlook on things. A lot of people think it just doesn't carry through. Men that have been in the service—if we take the bunch which went through the last war—when they got out not many had any hankering to start fighting again.

GEORGE: I was thinking of regimentation of thought—not war as a good or bad thing. For example, the tendency of the American people to think every which way, to go around in a circle and off in all directions. The tendency of the army to create a relationship between doing certain things and not doing certain things—respecting higher authority, the aristocrat— more so than the elected authority—that type of thing.

TEACHER: Oh, then you don't mean, George, that UMT would teach aggressiveness—you mean perhaps it would promote the development in civilian life of a caste system, a group who are habitually willing to obey and a group accustomed to commanding—like the Prussian social structure perhaps?

GEORGE: That's right.

Helping to Overcome Concealment. Communication may be hindered because a student hesitates to say what he really has in mind. A thought is lurking in the back of his head of which perhaps he is a little afraid, or which he does not quite understand, so he tries to phrase his comments so as to conceal what is actually there. Often such hidden thoughts include ideas which the student fears are extreme, unpopular in his community, or so lacking in grounds as to be open to attack. He may welcome a chance to examine these ideas critically if he can be helped to do it somewhat painlessly.

Sometimes a teacher can infer what a student is really thinking and state it himself, thus helping a student clarify his own ideas.

MARJORIE: The trouble with most parents is, they are old fogeys. They don't understand how the world has changed.

TEACHER: What do you mean, Marjorie?

MARJORIE: Well, they don't want you to do anything. It's always "don't do this" or "don't do that."

TEACHER: What, for example?

MARJORIE: Well, like going out on a date. They want to know all about the boy—his pedigree for ten generations. (laughter) And if they find anything wrong—and usually they do—they make you stay home.

TEACHER: Do you think high-school students should be allowed to choose their own associates?

MARJORIE: Sure, why not?

TEACHER: Do you think high-school girls should be free to go out with older men—say men of 30 or 40?

MARJORIE: (pause) Well, I guess a lot of people frown on that sort of thing.

TEACHER: But, if students are going to be really free to pick their own associates, then they should be free to run around with anyone they please—no matter what age—

MARJORIE: If I said yes to that—well, I know what people would think—

TEACHER: (laughing) Well, do you stand by your principle of freedom or don't you?

MARJORIE: I might as well be honest—sure I do—but that doesn't mean I'm planning to start dating married men.

TEACHER: But you feel you have a right?

MARJORIE: Yes.

ASSISTING TOWARD SOLUTION OF A PROBLEM

A group needs to be helped to conclude successfully each stage in the process of thought without serious logjams or bottlenecks and to move on to the next stage. A problem-solving discussion has direction and moves—even if sometimes by a circuitous route—toward some sort of conclusion. Some ways in which a leader can assist a group are described and illustrated below. In the next section, we shall describe and illustrate in more detail how each step of a problem-solving discussion may be handled.

Orienting a Group in the Nature and Purpose of Problem-Solving Discussion. Sometime in each course, a social-studies teacher should encourage discussion on the subject of discussion itself, in order to clarify the nature of reflective method, show how reflection may be served by discussion, show the logical pattern of problem-solving discussion, and treat problems of technique required for effective discussion. In most cases, such critical examination should be held early in a course; but with immature students it may be delayed until after the group has had considerable experience in dealing reflectively with content. But in every discussion—no matter how seasoned a group may be—it is always appropriate to raise questions about matters of methodology if thinking would be furthered thereby. The following excerpt illustrates a departure from the formal theme for the purpose of examining basic methodology:

WILLARD: I think I learn more in classes where the teacher lectures and gives definite assignments.
TEACHER: How do the rest of you feel about that?
JAMES: Well—this isn't meant as a criticism of this class—but it seems to me that we often go round and round. Sometimes I can't tell what I've gained from it.
TEACHER: Have our discussions been worthwhile? Has the class learned anything of value from them?
ELAINE: I think it has done me some good just to hear the opinions of other people.
WILLARD: But all you do hear is opinion. I want something more definite than that.
TEACHER: If our discussions have sounded like mere airing of opinion, something must be wrong. There should be some other ends that can be served by discussion if it's done right. What do you think we ought to aim for when we discuss?

Guarding Against Superficiality and Promoting Critical-Mindedness. Unless taught otherwise, secondary-school students are likely to be highly uncritical. But critical-mindedness is an essential of successful reflection. Closely related to lack of a critical faculty is the tendency to study issues superficially. Students actually may resist digging beneath the surface as a result of repressions, laziness, or habits acquired in previous courses. It is always legitimate for a teacher to press students for evidence whenever they come forth with sweeping generalizations or dubious facts. And whenever an opportunity presents itself, a teacher should ask questions designed to expose inconsistency, conflict, or faulty logic, and questions that are probing enough to prevent discussion from confining itself to surface or peripheral matters. Of course, he should not become so much of a gadfly that students become hostile, discouraged, or withdrawn. Questioning should be good humored and tactful and should not go so far as to undermine essential permissiveness.

In the following excerpt a teacher tried to raise questions about an assertion of fact made by a student and in the process achieved a much deeper analysis than would have occurred if the teacher had remained passive.

RAMON: I don't see how we could get by without a protective tariff, that is, not unless we are willing to equalize our standard of living with other parts of the world. And I don't think the people in our nation are ready or willing to do that.

TEACHER: What do you mean by equalizing the standard of living?

RAMON: Well, putting everyone on the same level.

TEACHER: You mean everyone having the same real income—the same buying power?

RAMON: I guess that's it—the same number of cars and radios per capita, the same number of bathtubs, and that sort of thing.

TEACHER: Is it all right if we pursue this question a little farther—it interests me. What is the basis of a worker's income—that is, what determines how much he earns?

RAMON: His wages? Well, if he belongs to a union he is likely to get more. And the more profits an employer makes, the more he can afford to pay.

TEACHER: Maybe we can approach the question better if we try another way. A century ago a factory worker in the United States was lucky to make ten dollars a week; today factory workers average about seventeen or eighteen dollars a day. How do you explain that?

HAROLD: Price inflation probably has something to do with it. And like Ramon said, unions.

TEACHER: But does the average factory worker live better today than he did a century ago? More cars and radios, more bathtubs, better homes and the like?

HAROLD: Oh, sure.

TEACHER: Do you think all of the gain has been due to unions—all the gain in standard of living, I mean?

ELAINE: I think our ability to produce more has a lot to do with it—each worker now turns out a lot more in a day. Because we have better machines than they did then. And mass-production industries.

TEACHER: Elaine is saying that the average worker lives better now than he did a century ago because he is more productive. Is productivity a basis for wages—does the amount a worker can turn out have something to do with what his employer can pay him—and what his standard of living will be?

HAROLD: Naturally. Where is this leading us?

TEACHER: Well, is the labor force of every nation equally productive? I mean, does the average American worker produce as much as, say, the average Chinese worker? What about that, Ramon?

RAMON: I would say the American is much more productive. What has this got to do with the tariff?

TEACHER: I'll try to tie it in. Would you say that eliminating tariffs—pursuing a policy of free trade—would make the Chinese worker as productive as the American?

RAMON: Well—I don't know—I don't see why it would.

ELAINE: I think I get your point—there would still be different levels of productivity under free trade, therefore the people of the most productive nations would continue living better than the rest. Free trade couldn't equalize our standard of living with other parts of the world like Ramon said.

We shall illustrate one other means of helping to induce critical-mindedness—getting qualifications attached to overly broad generalizations.

RAMON: Well, I guess I'm one of those reactionaries who believes that you can't change human nature.
TEACHER: I don't know whether holding that belief makes you a reactionary. If so, I would guess that you have lots of company. I would be interested in knowing just what you mean, though, when you say that you can't change human nature.
RAMON: Well, I mean that people are basically the same now as they were as far back as we have any records—as far back as the ancient Egyptians, for example.
TEACHER: Do you mean people have the same customs now?
RAMON: No, not the same customs—oh, I guess some customs haven't changed much.
TEACHER: Do you mean people have the same beliefs today as they had in ancient Egypt—about politics, economics, religion, sex, and so on?
RAMON: No, I don't mean that—you can't say that people haven't changed. But there are some things that don't change.
TEACHER: For example?
RAMON: People have always been and always will be basically selfish. And they still fight wars.
TEACHER: Then you would say that there are a few drives or motives that remain the same?
RAMON: Yes.
TEACHER: Would you say man has changed in more ways than he has remained the same, or remained the same in more ways than he has changed?
RAMON: Well, you've got me there. I suppose I will have to take back part of it. It wasn't a very careful statement.

Keeping Students on the Subject. A teacher should try to hold his group to the point of the discussion, although at times a wise teacher will decide that the point should be changed in midstream. Closely related to this problem is the need to prevent members of a group from obstructing emerging lines of thought with trivial or facetious remarks. Below is an example of how a teacher may prevent discussion from moving in irrelevant directions.

AL: Aren't we giving too much of a superman quality to the atom bomb and too little importance to old-fashioned infantry? I don't think the infantry will ever be replaced, even if only for mopping up operations—
GEORGE: My brother was in Japan and he talked with Japanese people around

Hiroshima and also some who lived in Tokyo. Their worst fear—even after the atom bombing—was incendiary bombs.

AL: Our tendency to overrate new weapons is one reason why I'm in favor of UMT. We need a large, well-trained army of foot soldiers—

GEORGE: Can someone explain the principle of the H-bomb? I know the details are all secret, but the general idea has been published I think—can you?

TEACHER: That is a good question—but I am wondering if trying to answer it wouldn't be sidetracking us from the topic of discussion, which is UMT. The effectiveness of the H-bomb is, of course, important to us—but probably not the scientific principles. How about seeing me after class—I can explain all I know in a few minutes.

Keeping Discussion Unified So That Form and Direction Will be Clear. Discussions can easily become loosely jointed, if not dismembered. A few tangents, a few repetitions, and a group becomes confused. Points of confusion are usually sensed and sometimes openly revealed by questions such as "Where are we?" A teacher may keep confused wandering to a minimum by (1) making free use of the blackboard, (2) introducing at strategic points brief summaries and reviews, and (3) reminding the group of the object of the discussion.

TEACHER: So far in our discussion of Universal Military Training, we have talked about its cost, its possible effect on young men, and whether there is a genuine military threat to the United States from enemy nations. Are there any other big questions which would have to be answered in order for a person to take an intelligent stand either for or against UMT?

TEACHER: Do you have the feeling that we are going around in circles, that we need some way to pull the discussion together and see where we are, and decide where we want to go? We began with the question of whether the federal government or private power companies ought to develop Hell's Canyon. Now we are on the government farm program. Did we talk about Hell's Canyon to the point where you feel the significant facts and the chief competing opinions got out in the open? Did we reach a point where you would want to draw any conclusions, or is it still hanging?

Leading a Group Through the Steps of a Complete Act of Thought

As was pointed out in Chapter 8, it is assumed that all legitimate teaching techniques operate to move students through one or more of the steps of a complete act of thought, in accordance with the requirements of scientific methodology. Thus, problem-solving discussion begins by raising questions about established beliefs, and, if enough doubt appears to justify further exploration, moves a group through the formulation and testing of hypotheses and the drawing of conclusions. Very often problem-solving discussion must be combined with other techniques, particularly research activities, if it is to be of maximum fruitfulness.

More specifically a problem-solving discussion may be regarded as including these steps, though not necessarily in this order:

Step 1: Selecting and introducing the discussion topic.
Step 2: Clarifying and defining the problem.
Step 3: Developing and refining hypotheses.
Step 4: Testing hypotheses.
Step 5: Drawing conclusions.

STEP 1: SELECTING AND INTRODUCING THE TOPIC

Criteria for selection of topics for study presented in Chapter 8 included the suggestions that beliefs which are to be reflectively examined in classrooms should relate to social issues of wide concern, should have controversial aspect, should be held by a considerable proportion of students, and should, in the judgment of the teacher, lend themselves to frutiful study. We shall focus our main attention here on the mechanics of introducing topics which have already been chosen.

The first task of discussion is to confront students with statements which correspond to or bear an evidential relationship to their own beliefs or knowledge. These statements are the discussion "topic" and getting them before students is what we mean by "introducing the topic." The statements correspond to the established beliefs or preconceptions of step 1 of a complete act of thought as described on pages 68 and 69.

There are two basic procedures for placing before students propositions (or questions) for discussion. One is to get students to make statements about their own beliefs or purported knowledge, as in the following examples:

TEACHER: Tom, as I recall, you had something to say about this question the other day—can you repeat it?

TOM: Well—I think I said that, if we went on a free trade basis we would have another recession—or I guess you would call it a depression—like we had starting in 1929.

TEACHER: That is your considered judgment—that a business depression would follow any general removal of tariffs?

TOM: That's right.

TEACHER: Nancy, without wanting to put you on a spot, I am wondering if you could state your opinion on whether morality is correlated with religious faith—that is, whether people who hold definite religious beliefs are more likely than nonbelievers to follow our conventional moral codes?

NANCY: I understand the question all right. Actually, I've never known many people who were nonreligious— Oh, I guess quite a few people I know aren't really deeply religious—it's on the surface pretty much—but at least they claim a religion.

TEACHER: Maybe I'd better rephrase the question. Do you think people who seem deeply religious lead more moral lives, in the conventional sense, than those who take their religion pretty much for granted?

NANCY: Well—I don't know—I think the deeply religious person is more likely to conform to some of the standards that the churches talk about—like not drinking or gambling. I don't know whether what they say is immoral really is or not. For example, I think I approve of social drinking, at least my parents do it.

TEACHER: Would you say then that a deeply religious person is more likely to conform to conventional middle-class moral standards than a person who is only mildly religious?

NANCY: Yes, I think I would go along with that—so long as you'll let me make room for some exceptions.

In the two illustrations, the teacher has succeeded in getting statements of belief before the group. These particular beliefs may or may not be widely shared in the group, and it is evident that in the latter instance the student expressing the belief does not feel very deeply committed to it. In both cases, fruitful discussion of the belief may be possible, provided most other students in the class also have beliefs (including, we might hope, contrary ones) about the same subject.

A second basic procedure for confronting students with statements of belief is to introduce them from outside. Material introduced from the outside will be meaningless unless it is somehow related to previous experiences of students; that is, they must have beliefs of some sort about the material. Psychologically, the role of material introduced from outside is to bring students to recall and formulate more clearly what they already know and believe. Discussion of such material, although on the surface it may appear to be devoted only to testing propositions suggested by the material itself, will have the effect of making students reexamine and perhaps revise or add to their own beliefs, provided, of course, that the material is relevant.

There are certain advantages to using materials introduced from outside as springboards to discussion. If statements of belief analyzed in class are—in appearance—those of outsiders, then a less threatening emotional climate results. Students do not see their own ideas as under direct attack and can thus remain more relaxed and perceptive. Of course, unless students do make their own connections and view their own notions more critically, the discussion will not have accomplished an educational purpose. A teacher can often tell what is going on in the minds of students by listening to what they say or observing the level of interest which develops.

If a problem-solving discussion is to be instigated through materials introduced from outside, introduction of the subject may, on the surface, seem quite conventional. Students may be asked to read something, to bring reports, to watch a movie, or simply to pay attention while the teacher reads or describes some situation. Any of the conventional sources of content may be used—textbooks, films, clippings, speakers, and trips—provided the content presented contains ideas, facts, or expressions of belief which can be related evidentially to the present beliefs of students. Techniques of presenting such materials may also appear similar to those of conventional subject-centered teaching, except that through questioning or explanation the teacher makes certain that students see clearly the propositions stated or implicit in the materials. The following may demonstrate this point:

TEACHER: Class, I have with me yesterday evening's edition of the comic strip "Blondie." How many of you have read it?
MARGE: Oh, is that where Blondie came home with the new hats?
TEACHER: Yes, how many of you saw that? (Several hands go up) Since some of you missed it, I'll read it. (The gist of the strip is that Blondie has spent a lot of money for foolish-looking hats while Dagwood, who supplies the cash, feels persecuted)
TEACHER: (after reading) What big point, or idea, do you think the cartoonist is trying to communicate?
MARGE: Well, to me the comic strip means that men don't always appreciate women's ideas of style the way they should. Personally, I think Blondie had a right to buy those hats.
TOM: I can't accept that interpretation at all. I think the cartoonist is trying to say that women are slaves to style and that they don't spend money wisely.

STEP 2: CLARIFYING AND DEFINING THE PROBLEM

This step involves getting clearly in mind what the problem is—that is, what it is that is blocking fuller understanding. A danger in discussion is that students will not come to feel involved in a problem—that the problem is only in the mind of the teacher. Step 2 tries to surround with doubt the beliefs or purported knowledge introduced in step 1; or it tries to expose incompatibilities or conflict in students' conceptual patterns. The function of discussion leadership in step 2 is—through questioning or other techniques—to expose inadequacies in the beliefs and knowledge of students, to help students see how their beliefs may be confused, contradictory, or ungrounded. Questioning seeks to make these inadequacies explicit—to define them so clearly that, if it seems desirable, they can be written on the blackboard. A teacher's intention is to raise doubts of the general form "If the one thing is true, how can the other be true also?" If he is successful in revealing to students discrepancies in their thinking, questions such as these will inevitably enter their minds: "Where is the flaw in my thinking?" "What is the right (or a better) answer to this?" and "How can I find out?"

The following example shows how a teacher may reveal inconsistencies through questioning:

TEACHER: (who has just read to the class a story in *Time* magazine about a son in an old, aristocratic New England family—the Stantons—who has been disinherited because of marrying a girl from the slums) What do you think of this story?

ANNE: I guess something like that could happen only in New England.

RUTH: Why not in San Francisco? We have a high-society crowd out here that think they are just as important as the upper crust in Boston—

BILL: Going back to the story, I don't think his parents had any right to cut him off from the family fortune—I thought this was a free country—that anybody had a right to marry anyone he wanted to. If I decided I wanted to marry a migrant farm laborer living in a tent—well—no one had better try to stop me.

TEACHER: Do you girls share Bill's feeling that the young man in the story should be allowed to marry anyone he pleases, no matter what her social rank?

EILEEN: I think so. I think it's none of his parents' business.

ANNE: Oh, naturally his parents would be interested—but I think he had the right.

RUTH: I agree—some rich man's son might propose to me sometime. (laughter)

TEACHER: Let's carry this a little farther. From your answers, I take it that most of you don't think much of the idea of some people setting themselves up as better than others—the social arrangement you have when some people are "high society" and feel they are above the common crowd.

EILEEN: Doesn't the Declaration of Independence say everyone is equal? That's a principle of democracy.

TEACHER: Do you take that to mean that they are socially equal, equal in ability, or what?

EILEEN: Well, to me it means equal opportunity for everybody to do what he wants and live a happy life—but I think it means social equality too.

RALPH: I'm not upper crust, but then I don't come from the lower-lower class either. I try to treat everybody alike—no matter which side of the tracks they come from.

TEACHER: Then do all of you go along with the idea that any kind of social discrimination is bad—that we shouldn't have social barriers or social classes based on the feeling that some people are better than others? ("Yes's" and nods indicate general assent)

TEACHER: You have me really interested now. May I ask you some questions along a slightly different line? You may not see right away how it ties in, but I think you will later. How many of you expect to go to college (A majority hold up hands) All right, fine. Eileen, you say you are going to college—I am wondering if you will be interested in joining a sorority then— if you will agree to go in.

EILEEN: Well, I don't know just what you are thinking of. I probably wouldn't have the money.

TEACHER: Let's assume you could afford it—I know they are often expensive. If you could afford it, and were invited, would you join a sorority?

EILEEN: Well, I don't know for sure—it's quite a long way off. But probably.

TEACHER: How about the rest of you girls? Ruth? Anne? Sarah? (Most girls answer a qualified yes—if they are asked, if it doesn't cost too much, etc.)

TEACHER: Why would you want to join a sorority? Can you tell us, Eileen?

EILEEN: That's a hard question (laughs). I guess it's just the thing to do—it's part of going to college.

TEACHER: There must be a more definite reason than that.

EILEEN: If you were asked, and could afford to join and didn't, then people would think you were a little strange—stand-offish or something.

SARAH: Well, if you go to State—that's a pretty big place—I think you'd feel a little more like somebody, if you joined a sorority.

TEACHER: Oh? What do you mean "You'd feel a little more like somebody?"

SARAH: Well—I don't know exactly—it's hard to explain. I guess you'd feel a little more important.

RUTH: I think maybe Sarah means that people would sort of look down on you if you didn't belong—

TEACHER: What people?

RUTH: Oh—other students—the important students on the campus—the leaders —you know, those who are officers in organizations.

TEACHER: And maybe sorority girls too—would they look down on you if you remained outside a sorority?

EILEEN: I suppose they might—

TEACHER: And, if you joined a sorority, would you look down on girls who didn't get in?

EILEEN: Well—I might feel sorry for them. I wouldn't really look down.

TEACHER: Let me ask this question: Do most of you feel that a sorority or fraternity is a means by which students try to raise themselves in the eyes of their fellow students?

ANNE: I think so. One means.

TEACHER: Suppose I changed the wording of the question, and said, "Is joining a sorority or fraternity a means of raising your social position?"

EILEEN: I don't like the word *social position*. That sounds like society again.

ROGER: If a person raises himself in the eyes of his associates, then doesn't he have a higher social position?

TEACHER: Eileen, your use of the term *society* interests me. You mean society people, like the Stanton family in the *Time* magazaine story?

EILEEN: Well, yes, I guess so.

TEACHER: Do you ever read the society page in the newspaper?

EILEEN: Sometimes. Mother always reads it before anything else.

TEACHER: Have you ever read about the affairs of sororities on the society page—about their parties and what the girls wear and that sort of thing?

EILEEN: Why, yes.

TEACHER: Could that be one reason girls join sororities—to get their pictures and names in the society pages?

ROGER: May I say something? You girls say you are opposed to social class, social discrimination, and things like that. You think it's awful if old man Stanton gets mad at his son for marrying someone who's socially below him. But sororities do the same thing—I know because I have a cousin who's in one and she now thinks she's top of the heap—

ANNE: I think maybe we've been trapped—you (looks at teacher) deliberately maneuvered us into that—some of us anyway. I think what you are trying to get across is that a lot of sorority girls are trying to accomplish the same thing through their sororities that Mr. Stanton was trying to do when he disinherited his son.

TEACHER: I wasn't trying to trap you. I only wanted you to think about it and see for yourselves.

EILEEN: I guess I will be a different kind of sorority girl—if I ever join one.

TEACHER: Maybe some of you would want to take back what you said about social equality—maybe it isn't always a good idea.

ROGER: I think practically everybody—especially girls—would be snobs if they had half a chance—it's human nature.

EILEEN: Why does Roger pick on the women? Men are just as bad.

RUTH: I wonder—maybe we all violate the idea of equality every day.

In the following example, the teacher tries to expose through questioning a contradiction in the editorial policies of a newspaper. Because he is using outside materials of an impersonal nature, rather than the stated beliefs of students, he can expose the conflict more quickly and directly. Less caution is needed, because students are less likely to feel their personal beliefs are in public jeopardy.

TEACHER: Chapter 19 of your textbook—which you are assigned for tomorrow—discusses the Department of the Interior, and in connection with that the work of the Federal Bureau of Reclamation. I want to start your thinking about some of the issues involved by reading two editorials which I clipped from the local paper. The first has to do with the generation and sale of electricity in federal projects. (Teacher reads from editorial, which begins as follows: "The cost of federal irrigation water would be prohibitive in most areas if not for income from the sale of government-generated power. The power features of Reclamation projects have to date made the projects feasible for water users. To argue, as Senator ———— has, that Reclamation should sell its power at cost to private utilities, and that in future projects Reclamation ought to stay out of the power business entirely, is to argue against the very future of the West. The Senator's contention that such projects are socialistic is matched only in absurdity by some of his other arguments. . . . Etc.")

TEACHER: What do you make of this editorial? What is the writer saying?

TOM: It seems clear enough—he thinks the Reclamation Bureau ought to keep on generating power and selling it at a profit. And applying the profits on the cost of the project.

TEACHER: Does the editorial writer think government generation of power is an example of socialism?

VERNON: He says—as I interpret it—that Senator —— is crazy—or words to that effect—for using the term *socialism*.

TEACHER: Well, I want to read you an editorial from the same paper—not the same issue, but one which came out about a week later. This editorial is about a different subject—it seems—the present labor government in Britain. (The editorial starts as follows: "It is now the expressed intention of the labor government to nationalize British steel. Thus, one of Britain's most important manufacturing industries seems destined to go the way of coal, electricity, communication and transportation, and all the other industries that have felt the socialistic ax. How long will it take the labor government, we wonder, to realize the disastrous consequences of government ownership. . . . Etc.")

TEACHER: Now, what would you say the attitude of the writer is toward the nationalization of industry?

ANNE: He obviously doesn't think much of it in England—he's very bitter I would say—

ARNOLD: I would say he doesn't think much of it anywhere.

TEACHER: What, exactly, do you persons understand by the term *nationalization?*

TOM: I think it means the government taking over and operating business—doesn't the editorial say socialism and nationalization are the same—that is, nationalization leads to socialism?

TEACHER: All right. Let's say it means the socializing of industry. Industry is socialized when it comes under government ownership. Now, I want you to compare these two editorials, to consider them side by side. Do you see any inconsistency—anything which doesn't seem to jibe?

VERNON: Will you read the first one again—or part of it? (Teacher rereads editorial) Well, it seems to me that one editorial attacks government ownership and the other one praises it.

RALPH: But they are talking about government ownership in different fields—steel and electric power.

TEACHER: Would you say that when the government goes into the electric power business that is socialism?

TOM: It depends on how the government does it—if it benefits all the people, it isn't socialism.

TEACHER: Then you would say that Shasta Dam is not an example of socialism?

TOM: Well, it was built for all of us—it was authorized by a democratically elected Congress.

VERNON: Tom has already said that when the government takes over an industry, that is socialism. I don't see any difference between government ownership here and any place else.

TEACHER: You mean it's all socialism—by definition?

VERNON: Sure.

TEACHER: Getting back to the editorials—how many of you think that the writer—if it was the same man—was contradicting himself when he said one time that government electric power in the United States is not socialism, but government steel in England is?

TOM: Maybe there's a contradiction—but I wouldn't want to call Shasta Dam socialism—then I would have to be against it. (laughter)

TEACHER: Do you feel that perhaps some people in this country think that government ownership of industry in a foreign nation is socialism, but that when it happens here it is merely economic progress?

TOM: Just what is socialism, anyway? Everyone seems to think it's so bad, but, if Reclamation Projects are socialism—well, I don't know. I'm all confused, I guess.

STEP 3: DEVELOPING AND REFINING HYPOTHESES

This step is initiated by asking students general questions such as "Do you have any ideas which explain this discrepancy?" "Can you think of any solutions?" or "What are some possible answers?"

It is necessary to illustrate two procedures which are associated with step 3. One illustration will be of procedures used in moving from judgments of value which are at issue to judgments of fact capable of serving as hypotheses. The other will show how a group may refine judgments of fact in an effort to remove ambiguity. If step 2 deals only with judgments of fact, then step 3 will normally confine itself to their refinement. That is, the initial statements of belief brought under inquiry *become* the hypotheses of step 3. Step 3 involves the formulation of new ideas only when the judgments treated in step 2 are normative in content and not susceptible to the direct test of empirical data.

TEACHER: Yesterday we were discussing the pros and cons of drinking. I think you were concerned mainly with teen-age drinking. I gathered that a number of you were somewhat on the fence—you still hadn't made up your minds one way or another. Just what were some of the issues that came up?

MURIEL: Spud was arguing—I don't know if he meant it—that it's okay for anyone who is a senior in high school to do social drinking—with his parents maybe—like a glass of wine before dinner, or a cocktail in the evening.

TEACHER: Was there any opposition to Spud's opinion?

SPUD: Several people—Marion was one—thought that nobody, young or old —anyplace or anytime—should ever drink anything alcoholic. I suppose she might except vanilla extract when it's used in cooking—

TEACHER: Was the issue, then, between social drinking and total abstinence? I thought maybe some of you were concerned with drinking in still a different situation—

DAN: We were talking about the drinking high-school kids do on dates and at parties—or at games. I don't think we got very far into the morals of that.

TEACHER: Well, then, we have represented in class the opinion that no one should take alcoholic beverages in any situation. Let's get that idea down first. (Writes this on blackboard) And didn't someone also say yesterday that it's okay for adults to drink—persons over 21—but not for teen-agers?

MURIEL: Yes, that point was made. I think it was Anne.

TEACHER: (Writes statement on board) These two opinions both state that it is wrong for teen-agers to drink. Now what were some of the ideas on the other side?

SPUD: Put down mine—that social drinking done temperately and with adult supervision ought to be accepted.

TEACHER: (Writes: Supervised social drinking among high-school youth is proper.) Is there anyone who approves the idea that unsupervised drinking is okay—at parties or on dates?

LOWELL: I know some kids who do it—quite a few in fact. They talk older people into buying the stuff for them.

TEACHER: Do you approve it?

LOWELL: Well, that's a hard question. Probably not—but a lot of pressure is put on you sometimes. It's hard not to go along with the crowd.

TEACHER: Shall I put this down anyway, as a possible position one might take? If none of you accept it, there must be some teen-agers who do. (Writes)

TEACHER: Well, shall we begin with the first of these beliefs—people should not drink under any circumstances? What are some reasons for holding this belief? Marion, you ought to have first chance.

MARION: Well, I think drinking is wrong—immoral.

TEACHER: Is that saying in different words the same thing we have down—or at least not going much beyond it? I think we would be interested in some of the reasons *why* a person might think it's immoral.

MARION: Well—that's what my parents have always said. They don't drink.

TEACHER: Hm-m-m. Maybe you can tell us why your parents hold their opinion.

MARION: Well—they talk about it at home. I guess mother would say that most broken homes are caused by drink, and when a person starts he can't stop. She has a brother—well, I'd better not talk about that. (laughter)

TEACHER: Shall I write down these two reasons for not drinking, then? Drinking leads to broken homes and anyone who drinks at all is likely to become an excessive drinker?

MARION: That about sums it up, I guess.

TEACHER: Are these statements which we could show to be true or false?

MURIEL: I should think so. Wasn't there something in the textbook about drinking and the divorce rate?

The following illustration shows the equally important, and even more difficult and painstaking, job of refining judgments of fact in the direction of usable hypotheses.

TEACHER: We have on the board the proposition "The excess profits tax stifles business initiative." Is the meaning of this statement clear enough so that you are ready to begin talking about its truth or falsity?

ANDY: It isn't clear to me. I know in general how the excess profits tax works —we have already talked about that. But that word *stifle* bothers me.

JAMES: I should think it might mean stop or shut off.

ROBERT: Then you would have to throw the statement out. Business hasn't been stopped or shut off—that sounds like destroyed—by the excess profits tax.

ELAINE: Well, maybe we could define it to mean simply slowed down.

TEACHER: Slowed down in relation to what?

ELAINE: Well, in relation, say, to what is possible.

TEACHER: Then could we define stifle in this case to mean slowed below the maximum possible amount of initiative? (Teacher rewrites statement.)

ANDY: That is certainly a more cautious statement—it's a lot clearer. But I doubt if it's true.

ANDY: Let's try to get the proposition worded right before deciding whether it is true. I don't know for sure what business initiative means.

TEACHER: A good point. Does anyone want to try to define it?

JAMES: Well, it means a willingness to go ahead.

TEACHER: To go ahead? Is that clear to everyone?

AL: What does he mean by go ahead? It seems to me that taking risks is a better term.

TEACHER: Then you would want to say, The excess profits tax reduces willingness to take risks below what it would be without the tax?

ELAINE: I don't like the use of the term *willingness*, but I'm not sure why.

TOM: I don't see how you could measure anything like willingness—we are trying to get a statement which we can prove one way or another.

ELAINE: How about this—suppose we said, The excess profits tax slows down the rate of expansion of business below the maximum possible rate. Willingness to take risks produces expansion, but expansion is something you can talk about more objectively.

TEACHER: Would you go along with a little simpler statement, say, When an excess profits tax is in effect, business expands more slowly than at other times?

STEP 4: TESTING HYPOTHESES

A teacher's first move in connection with step 4 usually is to ask, "How can we go about deciding whether this idea—or solution—is a good one?" or "What kind of information do we need and where can we get it?" Questions like these place responsibility on students for determining methods of testing. This helps them visualize better the procedure they are following, helps them develop a more critical outlook toward use of evidence, and helps to train them in the full use of the problem-solving method.

Of course, there may be no means of testing the hypothesis. Or the available evidence may be so complex or so difficult for students to comprehend that testing is impossible. When no tests can be devised, discussion will end without fulfillment of step 4. In this case, a group may discover that the only conclusion it can draw is that no conclusion is possible.

The following illustration shows how one group of students approached step 4.

TEACHER: Here is the proposition before us: When an excess profits tax is in effect, business expands more slowly than at other times. How are you going to test it? What sort of data would you need?

HAROLD: You could check the rate of expansion of business during the years in which the excess profits tax has been in effect and you could compare that with rates of expansion before that time.

JAMES: I don't think your results would be very dependable. There are too many things which might enter in to throw it off—like wars, for example.

TEACHER: How could war affect it?

JAMES: If you have an excess profits tax only during a war, then business might be expanding pretty rapidly due to government spending and the pressure of war necessity. The rate might be higher than in peacetime, but how would you know that the rate would not have been still higher without an excess profits tax?

HAROLD: I know the approach has its weaknesses—but it might give you some clue.

GEORGE: There is a lot of literature on both sides—I don't know just what all the arguments are, but probably some of the literature discusses the tax in relation to the rate of business expansion—or maybe it talks about incentive.

ELAINE: If the literature does nothing but argue about the effect of the tax on incentive—or initiative—that won't help much. That's dealing with personal motives and not necessarily behavior.

GEORGE: Well, I never really got finished. I was going to say that we might try to get hold of some pamphlets—publications of, say, the CIO on the one hand and the NAM on the other.

JAMES: Or you could read the *Wall Street Journal*.

GEORGE: The literature could be analyzed for whatever it's worth.

RALPH: Somebody told me a long time ago that the surest way to find out something is to go and ask someone. If you want to know if this tax slows down business, the most direct way—of course, it would take time and people —would be to ask a number of business leaders themselves. Ask them, "Do you have any plans for expansion that you are holding up because of the excess profits tax?"

TEACHER: You could organize a committee here in class—is that it—and they could go down town and talk with some businessmen?

RALPH: On the local scene: Yes—

JAMES: If you do, take along a good supply of salt. (laughter)

RALPH: What I first had in mind was to write letters to some national business leaders and—

ANDY: Yes, and I know exactly what all of them will say. They will say, "Yes, it has stifled my business—I'm not expanding because of it." I'll venture to say that very few would tell the truth.

RALPH: Well, the excess profits tax—as I understand it—doesn't affect very many corporations at all in the United States.

ANDY: I still don't see how that would make your results any more objective. They all damn it because they're opposed in principle—they just assume that an excess profits tax is automatically a damper on production.

TEACHER: Does anyone else have a suggestion for testing the proposition before us?

ROGER: Have any other countries tried an excess profits tax similar to ours? If so, we might be able to get information on how it worked, whether it curtailed industrial expansion—or whether economists thought it did.

HAROLD: That suggests something else—why not look into some textbooks on taxation—something written by an objective tax expert—if there are any. I'd like to know what an economist would say.

TEACHER: Any other ideas? (pause) Then how would you like to handle this? Which of the things suggested do you want to try, and how should we organize ourselves?

The above illustration is of a situation where the pooled experiences of a group are not sufficient to test a hypothesis. In the following example, a group pools its present information on a subject and finds that a reasonably adequate conclusion is possible on the basis of it.

TEACHER: So advertising much of the time is not entirely honest, you feel? What kind of support do you have for such an idea?

BETH: Well, I was at a drive-in last night and there was some advertising on the screen before the show—it showed a car that was running on regular gas going up a hill and the motor made an awful noise—like a death rattle. Then it showed the same car pulling up the grade with ethyl gas in the tank and you could hardly hear the motor it was so quiet.

TEACHER: Was that dishonest advertising?

BETH: My dad is a garageman and he says that, unless you have an extra high-compression motor, regular gas is better for your car than ethyl. I don't know why—I don't know anything about cars—but I think he said the motor stays cleaner with regular.

ROD: What about power? I'll bet you get more power with ethyl—

BETH: I don't think so—I've heard dad mention that too.

TEACHER: Just what did the advertising claim—did it claim that ethyl kept your motor cleaner—or had more power?

BETH: Come to think of it, it didn't say so directly. But it sure implied that.

TEACHER: Does anyone have any more examples of what you think is dishonest advertising?

MAYNARD: I read an article in a magazine that said chlorophyll has no medical value—it doesn't stop bad breath, it doesn't keep your teeth from rotting
out, or anything else that the ads say. People have been eating chlorophyll for
millions of years—everytime they eat green plants.

MARGE: I saw a funny cartoon about that—a farmer was planning to give his
cows chlorophyll to keep their breath sweet—and here they were standing
knee deep in grass.

TEACHER: Is the manufactured chlorophyll—the kind which comes in med-
icines and cosmetics—the same chemically as when it occurs in nature? What
I'm getting at is that maybe the two forms don't have the same effect on you.

MAYNARD: I suppose that could be true—but the article I read didn't say anything about it.

RUPERT: What magazine was that in—was it a probusiness magazine or an
antibusiness magazine?

MAYNARD: Well—I don't remember for sure where I saw it—I think it was
Reader's Digest.

TEACHER: Martha, you had your hand up a moment ago.

MARTHA: I think one of the best examples of misleading advertising is in the
cigarette ads. They advertise that a particular brand won't irritate your throat
or make you cough. But doctors say that there is no way to keep any tobacco
from having an irritating effect.

STEP 5: DRAWING CONCLUSIONS

Some pitfalls in the use of evidence may be avoided if a teacher is familiar with rules of evidence and criteria of a good conclusion as described in
Chapter 5. Although it is assumed here that permissiveness is to be observed in the sense that students are allowed full intellectual independence
in examining evidence and drawing conclusions, it is also assumed that a
teacher should ask questions and make recommendations intended to
prevent superficiality of thought. A teacher is obligated to prevent
students from overlooking important evidence or neglecting established
rules of evidence in drawing conclusions. Groups of younger children
and groups inexperienced in problem-solving methods require more help
and criticism than those accustomed to the discussion methods described
here.

A conclusion of an act of thought may be only a restatement of an idea
brought before the group at the start; what was presented at the start as
established knowledge remains established knowledge. It is now seen in a
different light—better grounded and more fully understood—and has
therefore shifted in status from a preconception to a conception (but will
function as a preconception in the next act of thought in which it is involved). In other instances, a conclusion modifies an original statement or
preconception, often in the direction of greater precision and clarity of
statement or in the addition of qualifications. In still other cases, a con-

clusion will affirm an entirely new idea—perhaps something quite contradictory to the original belief.

In the following illustration, a class achieved consensus on one point but remained in disagreement on others:

TEACHER: I wonder if it would be possible for us to draw any conclusions at this point—sum up your thinking if it has jelled at all.

ROGER: It seems to me that we have been moving steadily toward agreement on one point—and that is, that there should be a general lowering of tariffs, in order to stimulate imports and build up dollar balances abroad.

ROBERT: No one has maintained that the United States should continue its gifts in dollars and goods to foreign nations indefinitely, and yet I think it is generally felt that the only way this can be avoided is to help these nations pay their own way. They can do that only by increasing their exports to this country.

TEACHER: Is it the consensus, then, there should be a general lowering of tariffs? (Nods indicate agreement. Teacher writes this on the board) All right. Is there any general agreement as to how much they should be lowered —is it a general abolition of the protective principle itself that we want?

JAMES: Absolutley not. I maintain—and I think there are two or three who agree—that tariffs should remain protective on most products. We might except a few—those that are not particularly important to us but mean a lot to the economies of certain other countries—like lace making, garlic, or handmade rugs.

TEACHER: Okay—we still have our protectionist group. (Writes this conclusion on the board) Any freetraders?

ANDY: I don't think anyone has argued for free trade, although I was pushing in that direction at the beginning of our discussion. I think that now I would favor a tariff for revenue only on most items, but would approve tariffs on the products of essential war industries—like synthetic rubber—if the industry can't compete in foreign markets without tariffs.

TEACHER: Have any other positions emerged from the discussion?

Note that two of the conclusions were carefully qualified. As a result of discussion, students who had advocated without qualification the protective principle had become willing to accept less protection than at present and to exclude one category of items entirely. Freetraders had modified their original stand to permit protective tariffs on essential war industries and to allow for low and income-producing duties generally. Note also that conclusions are in the form of value judgments or policy statements. No proof was adduced for the belief that tariffs should be lowered, but the discussion did apparently help students see that, in order to achieve one of their values (a preference for Europe's paying its own way), it would be necessary to lower tariffs.

The following illustration shows even more clearly how conclusions in the form of value judgments may be formed, and how a teacher through questioning may help students see just what they are doing as they move from value judgments to judgments of fact and back again.

MARION: The conclusion that I've reached as a result of our discussion is that our present treatment of criminals is all wrong.

TEACHER: Oh, why did you reach this conclusion?

MARION: Because of the figures we had showing how many minor and one-time offenders who serve prison terms become big-time criminals after they are released. They are taught to commit the big offenses—and how to go about it—by the criminals they come in contact with in prison.

TEACHER: Then the reason you feel our present method of dealing with criminals is bad is because you think it makes more criminals—multiplies the problem?

MARION: That's right.

TEACHER: There is an assumption there—what it is you are assuming?

MARION: Oh—well—I don't know—

JOHN: Isn't she assuming that it's bad to make more criminals?

MARION: Yes, of course—I thought that was obvious.

TEACHER: Perhaps, but I want to make sure you know exactly what you are doing. You want minor criminals to be reformed rather than turned into big-time crooks and habitual offenders—and you see prison reform as one means to this end. Could you prove that your chief aim here is good—are there any facts, I mean, which would prove it?

MARION: That we ought to try to reduce crime? Well, I guess that's only an opinion—but is there anyone who questions it?

HARRY: There are a lot of people who make a living out of crime—the bigger and oftener the crime, the better—so far as they are concerned. I'll bet they wouldn't agree with you.

MARION: Are you people trying to get me to say I favor more crime?

TEACHER: No—I only wanted to show that our desire to reduce crime is one of our values—although certainly a very widely held one. You can't prove it true or false the way you can a statement about conditions in a prison or the effect of prison life on a man's behavior. That doesn't mean it isn't a good value, of course.

DISCUSSION QUESTIONS AND EXERCISES

1. Studies which have been made of class time spent in different activities suggest that in the social studies relatively little time is given to problem-solving discussion. Some reasons commonly given by teachers for not engaging in discussion more often include:

   a. Discussion is an inefficient means of learning.

   b. Discussions tend to fail because students lack the necessary informational background.

   c. It is difficult to prevent discussions from becoming disorganized and heading off at tangents.

  d. It is difficult to control students during discussion.
  Evaluate each of these arguments.
2. Recalling discussions in which you have been a participant, what would you say were their chief inadequacies? How would you rate them from the standpoint of learning effectiveness? What rules or cautions would you suggest in order to eliminate the chief weaknesses which you have observed?
3. Select a topic which you judge to be suitable for problem-solving discussion in a senior high school and develop a plan for leading a discussion on this topic. Make your plan as concrete as possible, including key questions which you would ask and anticipated responses of students.

REFERENCES

BAIRD, ALBERT C., *Discussion: Principles and Types,* New York, McGraw-Hill, 1943.

A good discussion of different kinds of discussion and the principles which apply to each.

CANTOR, NATHANIEL, *Learning Through Discussion,* Buffalo, N.Y., Human Relations for Industry, 1951.

Application of nondirective therapy to group discussion situations.

McBURNEY, JAMES, and KENNETH HANCE, *Discussion in Human Affairs,* New York, Harper & Row, 1950.

One of the most useful texts on discussion which centers upon clarification of social issues.

NICHOLS, ALAN, *Discussion and Debate,* New York, Harcourt, Brace & World, 1941.

Remains a good reference for students of debate.

CHAPTER II

Evaluating the Results of Reflectively Oriented Teaching

WE HAVE proposed that the foremost purpose of social studies should be to promote reflective analysis of problematic areas of American culture. This purpose has been defended by indicating the chief consequences of achievement. The role of evaluation is to measure the extent to which consequences predicted from a theory of teaching actually follow. If evaluation is to be successful, it is necessary to define these anticipated consequences concretely.

Although they represent two sides of the same coin, we may say that consequences of any approach to teaching fall into two broad categories: (1) social consequences and (2) individual consequences. Social consequences refer to what happens to a social group as a result of its educational practices and are reflected in the functioning of institutions of government, economics, and social life. If our schools were to achieve greater success in promoting reflective study of areas of irrational belief and behavior, we may infer that eventually this would be reflected in social phenomena such as more general acceptance of the democratic core values of the culture, greater social cohesion and stability, enhanced ability of society to solve its problems, and closer correspondence between the professed ideals and behavior of society. Social consequences of an approach to teaching are hard to measure reliably. It is always difficult to determine the role of formal education in producing a given social condition—for example, if Americans should vote a Fascist or Communist into the presidency, what part of this behavior could be attributed to the kind of teaching which they have experienced? In any case, the attempt to evaluate the success or failure of education in terms of social consequences is a long-range procedure. Today's teaching may not begin to show observable social effects for half a century.

Because of such difficulties, evaluation of teaching must, for the most part, confine itself to more-or-less immediate consequences as reflected in the thinking and behavior of individual students. But if this kind of evaluation is to show results, anticipated outcomes must be defined with great care. We assume that consequences such as the following may be expected from teaching which emphasizes the reflective analysis of social issues and personal beliefs:

1. Learning of meaningful generalizations (concepts, ideas, theory) in relation to critical areas of controversy; and learning of relevant facts as data—i.e., in their evidential relationships to ideas.
2. Achieving generalizations and supporting data which tend (a) to be internally consistent and (b) to reflect all available and obtainable evidence, both experiential and experimental.
3. Acquiring an understanding of the nature and implications of reflective methodology, and forming the habit of a reflective approach when faced with a problem.

For a social-studies teacher pursuing a reflective approach to teaching, evaluation takes the form of trying to determine how well students are achieving beliefs and behaviors in line with predicted consequences such as those given above. Such a teacher will try to determine the degree to which students are conceptualizing (in contrast to memorizing isolated facts), achieving more consistent and better-grounded beliefs, and learning habitually to tackle problems reflectively.

Evaluation also tries to expose reasons for achievement or lack of achievement of goals. This is its *diagnostic* function. Evaluation therefore employs two basic types of tests, achievement and diagnostic. However, many tests perform both functions with considerable adequacy. In the present chapter, we shall be concerned with techniques which have been developed for measuring achievement in situations dominated by reflective teaching; in general, the same techniques can serve valuable diagnostic functions.

Unfortunately, techniques of evaluation so far devised for the purposes we have in mind are not entirely adequate. Although we have tests designed to measure consistency in attitudes, and ability to use reflective processes, their accuracy is open to doubt. Some tests make different assumptions from those we have made. Many tests designed for use in social-studies classes bear but lightly on critical social issues as exemplified in the closed areas of culture.

The Measurement of Understanding

In Chapter 4, we dealt generally with the nature of concepts. From that discussion it should be apparent that a student who is able to say that "an income tax accords with the principle of ability-to-pay" does not necessarily understand an income tax. If we want to know whether he has achieved worthwhile conceptualization, we shall have to ascertain more about his thought processes than merely whether he can state a textbook definition. This does not mean that recall is never involved in the measurement of conceptual learning; but recall alone is not evidence of conceptualization. We do have evidence of conceptualization when a student demonstrates ability to *use* something he has learned in a novel situation: when he generalizes from data, when he makes inferences, and when he applies principles fruitfully in new confronting situations. These same operations may also be taken as evidence of the presence of thinking. In other words, thinking rather than mere recall during a testing situation is the kind of behavior most likely to be taken as evidence of conceptual learning.

We shall discuss later various tests for measuring thinking processes of students. These instruments are intended to measure a certain kind of concept—that is, the extent to which a student has conceptualized the thinking process.

In the present section, we want to find out how a teacher may measure the learning of many other concepts. An instrument which measures a student's understanding of events in American history requires a student to think. But it does not measure only how well he thinks. It measures, too, the conceptual results of his thinking. It tells us how well he had thought about the significance of certain events in American history.

As indicated above, techniques for measuring the amount and quality of conceptualization achieved in particular subject areas remain primitive when compared with techniques used to measure mere recall of arbitrary associations. Much of the progress which has been made consists of refining objective or short-answer types of examination so that they will have fewer clues which enable a student to guess or merely to recall a correct answer. Less progress has been made in devising new instruments. We shall first survey some of the refinements made in standard testing items such as true-false, multiple-choice, and matching questions.

IMPROVEMENTS OF TRUE-FALSE EXAMINATIONS

Various studies have shown that true-false examinations have contained specific determiners which provide a test-wise student with a basis for guessing the correct answers. Hawkes, Lindquist, and Mann have summarized these studies as follows: "Four out of five statements containing 'all' were false. Four out of five statements containing 'none' were true. Nine out of ten statements containing 'only' were false. Three out of four statements containing 'generally' were true. Four out of five 'enumeration' statements were true. Two out of three 'reason' or 'because' statements were false. Three out of four statements containing 'always' were false. The longer the statement, the more likely it is to be true." [1]

These results were based on studies of examinations actually constructed and used by teachers. The point is not that teachers should avoid statements including the use of "all" and other terms indicated above but rather that, in a given examination, at least half the statements using a particular "cue term" should be false and half should be true. This kind of reform would not guarantee the measurement of understanding but it would reduce the chances that a student could guess the correct answer.

In addition to this reform a teacher would have to test for interpretive and inferential, as well as purely descriptive, facts. True-false items may indicate various degrees of understanding, including understanding of descriptive facts, interpretive facts, and inferential facts. The following three items represent these three levels of understanding:

T F   The United States makes use of protective tariffs. (descriptive) (true)

T F   A rise in the cost of living reduces the gold backing of a dollar. (interpretive) (false)

T F   During World War II the inflationary spiral was characterized by a series of wage increases. Each wage increase was followed by a price increase. It has been argued that labor unions were largely responsible for wartime inflation. Is it true or false that this argument assumes that there would have been very little inflation had the government frozen wages? (inferential) (true)

The validity of a true-false item is reduced when it is subject to two conflicting interpretations, the more obvious one being keyed as correct. Inferior students are more likely to respond to the obvious meaning of such an item, and mark it accordingly, whereas students with greater depth of understanding may respond to the hidden meaning. As a result, a student who has thought carefully about the subject may get a lower score on a true-false examination than a mediocre student. If it is depth of understanding which we are trying to measure, then tests of this sort violate the purpose of evaluation. To a large degree, careful phrasing of items will eliminate this problem.[2]

Another common error in the construction of true-false items is the practice of burying a minor false item in a statement the major elements of which are correct. The following, taken from Hawkes, Lindquist, and Mann, are examples of good and poor items:

[1] Herbert E. Hawkes, E. F. Lindquist, and C. R. Mann, *The Construction and Use of Achievement Examinations*, Houghton Mifflin, 1936, p. 72.

[2] *Ibid.*, p. 55.

Bad   T F 1. The Sherman Anti-Trust Act, passed in 1870, declared com-
           binations in restraint of trade illegal.

Better   T F 2. The Sherman Anti-Trust Act, which declared combinations in
           restraint of trade illegal, was passed in 1870.[3]

Experience with items of this kind indicates that students, whether
they are inferior or superior in depth of understanding, tend to mark the
first example true since the major elements are true. This first example is a
"catch" question; such questions, contrary to opinion, are unlikely to
measure understanding. One does not measure depth of insight by deliberately distracting a student's attention from the crucial elements in an
examination question. As Hawkes, Lindquist, and Mann have explained:
"They [statements of this kind] tend to trip up the student whose knowledge is sound but who naturally ignores what should logically be minor
or unimportant elements in the statement and who interprets a statement
in the straightforward fashion characteristic of ordinary reading. Statements of this kind tend to test for the student's mental alertness or 'test-
wiseness' rather than for his knowledge or understanding of the subject
matter involved." [4]

The same kind of reasoning applies to the construction of true-false
items which contain a "reason" or a "because" element. The false element, if there is one, should be in the "reason." The following is an
example of good and bad practice:

Bad   T F 1. Grant's administration was marked by very little political scan-
           dal, because his own honesty was an incentive to those holding
           political offices.

Better   T F 2. Grant's administration was marked by serious political scandal
           because . . . (either correct or incorrect reason may be pro-
           vided).[5]

The second item is better than the first because the false element, if
there is one, is left until the last. If the first part of such an item were
false, and the last part true, some students—and not necessarily those with
the least knowledge or understanding—would be "caught" by the item.

Even the most careful construction of true-false items leaves much to
be desired. Test makers have steadily lost confidence in the technique
because of the difficulty of eliminating ambiguity and reducing guessing.
Hawkes, Lindquist, and Mann are of the opinion that much of the ambiguity of true-false items is inherent in the technique. It also seems prob-

---

[3] *Ibid.*, p. 156.
[4] *Ibid.*, p. 157.
[5] *Ibid.*, p. 156.

able that frequent use of this technique encourages students to do "either-or" thinking.

Despite the inadequacies of the true-false technique, Hawkes, Lindquist, and Mann suggest two circumstances in which true-false items may be justified:

The true-false test appears to be particularly well adapted to those situations in which one wishes to test for the persistence of popular misconceptions or superstitious beliefs, where the suggestion of a correct response will make a multiple-choice item too obvious. It is also well adapted to the situation in which it is impossible or extremely difficult to find enough plausible alternate responses to make a multiple-choice item, or in which there are only two *possible* responses, as in the following item: "In a lead-zinc cell, the lead plate is *positively* charged." Here there are obviously only two possible forms of the statement—"is positively charged" and . . . "is negatively charged"—and the construction of a multiple-choice item would be impossible.[6]

IMPROVEMENT OF MULTIPLE-CHOICE ITEMS

The multiple-choice technique has grown in popularity and there is no doubt that it is generally superior to the true-false scheme when one's purpose is the testing of certain kinds of understanding. It is, however, subject to misuse, and there is nothing in the technique itself which guarantees measurement of understanding. If it is used largely for the asking of *who, what, when,* and *where* questions, it is no better than the true-false technique. On the other hand, it may ask *how, why, with what consequences,* or *of what significance* questions, which require students to interpret events, institutions, and personalities. True-false items are generally ill adapted to asking the latter type of question.

Hawkes, Lindquist and Mann feel that multiple-choice items are better than any other short-answer form for the measuring of inferential reasoning, reasoned understanding, and judgment or discrimination. However, unusual care is required in their construction.

An example of the direct-question multiple-choice item is the following:

Which of the following U.S. industries is characterized by relatively free price competition?

...... 1. steel
...... 2. petroleum
...... 3. nonsupported agriculture
...... 4. farm machinery manufacturing

An example of the incomplete-sentence form is as follows:

Labor in the U.S. is generally more productive than labor in foreign countries because

[6] *Ibid.,* p. 154.

...... 1. American workmen have higher IQs than foreign workmen.
...... 2. American factories use more capital per worker.
...... 3. American laborers work more strenuously than foreign laborers.
...... 4. Americans are more inventive and ingenious than foreigners.

The direct-question form is generally thought superior to the incomplete-sentence form because it is less likely to be ambiguous and to contain clues which give away the answers. (The foregoing example, however, is of a type which could just as well be handled through true-false items.) If the incomplete-sentence form uses an initial statement which is the equivalent of a direct question, then these weaknesses may be eliminated. To be avoided is the type of incomplete-sentence item which is essentially a collection of true-false items, each beginning with the same phrase, as in the following example taken from Hawkes, Lindquist, and Mann:

The Declaration of Independence (1) was drafted by Thomas Jefferson, (2) was signed in 1778, (3) contained an indictment of the English king, (4) was signed by all the members of the First Continental Congress.[7]

As with other types of short-answer questions, multiple-choice items must be phrased so they will not contain irrelevant clues to the correct response. For example, it is advisable to avoid the use of textbook language or pat questions and answers; unfamiliar phrasing is more likely to insure that questions will be answered in terms of underlying meanings rather than simple recall. If stereotyped phrasing is used, it should be used in the incorrect responses. Such practice can mislead rote learners and reveal their lack of understanding. Another type of clue is the tendency of teachers to make the correct response consistently longer or shorter than incorrect responses. When this is done regularly, students soon "catch on."

Inclusion in the correct response of the same word, words, or phrases as are contained in the question or introductory statement forms another irrelevant clue. Because of its phraseology, a student with no understanding of government regulatory agencies should be able to answer the following item.

Railroad companies and other companies carrying on interstate commerce are now regulated by a commission appointed by the President of the United States. This commission is called

...... the Civil Service Commission
...... the National Chamber of Commerce
...... the Interstate Commerce Commission[8]

[7] *Ibid.*, p. 140.
[8] *Ibid.*, p. 70.

Of similar nature is the error of making one or all incorrect responses grammatically inconsistent with the introductory question or statement. For example, the verb of an introductory statement might call for a plural noun in any correct choice but the test maker might inadvertently use singular nouns in some of the wrong choices.

One further irrelevant clue is the tendency habitually to place the correct choice in a particular position with reference to other choices. For example, a test maker is likely to think of the correct choice first, and unless he guards against it, he may place a predominant number of correct choices at the beginning of the group of choices. Students soon sense any uniformity in placement of correct answers.

An important rule for the construction of any multiple-choice item is that all choices be made to sound plausible. Any choice which is obviously incorrect is eliminated on sight by students taking the test, and therefore should not be included in the first place. The following item illustrates this error:

According to most labor economists, what is the central aim of organized labor in the United States today?

...... 1. to achieve basic social reforms, such as elimination of slums
...... 2. to improve wages and conditions of employment
...... 3. to elect government officials who are sympathetic to labor
...... 4. to destroy the American economic system

To any normally bright student the last choice will appear so farfetched that his thought will immediately focus on the first three. In effect, the foregoing item is a three-choice one. Occasionally a multiple-choice item is so constructed that all but the correct choice seems implausible. Such an item measures nothing except the ability of a student to read. A teacher must be careful, however, not to make wrong choices so plausible that an item is negatively discriminating, in which case it will be checked incorrectly more often by good than by poor students.

An item may discriminate negatively for several reasons. In the following example, students who selected choice number 1 were on the average superior in achievement to students who selected choice number 4, the correct answer.

What was one of the immediate results of the War of 1812?

(1) the introduction of a period of intense sectionalism
(2) the destruction of the United States Bank
(3) the defeat of the Jeffersonian Party
(4) the final collapse of the Federalist Party [9]

Hawkes, Lindquist, and Mann explain this response as follows:

[9] *Ibid.*, p. 59.

. . . The pupils selecting the first and incorrect response apparently did so because of positive but insufficient learning. They knew that a period of intense sectionalism did set in before the middle of the century, and therefore chose the first response. Apparently, they did not know, or failed to recall, that a short period of intense nationalism was an immediate result of the Second War with Great Britain, and that this war, therefore, could not be considered as "introducing" an era of sectional strife. Other pupils, with less knowledge in general, were able to select the correct response since they were not attracted to the first response by a certain knowledge that intense sectionalism did develop in the nineteenth century. . . .[10]

Negative discrimination may sometimes result from misinformation on the part of a test maker. The following item illustrates this effect:

In the second half of the fifteenth century the Portuguese were searching for an all-water route to India because:

    (1) They wished to rediscover the route traveled by Marco Polo.
    (2) The Turks had closed the old routes.
    (3) The Spanish had proved that it was possible to reach the east by sailing westward.
    (4) An all-water route would make possible greater profits.[11]

A superior student might reject the answer keyed as correct (number 2) because of acquaintance with recent historical research, which regards the second response as insufficient explanation of Portuguese attempts to round Africa.

A similar result may be obtained when an item deals with a controversial subject for which the authoritative answer is at variance with popular opinion. The following item discriminated negatively because its keyed answer (number 3) conflicts with the popularly held belief—also expressed in some textbooks—that altruistic motives were primarily responsible for our entry into World War I:

America's entry into the World War was largely caused by the
    (1) fear that the defeat of the Allies would lead to the overthrow of republican government in France.
    (2) violation of Belgian neutrality.
    (3) fear of losses by the moneyed interests if the Allies were defeated.
    (4) declaration of war by Italy.[12]

The foregoing examples illustrate the fact that a multiple-choice item may fail to measure what it is intended to measure. The fundamental

[10] *Ibid.*, p. 60.
[11] *Ibid.*, p. 63.
[12] *Ibid.*, p. 64.

problem is stated by Hawkes, Lindquist, and Mann: "In a general achievement test intended for a given group . . . an item testing for a high level of understanding will function effectively only if there is in the group a significant proportion of students who have actually attained that high level. If the group tested does not include a reasonable number of such students, the item not only will fail to discriminate as it should but may discriminate in the wrong direction." [13]

The kind of invalidity discussed above will be reduced to the extent that a teacher makes successful use of the reflective method. Such a teacher need not construct items pitched at a low level of understanding. He can test for a level of conceptual learning which the commercial publisher of standardized tests cannot, for the latter must take into account the generally low level of understanding which is characteristic of his mass market.

THE IMPROVEMENT OF MATCHING ITEMS

A matching item is fundamentally a variation of a multiple-choice item, just as the latter is a variation of a true-false item. Matching items are not as well adapted to the testing of understanding as are multiple-choice items. The chief use of matching items is testing for descriptive information. However, some measuring of understanding may be achieved when one column consists of principles or laws, and the second column consists of situations which can be explained when they are matched with the appropriate principle or law.

A matching item is more susceptible to technical imperfections than is even a multiple-choice item. One of the most common sources of difficulty is the use of incomplete sentences, which makes it possible for a student to respond correctly by looking for grammatical consistency. The following example illustrates this bad practice:

......	1. Most normally green-plants lose their color when	a. through their stomata
......	2. The common characteristic of flowering plants is	b. contracts into a rounded mass
......	3. Almost all plants which form coal	c. grown in the dark
......	4. When an expanded amoeba is strongly stimulated it	d. are now extinct
		e. the formation of a reproductive body [14]

Another kind of clue is offered when a matching item lacks homogeneity. When an item possesses heterogeneity, alternate responses lack the plausibility they should have in order for the item to be valid. Since a

[13] *Ibid.*, p. 61.
[14] *Ibid.*, p. 69.

matching item is really a multiple-choice item which employs the same
responses several times, the ideal exercise is one in which each particle in
one of the columns is a plausible answer for all particles in the other column. The following are examples of wrong and right practice respec-
tively:

...... The law that forbade slavery north of the Ohio	1. Mason and Dixon line
...... A boundary between two colonies, that later became famous as the division be-tween slave and free states	2. Dred Scott Decision
	3. Spanish Armada
...... The fleet whose defeat in 1588 gave England control of the Atlantic	4. Ordinance of 1787
	5. Missouri Compromise [15]

...... A boundary between two colonies, that later became famous as the division be-tween free and slave states	1. Mason and Dixon line
	2. Missouri River
...... Marked the northern boundary of slave territory in the area immediately west of the Alleghenies	3. Ohio River
	4. $49°$
...... Was intended to be the boundary be-tween free and slave territory in the Louisiana Purchase	5. $36° 30'$ [16]

The second item will have more discriminating power than the first
because students will be unable to guess the correct responses so easily.
Both items have the advantage of listing more particles in one column
than in the other, which reduces the chances that students will reach a
correct answer by elimination.

ESSAY EXAMINATIONS

Some educators believe that essay examinations are superior to any
short-answer technique for the testing of understanding. They deplore
the tendency of teachers to use short-answer examinations virtually to the
exclusion of oral or written examinations which require students to organize and express ideas. Opposition to declining use of essay examinations is probably greatest among college and university faculties. High-
school teachers by contrast have made what seems to them a necessary
compromise with the exigencies of student overload. A high-school
teacher who teaches five classes a day, each with thirty or more students,
feels he does not have time to read carefully answers to essay examinations.

[15] *Ibid.,* p. 172.
[16] *Ibid.,* p. 173.

This compromise does not appear as a solution when one remembers that the time saved in grading short-answer examinations would be more than canceled if the teacher were to exercise proper care in their construction. It takes hours of reflection to build a good short-answer test, and further hours of labor to keep it up to date. If teachers are to justify the displacement of the essay examination, they will need a more convincing argument than the claim that they are too busy to read essay examinations.

Any proper assessment of essay examinations must take into account the different kinds of questions which may be asked on them. Some common kinds of questions could be asked just as well on a short-answer examination. It would be better to ask such questions via a short-answer examination and thus make possible the asking of more questions and consequently the covering of a larger sample of understandings or facts. A question such as "Describe the chief features of the Treaty of Versailles" calls for a highly factual response which could be covered more effectively in a short-answer test. It is important to remember that one of the criticisms of essay examinations has been the unreliability of scoring. If a factual outcome in learning can be covered in a short-answer test, which is reliably and objectively scored, a teacher gains nothing by asking the same question on an essay examination, which is more difficult to score objectively.

Sims has made a study of the kinds of questions asked on essay examinations, and most of them do not require a thoughtful handling of materials in answering.[17] He found three types of essay questions: (1) simple-recall, (2) short-answer, and (3) discussion. Obviously, the first two do not require a student to manipulate ideas creatively. They ask him *who, what, where,* or *when* questions, or they ask him to *list, state, name,* or *find.* The descriptive material covered in such items could be covered more objectively and more fully in a short-answer examination. Questions which ask students to *discuss, explain, describe, compare,* or *outline* are more likely to reveal the extent and quality of conceptualization, but even this would depend on how a teacher and his students interpreted the questions. For example, for some persons the term *explain* can have a meaning which amounts to recall rather than reflection. When asked to explain an event some students will simply list three causes from the textbook. Others will carry on a discussion comparable to a scientist's attempt to explain in laboratory terms. It is undoubtedly more difficult to control a student's mode of response in an essay than in a short-answer examination.

[17] Verner Martin Sims, "Essay Examination Questions Classified on the Basis of Objectivity," *School and Society,* January 16, 1932, pp. 100–102.

Apparently the worth of an essay examination depends very much on what kinds of questions are asked and how a student interprets them. Also important is the manner in which students are accustomed to approach examinations. Although an essay question may be designed to evoke a reflective response, few students may respond in this way because of contrary habits. If one is accustomed to parroting a textbook, or to displays of empty rhetoric, an essay question may reveal little more about his depth of understanding than will a short-answer question. Also, students who are unable to express themselves on paper may fail to reveal the actual conceptualization which they have achieved. Limitations of time may handicap slow writers and prevent their answers from reflecting fully the quality of their thought.

A recommended reform has been the "open book" examination, which may even be taken outside the classroom and at a more leisurely pace. It is possible to ask questions which cannot be answered straight from a book but only after a student has reflected upon ideas in a book. An even more promising procedure may be the assignment of a short research paper. This paper can be written as leisurely and reflectively as an "open book" examination. Either short research papers or "open book" examinations are probably preferable to traditional essay examinations.

If one views the short research paper as a superior form of essay examination, there is no issue between short-answer and essay examinations. Both can be used for reflective and conceptual ends if the intent and skill of a teacher permit. The only advantage that a short-answer examination would have would be in the objectivity of its scoring and the greater scope of its coverage. Useful techniques have been developed for objectifying the scoring of essay examinations,[18] and some of these could just as well be applied to the grading of a short research paper. What a short-answer examination contributes in scope of coverage a short research paper can contribute in depth of treatment. These techniques can be used effectively in combination for measurement of conceptual understanding.

The Measurement of Attitudes

For practical purposes of measurement there is no difference between an attitude and a value. We may define an attitude as a persistent feeling tone with reference to some object or process in the environment, and value as an attitude which has been intellectualized or clarified as a result of reflective scrutiny. When a person thinks about an attitude, so that he is

[18] See Verner Martin Sims, "The Objectivity, Reliability, and Validity of an Essay Examination Graded by Rating," *Journal of Educational Research,* October, 1931, pp. 216–223. Also see Hawkes, Lindquist, and Mann, *op. cit.,* pp. 207–209.

fully aware of it and of its implications, we say that he has acquired a value. However, a statement of preference (value judgment) may reflect either an attitude or a value.

We assume that it is possible to discover attitudes (or values) of a student by requiring him to respond to a series of preference statements (i.e., value judgments). For example, suppose a student is confronted with the statement "The United States made a big mistake when it joined the United Nations" and says he agrees. Assuming he understands the thought expressed in the statement, and that his answer is sincere, we may infer that he has a negative attitude toward membership in the United Nations.

To date, measurement of attitudes has commonly taken the form of asking students to respond to series of statements of the general type indicated above. Although several weaknesses of this procedure have been identified, probably the greatest obstacle to overcome is lack of sincerity on the part of students. Because teaching is so often authoritarian (even when teachers do not intend it to be), students come to feel it expedient to respond to attitude tests in what they see as "respectable" ways. When confronted with a value judgment, they are likely first to decide what response would be most pleasing to the teacher or other adults who might learn of the test results. Attitudes thus remain concealed.

To acquaint readers more fully with what has been done in the field of attitude testing, and to indicate more specifically what some of the problems are, we shall review some of the attitude scales which have been developed in the United States.

SCALE OF BELIEFS 4.21 AND 4.31

This instrument was developed by the Evaluation Staff of the Eight Year Study. It is intended to gather evidence on the liberalism, conservatism, uncertainty, and consistency of student attitudes in areas such as democracy, economic relations, labor and unemployment, race–nationalism, and militarism. There are a number of items for each area on each of the two forms, 4.21 and 4.31. The six areas mentioned above were considered among the most controversial at the time the test was developed. No doubt a similar instrument constructed now would include areas not covered in the original scale.

In this test a liberal point of view is revealed when students subscribe to statements which endorse "freedom of speech; democratic processes in government; responsibility of the government for promoting the welfare of all groups in society with respect to health, security for old age, and the protection of consumers; and reinterpretation of the Constitution and other basic laws in keeping with present-day social and economic demands." [19] A conservative cluster of attitudes is revealed when students

[19] For a fuller treatment of this problem as well as for a more complete discussion

"approve restrictions on freedom of speech," [20] and when they say it is all right "to limit the responsibilities of government for social welfare, and to favor a strict interpretation of the Constitution." [21] These are the definitions of liberalism and conservatism for the first part of the test, which deals with democracy and its interpretations. There are similar definitions of liberalism and conservatism for each of the other five parts of the test.

Each form of the test, 4.21 and 4.31, has 100 statements. Students are asked to indicate whether they agree with, disagree with, or are uncertain about each statement. Agreement with certain items along with disagreement with certain other items indicates liberal attitudes. Likewise, there are items with which agreement or disagreement indicates conservatism.

The uncertain responses, although easy to count, are difficult to interpret. A student may mark a particular statement "uncertain" for one or more of three reasons: He may not understand the statement; he may understand it but be uncertain of his attitude toward it; or he may be afraid to reveal his position to the teacher.

Consistency is measured by comparing the responses on 4.21 with the responses on 4.31. For example, statement 97 on 4.21 reads "It is all right for Negroes to be paid lower wages than whites for similar kinds of work" while statement 192 on 4.31 reads "The same wages should be paid to Negroes as to whites for work which requires the same ability and training." If a student agrees with both statements, or disagrees with both, or agrees or disagrees with either statement when he is uncertain about the other one, such response is taken as evidence of inconsistency. A consistency score is easier to interpret than an inconsistency score because of the difficulties posed by the uncertainty response. Obviously, agreement-uncertainty as a paired response is not the same degree and perhaps not the same kind of inconsistency as agreement-agreement.

Consistency is counted as a percentage of the total items on either form. A consistency score can be derived for each of the six areas as well as for the whole scale. The least consistent areas are the ones within which students need the most clarification. However, any growth toward greater consistency must be interpreted with considerable care. It is customary to administer the two forms at the beginning and end of a school year (at the beginning and end of a unit of work is not good practice since the span of time covered by a unit is usually too short for significant change in attitudes). A higher consistency score cannot always be taken as

---

of Interpretation of Data 2.51 and 2.52, see Eugene Smith and Ralph Tyler, *Appraising and Recording Student Progress*, Harper & Row, 1942, p. 217.

[20] *Ibid.*

[21] *Ibid.*

evidence that reflective clarification of attitudes has occurred. The internal structure of the test is such that a student who becomes more liberal or more conservative will also become more consistent. If a student has been thoroughly indoctrinated by a conservative or a liberal teacher, his responses to the test at the end of the school year may be more certain and more consistent even though he has not reflected very much on his attitudes.

It has been many years since the Scale of Beliefs was constructed, and rather than use the original form teachers should build new forms based upon the original structure and capable of sampling attitudes in closed areas. In constructing any scale of this kind certain precautions are necessary. The definition of democracy implied by the scale should be explicitly recognized by the teacher when he formulates items. In the attempt to measure consistency a teacher should not make contradictions too apparent. The statements "Negroes should not be paid as much as whites" and "Negroes should be paid as much as whites" present a contradiction which is too easy because it is too sharp. The example given earlier is more illustrative of correct phrasing and a desirable degree of contradiction.

THURSTONE SCALES FOR THE MEASUREMENT OF SOCIAL ATTITUDES [22]

These scales consist of weighted items and therefore are intended to measure the depth of an attitude. Each scale has a list of statements dealing with the same general topic. There are usually twenty or more statements, each with a point value assigned to it by a jury of adults. The higher the point value the more unfavorable the attitude expressed by those who check the statement. The scale for measuring the attitude toward war is typical of Thurstone's technique. The following is an excerpt from this scale:

(2.7) 1. The benefits of war outweigh its attendant evils.
(7.8) 6. The misery and suffering of war are not worth its benefits.
(9.4) 16. It is difficult to imagine any situation in which we should be justified in sanctioning or participating in another war.
(10.6) 20. He who refuses to fight is a true hero.
(10.7) 22. It is the moral duty of the individual to refuse to participate in any way in any war, no matter what the cause.[23]

The numbers in parentheses indicate the point value assigned the statements by the jury. The student checks the statements with which he

[22] L. L. Thurstone and E. J. Chase, *The Measurement of Attitudes,* University of Chicago Press, 1929.
[23] L. L. Thurstone, *Attitude Scales, Attitude Toward War,* Form A, University of Chicago.

agrees, and his score is the median point value for all the statements he checks. The scale for measuring a student's attitude toward war is indirectly a measure of his pacifism. The higher his score the more pacifistic he is. The directions tell students that there is no right answer to the test.

In addition to this scale, Thurstone also has scales on God, Church, Negro, Treatment of Criminals, Constitution, Birth Control, Chinese, Germans, Sunday Observance, Law, Censorship, Evolution, and Capital Punishment, all constructed in roughly the same way.[24]

REMMERS ATTITUDE SCALES

These scales, like the ones developed by Thurstone, consist of weighted items. Both Remmers and Thurstone make use of the technique of equal-appearing intervals. The construction of a scale based upon equal-appearing intervals follows steps analogous to certain practices in psychophysics. First, a large number of statements of opinion concerning some attitude-object are formulated. Second, these statements are given to a jury, or group of judges, who are asked to rate each statement on an eleven-point scale. The neutral statements are sorted into the midpoint of the scale. The very favorable statements are placed at one end of the scale at varying distances from the midpoint of neutrality. The unfavorable statements are distributed from the center to the other end of the scale. If there are 100 judges, there is likely to be some disagreement over the weighting of each statement. The average weight assigned to each statement is taken as the correct weight. Some of the statements may be given radically different weightings, and these are discarded. The third step is the arrangement of acceptable statements on the attitude scale. Remmers arranges his statements according to decreasing favorableness, i.e., the first statement is the most favorable one. Thurstone prefers a random arrangement of statements.[25] Research with the two scales indicates no particular advantage for either arrangement.

The Remmers scales are more general than those by Thurstone and are advertised as Master Attitude Scales. They purport to measure attitudes toward attitude-objects such as Any Disciplinary Procedure, Any Proposed Social Action, Any Teacher, or Any Racial or National Group.

---

[24] For a good discussion of these scales, the difficulties involved in their construction, and criticisms of their validity see Marie Jahoda, Morton Deutsch, and Stewart W. Cook, *Research Methods in Social Relations, Part 1 Basic Processes,* Dryden Press, 1951, pp. 190–194.

[25] For a much fuller discussion of how to construct an attitude scale based upon equal-appearing intervals see H. H. Remmers and N. L. Gage, *Educational Measurement and Evaluation,* Harper & Row, 1943, pp. 390–392. For a fairly complete list of both Remmers and Thurstone scales see the same work, pp. 392–393.

Students are told to write in the name of the teacher, the social action, or the racial group toward which they have been asked to respond.

The following excerpt from *A Scale for Measuring Attitudes Toward Any Proposed Social Action, Form A*,[26] illustrates the nature of the Remmers approach:

(10.9)   1. Is the best thing that can ever come into existence.
 (9.3)   7. Is greatly needed.
 (8.5) 15. Is sure to be effective.
 (6.1) 30. Cannot do any serious harm.
 (3.8) 40. Dodges the real issue.
 (2.8) 44. Is based upon an unsound principle.
 (1.2) 50. Is perfectly absurd.

THE LIKERT SCALE

This scale is also intended to measure the intensity of an attitude. Students are presented with a list of statements and indicate the extent to which they agree or disagree with each one. They are usually instructed to mark each statement as follows: agree strongly, agree somewhat, uncertain, disagree somewhat, or disagree strongly. The Likert Scale is easier to construct than the Thurstone or Remmers scales as it does not require the cumbersome use of a jury. Sometimes an evaluator will use some variation of the Likert Scale, with a six-point rather than a five-point rating scale. The following excerpt from the F Scale used in a study of the authoritarian personality is illustrative of one variation:

Mark each statement in the left margin according to how much you agree or disagree with it. *Please mark every one.* Write in $+1$, $+2$, $+3$, or -1, -2, -3 depending on how you feel in each case.

1. I AGREE A LITTLE	1. I DISAGREE A LITTLE
2. I AGREE PRETTY MUCH	2. I DISAGREE PRETTY MUCH
3. I AGREE VERY MUCH	3. I DISAGREE VERY MUCH

 1. Human nature being what it is, there will always be war and conflict.
 4. It is up to the government to make sure that everyone has a secure job and a good standard of living.
11. When a person has a problem or worry, it is best for him not to think about it, but to keep busy with more cheerful things.
16. Men like Henry Ford, or J. P. Morgan, who overcame all competition on the road to success, are models for all young people to admire and imitate.[27]

[26] H. H. Remmers, Division of Educational Reference, Purdue University, Lafayette, Indiana.

[27] T. W. Adorno, E. Frenkel-Brunswik, D. J. Levinson, and R. N. Sanford, *The Authoritarian Personality*, Harper & Row, 1950.

Unlike Remmers and Thurstone, Likert has not prepared attitude scales for commercial distribution. His chief contribution has been the idea of a five- or six-point rating scale for each statement in an attitude test. Ideally, the rating scale is repeated after each statement instead of being presented once at the beginning of the test as we gave it above. In common with the Remmers and Thurstone scales, the Likert Scale attempts to measure intensity without trying to measure consistency.

VALUE ANALYSIS

Attitude scales are sometimes criticized for the rigidity of their structure. Some authorities believe that students are more likely to reveal their attitudes in an unstructured situation. Actually, no testing situation is completely unstructured; what these authorities probably want is a situation which is structured so that individuals are relatively free to express attitudes in their own manner. Value analysis as it has been developed by Louis E. Raths and Newton Hodgson may be an answer to the need for a more valid measure of attitudes.

This technique involves placing students in some kind of situation to which they are asked to react by writing answers to certain questions. They may be placed in the situation by teacher assignment, or they may help determine the situation through teacher-pupil planning. Possible situations would be visiting a public housing project, observing a legislative committee at work, taking part in a cleanup campaign, trying to get signatures on a petition. The situations selected are supposed to be ones likely to elicit attitude expressions from students. Students are asked to write answers to questions such as the following:

1. What did you like or approve in the situation?
2. What did you dislike or disapprove in the situation?
3. What recommendations do you have for improving the situation?

A teacher may vary the questions, but he always tries to get evidence on students' feelings of approval and disapproval and recommendations for change. This method may be criticized on the ground that it does not yield a neat quantitative score susceptible to several kinds of pretty statistical juggling. However, it is not entirely free from quantitative features. It is possible, for example, to count the number of things which the writer of a certain response is against as compared to the number of things toward which he is favorable. It is even possible to combine certain responses to form categories. Certain responses when placed together may be taken as evidence of a person's attitude toward government, human nature, and a variety of other objects or processes.

A few observers of this technique have argued that it has the virtue of taking its categories from the free responses of students rather than forcing students to respond to certain predetermined categories, as they are obliged to do on attitude scales. However, any teacher can take the free responses of a student and force them into certain categories which are just as predetermined as the ones implicit in the attitude scale. But the fact that the "forcing" is done after the student has responded rather than before can mean that the student has felt more free to express his attitudes and therefore that the teacher has more valid data in his predetermined categories.

Almost any student paper or report can be value-analyzed provided it deals with some problem or issue about which its writer has some strong feeling and genuine interest. The technique may also be used with movies or recordings. After viewing a movie, a group may be asked to write answers to questions like the following:

1. Some incidents in the movie are more important than others. Which incidents or scenes seem to you to be the most important? (Do not name more than *three*.)
2. Why do you think these incidents are important? What makes them significant as far as you are concerned?
3. How could each situation be improved so as to contribute to the growth of everyone in the situation?

The Measurement of Thinking

As we have seen, there is a difference between thinking about the subject matter of the social sciences and thinking about thinking. It is necessary that students think about thinking if they are to acquire more effective habits of thinking. Those who examine reflectively beliefs in closed areas will not necessarily acquire thereby a complete and rounded conception of the thinking process. Whether they do or not will depend on the extent to which teachers promote examination of the process by which they reach conclusions. A teacher who promotes reflection about reflection will want to know whether his students are improving the quality of their thinking. In other words, he will want to use tests which measure achievement in reflective thinking.

The following tests require a student to apply what he knows about thinking just as the tests described earlier require him to make some application of his social-science knowledge. However, it is impossible to divorce tests of conceptual achievement and tests of how well reflection itself is understood. Most of the tests described in the present section, for example, not only test a student's understanding of thinking but also measure his understanding of certain social-science concepts.

Prior to the Eight Year Study not much was known about the evaluation of thinking. The Evaluation Staff was interested in getting evidence on achievement of the more intangible outcomes of education. Improved thinking was one of these outcomes. The staff took the position that they could not measure progress toward any educational objective unless that objective was given an operational definition. That is, they believed it would clarify what they were trying to evaluate if they could identify the overt behavior which could be taken as evidence for the presence or absence of thinking.

In their judgment, a person who thinks conducts operations such as interpreting data, using principles of logic, identifying assumptions in an argument, recognizing evidence and seeing its relationship to a hypothesis, making hypotheses and inferences, and applying principles to new situations. They devised instruments for measuring many of these behaviors. An understanding of these instruments not only is basic to an understanding of the Eight Year Study but helps to clarify the nature of thinking; it also helps the more creative teachers to devise better means of getting evidence on these and other aspects of thinking.

INTERPRETATION OF DATA 2.51 AND 2.52

This instrument was developed by the Evaluation Staff of the Eight Year Study for the measurement of a student's ability to interpret data. Intended for use with high-school students in grades 9 through 12, it has also been used with freshmen in college, and some high-school teachers have developed forms for use with junior-high students.

Each form of the test consists of ten exercises. Each exercise presents a set of data in the form of a table, a graph, a chart, or a prose description and is accompanied by fifteen statements, each of which represents a possible interpretation of the data. Students are directed to mark each statement according to whether it is true, probably true, false, probably false, or unsupported by sufficient data, limiting their judgment of each statement to the data given them in the test item—that is, not intruding any other data which may be known to them. In other words, this test tries to discover whether a student can determine the limits of the data supplied to him.

A student who takes an interpretation-of-data test receives four different scores—a general accuracy score, an overcaution score, a going-beyond-the-data score, and a crude error score. The general accuracy score indicates the extent to which the responses of a student agree with the test key. The other scores are diagnostic, as they indicate the nature of errors made. The most frequent error of students who took this test in the Eight Year Study was a tendency to go beyond the data. Most students found it tempting to infer a meaning which was not justified by the data they were asked to interpret.

High-school students were at their best when they had to distinguish between true and false interpretations. They were weakest in distinguishing between the true and the probably true, the false and the probably false. One may infer that high-school students are not learning adequately to distinguish different degrees of probability. Their tendency to think in terms of either-or categories presents serious difficulties in understanding today's world.[28]

The following is an example of an exercise from an interpretation-of-data test constructed by one of the authors for use in a high-school social-studies class. The example is keyed and each item is followed in parentheses by an explanation of the principle being tested by the item:

Study the given facts carefully. Read each statement carefully. In answering each statement, *stick to the given facts*. Refer to the facts each time and place a number in front of the statement:

Mark it *1* if the facts given make the statement true.
Mark it *2* if the facts given make it probably true.
Mark it *3* if the facts given do not make it possible to judge the statement one way or another.
Mark it *4* if the facts given make it probably false.
Mark it *5* if the facts given make the statement false.

Statement of Facts:

The following table represents the relationship between yearly income of certain families and the medical attention they receive.

FAMILY INCOME	PERCENT OF FAMILY MEMBERS WHO RECEIVED NO MEDICAL ATTENTION DURING THE YEAR
$1,200 to $3,000	40%
$3,000 to $5,000	33%
$5,000 to $10,000	24%

Interpretations:

(3)   1. Many family members do not receive medical care because they cannot afford it. (Assuming Cause)

(3)   2. The members of wealthy families require less medical care than the

members of other families because they are well-fed and well-housed. (Assuming Cause)

(2) 3. At least 70 percent of the members of families with incomes of $11,000 a year receive some medical care during the year. (Extrapolation)

(2) 4. The members of families with incomes of $1,500 a year receive less medical care than members of families with annual incomes of $3,500. (Interpolation)

(5) 5. The lower the family income, the greater is the percent of family members who receive medical care. (Recognition of a Trend)

(3) 6. If those families with incomes under $3,000 a year would double their income, fewer of their family members would go without medical care. (Assigning Effect)

(2) 7. A smaller percent of members of families with incomes of $10,000 to $15,000 a year received no medical attention than did members of families receiving $1,200 to $3,000 a year. (Extrapolation)

(3) 8. The government should give free medical care to families with low incomes in order to improve the health of the nation. (Value Judgment)

(3) 9. John's father makes $1,500 a year while Jim's father makes $3,000 a year. Jim receives medical attention more often than John. (Sampling)

(4) 10. Families with incomes of $8,000 a year had a greater percentage of family members who went without medical care than did the members of families with incomes of $4,000 a year. (Interpolation.) [29]

Sometimes a teacher who uses an exercise like the one above is tempted to review the test, item by item, with his students. If he succumbs to this temptation, he may teach his students how to take the test instead of how to interpret data. In teaching students how to take a test a teacher destroys the future usefulness of the test and tests similar to it. An alternative to going over a test is to teach students principles of interpretation which they have a chance to apply when they take almost any kind of thinking test.

APPLICATION OF SOME PRINCIPLES OF LOGICAL REASONING TEST, FORM 5.12

This test, developed by the Evaluation Staff of the Eight Year Study, tests a student's ability to apply certain principles of logic and to take note of relationships between assumptions and conclusions. It does not examine students on all principles of logic but is restricted to the following five:

1. Do students recognize the necessity for defining precisely certain key words and phrases?

2. Do students understand the conditions necessary to the soundness of an indirect argument?

---

[29] *The Ohio Thinking Check-Up*, issued by Bureau of Educational Research, The Ohio State University, 1945. Constructed by Lawrence E. Metcalf and Louis E. Raths.

3. Do students understand the invalidity of name calling?

4. Do students see the relationship between premises and conclusions when they are asked to assess an example of if-then reasoning?

5. Do students understand the necessity of determining whether a sample is representative of a larger population about which they are trying to reach a conclusion?

The student is given a series of exercises toward which he is asked to react logically. In the total test, he deals with ten different exercises, two for each of the five principles of logic. Each exercise has three possible conclusions and twelve possible reasons. The reasons consist of: (1) general or abstract statements of the logical principle involved, (2) specific statements of the logical principle involved, and (3) general or specific statements of logical principles which are irrelevant to the conclusion selected. A general accuracy score is obtained by computing twice the number of correct responses (both conclusions and reasons) minus the total number of wrong responses (both conclusions and reasons).[30]

Form 5.12 is no longer available for distribution, but in 1950 the Educational Testing Service published a Logical Reasoning Test which follows the pattern of the original instrument. The following is an example taken from the Logical Reasoning Test Form A, Test Number 282-42-1:

PROBLEM III

John L. Lewis, head of the United Mine Workers, once described the results of a conference on unemployment which a union delegation had with Frances Perkins, who was then Secretary of Labor. Secretary Perkins had assured the delegation that the unemployment situation was less critical than they had believed and that the government was taking steps to solve the problem.

"After three hours," Lewis related, "the delegation went away woozy in the head, just like the good woman who is Secretary of Labor." Lewis remarked that he believed Miss Perkins would "make a good housekeeper" but he added, "I don't think she knows any more about the economic problems of this country than a Hottentot does about the moral law."

Directions:

Examine the conclusions that follow. Accept as true the charges made by Mr. Lewis, and choose the conclusion which you believe is justified.

Conclusions:

X The charges made by Mr. Lewis proved that the statements made by Secretary Perkins to the union delegation were wrong.

Y The charges made by Mr. Lewis did *not* prove that the statements made by Secretary Perkins to the union delegation were wrong.

Z More information is needed to decide whether or not the charges made by

[30] This test is discussed by Smith and Tyler, *op. cit.*, pp. 111–126.

Mr. Lewis proved that the statements made by Secretary Perkins to the union delegation were wrong.

Mark in Column:

A: Statements which explain why your conclusion is logical.
B: Statements which do not explain why your conclusion is logical.
C: Statements about which you are unable to decide.

Statements:

1. Since we assume that the Secretary of Labor was really as incompetent as Mr. Lewis implied, we must conclude that her statements to the union delegation were wrong.
2. When Secretary Perkins assured the union delegation that the unemployment situation was less critical than they believed, she was obviously wrong.
3. Before we can decide whether or not Mr. Lewis proved his point, we must know what he meant by such terms as "woozy," "Hottentot," and "moral law."
4. To make a sound argument, Mr. Lewis would have to consider Miss Perkins' knowledge of all the other possibilities including social problems.
5. Even if Miss Perkins were shown to be ignorant of economics, this would not prove that the particular statements which she made to the union delegation were wrong.
6. An attack upon certain aspects of a person or institution, even though justified, is not enough to prove the lack of all merit in that person or institution.
7. The soundness of an indirect argument depends upon whether all the possibilities have been considered.
8. A changed definition may lead to a changed conclusion even though the argument from each definition is logical.
9. In order to prove a point, one must direct his argument to the point and not attempt to discredit those who think otherwise.
10. The statements quoted give only a sample from Mr. Lewis' remarks, and so no logical conclusion can be drawn.
11. A sample does not necessarily represent all of the data which may apply to a situation.
12. Whether or not Mr. Lewis' accusations are true, they do not apply directly to the issue of whether the statements made by Miss Perkins to the union delegation were right or wrong.[31]

In the above example the correct conclusion is Y, and the correct reasons are 5, 6, 9, and 12. This exercise tests a student's ability to resist name calling as a method by which to reach a conclusion. The list of reasons in the exercise includes all five of the principles of logic used in the test so that a student has an opportunity to distinguish among them.

[31] *Logical Reasoning Test, Form A,* Cooperative Test Division, Educational Testing Service, Princeton, New Jersey, and Los Angeles, California, Copyright 1950, pp. 6–8. This test is no longer available for distribution, but rights to reproduce it may

NATURE OF PROOF, 5.21 AND 5.22

Understanding the nature of a proof has been an educational objective in the teaching of geometry for a great many years. However, restricting the teaching of the nature of proof to geometry classes appears unreasonable to teachers who recognize that their students are exposed every day to a variety of arguments, all of which try to prove something to students and hence induce them to act in certain ways. Newspaper editorials, public speeches, advertisements, books, magazines, movies, radio and television programs—all make such appeals. These appeals are not equally sound in their intellectual content. No doubt there are many persons "taken in" every day by unsound arguments because they lack ability to analyze the nature of the proof which is offered them. This ability can be acquired from a study of various examples of proof.

Schools which participated in the Eight Year Study tried to develop in their students improved ability to analyze arguments and proofs. The Evaluation Staff developed some instruments for evaluating understanding of proofs. Prominent among them were Nature of Proof, 5.21 and 5.22.

In Nature of Proof, 5.21, students are presented with a series of exercises each of which includes a conclusion which they are asked to accept. This statement of problem and conclusion is followed by a list of fourteen statements. In Part I of the exercise students are directed to mark each statement as follows:

1. With an *A* those statements which either support or contradict the conclusion. These are the relevant statements.
2. With a *B* those statements under *A* which support the conclusion.
3. With a *C* those statements under *B* which students do not consider satisfactorily established by whatever general knowledge they have but which must be included in their argument if the conclusion is to be acceptable.

In Part II students are directed to indicate whether they are inclined to accept the conclusion, to reject it, or to be uncertain. They also indicate on their answer sheet which of the statements marked with a *C* in Part I might cause them to reconsider their decision if more information were made known to them. These statements are marked with a *D*. Statements marked with a *D* represent what a student believes to be the crucial assumptions, the truth of which he is willing to question.

The following excerpt is from Nature of Proof, 5.21:

---

be obtained for some purposes. It is very desirable that teachers study this test in order to learn how to build their own tests of logical thinking.

PROBLEM IX

In a radio broadcast the following story was told: "The people in a little mining town in Pennsylvania get all their water without purification from a clear, swift-running mountain stream. In a cabin on the bank of the stream about half a mile above the town a worker was very sick with typhoid fever during the first part of December. During his illness his waste materials were thrown on the snow. About the middle of March the snow melted rapidly and ran into the stream. Approximately two weeks later typhoid fever struck the town. Many of the people became sick and 114 died." The speaker then said that this story showed how the *sickness of this man caused widespread illness, and the death of over one hundred people.*

Statements:

ABCD   1. Typhoid fever organisms can survive for at least three months at temperatures near the freezing point.

       2. Good doctors should be available when an epidemic hits a small town.

ABCD   3. Typhoid fever germs are active after being carried for about half a mile in clear, swift-running water.

A   4. There may have been other sources of contamination by waste materials containing typhoid fever germs along the stream or at some other point in the water supply of the town.

AB   5. The waste materials of a person who has a severe case of typhoid fever contain active typhoid organisms.

AB   6. Typhoid fever is contracted by taking typhoid organisms into the body by way of the mouth.

       7. Only a few people in this town had developed an immunity to typhoid fever.

A   8. Typhoid organisms are usually killed if subjected to temperatures near the freezing point for a period of several months.

       9. Sickness and death usually result in a great economic loss to a small town.

ABCD 10. The only typhoid organisms with which the people in the town came in contact were in the water supply.

    11. Vaccination should be compulsory in communities which have no means of purifying their water.

ABCD 12. The worker's waste materials were the only source of contamination along the stream.

A   13. There may have been other areas of typhoid fever germs in the town such as milk or food contaminated by some other person.

AB   14. The symptoms of typhoid fever usually appear about two weeks after contact with typhoid germs.[32]

[32] Smith and Tyler, *op. cit.,* pp. 133–134.

Statements 2, 7, 9, and 11 are irrelevant to the conclusion. If a student marks any of these with an *A*, he has failed to relate assumptions to a conclusion. A general accuracy score on this test does not mean very much. Separate scores which get at separate behaviors have more meaning. One such score indicates the extent to which students recognize the relevant aspects of an argument. The above form of the Nature of Proof Test is so constructed that the total performance depends on how well a student does on the early parts. A later revision of this test, Form 5.22, takes care of this difficulty so that each part of the test can be scored separately.[33]

The data yielded by nature-of-proof tests supply answers to questions such as the following:

1. To what extent does a student recognize relevant phases of an argument and distinguish between considerations which support and ones which contradict a stated hypothesis or conclusion?
2. To what extent does a student challenge the assumptions underlying an argument and distinguish between assumptions which, from the point of view of a committee of adults, should and should not be challenged?
3. How do the conclusions reached by a student compare with those reached by a committee who made the test?
4. To what extent does a student recognize the relevance of proposals for the further study of a problem?
5. To what extent does a student judge the relevant activities as practicable, i.e., distinguish between activities which, from the point of view of a committee of adults, are and are not practicable? [34]

The fourth and fifth questions above are not treated in Form 5.21. Teachers who are interested in these two questions should consult and study a sample exercise from Form 5.22.[35]

Both 5.21 and 5.22 emphasize the subject matter of the physical sciences, but many of the exercises also recognize social aspects. Teachers of the social studies may be more directly interested in a special form of the nature-of-proof tests called Analysis of Controversial Writing (Form 5.31).[36] This test is designed to show whether students can make logical analyses of propaganda materials. The behaviors on which the test focuses are:

a. Recognition of the purposes of authors of propaganda—that is, ability to make more discriminating judgments as to the points of view which it is

---

[33] For a full discussion of nature-of-proof tests see *ibid.*, pp. 126–156.
[34] *Ibid.*, p. 143.
[35] *Ibid.*, pp. 136–139.
[36] Discussion and sample exercises may be found in *ibid.*, pp. 148–154.

intended a consumer should accept or reject. (In a broad sense, this refers to the generally accepted concept of "reading comprehension.")

b. Identification of the forms of argument used in selected statements of propaganda. (This refers to reading comprehension in a different sense.)

c. Recognition of forms of argument which are considered intellectually acceptable and which are not employed in certain statements.

d. Critical reaction to the forms of argument which represent typical devices employed in propaganda.

e. Ability to analyze argument in terms of established principles of proof.

f. Recognition of the relation of propaganda to the social forces which breed it.

g. Knowledge of the psychological mechanisms involved in the susceptibility of people to certain language symbols.[37]

APPLICATION OF PRINCIPLES TEST, FORM 1.5

Students who can think effectively and who have conceptualized their learning are able to apply principles (i.e., generalizations) in a variety of new situations. The Application of Principles Test measures two related kinds of achievement: logic of thinking and understanding of social principles, or social theory. This test, constructed by the Evaluation Staff of the Eight Year Study, overlaps somewhat the Nature of Proof Test and the Application of Some Principles of Logic Test, but it differs in its emphasis upon measuring understanding of certain social principles. Smith and Tyler state the purpose of the test when they say:

> The analysis of the objective resulted in the following list of important types of behavior to be evaluated: (1) *The ability to see the logical relations* between general principles and specific information on the one hand and the issues involved in a given social problem on the other; i.e., to see whether a statement supports, contradicts, or is irrelevant to a conclusion. (2) *The ability to evaluate arguments* presented in discussing a specific social problem, and in particular, to discriminate between statements of verifiable fact, statements of opinion and common misconceptions. (3) *The ability to judge the consistency of social policies with social goals;* i.e., to judge the appropriateness of certain policies for achieving certain social aims.[38]

The following sample taken from Application of Principles Test, Form 1.5, illustrates how the test measures achievement of the above objectives.

PROBLEM:

Housing is one of the problems of concern today. Many schemes have been suggested as a means of improving housing conditions. In general there are two major ways in which government can aid in solving this problem: (1) by set-

[37] *Ibid.,* pp. 149–150.
[38] *Ibid.,* pp. 197–198.

ting standards for and regulating the construction of private housing, and (2) by building houses at public expense, contributing either part or all of the funds necessary. Nevertheless, many people believe that the *government should build houses at public expense to rent to those sections of the population with the lowest incomes.*

1. Directions:

For each of the following statements, place a check mark in one of the columns labeled Part I. Place the check mark opposite the number which corresponds to the number of the statement in:

Column A if the statement *may logically be used* to support *the underlined* conclusion.

Column B if the statement *may logically be used* to contradict *the underlined* conclusion.

Column C if the statement neither supports nor contradicts *the underlined* conclusion.

Check each item in only one column. In case of doubt, give the answer which seems most nearly right.

In this part of the exercise, assume that each statement is true.

Supports Assumption	1. Whenever houses are not available to the public, society should assume the responsibility for making it possible for everyone to have a decent place to live.
Contradicts Misconception	3. Government-built houses are more expensive to construct than comparable houses built by private companies.
Supports Misconception	11. It has been demonstrated that the federal government can build adequate houses for the lowest income group cheaply enough so that they can be paid for out of income from rent.
Contradicts Accurate	14. Individuals who have heavy investments in slum property would probably suffer heavy losses if a broad program of federal housing went into effect.
Contradicts Assumption	17. The system of private initiative in business should not be jeopardized by the socialization of any of the fundamental industries.
Supports Accurate	20. Under present conditions, at least 50 percent of the people cannot easily afford to own a decent home; at least one-third of the population cannot afford to rent decent homes.
Irrelevant Accurate	22. Comparable houses can frequently be rented in the suburbs for somewhat lower rentals than in the city.

II. Directions:

Go back over the statements. In the columns labeled Part II place a check mark opposite the number which corresponds to the number of the statement in:

Column D if you believe the statement can be proved to be true.
Column E if you believe the statement can be proved to be false.
Column F if you believe the statement cannot be proved either true or false.

Check each item in only one column. In case of doubt, give what seems to you to be the one best answer.

When you have finished Part II, go on to Part III.

III. Directions:

In the column labeled Part III opposite the number which corresponds to the number of the statement, write: *A plus sign if it expresses a type of action which you think* would improve the housing conditions of that third of the population with the lowest incomes. *A zero sign if it does not express a type of action which you think* would improve the housing conditions of that third of the population with the lowest incomes.

1. New buildings should be required to measure up to higher minimum standards for construction.
2. Credit for housing should be supplied in larger quantities and at lower rates of interest.
3. All city land should be reassessed.
4. Laws should be passed requiring the destruction of all slum areas.
5. The government should subsidize housing for lower income groups.[39]

This excerpt does not represent a complete exercise from the Application of Principles Test, but it indicates the nature of the test. The comments to the left of the statements in Part I represent the key for that part of the test and for Part II. Part III, which consists of true-false items, is also keyed. This is an old test and some of the statements contain obsolete statistics. Nevertheless, teachers may profitably study it for ideas in constructing their own versions.

In constructing this test it is necessary to exercise certain cautions. If the material used in the test is not new, students may be able to respond correctly on the basis of memory rather than application and interpretation. If the situations in the test are too novel, students may not be able to make application at all. Ideally, a teacher should have several forms, each testing at a somewhat higher level. From the use of different forms he can get some notion of how deep and complete is students' understanding of certain principles.

In order to interpret test results it is helpful to know something about the factual background of students. If they do not know the relevant facts on the housing problem, they may fail to apply a principle even though they have studied it in connection with some other social problem for which they have factual background.

Besides ability to apply social facts and social generalizations to a social problem teachers are concerned with the application of social values

[39] *Ibid.*, pp. 199–202.

Social Problems, Form 1.41 and Form 1.42, is an attempt to measure ability to apply social values to social problems. The following is an illustrative excerpt:

Cotton Picker.

Cotton has been picked by hand which is a slow and expensive process. Recently, the Rust brothers invented a machine to do this work. It would pick in 7½ hours as much cotton as one hand picker could pick over a whole season of eleven weeks. The cost of production of cotton could be reduced from $14.52 to $3.00 per bale. To date, this machine has not been placed on the market. What should be done with this machine?

Solutions: (Check one or more which you think are desirable)

...... A. The machine should be placed on the commercial market for immediate manufacture and sale.
...... B. The machine should be made available under some form of public control and provisions made for establishing in other jobs the cotton pickers who are thrown out of work.
...... C. The machine should not be put to use at the present time.

Directions:

Write in the space below the reasons which you would use to support the solution or solutions you have checked. Be sure to write all the reasons you can think of.[40]

TEACHER-MADE TESTS OF THINKING

Tests developed as part of the Eight Year Study are no longer available. Even if they were, it is doubtful if public-school teachers could make much use of them because many of the data contained in them are now obsolete. Nevertheless, familiarity with these tests should be of value to teachers. They represent the profession's most mature achievement to date in evaluating thinking and incorporate the most adequate operational definitions of thinking yet reached.

Even though a teacher may feel that he lacks technical competence necessary to construct formal tests of thinking, the Eight Year Study tests can show him what to look for when he attempts to make informal judgments about his students' thinking. Informal judgment ought always to accompany the use of formal instruments. The following are some of the things to look for when one is interested in analyzing student thinking:

1. Are students confusing values with facts?
2. Are students attributing purpose, cause, or effect when the data do not warrant their doing so?

[40] *Ibid.,* p. 178.

3. Are students able to distinguish between that which is true and that which may be true? Between that which is true and that which is probably true? Between that which is probably true and that which may be true?

4. Are students able to see the relationship between a conclusion and related assumptions?

5. Are students able to use simple principles of logic in reaching a conclusion? Are they familiar with the simple rules of evidence and the characteristics of a hypothesis?

6. Do they know what a theory is and how it is different from a hypothesis? Do they ever confuse the theoretical with the ideal?

7. Are students given to believing what they want to believe even when the data are contrary?

8. Do students have tenable reasons for the policies they recommend?

9. Are students able to apply their values in ways which lead to goals implied in the values?

10. Are students relatively free from rationalization?

It does no good, of course, to ask these questions if instructional procedures are such that the answers cannot appear. A teacher who uses the reflective method of teaching the social studies will find, however, that the answers do tend to appear, particularly when reflection is focused on beliefs in the closed areas.

DISCUSSION QUESTIONS AND EXERCISES

1. Why is the measurement of understanding more difficult than the measurement of arbitrary associations?

2. Summarize what you have learned from this chapter about the measurement of understanding. Measurement of thinking. Measurement of attitudes.

3. What relationship exists between the validity of the attitude tests described in this chapter and the classroom atmosphere within which the tests are administered?

4. How could results obtained from administering the Scale of Beliefs be used by a social-studies teacher who is preplanning what to teach?

5. What use could be made of results obtained from the Interpretation of Data Test?

6. What should be the aim of a teacher in the area of attitude education?

7. To what extent should a teacher depend upon pencil-and-paper instruments as a means for getting evidence on the effectiveness of the reflective method? To what extent upon techniques of a more casual nature—such as teacher observation?

8. How is the teaching of history different from the teaching of thinking? Can both be taught in the same course and at the same time?

9. Can thinking be taught? Can thinking be evaluated? Should we teach that which we cannot measure or evaluate? Should we teach only that for which we have adequate evaluative techniques?
10. What is the difference, if any, between measurement and evaluation?

REFERENCES

BLOOM, BENJAMIN S., ed., *Taxonomy of Educational Objectives*, New York, Longmans, Green, 1956.

Contains many examples of test items for determining progress toward different kinds of educational objectives.

HAWKES, HERBERT E., E. F. LINDQUIST, and C. R. MANN, *The Construction and Use of Achievement Examinations*, Boston, Houghton Mifflin, 1936.

This thirty-year-old book remains one of the best references on testing achievement.

SMITH, EUGENE R., and RALPH TYLER, *Appraising and Recording Student Progress*, New York, 1942.

The only book which describes the thinking and attitude tests of PEA Eight Year Study.

PART IV
The Social-Studies Curriculum

CHAPTER 12

The Content of the Social-Studies Curriculum

THE TERM curriculum has long been bothersome. Many experts define the term as "all the experiences which emerge from a student's presence in school." This might be a useful definition, if it were not so all-inclusive. A boy making a date, a love note passed in class, a piece of chalk thrown, a jostling of shoulders in the hall, going to the toilet—a thousand events—would be included. And perhaps they should be; but when "curriculum" encompasses *all* of a student's experiences, we have an unmanageable term. A more limiting definition seems better for our purposes. We shall consider the social-studies curriculum as all the content to which students are exposed in courses labeled social studies, and such extraclass activities as may be *clearly* of a social-studies nature—such as a current affairs or a political science club. Certain all-school assemblies might come under the same head, as when a representative of the local American Legion speaks to students about the meaning of patriotism.

A Brief Historical Background

Some historical background is needed to fully understand contemporary practices and new developments. Space permits only a brief and over-simplified recounting of the historical growth of the social studies. Students who would prefer a more detailed and scholarly treatment should refer to any good book in the history of education.

NINETEENTH- AND EARLY TWENTIETH-CENTURY PATTERNS

Courses which were developed and most emphasized in the academies and public high schools were history, geography, and government. Economics, sociology, social psychology, and anthropology were either unknown fields of inquiry or not sufficiently complete or organized to be introduced into the curriculum. Economics was an exception, but was rarely taught except as a college or university subject. We are referring to the greater part of the nineteenth century: by the 1880s and 1890s, sociology was fairly well established, although, again, almost exclusively as a college subject.

Economics was labeled the "dismal subject," but sociology—early in the twentieth century—developed a certain sparkle, largely because of clashes in points of view. Charles H. Cooley, in *Human Nature and the Social Order* (1902) and *Social Organization* (1909) introduced modern sociology. Much of what Cooley said makes more sense today than what is published in sociology texts of the 1960s. On the other hand, there was William Graham Sumner, who was inspired by Herbert Spencer's Social Darwinism. He is best remembered for his *Folkways* (1909), but much of his writing effort was devoted to a defense of Social Darwinism and laissez faire (as in his "The Absurd Effort to Make the World Over," in his 1933 volume *War, and Other Essays*).

Turning to high-school subjects, history, geography, and government were taught, early in the twentieth century, by a process of drill dating from the Latin Grammar Schools of colonial times. The emphasis was on facts—most of which, in the light of modern knowledge, were wrong. History was taught as a chronological narrative of facts which stressed the political, diplomatic, and military. "Social history" was then largely an unknown subject. Although a somewhat sociological approach to history was developing, e.g., the British historian Henry Thomas Buckle and his famous *History of Civilization in England* (1872), this approach apparently was unknown to high-school teachers in the United States. Perhaps this was for the best, since Buckle's generalizations were wrong more often than not.

Geography, likewise, was taught early in the century more as a physical than a social science. It was often part of a subject labeled "natural philosophy," and emphasized the memorization of place names, climates, location of areas, nature of terrain, astronomy, and the like.

Government was taught as structure, not process. Psychological factors largely were ignored. Both government and history were didactic and slanted, with strong emphasis on "patriotism." We might justifiably conclude that much of the curriculum of the social studies in the nineteenth century and early twentieth century was a collection of fairytales.

Contrasting influences affected social-studies content during the first third of the twentieth century. John Dewey's impact was beginning to be felt; he tended to reject most that had gone before in favor of reflective teaching. However, Edward Thorndike's mechanistic, fact-memorizing approach proved more influential. Dewey was erroneously tied in the public mind to the Roussellian-oriented "Progressive Education Movement" and eventually found it necessary to disclaim this affiliation in forceful terms.[1]

The number of social-studies subjects steadily increased. Geography was split into general, economic, and physical. History proliferated into a greater variety of specialties, as did government. High-school history and government texts became slightly less didactic and ethnocentric but still left much to be desired.[2]

CHANGES OF THE 1930S

In the 1930s, significant content innovations appeared. We may attribute this to the Great Depression, a national state of despair and social rebelliousness, and to the eradication of complacency from the thinking of many professors and high-school teachers. One innovation in social studies was "social reconstructionism." The concept of reconstructionism evolved from the basic notion that social change is inevitable: (1) The course of social change may result from undirected "drift" or it may be led in more-or-less directed fashion by some group or cooperating groups in the society. (2) It is better that social change be directed. (3) Since the future decrees some sort of collectivism—the choices being authoritarian (Communism, Fascism) or democratic—some group needs to push for democratic collectivism. (4) There are many groups eager to direct social change, most of them in an authoritarian direction; and, in the presence of a vacuum in leadership, they will do so. (5) The group most dedicated to democratic values, most knowledgeable about cultural trends, and in the most strategic position to direct social change, is school teachers. (6) School teachers, therefore, should be the architects of the new social order. George Counts was one of the most forceful proponents of social reconstructionism at this time.[3]

THE 1940S AND 1950S

The war years saw little change. The war crowded out opportunities for fresh thought and classroom experimentation, although some truly original thought was occurring in a few places. Perhaps the most notable example was Ohio State University. Under the inspiration of Boyd Bode, the late Alan Griffin, a highly original thinker, applied in a way not previ-

[1] His most pointed critique of Progressivism is probably in *Experience and Education*, Macmillan, 1938.
[2] For one revealing study, see Arthur Walworth, *School Histories at War*, Harvard University Press, 1938.
[3] See his *Dare the School Build a New Social Order?*, John Day, 1932. Theodore Brameld is probably the leading exponent today.

ously tried in the social studies Dewey's concept of reflective teaching.

And then the McCarthy era struck. There is little to say about this period, except that it resembled closely the suppression of academic freedom which accompanies or closely follows most major wars. The first half of the 1950s seems particularly disastrous, however, because it forced teachers into the pattern of meaningless, neutralized fact memorizing which had been fought by many leaders in education for half a century.

THE "NEW" SOCIAL STUDIES

Shortly after the Russians placed Sputnik in orbit, the public-school curriculum became an object of serious concern to those American power centers that felt that we had been outpaced in the field of science teaching. Harsh criticisms were aimed at educators, who were charged with being exclusively concerned with "progressive education," "core curriculum," "life adjustment," and "problem solving." With encouragement from government and private foundations, curriculum projects were developed in physics, chemistry, biology, and mathematics. Each project was richly endowed with the resources that only money can buy. In each discipline, an attempt was made to identify basic concepts and theory, and then to develop instructional materials with which to make this new content clear to students. The objective in each project was not only to teach theory but also to get students to think like scholars and to begin to appreciate a discipline as a discipline. A discipline was defined both in terms of its basic concepts and its distinctive methodology. As one observer put it, "We want students to learn theoretical physics, not how to make soap or toothpaste, and to learn physics by thinking the way physicists think. After all, that's the way physicists learned it in the first place."

Under the influence of Jerome Bruner, many of the projects acquired a taste for a method of teaching called *discovery*, later to be designated *inductive teaching*. The fact that this "new" method was as old as Plato was not generally recognized.

The trend in content was away from "problems," except for problems in theory, and toward "subject matter." This development reversed the trend of the 1930s which had been toward "problems" and away from "subjects." It was not the same old subject matter, however. The old subject curriculum had emphasized facts and their memorization. The new centered upon concepts, meanings, and theories. Whenever inductive teaching became truly reflective, analysis rather than memorization became the chief mental activity of students.

Subject matter came to be regarded as "the basic structure of a discipline" and "discovery" was viewed as the best teaching method by which to communicate "structure." Scholars could not always agree on

THE CONTENT OF THE SOCIAL-STUDIES CURRICULUM

the structure of a given discipline. In biology, for example, a national curriculum project produced three versions because biologists could not agree on one. A number of mathematics projects varied in their proposed content and sequence. Chemists also produced more than one solution. Only the physicists were able to offer a monolithic solution to the problem of structure.

Confusion was also exhibited over the meaning of inductive teaching. It is still a matter of dispute whether it is the same as reflective teaching, as defined by John Dewey. Most advocates of inductive teaching, because they identified John Dewey with the mistakes of child-centered progressive education, never became students of his concept of reflective teaching. Yet much of their "induction" looked reflective when honestly practiced. Regardless of what the terms meant, a bandwagon movement took charge, and it became fashionable within science and mathematics education to use "discovery" and "structure" as slogans and rallying cries.

It was not long before social studies got into the act. The heavy attention given to science and mathematics by government and foundations resulted in the charge that a lack of balance had appeared in the curriculum. Devotees of the arts, humanities, and social sciences demanded equal attention. By the mid-1960s, there were more than thirty projects in social studies alone. Many of these attempted to follow the model set by mathematics and science, and were centered around a discipline and the method of discovery.

One of the first disciplines to enter into curriculum-reform competition was economics. Led by the Committee for Economic Development, the Joint Council on Economic Education, and the American Economics Association, a national task-force report outlined the basic content for a high-school economics course. The recommended content was conceptual-theoretical, and the preferred method of teaching resembled the concept of reflective thought found in Dewey's *How We Think*.

Other projects developed—in anthropology, geography, sociology, and history. One project, headed by Donald Oliver at Harvard, centered on the analysis of controversial issues. It came closer than any other to Dewey's concern with controversy, values, and reflective thought.

Most of the social-studies projects are still in existence; and because they have not completed their work, it is difficult to assess their quality or effect. A few observations, however, seem warranted. First, there is in most of the projects a healthy emphasis on meaning as opposed to traditional valuing of facts and memorization. Second, it is not clear whether inductive teaching as practiced in some of the projects is a royal road to learning, or a primrose path down which students are led to predetermined conclusions. Third, the projects, with few exceptions, are nonexperimental. Rather than test hypotheses, projects have developed "new" and "exciting" instructional materials based upon unexamined assumptions. One of the unexamined assumptions is the idea that knowledge of the structures of disciplines is an essential part of a general education. Little effort has been made to evaluate systematically the learning that results from teaching the new materials. It is very doubtful whether these new materials are useful for any but the most gifted of students. Fourth, many of the project directors have been stridently insistent that they are leaders of a curriculum revolution. But not much effort has been made to disseminate far and wide the new materials, nor have project directors laid claim to definitive answers to the persistent problems in curriculum and instruction. Consequently, their "revolution" has occurred, if at all, in a few pilot schools or involved only isolated teachers. Teaching, in general, continues to emphasize memorization of facts with consequent neglect of concepts, generalizations, and inquiry.

Within the next ten years, a rigorous assessment of these new projects will no doubt occur. This assessment will put the profession in position to determine what to disseminate to whom, and to evaluate the import of these projects for the reform of teacher education.

In the history of social-studies education, content emphases have gone through a number of gyrations influenced by the changing cultural climate and the expanding ideas of those earnestly seeking to innovate. There is little evidence that the outcome of social-studies education is today much different from what it was a half-century or more ago. The outcome for the typical student still is the acquisition of a hodgepodge of memorized, largely standardized facts, most of which he quickly forgets because they have little value in out-of-school situations.

Qualification, of course, is mandatory. There are many individual schools and school systems, as well as thousands of individual teachers, who accomplish worthwhile results. But there are many more schools, school systems, and teachers who do more harm than good. The situation has not changed fundamentally from the time three decades ago when J. Wayne Wrightstone asserted that social-studies courses had so little impact on students that they could be eliminated from the curriculum with little or no difference for important educational outcomes.[4]

We need strikingly different approaches to content selection, organization, and methodology if we are to educate youth concerning *social* problems at a fast enough pace to prevent the problems created by a presently out-of-hand technical and scientific world from engulfing us. Sometimes a "new" approach has seemed fresh only because of obscuring gimmickry or new terminology. With the possible exception of the Oliver project at

[4] Morris L. Bigge and Maurice P. Hunt, *Psychological Foundations of Education.* Harper & Row, 1962, p. 3.

Harvard, current projects do not promise a sufficiently radical change in the aims, content, or methods of social-studies education. The remainder of this chapter will suggest a way of cutting loose from traditional approaches.

Content as the Data of Reflection

Instead of restricting our concept of the content of learning to predetermined, formally organized bodies of knowledge, we may think of content as the subject matter which functions in the thinking process. *The content of learning may be regarded as the data of acts of reflective thought.*

The content of reflection—in contrast to the content of history, political science, geography, and so on—includes every relevant aspect of the mental and physical environment in which a given act of thought occurs, everything a thinker brings to bear on a problem. General ideas or principles are prominent among the resources applied to any act of reflection. These generalizations supply the assumptions, the hypotheses, and to a degree the factual data of an act of thought. They represent the previous experience of a learner, as captured in his conceptual structure. An act of thought also makes use of concrete sensory data (observations) which are either recalled from past experience or obtained through new experiences implied by the problem. In short, the content of a given act of thought includes one's own personal resources plus pertinent data from the social and physical environment.

A given act of thought also employs facts, values, and assumptions about the nature of thought itself. A person may not be aware of the methodological assumptions he is making; he may not realize that if he thinks reflectively he is selecting an approach to knowing which is fundamentally different from other approaches he might have selected. Nevertheless, whether explicit or not, whenever thought is undertaken such assumptions operate. This fact suggests an idea of crucial importance: a comparative study of methodologies should be an important part of any course in social studies.

Any act of thought involves *selection* of resources. A thinker may use only those mental, cultural, and physical resources which are pertinent to solution of the problem at hand—and no other. He must be able to distinguish what is relevant from what is not. He must learn to keep irrelevant resources in the background lest they clog the mind and impede thought.

Content assumes an *emergent* character. From the standpoint of ₐ learner, it comes into existence as it is needed; it does not have a life independent of his own. During an act of thought, a learner searches for usable data. The data which he locates and uses were not data before that time. The factual materials from which he draws data may, it is true, have functioned as data for a great many other persons. But to an individual learner, factual materials are nothing until their function in thought is seen. In a very real sense, *knowledge does not exist before learning begins.*

SOME EDUCATIONAL IMPLICATIONS OF VIEWING CONTENT AS THE DATA OF REFLECTION

What does our proposed revision of outlook mean in practice? It suggests that a prominent part of the content of each learning problem will consist of items from the conceptual backgrounds of students: knowledges, values, and habits which have been acquired in former experience. As new problems arise, this conceptual equipment comes into play in new ways. We have discussed how necessary it is that teachers understand the background students bring with them to a classroom. This aspect of the content of any given learning problem is fully as important as content which comes to a student from outside himself.

When a student views learning materials proffered from outside—as through a teacher's lecture—he sees as content only that part which is sharply pertinent to his learning problem. Content functions as *data* or *evidence,* or it is not to be regarded as the content of learning. Unless it functions literally as data, it is mere stuff—irrelevant, useless. Now what happens if we try to apply such a criterion to the traditional content of high-school social studies? It is quite probable that, whatever the problem under scrutiny, some traditional subject matter of the social studies will be serviceable; but it is also probable that much needed content will not be available through the traditional subjects (or will be inaccessible) and must be sought. Some of the current projects in social studies promise more serviceable content.

Traditional organization tends to provide materials which are irrelevant and to deny use of those which might be pertinent. At first glance, it might seem that, if we adopt the idea that the proper content of social-studies education is the data of thought, we have rejected all possibility of planning courses or preparing teaching materials in advance of actual learning situations. However, even though the particular problems which a class will study may not always be predicted with certainty, and even though, when a problem has been selected, all needed data cannot be ascertained in advance, principles do exist for partially solving this dilemma—they will be treated later.

INSEPARABILITY OF METHOD AND CONTENT

The curriculum of teachers' colleges and university departments of education is usually separated into two parts: (1) subject-matter courses, in which prospective teachers are taught "content," and (2) methods courses, in which prospective teachers are taught something called "teaching methods." This distinction might be a useful convenience if everyone recognized its basically fictional character. As it is, the distinction does great damage because almost everyone takes it literally.

The task of selecting and organizing content is methodology in its intellectual and pedagogical sense. The right selection and organization of content virtually guarantees that reflection will occur among those who are exposed to it. If content is properly selected and organized, the technique of presentation is not likely to be so bad as to prevent reflection. Conversely, the smoothest use of technique cannot produce reflection if content is irrelevant, trivial, unintelligible, or otherwise inappropriate.

Therefore, the statement that a method of teaching is wrong ought to mean that the content is wrong, and the statement that content is wrong ought to mean that it cannot advance the use of a desired intellectual method. A realistic discussion of what constitutes desirable content ought to show how that content is going to function in a learning situation, just as a realistic discussion of a particular intellectual method ought to reveal the kinds of content most appropriate to it.

If the inseparability of method and content is understood by all, then it should be fairly easy to appreciate the significance of the idea that the content of education should be regarded as including only the data of thought. For this is the same as saying that content, if it is meaningful and useful, must be related to an intellectual method appropriate to it. When we say *that the content of learning is the data of reflection we are saying, in a different context, that no content has meaning apart from the method by which it is verified and used, an assumption that is basic to many of the current projects in social studies.*

Individual Needs Versus Social Needs:
A False Issue

Viewing the content of learning as the data of reflection, rather than as predetermined collections of facts, poses difficult problems for teachers and textbooks writers; it seems to exclude the possibility of selecting subject matter in advance of the reflective acts in which it is to be used. A way around this dilemma would appear to be an authentic problem-centered approach, in which teaching materials are selected—and textbooks written—so as to incorporate data which are relevant to existing or potential problems of students. Such content may be regarded as truly problem centered; *it has the general characteristic of presenting contrasting or conflicting ideas and the factual data pertinent to them.*

There still remains the question: Which problems are to be selected for study? We have suggested elsewhere that problems should be selected in such a way that they will involve beliefs that are widely held by students and have broad social significance. This principle, although useful, does not, without further clarification, move us entirely out of the woods. High-school students have acquired hundreds, if not thousands, of beliefs about matters which might be judged socially important. Limitations of time and energy make it impossible to raise for reflective examination propositions corresponding to all of them.

The fact that many beliefs can never be challenged is less disturbing if, in the process of testing some beliefs, students have conceptualized a method of problem solving which they can apply widely. As suggested earlier, a study of reflective methodology per se should make up an important part of the social-studies curriculum.

Does this mean that so long as students can be taught a general methodology it does not make much difference what specific subjects they study? Undoubtedly, if the sole aim of a teacher is to get reflection along with some conceptual understanding of the reflective process, one item of subject matter (so long as it conforms to the general requirements of reflective content) may serve as well as another. If a teacher's only aim is this, his students may do as well by concentrating on the study of football plays as by concentrating on, say, the behavior of Congress.

However, most persons believe that some ideas and issues of American culture are in greater need of reflective scrutiny in our schools than are others. This view demands some discussion of the whole notion of *need* and the controversy which surrounds this term.

EDUCATION AS BASED ON NEEDS OF CHILDREN

Almost everyone agrees that public education should in some way take cognizance of the needs of children and youth. But not everyone agrees on what children need or on just how education should deal with needs, even if they could be determined. One group of progressives has insisted that no one can know the needs of a child better than the child himself. According to this group, children should be encouraged to tell about the problems that they feel right now, and school programs should be adjusted to deal with them.

Other groups feel that, although schools should not ignore immediate felt needs of pupils, other needs, of which children and youth are largely unaware, should be served by the curriculum in whatever ways adults deem best. For example, children have a need (which often they do not recognize) to prepare for various aspects of adult life; and only adults are likely to understand such a need. Children also need (which they seldom understand or appreciate) to become wise citizens. This need must be met if the standards of the social group are to be served.

EDUCATION AS BASED ON NEEDS OF SOCIETY

We may identify another position, which tends to disregard, or at least offer a different interpretation of needs of children as a criterion for selecting content: Educationists should look first at the social order before trying to construct curriculums. They should seek to identify the most pressing societal needs and then see that children are so educated as to meet them.

For example, it might be ascertained that the nation has failed badly in relation to some goal which is generally acceptable. Democratic principles may be in process of violation. Economic difficulties or the specter of war may confront us. Youth should study these problems and should be taught the necessary knowledges and skills which will enable them, as adults, to reduce them.

This general point of view is not much different from the modification of the outlook first stated in the foregoing section, to the effect that although the needs of children and youth should be the basis for curriculum building, adults are best able to determine what these needs are. The focus is somewhat different, however; the one position focuses on students, the other on the social order.

EDUCATION AS BASED ON PERSONAL AND SOCIETAL NEED

There is a third position which reconciles the two approaches described above. If one accepts the culture concept of sociologists and anthropologists, it follows that an individual personality is always a product of its surrounding culture. Without culture (in the sociological sense of a total way of life) a human being is devoid of personality—and, one might add, of needs. According to the culture concept, the personality of each individual is simply an extension of the beliefs, customs, attitudes, needs, values, and habits of the group in which he lives. This does not mean that there is no such thing as individuality, but that even the most rugged of individualists derives the greater part of his personality from his social environment.

The aspirations and frustrations of any individual are likely, therefore, to resemble closely those of numerous other members of the same culture, or subculture. Personally felt problems will have a large element of commonness and be closely related to pervasive social conditions because they are a result of *problem-generating features of the culture*. Individual emotional conflicts, for example, develop from discrepancies and inconsistencies in the surrounding social situation. A culture which was integrated in its central values, or which possessed a satisfactory means for dealing with inconsistencies, would not produce personalities torn asunder with emotional conflicts.

Acceptance of this third position enables one to avoid certain dilemmas involved in acceptance of either of the other two positions. Curriculum planners often develop two lists of problems, one "personal" and the other "social," implying that social problems are not personal and that personal problems are not social. Yet it should be apparent that a problem of any kind is always personal in the sense that it is held by a person, or persons, and that every personally held problem has social consequences. A person who is unemployed, unable to support himself and his family, and looking for work certainly has a personal problem. But the fact that he is unemployed stems from a social problem and in turn produces certain social effects; and the way he solves his problem will have still other effects.

Likewise, a person who is expected to study unemployment as a social problem will not be motivated to do so except as he comes to feel personally that this social problem is his problem. Not that he must become unemployed in order to feel the problem of unemployment. As a matter of fact, the most objective and highly motivated studies of unemployment have been made by employed persons. But such a person must be able to identify with the unemployed person. He must have enough imagination to see how the unemployment of any person tends to affect his own income, cost of living, job opportunities, chances for war or peace, and so on.

This analysis illuminates the fact that means and ends are so continuous with one another that the actual meaning of any need is found in the means for achieving it. Thus it is unrealistic to categorize needs as social and biological. The need for food, for example, is usually considered biological, but a moment's reflection will show that this need has no meaning until food is defined. In some cultures, a plate of fried grasshoppers would meet the need for food whereas a broiled steak would be more acceptable in the American culture.

Cultural analysis of personality and the problem of needs makes it clear that *there is a large class of problems which in content are at the same time both individual and societal*. Any problem of this class will be felt personally by large numbers of individuals; it will also correspond to one or more broad social issues. Education concerned with these serves at the same time the needs of individual students and the larger social group, and meets both felt and imputed needs. This does not mean that the content of education is never imposed, for an individual often fails to see a relationship between his frustrations and the broader social maladjustments in which they are rooted.

UNRECOGNIZED CULTURAL CONFLICTS

According to the cultural approach, the term *need* is a value term in the sense that the culture (1) values the absence of certain frustrations and (2) cherishes certain means for reducing frustration. The larger American culture, for example, does not condone a person's meeting his need to achieve by robbing banks. Because needs are cultural in their origin and social in their meaning, there is no escape from the practice of imposition in education. Much trouble today arises from the fact that the culture through its schools imposes conflicting values upon individuals with the result that many persons do not know what they need.

In the United States today, there are many problems which cause great emotional disturbance in individuals in spite of, or perhaps because of, the fact that they are but dimly sensed or understood. Persons with such problems know that there is something wrong with their lives. They feel unhappy, lonely, frightened, or insecure and yet cannot tell why. Some of this confusion is plainly due to the fact that the culture tends to obscure and conceal from them the sources of their difficulties.

Since personal problems which are rooted in unrecognized cultural conflicts cannot be effectively verbalized by troubled individuals, certain psychoanalysts have turned to a study of culture as they seek to clarify the role of the unconscious in the neurotic lives of their patients. In their therapy, they recognize that an untrained individual finds it difficult to analyze the culture objectively; he takes the culture for granted, assuming that because it is so familiar to him its structure must be logical, right, and natural. Cultural anthropologists and psychiatrists know better; they know that the culture may generate severe conflicts, which are understood but dimly, if at all, by persons suffering them.

In the future, curriculum making probably will rely heavily on data supplied by sociologists, anthropologists, psychologists, and psychiatrists. A number of professional educators are already working closely with scientists in these fields. The field of psychology has, of course, been an adjunct of education for more than half a century, but in the main its contribution has not been of the kind suggested here. Only recently have psychologists become interested in discrepancies of the culture as a source of intrapersonal conflict.

A Recommended Approach to Selection of Subject Matter in the Social Studies

We are now ready to suggest a purpose for social-studies education which takes into account both method and content: *The foremost aim of instruction in high-school social studies is to help students reflectively examine issues in the problematic areas of American culture.*

According to this statement of purpose, teaching materials should be drawn from a selection of conflicting propositions in such controversial areas as race and minority-group relations, social class, economics, sex, courtship and marriage, religion and morality, and national and patriotic beliefs, plus a wide range of relevant data to be used in testing them. Many of these propositions will be derived from, or correspond to, the values, beliefs, and attitudes of high-school students. One might say, therefore, that in any given learning situation teaching materials should be drawn from (1) broadly social and highly controversial issues of the culture; (2) knowledges, values, and attitudes of students; and (3) relevant data of the social sciences.

One reason why social-studies education should focus on issues in problematic areas is that it is here that personally felt problems (particularly intrapersonal conflicts) tend to intersect with pervasive and troublesome cultural issues. To study such problems provides a way of meeting both individual and social needs, by reducing the amount and intensity of intrapersonal conflict and by making such conflict more manageable as it arises. It is to be hoped that society will thus gradually achieve a clearer sense of direction, more harmony and cohesiveness, and fuller realization of the democratic idea.

Many objections will be raised to the above statement of purpose, method, and content. Some persons will argue that, if a policy of reflective learning is to be pursued at all, it should be followed only in connection with problems unaffected by strong emotional blockings; that further attempts to study problematic areas in the schoolroom not only will inflict on teachers the wrath of organized interest groups in the community but, because the same taboos operate in the minds of students as in the minds of parents, will necessarily be unsuccessful. It is thought that students, like their parents, believe what they want to believe—particularly in the problematic areas—and that attempts to produce reflection will not overcome this habit.

The task of getting students themselves to reflect on highly controversial matters has at least been made easier by knowledge gained from experience in psychiatry and group dynamics (see Chapter 9). Our concern now is to examine whether a teacher may reasonably expect to succeed (i.e., to produce reflection and help students achieve more harmonious and adequate beliefs), if he focuses his instruction on problematic areas. Assuming that the proper emotional climate has been achieved, there are at least two reasons why a teacher can expect success.

First, it is impossible to induce serious reflection in students unless they can be made to *feel* a problem. Reflection is hard and often painful work. Unless a fairly pressing or enticing reason has emerged, very few persons will willingly engage upon it. It is in the problematic areas that the great controversies, perplexities, and doubts of adolescent youth occur. A skillful teacher should be able to produce a higher level of motivation through study of issues in problematic areas than through study of almost anything else. It is true that beliefs in these areas are deeply cherished and that this may produce a serious barrier to reflection; but, by the same token, a teacher can usually create a reason for reflection by showing how one cherished belief is incompatible with an equally prized one.

Second, young people are reputedly more flexible and open-minded than adults. There are no problematic areas at all in the outlook of a very small child. It is education, both formal and informal, which gradually closes certain areas of living to rational discussion. However, the high-school period is also a time when youth begin to wonder about many of the beliefs they have learned to take for granted. Intellectual interests of many young persons reach their peak at this time. Serious doubts develop as it is noted that adults do not always practice taboos which they have taught children to embrace. Faith in the omniscience of adults is shaken and one may note a general tendency to rebel against parental authority. Given the storm, the stress, the uncertainty, and the rebelliousness of this period, a serious threat to social stability results from any educational program which fails to take advantage of the motives for reflective study which develop during the high-school years.

Many adults fear that tender young minds will not be able to understand the more serious controversies of life. Actually, the so-called tender young minds are more likely than adult minds to profit from reflective study of deeply controversial issues. If it is postponed until adulthood, such study never is likely to occur.

The fear that youth will accept "wrong" beliefs if they open their minds to new ideas is actually only a fear that they will accept *different* beliefs. This is not necessarily the outcome. Reflection may fortify or it may undermine conventional beliefs. There are no prior guarantees as to what conclusions it will produce, but a great many conventional beliefs can emerge from reflective scrutiny more strongly accepted than before. The aim of reflection is never to destroy a belief, but to evaluate it in light of the best evidence and logic. Reflection can only guarantee the emergence of beliefs which are relatively more adequate and harmonious than the ones young persons normally hold.

Curriculum Organization for a Reflective Approach to Learning

STANDARD SUBJECTS AS BURDENED WITH IRRELEVANT CONTENT

Much of the subject matter of standard social studies is irrelevant to problem solving in areas of ideological controversy. Learning materials are relevant when they can set and clarify problems for students or move them toward conclusions, preferably in the form of generalizations which have predictive value. If materials are unrelated, or cannot be related, to any imaginable values, beliefs, or attitudes of students, it will be difficult and probably impossible for them to supply content for reflection. This does not mean that a student must have an attitude toward the tariff, for example, in order to learn reflectively about the tariff. He may have an attitude toward something else—say, the cost of living—which can be clarified by his introduction to scholarly studies of the tariff.

Inclusion in the standard subjects of irrelevant material is not in itself an argument against a curriculum of separately organized subjects. We might retain our history, geography, and civics courses and, by proper revision of the subject matter in each, create courses far more provocative and useful than anything we now have. There is another respect, however, in which a curriculum of separately organized courses is less than ideal.

LIFE PROBLEMS AND SUBJECT-MATTER BOUNDARIES

The content of any act of thought is likely to cut across subject-matter boundaries. Life problems of students almost invariably extend across more than one field of inquiry, unlike textbook problems of history, political science, economics, or any other social-science subject. If any issue of broad social import is to be understood, probably it can best be done through study of data from several of the social sciences and perhaps a number of other fields as well. For example, problems of race cut across the fields of politics, economics, religion, biology, psychology, and probably others. In commenting on the curricular consequences of a separate-subject organization, Professor Harold C. Hand said:

"In consequence of this conflict of inner logic—i.e., the inner logic of real-life-problem-solving vs. the inner logic of standard subjects which at best admits of but incidental attention to such problems—efforts to functionalize the traditional high school subjects invariably and inevitably result in asking the teacher simultaneously to serve two contrarily-oriented masters. That this is frustrating in the extreme, there can be little doubt—as any number of intelligent and conscientious teachers will testify. What is more important, the traditional master almost invariably wins out in this unhappy and unequal struggle—to the educational neglect of society and youth, as we have demonstrated. If the course is labeled "English" or "social studies" or any other name identified with a recognized body of more or less standard subject matter, the teacher is conscience-stricken unless he gets across at least a respectable minimum of whatever this subject matter may be. This he usually does regardless of the fate of the problems with which he is also supposed to be dealing. But this neglect of problems also induces feelings of guilt, it must be recognized. What this adds up to is scarcely a recipe for good mental health." [5]

THE LOGIC AND PLAN OF THE CORE CURRICULUM

The core curriculum, or course in "common learnings," has been proposed as a solution to this conflict. Although many of the standard school subjects are retained for purposes of specialization, the most important offering of the curriculum focuses deliberately on problems of living. A block of time, two or more hours, is reserved for their study, and teachers responsible for this are freed from other subject-matter commitments. Experience to date suggests that teachers working with a core curriculum have not always understood the pedagogical implications of a reflective approach to learning. Teachers who are free to organize a core along lines most congenial to a reflective approach may be helped by the following suggestions: *A core should be problem centered, and organized on the basis of a series of apparent contradictions in belief in problematic areas of the culture which we might expect to be shared by most students.* Work should be organized in a sequence of blocks, one on the study of discrepancies in our racial ideology, another concerned with discrepancies in our beliefs about government and politics, another with discrepancies in our economic thinking, and so on. Ideally, all the major problematic areas would be covered in such a core, although probably not in any one year. In fact, it might be advisable to limit a single year to exploration of no more than two or three broad problem areas.

[5] B. Othanel Smith, William O. Stanley, Kenneth D. Benne, Archibald W. Anderson (eds.), *Readings in the Social Aspects of Education*, Interstate Press, 1951, pp. 387–388.

Although a core of this sort would inevitably "integrate" the social studies and embrace data from fields such as literature, psychology, philosophy, human biology, and perhaps other fields, it would not integrate simply for the sake of integration. The focus would always be *on a problem and what is needed to study it.* Irrelevant material would be rigorously excluded. The study of a particular issue might be regarded as a "unit of work," provided *unit* is defined broadly to refer to the experiences related to reflective study of an issue.

ACHIEVING A "CORE APPROACH" IN SUBJECT-CENTERED COURSES

Some teachers have revised their traditional courses in an attempt to make them serve better the needs of reflection. One teacher who had been teaching literature for thirteen years was assigned in his fourteenth year to a class in eighth-grade geography. Since he knew very little geography, he found it convenient to cover the textbook page by page in traditional recitation style. However, it soon became evident to the teacher that only a few of his students understood what was covered, and that student interest was lagging.

He solved this problem by sharing it with his students. Exploring with them the problem of making the course more worthwhile, he discovered that they were much interested in understanding conflicts between the United States and the Soviet Union. He and the class agreed that some knowledge of geography would help them to understand these conflicts, also that knowledge other than the "purely geographical" would be essential. It was decided to make a rather thorough study of conflicts between the two nations and to utilize geography only as needed.

As study developed, students learned relevant history, economics, philosophy, political science, and geography. They also acquired skill in letter writing, public speaking, interviewing, chart and map interpretation, and simple statistics. The course ceased to look like geography. The casual visitor would have thought he was observing a class in contemporary problems. A geography class altered in this way may acquire many characteristics of a core. In fact, it may achieve a more fruitful integration of data than a "core" taught by a less understanding teacher.

Some Specific Problems in Curriculum Making

We have suggested that curriculum making in the future will involve (1) problematic areas of culture; (2) attitudes, values, and beliefs of students; and (3) data relevant to the testing of student attitudes, values, and beliefs in the problematic areas. Each of these tasks presents its own problems, but in no case are the problems insurmountable.

WHAT IS A PROBLEMATIC AREA OF CULTURE?

In order that we may communicate with full clarity our position toward curriculum making, it is essential that the reader have no doubts concerning what we mean by the expression "problematic areas of culture." As we define this expression, it has at least two broad dimensions. *First,* it is an area of culture in which attitudes, values, beliefs, and purported knowledge are frequently and often highly contradictory. Put differently, it is an area of culture ridden with uncertainty—an area fraught with "loose ends." Ideas simply do not jibe or "add up." Perhaps an apt term would be "irrational," except that the concept, irrational, covers somewhat more than what we intend. Our focus is upon inconsistency and ensuing confusion. *Second,* a problematic area of culture may or may not be characterized by widespread closed-mindedness. If an individual exhibits such a rigid personality structure in certain areas of interest that he finds it psychologically impossible to entertain new evidence, then, for this person, the area of interest concerned properly can be labeled a "closed area." It is not open to reflective inquiry; insecurity prevents entertaining doubt concerning traditional views and hence any effective thought about how problem solving might proceed.

Since we will use the concept of closed areas of culture from time to time in this and ensuing chapters, some qualifications are necessary. A touchy area of cultural interest—such for example as race relations—is always *more-or-less* closed. Many persons are able to reflect upon the problems involved with minimal prejudice—a prime example, perhaps, being cultural anthropologists. On the other hand, persons with a strong racist orientation are quite likely to be unable to think reflectively about any aspect of race—their capacity for reflection is, so to speak, in a state of paralysis. These same persons, however, might be able to cast and test hypotheses reflectively in many other areas of interest—for example, in directing a business enterprise.

Almost everyone has at least a few closed areas but some persons have a great many more than do others and what is closed to one person may be quite open to another. Nevertheless, in the chapters of cultural analysis which follow, we shall suggest those areas for which evidence suggests that large numbers of persons have minds closed to factual evidence. All of the cultural areas which we shall treat are problematic, however, in the sense that whether or not they may represent closed areas to many persons, they are at least areas in which a great amount of inconsistency, confusion, and ignorance are apparent.

WHAT PROBLEMATIC AREAS SHOULD BE STUDIED?

How should a curriculum maker select which problematic areas to treat in the social studies? Answering this question is not as difficult, perhaps, as it seems. A teacher needs to ask questions such as, "Is this an area of wide social concern, an area generating problems for large numbers of Americans?" "Is this an area which, in addition to widespread concern, is also of concern to my own students?" "If it is not of concern to my students, am I likely to have reasonably good luck in getting them concerned?" "Is this an area which I am capable of handling competently?" "Will we have in this school and community, or in what we can secure from elsewhere, teaching materials containing sufficient relevant factual data so that beliefs may be tested reflectively?" And last, "Is this an area too touchy to treat openly in the classroom in this particular community?"

The eight problematic areas to be explored briefly in the following chapters were not selected arbitrarily. The authors feel that they all exemplify the criteria implied in the foregoing questions, except, perhaps, under certain circumstances, those of teacher competence and undue touchiness. Our main problem was to limit. For example, we would have liked to have written chapters on "Life and Death," in which we would have delved into issues such as euthanasia, suicide, abortion, the "funeral racket," and capital punishment; "The Puritan Ethic and Drugs," in which we would have explored the extent to which present-day beliefs are not based upon scientific knowledge but upon the notion that the use of any drug which contributes to pleasure is a sin and its use should be punished —without respect to the harmfulness physiologically of the drug—and (related to this) our extraordinarily irrational means of handling the "narcotics problem"; and "The Lower Third," in which we would have treated in a way impossible in the chapter on economics the poverty of hundreds of thousands of Americans, which in many cases equals that of the most impoverished of Asia, Africa, or South America.

Teachers will select for study whatever makes sense with any given class in any given year. Their selections will change from year to year. And this will only make social studies what they should be: evolving, fluid, relevant—and exciting.

Attitudes, Values, and Beliefs of Students

Here again, a review of definitions is in order. An *attitude* is an unverbalized tendency to act in a given way in a given situation. Since attitudes are unverbalized, we can not work with them directly. We must help students verbalize their attitudes. But when an attitude is verbalized, it then is on the way to becoming a value. A *value* is a preference, a like or a dislike, which presumably a person has to some degree thought about. In any case it can be talked about, i.e., verbalized.

Without care in definition, the term *belief* can cause us the most trouble. To many persons, when reference is made to a person's beliefs, it is immediately assumed that what is meant is religious faith. But belief has broader meanings. According to Webster's *Third New International Dictionary*, a belief may be "a statement or body of statements held by the advocates of any class of views." Note the expression, *any class of views*. This means one could have beliefs about anything. A belief, then, can mean any statement that a person feels pretty sure is true. A belief is held on the basis of some kind of evidence, no matter how flimsy; otherwise, it should be called "an article of faith."

It suits our purposes better in this writing not to tie the term, belief, down to *extreme* conviction—a belief might be lightly held or a person might be willing to die for it. Furthermore, it serves us better not to limit belief to statements which are always highly value laden; otherwise, it would not make sense to say, "I believe my car is out of gas." The simplest definition of belief which Webster's dictionary gives is "[a statement to which one gives] intellectual assent." This is the definition we shall use.

Teachers need to know as much about the beliefs of students as possible. In fact, our major contention—we have said it differently elsewhere—is that the only justifiable purpose of instruction in the social studies and probably all other subjects is to encourage the reflective testing of beliefs. This can hardly be done if a teacher does not know what the beliefs are. Of course, in the process of learning, some teachers cooperate continuously with students in the forming of belief: these teachers can scarcely help but know.

The beliefs most important for learning are those students bring to school with them; these are also often the most difficult to discover. Beliefs are held at differing levels of privacy. These levels are depicted schematically below. Placement of rings away from the center reflects increasing "openness," or willingness to expose beliefs to others.

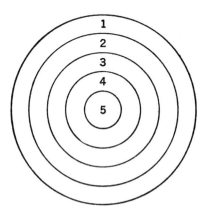

1. Beliefs a student is willing to expose to teachers, parents, and other adults.
2. Beliefs a student is willing to expose only to members of his peer group.
3. Beliefs a student is willing to expose only to a selected number of his peer group—an intimate clique or gang, perhaps.
4. Beliefs a student is willing to expose only to one or a very few of his most intimate associates—to his "best pal," let us say.
5. Beliefs a student is unwilling to expose to anyone.

It is our contention that students should be provided with data to test beliefs at all of these levels of privacy. It is easy enough to get at beliefs of type 1. We have no excuse for ignoring these. But how do we discover beliefs at the other levels? Simply as teachers, we learn a good deal—but not all—about student beliefs of type 2. We pick up a part of the general peer-culture belief pattern more-or-less accidentally—via the overheard conversation, the intercepted note, the occasional confidential statement made to us by students with whom we have exceptionally high rapport, etc.

But we suspect that often teachers know very little about belief patterns of types 3, 4, and 5. Yet, it is at these levels that student beliefs are most likely to pose problems both to students themselves and to adults. At level 3, for example, we may have a clique of half a dozen or so students who believe it morally acceptable for them to form a "sexual intercourse club," and translate this belief into action. Most problematic of all are beliefs of type 5. These are likely to involve severe conflicts and accompanying emotional disturbance. They may be highly individualized or may represent a somewhat common pattern within a particular peer group. If we could but know these beliefs, we might be able to make accessible to students data which would be of enormous value to them in helping them achieve a workable reconciliation of conflict.

THE FRESNO STATE COLLEGE STUDY OF STUDENT BELIEFS

This study, which attempts a unique method of exposing student beliefs in problematic areas of culture, with primary focus on beliefs in closed areas, is still in progress, and results have not yet been formally published. It was designed as a tool which any classroom teacher of the upper grades could use, although we concede that it is more likely to produce valid results on a college than on a high-school level.

Beginning in the fall of 1964, one of the authors (Hunt) conceived the idea of having his students write "tattle-tale" papers about other students. To ensure some degree of objectivity, the students reported upon were to be in no way identified, except by broad categories, such as sex, political affiliation, religious affiliation (if any), and age. The detailed assignment sheet, which has remained unchanged, requested students to report on others in the 18- to 25-year-old range. Furthermore, the assignment gives rather explicit instructions as to where—in a physical sense—to obtain information. Students are asked to keep ears and eyes open in any intimate, bull-session types of interactivity—e.g., sorority and fraternity houses, college dorms, parties, dates, campus coffee shops, and spontaneous gatherings.

In order to limit the number of subjects reported upon to a manageable number, the instruction sheet lists ten categories of assumed problematic areas; these are reproduced verbatim below.

1. Politics, political parties, and government (either local, state, or national). With respect to national government affairs, our foreign policy, among other things, would make for interesting comment.

2. Law, law enforcement, the courts—in short, our legal system. (Are the laws rational? Are they enforced as they should be? Is there justice in the courts? Is the Supreme Court doing a good job? Etc.)

3. The American economic system (report particularly on controversial matters, such as the proper role of the federal government, socialized vs. privately owned enterprise, taxation, monopoly, and the like).

4. Religion and the church. (How seriously do your fellow students take religion, what kinds of beliefs about religion do they have, what do they believe about church attendance, etc?)

5. Social class (report on whether students seem "class conscious," whether they take social status seriously, what they think about "social climbing," whether they think some groups of students are socially "better" than others, etc.).

6. Race and ethnic group (useful would be student opinion about how minority races should be treated, interracial socializing, dating, marriage, whether some races and ethnic groups are inferior to others, etc.).

7. Sex in any of its ramifications (relevant material would be student opinion on premarital sex relations, intimate petting, homosexuality, masturbation, and whatever else you may have heard opinions on).

8. Dating, courtship, marriage, and man-woman relationships generally (relevant would be opinions on "going steady," proper length of courtship, degree of intimacy desirable between betrothed couples, fidelity in marriage, who should be "head of the family" etc.).

9. Morality in matters other than sex (under this head, report student opinion on what some persons think of as "vices"—drinking, gambling, smoking, telling risque jokes, using earthy language [such as the "four-letter words"], swearing, reading so-called "naughty" books, etc.).

10. Education (relevant would be beliefs on such matters as whether students think their precollege schooling was worth much, what was good or bad about it, and what is good or bad about the colleges or universities they have

attended—thinking in terms of quality of instruction, usefulness of course content, adequacy of counseling, worth of extracurricular activities, etc.).

In an attempt to ascertain what students talk most about, they are instructed to select from two to four of the above ten groups—the two to four which they hear discussed *most frequently* in situations which are relatively intimate and uninhibited. The assumption underlying this instruction is that when away from adults, and among their peer group, a small clique of best pals, or one or two of their most intimate friends, they will reveal beliefs in categories 2 to 4 (see page 296).

Upon reading the first few papers received in 1964, an interesting phenomenon immediately became evident. Although students were warned rather sternly in the assignment to keep their own beliefs to themselves, and to report *only* beliefs expressed by others, it was obvious that they were revealing unwittingly many of their personal values and beliefs. Even though this had not been the original intent of the research design, students were, to put it bluntly, tricked into—to them unknown —giveaways. Papers received each semester since then increasingly confirm this tendency. Apparently, it is most difficult for a person to write about others without revealing much of himself.

Our tentative conclusion to date is that this approach to value and belief research has certain inherent weaknesses as well as strengths. First, results reflect (with some exceptions) the ideological patterns of but one region—the San Joaquin Valley of California. This is a conservative area because it is "rooted in the soil." Second, evaluation of results is subjective and the investigator may very well misinterpret the written material he has before him. On the other hand, a few semesters of practice with this device undoubtedly teaches the researcher a great deal about how to interpret—just as practice is required to interpret a Rorschach, TAT, HTP, and other tests which have as their purpose tricking individuals to reveal values and beliefs which they would not do if confronted with a direct Gallup-poll type of "What do you think . . . ?" question.

Although this study is still underway (it is projected as a five-year study), several tentative conclusions appear warranted:

1. After discarding all papers which seem shoddily done or "dreamed up" at the last moment, the researcher has obtained a respectable sample of what appear to be revealing papers—301 to be exact (through the spring of 1967).

2. By using inference—"reading between the lines"—the researcher can glean much from the papers other than what is overtly written. Despite the subjectivity of such inferences, they are informative. For example, does a girl who writes mostly about sex, but who inserts state-

ments deploring an interest in sex, have on her mind much of the time problems involving sex? One would presume so.

3. Except for two semesters, results have settled into a relatively stable pattern so far as prevalent student interests are concerned. The same is true of the pattern of beliefs revealed. The overall patterns and the deviations are shown in the three tables below.

4. Using as a base previous researches into student opinion elsewhere, we seem to be getting at Fresno a pattern which is more general, more national, and less regional, than was anticipated.

5. Within the Fresno student culture, there are certain small subcultures which deviate more from the norm than was anticipated.

6. Students are more candid than anticipated—except for about 25 percent who have strong religious attachments or other intellectual commitments which cause them to "clam up."

7. The device here reported appears to be a very useful adjunct to other established devices for studying relatively private values and beliefs. Its unique value lies in the fact that it lends itself more readily than other devices to classroom or other group use by teachers who lack time and training to use other depth techniques.

8. Probably much can be inferred about the beliefs of high-school students through studying those of college students. The age gap is not great. We assume that most high-school students tend to hold as "emergent beliefs" those which their older brothers or sisters in college have firmed up.

The three tables that follow indicate major areas of interest, by percentage, of "subjects most talked about in intimate situations." The first is a composite of all quality papers received to date. The second indicates the results of the fall of 1964 when there was a presidential election. The third shows the results of the spring of 1967 when, for some as yet unknown reason, religion outran sex as the most popular subject of conversation.

Some observations concerning what appears below seem desirable: the investigator at this time does not wish to push interpretation very far because it may influence results of the next two year's study (many of the students in his samples are likely to have read this.) One fact might at first glance appear puzzling to a reader. In each of the reproductions of statistics below, the percentages add up to far more than 100 percent. This is explainable on the basis that each student reported on more than one category—almost all on 3 or 4—and their responses therefore appear more than once.

One interesting fact is that, considering all useable papers tallied to date, an almost equal number of students report on religion and sex. Note, however, that in the spring of 1967, 54.7 percent reported religion as

COMPOSITE OF ALL QUALITY PAPERS RECEIVED TO DATE

Number in sample: 301

CATEGORIES ON WHICH STUDENTS WROTE	PERCENT REPORTING ON EACH SUBJECT
Politics	30.8
Law	8.6
American economic system	6.6
Religion	55.8
Social class	16.9
Race	39.8
Sex	59.8
Dating, courtship, & marriage	27.9
Morality	35.2
Education	32.3

QUALITY PAPERS, FALL, 1964

Number in sample: 40

CATEGORIES ON WHICH STUDENTS WROTE	PERCENT REPORTING ON EACH SUBJECT
Politics	92.5
Law	12.5
American economic system	20.0
Religion	70.0
Social class	45.0
Race	50.0
Sex	80.0
Dating, courtship, & marriage	45.0
Morality	65.0
Education	47.5

among the topics most frequently discussed but only 52 percent so reported on sex. In the fall of 1966 (not shown above) 65.1 percent reported on religion, 54.5 percent on sex. This marks a sharp reversal since during all preceding semesters (except fall 1964) sex was the subject reported as one of the most widely discussed among Fresno State College students. Are students at this school becoming more religious and less concerned with sex? A careful study of conversations reported reveal that this is *not* the case: if anything commitment to religion is decreasing while that of sex holds about steadily. Reasons for this will be published in a monograph after the conclusion of the study two years hence.

The reason for the high interest in politics in the fall of 1964 should be obvious: it was a presidential election year and at the time there appeared to be a very marked, and seemingly crucial difference, between the candidates. The fall of 1966 was a gubernatorial election year in California. The students reported that less than 28 percent of the time was politics a subject of conversation—apparently they much preferred talking about religion and sex than about Reagan and Brown.

QUALITY PAPERS, SPRING, 1967

Number in sample: 73

CATEGORIES ON WHICH STUDENTS WROTE	PERCENT REPORTING ON EACH SUBJECT
Politics	20.5
Law	6.8
American economic system	2.7
Religion	54.7
Social class	16.4
Race	38.3
Sex	52.0
Dating, courtship, & marriage	21.9
Morality	32.8
Education	30.1

To imaginative teachers, the research reported above may suggest other approaches more suitable for high-school use. For example, students might be asked to react to problematic case studies in writing. Much can be learned directly or through inference from such devices.

THE DATA OF REFLECTION

Data used to test student beliefs will include other student beliefs—often of the same student whose belief is undergoing test. If a student sees that he holds two mutually contradictory beliefs, then the process of testing has *begun*—even though it yet may have a long way to travel. Similarly, when, in discussion or in other teaching situations, the beliefs of a group of students bang up against one another, the process of testing has begun for many students. Material injected by the teacher—

anecdotes, statements of belief, reading of statements of others, and the like—also provide data to start the testing process.

But serious testing proceeds only with the use of factual data. As we have defined belief, it is impossible to draw a sharp line between the meanings of belief and fact (just as it is to draw a sharp line between opinion and fact). We will use the term, fact, with a definite connotation, however. It will refer to assertions that have been tested by those best equipped to do so—the experts in a given area. If specialists in demography agree that, according to the best available statistics, the population increased 2.4 percent in a certain year, then we can take this as a fact. Note that certain conditions must be present: The facts we use in the classroom are established by persons in the best position to know—experts. Second, there must be consensus among the experts or something very close to it. This matter of consensus is important; often, experts cannot agree—in which case we can only say there is an issue, not a fact.

Teachers will encourage students to gather their own facts—to discover for themselves what is true and what is not. This is the preferred way. But a great deal of help may be needed. Students need to be wary of the purported facts offered in any documentary material, but particularly in their textbooks. (This is a much greater problem in the social studies than in, say, the physical sciences.) It is inescapable that a teacher will need to offer many clues to source material, and perhaps even furnish some.

CONCLUSIONS

We have now presented in its basic form our recommendations for curriculum making in the social studies. Content selection should be based wherever possible on the criteria as implied in the questions on p. 294. Problems, units, projects, blocks of work—call them what you will —should focus on a problematic area of culture. It should be a problematic area where the concerns of large numbers of both adults and students intersect (or can be made to intersect). The primary teaching task is testing, with the most adequate data available, the beliefs of students. Insofar as they can be discovered, beliefs of a private nature should be given as much or more attention as those which are "open."

Such an approach does not require major disruption of present curriculum patterns. It does require that teachers conceive social-studies courses more broadly—history, for example, will include data from sociology, anthropology, psychology, and the like. But no overhauling of the present pattern of courses seems necessary in order to apply the problem-centered approach recommended here.

Finally, as a prelude to the chapters to come, each is designed to illustrate kinds of beliefs which are shared by adults and youth and are therefore appropriate for testing. Whether what we mention in each case would be appropriate in any school is an individual decision of the teacher; at times caution must dominate impulse. In some school systems, for example, sex may best be left alone—at least until the community can be educated to accept it as a proper part of the school curriculum. The same may be true of religion, etc. The ensuing seven chapters should be considered primarily *illustrative* and not in any sense a mandatory part of the social-studies curriculum. They merely demonstrate the ingredients: beliefs in problematic areas and samplings of relevant data with which to test them. Both cultural conflicts and confusions are illustrated, as well as closed areas. Study questions illustrate much about recommended technique, and are intended to be provocative, motivational.

Some readers will be tempted to read personal biases of the authors into the following seven chapters. The chapters are not intended to be coldly scholarly, to represent a fully balanced view of issues, or to be blandly soothing. Their content, to a considerable degree, is intended to be motivational. None of the seven chapters is written to carry a reader through a complete act of thought: If this were the case, the writing would negate the whole point of reflective teaching. The intent of the chapters is to demonstrate to teachers and prospective teachers the type of content which will arouse thought. In some instances, it has seemed best deliberately to inject what will seem to some little more than prejudice. Both content and the manner in which it is offered are intended to be provocative. To motivate students it is sometimes necessary to present the unpopular side of an issue—to "play the devil's advocate." How far this should be carried must be determined by each individual teacher, according to the situation in which he works. We have gone rather far in presenting the side of issues which many persons not only reject but prefer not to reflect upon. We hope this demonstration of the provocative will not confuse readers as to our intent. As a major qualification, however, we have documented wherever possible, and even though most of what we present will seem unpalatable to certain readers, *it is factual.*

As a last word, we believe readers will find these chapters *interesting* and wish that there were more. However, as a reverse twist on Parkinson's Law, in book writing, space creates its own limitations; the amount one wants to include does not automatically create its own space.

DISCUSSION QUESTIONS AND EXERCISES

1. What are some possible outcomes of simultaneous operations of trends toward both specialization and integration in the social sciences? Write a short essay on "What is ahead for the social sciences?"

2. It has been argued that it is dull, not bright, students who profit most from a traditional subject-centered curriculum and memory-level learning. The contention is that, since dull students are incapable of reflection, a problem-centered program is impractical for them. Evaluate this argument carefully.

3. Many persons will disagree with the propositions advanced concerning present content of social-studies subjects. For students who wish to perform research on this question, the following is suggested: Select several high-school social-studies textbooks in the field of history, civics (government), and geography. Include under each both recent titles and titles in use in the middle 1950s. Seek evidence pertinent to these propositions:

   a. In a given field, there is a body of standard content which is included in most textbooks.

   b. Except for considerable compression and simplification, much content of high-school texts resembles that of their college counterparts.

   c. In spite of changes in such aspects as organization, reading ease, format, and pictorial materials, the content treated has not changed significantly in the past decade or two.

4. Stuart Chase has said, "The culture concept of the anthropologists and sociologists is coming to be regarded as the foundation stone of the social sciences" (*Proper Study of Mankind*, p. 59). Why is the culture concept so regarded? Do you feel its significance is overrated? What applications might it have in education?

5. If one accepts the idea that, in any learning situation, the only content worth including is that which can function evidentially in reflection, how should a textbook writer pursue his task? Devise a plan for a textbook which would reflect the foregoing assumption.

6. Would you try to help students to intellectualize their methodology in connection with every attempt at reflective problem solving? Why or why not?

REFERENCES

BERELSON, BERNARD, ed., *The Social Studies and the Social Sciences*, New York, Harcourt, Brace & World, 1962.

A series of position papers on basic content in each of the social sciences.

BRAMELD, THEODORE, *The Use of Explosive Ideas in Education*, Pittsburgh, University of Pittsburgh Press, 1965.

The generally recognized leader of the social reconstructionist approach in education proposes that the gulf now existing between "educationists" and liberal arts professors could be breached if they adopted as a common integrating center a series of "explosive ideas." Although the number of examples given is limited by the book's relatively short length, it is sharply relevant to Part IV of the present book.

CARR, EDWIN R., *The Social Studies*, New York, Center for Applied Research in Education, 1965.

This little book is packed with information about curriculum, methods, materials, evaluation, and so on. The book is useful as a case study in showing why the social studies are in such sad shape.

CUBER, JOHN F., WILLIAM F. KENKEL, and ROBERT A. HARPER, *Problems of American Society: Values in Conflict*, 4th ed., New York, Holt, Rinehart & Winston, 1964.

This popular college text treats a large selection of problems of American life from the standpoint of contradictory values. A solid, reliable source, with good reference lists.

ELLSWORTH, RUTH, and OLE SAND, eds., *Improving the Social Studies Curriculum*, 26th Yearbook, Washington, D.C., National Council for the Social Studies, 1955.

Treats all the innovations discussed in the present chapter plus others, and presents numerous case studies. Students may draw their own conclusions as to how deeply these innovations have cut from the standpoint of changing the learning product.

FARBEROW, NORMAN L., ed., *Taboo Topics*, New York, Atherton, 1963.

An exceptionally provocative and interesting symposium on the difficulties which scientific researchers encounter when trying to investigate problematic areas in our culture. Chapters include the subjects of death, sex, suicide, peace, male homosexuality, religion, among others. Of the books of the 1960s, one of the most relevant to our theme.

FRASER, DOROTHY M., and EDITH WEST, *Social Studies in Secondary Schools*, New York, Ronald, 1961.

Chapter 2 is devoted to the social-studies curriculum in terms of present structure and trends. The authors present in detail the curriculum pattern recommended by the Connecticut State Department of Education and suggest that it is representative of the national pattern. Its "standardization" and failure to recognize the interrelation between subject and method bear out what is said about the social studies in the present book and indicate how little *real* change has occurred in this century.

FREEDMAN, LEONARD, and CORNELIUS P. COTTER, eds., *Issues of the Sixties*, Belmont, Calif., Wadsworth, 1961.

A better-than-average book of readings which treats social—and personal—conflict. Entire volume is excellent, but see especially Section 7, "The Changing American Character."

GROSS, RICHARD E., and LESLIE D. ZELENY, eds., *Educating Citizens for Democracy*, New York, Oxford University Press, 1958.

A book of readings, Part 2 of which is devoted to the social-studies curriculum. Note Chapter 4, "Orientation to Possible Solutions," by Nathaniel Cantor, whose highly original book, *The Dynamics of Learning*, Buffalo, Foster and Stewart, 1956, has become something of a classic.

HUNT, ERLING M., ed., *High School Social Studies Perspectives*, New York, Houghton Mifflin, 1962.

A book that updates conceptual and interpretative developments in history, social science, and area studies.

LEWENSTEIN, MORRIS R., *Teaching Social Studies in Junior and Senior High Schools: An Ends and Means Approach*, Chicago, Rand McNally, 1963.

Contains a very good short section on the structure of the social-studies curriculum, pp. 20–28.

LYND, ROBERT S., *Knowledge for What?*, Princeton, Princeton University Press, 1940.

One of America's greatest sociologists, in a profound book, questions the real worth of the social sciences, decides that as of the time of his writing they were not worth much, and proposes a fundamental reorientation. Like Robinson (below), Lynd proposes as focal points of study the forbidden areas of culture—the closed areas.

MAYER, MARTIN, *Where, When and Why: Social Studies in American Schools*, New York, Harper & Row, 1963.

Mayer, author of *The Schools*, New York, Harper & Row, 1961, and numerous articles on education, writes a devastatingly critical book on the social studies as taught in the 1960s. In many ways, his criticisms correspond to those found in the present book. Highly readable and provocative.

McDONAGH, E. C., and JON E. SIMPSON, *Social Problems: Persistent Challenges*, New York, Holt, Rinehart & Winston, 1965.

As of this writing, this clearly appears to be the best book of readings on the tensions of modern American culture. An extraordinarily useful reference source which should be in the library of every social-studies teacher.

PETERSON, WILLIAM, and DAVID MATZA, eds., *Social Controversy*, Belmont, Calif., Wadsworth, 1963.

Two University of California professors produce a valuable book of readings which focuses on several of our most troublesome closed areas.

ROBINSON, JAMES HARVEY, *The Mind in the Making*, New York, Harper & Row, 1921.

Influenced by John Dewey's philosophy, Robinson, the noted historian, wrote an enduring classic on the "whys" of education. Although not using the term, this is the first book we know which advocates the focusing of teaching on the closed areas of culture.

U.S. DEPARTMENT OF HEALTH, EDUCATION and WELFARE, OFFICE OF EDUCATION, *High School Curriculum Organization Patterns and Graduation Requirements in Fifty Large Cities*, Circular No. 587, Washington, U.S. Government Printing Office, 1959.

The "official source" of data on the frequency of offerings in high-school social studies, but inadequate because it ignores thousands of high schools in smaller cities, towns, and unified rural districts.

CHAPTER 13

Problematic Areas of Culture: Power and the Law

THIS CHAPTER deals with the "power structure" of American civilization and its supporting arm, the law. The term *power structure,* as referring to the power of some individuals and groups over others, is not in the vocabulary of the ordinary layman. What we treat here under the heading of power would, in the thinking of most laymen, comprise "politics." However, power in the United States today involves issues which go far beyond what laymen mean by politics.

That we have in the twin and integrally related subjects, power and the legal establishment, a closed area—or rather an entire congeries of closed areas—should be fairly obvious. First, most people have a very dim and confused view of how power operates in the United States; to the extent that they hold beliefs in this area, they are likely to be prejudiced and usually wrong. A combination of ignorance and closed-mindedness is the common condition. That law and the court system should be used to implement the power system probably has never occurred to the average citizen, although he may believe, without giving it much thought, that "money talks in court," i.e., the power of the court may be used to keep the rich on top and the poor on the bottom. Laymen do have innumerable opinions about justice and injustice and how the legal establishment promotes both. Much of the popular ideology on this subject is myth.

Background

In skimming briefly over the relevant historical background, we will use the convenient—although somewhat oversimplified—terms "Jeffersonian" and "Hamiltonian," by which we refer to the political beliefs these two men held at the time.

Jeffersonians, entranced by the ideal of a rural nation of independent small farmers governing themselves through a "one-man-one-vote" principle, each enlightened about the issues and voting intelligently, never envisioned the massive industrialization that was to come. Possibly much of the thinking of Jeffersonians was wishful and for good reason. They were in America, and fought and died in a combination civil war and rebellion against British control to escape what appeared to them the tyranny of centralized government and centralized economic institutions. They equated centralization with oppression, authoritarianism, and absence of freedom for the masses. Jeffersonians wanted a weak central government and a laissez-faire economy of small, competing units. They saw this as best realized in a rurally oriented nation and a central government with powers forever limited by a strong system of checks and balances. This was the "liberal" position of that time.

Hamiltonians took an opposite stance on almost every issue. Hamilton envisioned a strong central government; he even felt that the head of state should be titled "king" rather than "president." His sympathies were not with the small farmer, but with the industrialist—hence his advocacy of a protective tariff to enable the new nation to develop an indigenous industrial system. He wanted maximum independence for the central government, which he assumed would be controlled by a ruling elite. Hamiltonianism was the "conservative" position of the time.

Jeffersonianism was doomed from the start. In a rough sort of way, the westward frontier carried with it a flavor of Jeffersonianism—individualism, little or no centralized government of consequence, small-scale agriculture, handicraft industry, and the like. It is not surprising that the last traces of Jeffersonianism were seen in the Populist Movement whose geographical origins were in a largely frontier area—the Great Plains. We refer to Populism as bearing traces of Jeffersonianism because it was rurally based, its strength lay mainly in the small farmers of the south and the Great Plains states, it was against big business, against eastern financial power, and, particularly in the South, against a protective tariff. Populism, however, marked a fundamental change in belief from pure Jeffersonianism: It called for a *strengthening* of the federal power through intervention in the traditional monetary system; government ownership and operation of the railroads, and of the telegraph and telephone systems; demand for the creation of a sub-Treasury system; and other reforms, all of which could be conducted only by the federal government.

The elections of 1896 eliminated the Populists as a serious factor in American government. The Peoples' Party from the start had no real chance of success because, except for the brief and mild episode of the Jacksonian era, the country was already committed to Hamiltonian economic precepts even if it were not yet committed to the idea of strong federal power.

However, the demand for stronger federal power was to come—and from sources which would, in Jefferson's day, have seemed incongruous. It was to come from the masses—both farmers and urban labor. It was to come from those who had been dedicated to Jeffersonianism. The "new liberalism," which remains the liberalism of the late twentieth century, demands dynamic, aggressive, and increasingly strong federal power.

Only in a very general sense can an element of Hamiltonianism be seen in the new liberalism. Hamiltonianism called for strong federal power for entirely different reasons: Federal strength was sought as a shield to protect the privileged classes from the demands and the possible unruliness of the poor. The new liberalism sees federal power as the only practical shield to protect the under privileged from exploitation by the Business Establishment, by pressure groups of great variety, and even by elements within the federal government itself—such as the Military Establishment—which the lower classes and educated middle classes see as a threat. Pure Hamiltonianism, in its milder forms, is the "new conservatism"; in a more extreme and authoritarian form, it is "fascism."

To some it seemed that Goldwaterism was a revival of original Jeffersonian principles; but this particular movement contained too much chauvinism and courted too many friends among the authoritarian "right" to be construed as anything other than a kind of pseudo Jeffersonianism. This is the "new radical conservatism." (However, low-tariff policy remains "liberal," as do many other Jeffersonian preachments—such as the equality of men, strengthened public education, etc.)

It cannot be said however, that in the 1960s Hamiltonians are as scarce as Jeffersonians. The general posture of the conservative wing of the Republican Party—and we exclude the extremist Goldwater fringe—probably has some preference for high tariffs and favors permissive treatment of big business and other elements of the ruling elite, "sound" money, keeping the lower classes in their place, and so on. They are not however, consistent Hamiltonians; they do not like the idea of a strong federal government—and in that sense have a Jeffersonian flavor. But on this point they yield easily—a strong federal power is tolerable if they can achieve economic advantage through it.

The "great turning point" came with the Populist call for government ownership and operation of certain key industries, and with the rising socialist movement. The Socialist party nominated its first candidate for the presidency, Eugene V. Debs, in 1900—and with Debs still the candidate polled about 900,000 votes in 1912 and about 920,000 in 1920. Norman Thomas, as Socialist candidate, did almost as well in 1932 with about 885,000 votes. Most of the proposals on the Socialist party platform have since been adopted by either Democrats or Republicans and are now in effect.

So far as key legislation is concerned, the act creating the Interstate

Commerce Commission in 1887 and the Sherman Anti-Trust Act in 1890 were benchmarks. Hampered by a succession of Supreme Court decisions, the latter proved to be ineffective, although under it Theodore Roosevelt won at least two major "trust-busting" victories. It was not until 1914, during Wilson's first administration, that the basis of effective anti-trust action was established in the Clayton Anti-Trust Act and the Federal Trade Commission Act. Nor had the ICC functioned very well until, among other measures to bolster federal power, Roosevelt's administration passed legislation which strengthened it to some degree.

That all of this legislation contained loopholes, and could be enforced only if the administrative branch of the government chose and the Supreme Court permitted (which did not occur until the 1930s), does not nullify its importance. Weak as it was, this legislation established precedent and reflected the temper of the country—a fundamental change had occurred with respect to federal versus local power. Although it was not to be felt substantially until the 1960s, local power, except in rather small and insignificant matters, was doomed.

There is little point here in reviewing further background. From the first decade of the present century, the trend toward greater use of federal power has proceeded—slowly during Republican administrations, rapidly during Democratic. That those who deplore this trend most vehemently on an abstract level at the same time insist on it where concrete issues are concerned is but an indication of our inconsistencies. The balance of this chapter will be devoted to the specific points of conflict and confusion.

1. Sovereign Citizen vs. Power Centers

It is believed that ultimate power in our society lies in the voting power of individuals acting singly; but it is also believed that there are large power centers, such as "big business," "big labor," and "big government," which nullify the wishes of the people.

A belief in the citizenry as the ultimate source of power in a democratic state is very comfortable to live by. It justifies our going to the polls, gives us the feeling that we have done our duty by our country when we cast our ballot, and justifies forms of entertainment which many persons enjoy immensely—namely, the circus held every four years (labeled party nominating conventions).

Evidence of just what the popular vote means is in order.[1] From a

---

[1] The following material, unless otherwise noted, is drawn from Stuart Chase, *American Credos*, Harper & Row, 1962, chap. 7.

study conducted in 1960 using public-opinion polling techniques, re-searchers concluded that during a political campaign only about 25 per-cent of voters have enough interest to discuss it, only 7 percent ever attend rallies or dinners, only 4 percent contribute money, and only 3 percent ring doorbells or make telephone calls. The investigators in this study concluded that "homo Americanus . . . is not a political animal." [2] Chase also cites a New Haven Study of 1961, which demonstrated that for the typical voter many other areas of interest come before politics. This is true of politics on all levels—local, state, national, and interna-tional.

Turning to some of the public-opinion studies relating to ignorance, we find that a 1948 study reported by Chase revealed that 10 percent of voters did not know who the presidential candidates were, 50 percent could not name the vice-presidential candidates, about 66 percent had no knowledge of the respective party platforms or any ideas of where can-didates stood on issues. Studies made more recently show no significant change. In a 1958 study reported by Chase, only 50 percent of voters could name as many as one of the two candidates for Congressmen for whom they would be voting; also in 1960, 32 percent of voters could think of no political issues whatsoever that concerned them personally.

Reviewing the results of the famous study of voters at Elmira, New York, conducted by Berelson, Lazarsfeld, and McPhee, Chase suggests that at first glance it seems impossible that our system could function at all except by some quirk of chance or the "Grace of God." The large majority of voters are so ignorant of the nature of our government, of candidates and issues, that they cannot possibly vote with intelligence. In spite of this, we have managed to maintain a kind of democracy, falter-ing, shaky, and inefficient, perhaps—but we still have it. Berelson, Lazars-feld, and McPhee advance an interesting thesis to explain the success of American democracy, which space does not permit us to elaborate here, but with which social-studies students should acquaint themselves.[3]

Since apparently about 75 percent of American voters are both apa-thetic and ignorant, and since about 9 percent are extremists of authori-tarian bent—mostly of the political right—this leaves us with about 16 percent of the voting public that we can depend on to show both demo-cratic commitment and intelligence in voting.[4] We can only conclude

[2] Chase drew this material from Campbell, et. al., *The American Voter*, Wiley, 1960.

[3] See Bernard Berelson, Paul Lazarsfeld, and William McPhee, *Voting*, University of Chicago Press, 1954, Chap. 14.

[4] Gordon Hall, an expert on extremism, estimates there are about 7,000,000 politi-cal, racial, and religious extremists in the United States. Seymour Lipset agrees the figure may go this high. See "What Is an Extremist," *Look*, October 20, 1964.

that voters are a relatively minor force in the American power structure.

The evidence is somewhat confusing as to whether power in the United States emanates from a group of "power centers" or, as C. Wright Mills would have it, from a single, monolithic power center.[5] Confusion results from the fact that although Mills makes a rather convincing argument, it is obviously opinionated—which does not necessarily invalidate it—and lacks adequate supporting evidence. There are too many events which suggest that, if there is a single power elite, it is not monolithic in the Millsian sense: Persons who should see eye-to-eye on certain issues do not; the situation is fluid, dynamic, and what the case is one year may not be so the next.

We prefer the thesis that most crucial decisions in the United States are made by a system of power centers which may or may not pull in the same direction. We also feel that the 16 percent or so of responsible voters cannot be ignored; this figure seems destined to grow as educational levels rise.

In the discussion of the more significant of these power centers on the next few pages, an attempt has been made to list these centers in order of importance. But, since *in a given situation* this order may largely break down, it is meant only to be suggestive and provide a basis for further inquiry.

THE OFFICE OF THE PRESIDENCY [6]

By "Office of the Presidency" we are referring to the entire administrative branch of the federal government. However, the administrative branch belongs to the President; it represents a kind of extension of his person. Presumably his appointees reflect his views. The President may dominate the office in the sense that he is clearly the most forceful and influential member of the administrative branch—a genuine leader; then we refer to him as a "strong" President. Abraham Lincoln was a prototype. Or, a President may be forceful in carrying out his strictly defined Constitutional duties, but go no further; Grover Cleveland was a good prototype. In contrast, the president may not be strong-willed or a leader. Such Presidents may select strong-willed men for certain key posts and depend on them for leadership, as did President Eisenhower when he served under Secretary of State Dulles.

In the twentieth century, the Office of the Presidency has become a major power center, potentially overriding all others. In the 1960s it re-

---

[5] C. Wright Mills, *The Power Elite*, Oxford University Press, 1956. (Also a Galaxy paperback, 1959.)

[6] For many of the following ideas and facts, we are indebted to Sidney Warren whose excellent article, "New Dimensions in the Presidency," appeared in the *Saturday Review*, August 20, 1960. We take full responsibility for all conclusions stated.

mains a major power center even if the President himself is "weak." This is because of the multiplicity of self-sustaining agencies which are a part of the administrative branch and which are in a position to exercise freely power of great potency. These include, among others, the Military Establishment, the FBI, the CIA, the National Space Agency, the Federal Reserve Board. Sustaining many of these federal agencies—particularly the Military Establishment, the National Space Agency, and the National Science Foundation—is what might be called the "Scientific Establishment." [7]

What are the duties of a President, as of 1967? There are his strictly Constitutional duties: (1) serving as head of state—"the symbol of and spokesman for the entire United States"; (2) chief executive, charged with enforcing all laws; (3) legislator, who proposes laws to Congress and uses all the powers at his command to get them enacted; (4) maker of foreign policy; and (5) commander-in-chief of the armed forces.

The foregoing is only a beginning. As Warren suggests, since early in our history the President has been the leader of his political party. In modern times, he has become a molder of public opinion—a role greatly facilitated by modern means of communication. He is the caretaker of his people: In times of natural disaster, it is to the President that they turn. It is the President's responsibility to keep the economy unwaveringly dynamic. He is regarded as the repository of the public will—the one elected person who represents all the people. He is the country's chief diplomat, expected regularly to meet with other heads of state. Since the United States is the most powerful and influential nation in the world, the President is obligated to play the role of world leader to the best of his ability.

Any time we have a President with the physical stamina and the capacity for intellectual and moral leadership to do all these things with unusual effectiveness, he may well be the most powerful chief of state in the world. In the long run, however, he is answerable to the public at large, and even the strongest president is likely to be sensitive to public opinion.

THE POWER ELITE

This term refers to a closely knit, mutually supporting, group of individuals in official or unofficial positions, corporations, and arms of the federal government, which makes fundamental policy and implements it without authorization or much possibility of control by the citizenry at

[7] The best reference on this subject known to the authors is a symposium: Robert Gilpin and Christopher Wright, eds., *Scientists and National Policy-Making*, Columbia University Press, 1964. Most contributors are social scientists. See also Gilpin's *American Scientists and Nuclear Weapons Policy*, Princeton University Press, 1962.

large. A strong President is automatically a member of the power elite and may dominate it; but a weak President may not realize that such a power center exists; hence, he is subservient to it.

Whether a truly monolithic and unified elite exists is dubious. Perhaps the most telling argument against the existence of a monolithic power elite is that typical descriptions of it are oversimplified: Those who should be members of the power elite too often fall to quarrelling among themselves; the various elements frequently tend to develop divergent interests. A strong President who is committed to democratic decision making and the welfare of the masses is not likely to do anything to seriously injure the power elite, but he may take actions which they consider highly inimical to their interests. The so-called "traitor to his class," Franklin Delano Roosevelt, is a case in point. The scientific elite disagree among themselves, often violently: Edward Teller wants more, bigger, and better hydrogen bombs—Hans Bethe argues for disarmament. Despite its obvious lack of unity, we will continue to use the term, power elite, for this sprawled, ever-changing, power center of major significance.

THE SUPREME COURT AND THE FEDERAL COURT SYSTEM IN GENERAL

The federal courts play two highly significant roles in the power structure. First, they legislate by interpreting the Constitution and deciding what laws are in harmony with it. Historically, the general nature of court interpretation of the Constitution has been from conservative to liberal, from republican to democratic (not in a party sense). There tends to be a lag between court decisions and public opinion. When judges are slow to keep their interpretations in tune with public demand or with the public interest as the President sees it, the President can gradually change court opinion by appointing men of his own outlook as rapidly as court members die or retire.

It is rather hard to assess just where the court stands in the power structure. It can overrule both the President and the Congress on constitutional matters. This was dramatically illustrated during Franklin Roosevelt's administration; but, in the long run, Roosevelt prevailed by appointing new judges. The kinds of decisions made by the power elite are not expressed in law; therefore they do not come before the court for review. There are some exceptions to this, of course, but not a great many. We therefore feel it legitimate to place the court system third in the power hierarchy.

The second major role played by the court is dispensing justice. This will be treated later in the chapter.

SPECIAL INTEREST GROUPS

We refer here to what are commonly called "pressure groups," although some of the special-interest groups which we see as exercising major power are not regarded by the public at large as "pressure groups." Special-interest groups exist in large number and their power within the total power system varies according to circumstances. Their influence may be largely local, or it may be national or international. An example of a local group might be a citizens' committee to reform public education; of a national group, the American Medical Association; of an international group, a cluster of corporations with large foreign holdings.

A special-interest group can represent but a tiny minority of the population and yet manage effectively to control governmental decision: The AMA, for example, managed for decades to block attempts at expanding public medical services. Labor unions have secured much favorable—for them—legislation. The Ku Klux Klan has been a kind of "invisible government" in the Southeast. For a long period of years, the Roman Catholic Church decided, in effect, what motion pictures the American public could see.

Attempts to contain the federal government as a major liberal power center now lie largely in a minority special-interest group rather different from any previously known in the United States. This minority, because of strong financial support and extreme militancy, constitutes a power center stronger than its numbers suggest. We are referring to the bundle of "fringe groups," perhaps more accurately designated the "radical right." This group consists of mutually supporting organizations functioning either overtly as pressure groups or clandestinely as more-or-less underground conspiratorial organizations. How large in number the radical right is remains uncertain, as does the question of whether it is growing or declining in influence. The dedicated, militant radical right has been estimated as including directly somewhere between 3 and 8 million.[8]

The radical right would have little to stand on if it had not been able to create the impression that it was needed to prevent imminent takeover of the American government by American Communists. How accurate is this claim? The authors know of only one major scholarly work which is sharply relevant to this question.[9] The following analysis of the "Communist menace" is drawn from Shannon.

[8] Senator Frank Church, "Conspiracy USA," *Look*, January 26, 1965, pp. 21–37. See *Look* of October 20, 1964, p. 37, for a more solid figure of about 7,000,000.
[9] David A. Shannon, *The Decline of American Communism*, Harcourt, Brace &

The Communist Party received its greatest support at the polls in 1932 when its presidential nominee, William Z. Foster, received almost 103,000 votes. In local elections in large urban centers, Communist candidates have done much better proportionately, particularly in nonpartisan elections where their party identity was not indicated on the ballot.

According to Shannon, Earl Browder (one-time U.S. Communist Party leader) asserted that in 1945—when he was fired from leadership —actual party membership was in the neighborhood of 75 to 80 thousand. Many of those members were remiss in paying dues and were primarily interested in personal grievances. By 1948 the great "slide" began. Although the U.S. Communist Party declined largely from internal reasons—poor leadership and lack of a wide base of social discontent on which to build—, other factors were also significant: the debunking of Stalin, Titoism, anti-Semitism in the USSR, and the employment of Russian force in Hungary, among others. Anti-Communist hysteria during the McCarthy era perhaps delivered an unnecessary but final *coup de grâce*. The Party could boast no more than 20,000 members in 1957, most of whom were in New York City. By late 1958, the figure was down to 3000. Shannon concluded, "The conditions necessary for the growth of the American (Communist) Party certainly are not present today. . . ."

THE NATIONAL CONGRESS

We suggest that as a general rule the Congress falls lower in the power hierarchy than the groups previously mentioned because (1) it tends usually to bend before the will of a strong presidency, (2) it is impotent to thwart in major ways the aims of the power elite, and (3) all too often it has stood paralyzed in the face of pressures from special-interest groups. Yet, Congress is potentially a potent power center. It can, with full constitutional authority, reject presidential appointees, refuse to act upon legislative request, pass laws "over the President's head," and ignore or even take steps to weaken special interest groups. What it cannot do is dictate court decisions or, except in rare instances, muster the strength to take actions contrary to what most of the power elite demands. When Congress exercises its constitutional power rather fully, it is usually only as a result of the goading of an exceptionally strong President.

World, 1959. He traces the history of the party since 1945. Shannon's study was sponsored by the Fund for the Republic.

POLITICAL PARTIES

The individual voter who wants to make himself felt politically has his best chance working through the Democratic or Republican Party. The former is likely to provide more psychological rewards, since roughly two-thirds of Americans who affiliate with one of the two major parties are Democrats, and being on the winning side gives the individual a certain sense of elation. However, as pointed out on page 311, Americans in general are not much interested in politics. That the vote is largely meaningless, due to ignorance concerning candidates and issues, relegates the role of parties in the power structure to a position of relative unimportance.

It is necessary to qualify an assertion of this sort: The power role of a political party is difficult to assess. Most studies of party politics have focused on other matters. Opinion polling offers some interesting data. Most Americans see little difference between the two major parties. Nevertheless by the age of 30, 75 percent have settled, usually for life, into an identification with one party or the other. As Chase puts it, "In a fuzzy kind of way, voters believe that the Democratic party speaks for the poor, the Republican party for the rich." Many Americans are skeptical that a party will keep its campaign promises.

To conclude, it probably can be said that to the extent that the Congress is a significant power center—which as was suggested in the previous section, may vary from circumstance to circumstance—political parties can play a somewhat important role in the total power system by helping to assess public opinion and funnel it into the folds of the federal government. The persuasion of party leaders can influence decisions of Congress. Party leaders have access to the President himself, who is the titular head of his own party.

THE POWER OF IDEAS

We should like to inject one more thought about individual power (as opposed to power centers involving groups of persons). In the long run —and by this we mean what can amount to centuries or even millenia —it is *ideas*, usually originated or popularized by individuals, that shape man's destiny. We shall mention but two instances. An obscure, mild-mannered clerk, laboring only with mind and symbols in his room at night, evolved a body of physical theory which was to shake the world. The product of this thought, although highly complex, included an equation for the transmutation of mass into energy ($E = mc^2$). Life will never be the same again. Another mild-mannered, unobtrusive man worked for years in the British museum studying history, economics, and philosophy. Out of this emerged a book entitled *Das Capital*, which

presented in powerfully persuasive form the theory of dialectical materi-
alism and scientific socialism—a grossly perverted version of which we
now call Communism. Will the world ever again be the same? The heads
of state of all nations put together, and their power elites, have never
wielded such power as this.[10]

1.1 Do you think the growing power of the Presidential Office presents a fu-
    ture menace? Does it mean that a President who so intended could establish
    a dictatorship? If so, what steps would he need to take?
1.2 If anything resembling a power elite actually exists in this country, how
    would you expect it to differ from those of other countries? What addi-
    tional element of power—which we lack—would be a part of the power
    elite in a country like Spain?
1.3 In relation to most industrialized nations, the American electorate is no-
    tably apathetic and ignorant in the political arena. How do you explain
    this? If you see historical factors at work, what are they? What would be
    the best way to remedy the situation?

2. Law as Protection of the Weak vs. Law as a Weapon of Power

It is believed that ours is a society of law and that law protects the weak
against the strong; but it is also believed that many laws favor the rich
and powerful and act to keep the common man in his place.

While many are somewhat cynical about its truth, the typical American is familiar with the first idea. On the other hand, although most are
somewhat familiar with the second, few have considered in more than a
rudimentary way all that it implies. For example, the notion that "many
laws favor the rich and powerful," is rather widely believed but with
little idea as to *how much* American law does favor the rich and powerful. The idea that law may often be used as a weapon to "keep the common man in his place" introduces more clearly the idea of law as an integral part of the power structure—a possibility which probably has occurred only to some social scientists and a scattering of the most sophisticated lay observers.

Most Americans probably believe that basically most people are rascals
and the main function of the law is to control their overt behavior so
that an orderly society is possible; for example, everyone would be dishonest except that harmful dishonesty is illegal and people fear getting
caught. Laws are, therefore, a necessity; yet many individuals feel we
have too many of them. Laws which they feel unduly restrain their own

[10] See Max Lerner, *Ideas Are Weapons,* Viking, 1939.

"always-reasonable" desires should be erased from the books. But the very same persons who feel on an abstract level that we have too many laws are often the ones who continuously fight to have new laws passed —laws which will hedge in *other* persons.

It is historical fact that the American public, since the colonial period, has been rather contemptuous of law. Whenever they are reasonably sure they can get away with it, they break laws and boast about their cleverness. This has happened on a large scale, as when virtually every treaty—one kind of law—between whites and American Indians was violated. Settling disputes by violence rather than by legal means has a long history of respectability in the deep South, but no part of the country can claim purity on this score. Apparently, at all social ranks except possibly the lower-middle class, which to some degree takes upon itself the guardianship of morality, successfully breaking the law confers prestige.

Again citing Stuart Chase's *American Credos* (chap. 10), a study reported in 1950 indicated that 31 percent of the sample had never heard of the Bill of Rights, 36 percent had heard the name but couldn't define it, and another 12 percent described it inaccurately. Only 21 percent could describe with reasonable accuracy the nature of the Bill of Rights.

In public-opinion polls, when confronted with the chief tenets of the Bill of Rights on a purely abstract level, as in the question, "Are you in favor of freedom of the press?" virtually all respondents say, "Yes." It is evident that large numbers of Americans, however, when presented with specific instances, do not approve of the Bill of Rights and the Fourteenth and Fifteenth Amendments. A few sketchy examples will suffice. Thirty-three percent of respondents in one study would forbid newspapers from criticizing the American government. Twenty-five percent would not let the Socialist Party publish a newspaper. In a Gallup study in 1961, 49 percent of the sample wanted more television censorship and 31 percent more newspaper censorship.

Because of the known existence of some millions of persons who are either committed to or mildly "string along with" the radical right, most of these results are not surprising. But some results are. Chase reports a study made in 1958 which indicated that at a Labor summer school, 60 percent of union leaders would deny an atheist the right to teach in college; 50 percent would deny the same right to a Socialist. Perhaps more alarming were the results of the studies in depth over a period of years of some 7000 high-school students. Large proportions would deny some or all people most of the basic rights guaranteed in the United States Constitution.[11]

[11] H. H. Remmers, ed., *Anti-Democratic Attitudes in American Schools*, Northwestern University Press, 1963. See also the journalistically styled *The American Teenager* by H. H. Remmers and D. H. Radler, Bobbs-Merrill, 1957.

There is no reason to suppose that people are any less ignorant about federal, state, and local legislation than they are about constitutional law. Their knowledge of law, including protections guaranteed them, is negligible and limited largely to specific cases where they or their friends have become embroiled.

The entire picture is confused because the Legal Establishment seems ambivalent in its operations—reflecting, no doubt, ambivalent thinking in the culture. First, it is obvious that there are in state, local, and federal law many provisions for protecting the public against powerful vested interests. To name a few cases: The United States Supreme Court during its "liberal eras" has done much to implement the Bill of Rights and the Fourteenth and Fifteenth Amendments of the Constitution. We have pure food and drug laws, laws requiring honesty in labeling, laws requiring honesty in advertising, laws to protect against business monopoly, and the like. We have federal laws to protect soldiers against undue abuse by officers and to let those who object in principle to war plead their case for conscientious objector status. We have state and local laws to protect against police brutality, to provide the indigent with legal counsel, to provide sustenance for the helpless. Thousands of items of legislation of a "protective" nature could be named.

But these facts, in themselves, fail to provide a clear picture of the situation. To what extent are the protective measures of the Constitution enforced? Or those of federal, state, and local law? And if they can be shown to be enforced effectively, is there a contradictory body of legislation which is nonprotective in the sense that its purpose is to protect, not the underdog, but only the rich and well born, the corporations, the higher echelons of the military, the power elite and special interest groups in general from attack by reformers who represent the weak? Either lack of enforcement or a body of nonprotective measures would neutralize much of our protective legislation.

Granted that on certain occasions the Supreme Court and other federal courts—and state courts, also—are dominated by liberal judges committed to protection of those most likely to be persecuted unfairly, these occasions are limited. For example, the liberal "Warren Court" is definitely exceptional. Conceding this area of positive enforcement, to what extent do the main body of the law and the *overall* operation of our total court system (federal, state, and local) protect the public?

One often-forgotten fact is that the legal structure, save from written Constitutions, is legislated by groups which operate at some level in the power structure: the Presidential Office, the Supreme Court, the National Congress, state Supreme Courts, state legislatures, lesser state and local courts, county supervisors (or commissioners), city supervisors (or commissioners), schoolboards, and perhaps a few lesser agencies. Who are these people? At the top two levels, they are quite clearly VIPs of the first rank. At the Congressional level, they range from persons who operate from a very strong base of power to those of little consequence. At lower levels, the prestige and power of those who legislate is varied; but these groups *do* legislate and we are supposed to obey. Hovering behind this entire legislative structure is the power elite, ever striving to maintain its position.

No one in the foregoing groups wants to lose his place in the power hierarchy. No one in the foregoing groups is likely to try to influence legislation in a way that would endanger his own position in the power structure. To those in a position to legislate or influence those who do, many individuals or groups may loom as threats. Among these are labor unions, consumer organizations, racial and ethnic groups, small businessmen, and intellectuals—especially writers and iconoclastic types in the performing arts, teachers, and students. Ideas—which may stem from the foregoing intellectuals or from scientists whose new inventions threaten old but profitable institutions—are often regarded as dangerous. Both individual and organized crime are a threat. (Although powerful figures among the latter may have much in common and cooperate with specific members of the power elite, as well as with members of the Executive Office, the Legal Establishment, and legislative bodies.) The young may often seem a menace to the old. Women may seem a menace to men— and, in certain special situations, vice versa. Even the "modernist" clergy and their supporters may loom as threatening. The immigrant may seem a threat to the native born—and so on and on. In summary, the upholders of the status quo always feel under attack by any person, group, or idea that is unconventional, unorthodox, or in any way likely to upset things.

The point we are leading to is that there is a vast body of law, a deliberate—often fought for—absence of law, and a court system, including prosecuting attorneys, *whose purpose is to aid and assist those who have power over others to maintain that power.*

2.1 In its overall force, do you consider the law more as a needed means of maintaining order and protecting the underdog, or as a means of preserving the power of those who now have it? If law performs both functions, what does this suggest about the ways of thinking of Americans in general? Is ambivalence in this area a problem serious enough to be concerned about?

2.2 How do you explain the persistent tendency of the American people to violate legal statutes? Excluding the area of political "crime," is there more, or less, law violation in the United States than in other advanced industrialized nations?

2.3 How do you explain the general ignorance concerning law, especially Constitutional law? Would it help to teach more courses in government or civics in high school? If so, how would you revamp such courses to make them more effective?

3. Courts as Dispensers of Justice vs. Courts as Dispensers of Injustice

It is believed that the United States has the fairest system of courts in the world; but it is also believed that "money talks" in courts and anyone who has enough of it can buy his way out of trouble.

The popular mythology runs something like this: The United States is one country in the world where a person can be assured of justice. This is in large part due to the fact that every accused is entitled to trial by a jury of his peers. It is also attributable in part to the rather worshipful attitude people have toward judges. The very term, judge, has the rather magical connotations of a person of unusual wisdom, commitment to justice, impartiality, and the like. Conversely, lawyers are thought by large numbers of persons to be "slippery," cunning, untruthful, and mercenary. In spite of the widespread distrust of lawyers, there is still faith that the jury, with the guiding hand of the saintly judge, will ferret out the truth.

A more cynical belief, held by an unknown proportion of persons, says, in effect, that in the courtroom, "Money talks." In other words, the rich man who can afford to hire the best—i.e., the most clever and dishonest—lawyer is likely to go free even though patently he may be guilty. This cynical group evidently does not think very highly of jurors because it assumes that a "good" lawyer can sway a jury.

Another aspect of the popular myth is that most crime, and particularly serious crime—e.g., crimes of violence—are committed by lower-class persons. Lower-class persons, particularly the "lower lowers" are regarded as having no "moral sense." The myth would have it that these persons are defective in some way—they verge on feeblemindedness or insanity, or lack the innate conscience that is supposed to be part of the genetic inheritance of normal people.

So far, we have discussed the popular ideology with regard to courts and justice. What is this ideology with respect to the virtue of laws themselves? This is harder to ascertain, and there may be few strong feelings about laws in general. Where people exhibit strong feelings about law, it is usually a particular law, and one that has affected them personally. In the Fresno State College study of student beliefs, very few girls showed interest in questions of law, but a considerable number of male students did. They evinced two major complaints: (1) There was a strong feeling that traffic laws are "unfair." (2) Most were incensed over the laws of California governing sex, particularly the legal entity known as "statutory rape." Much less often mentioned, but still an irritant to male students, is the law making it illegal for anyone under 21 to purchase or drink alcoholic beverages.

Now that we have briefly explored the ideology of the law, courts, and justice, what are a few of the salient facts? The popular ideology is at best inconsistent and confused; at worst in diametrical variance with well-established facts. First, excluding the area of political crime, the American court system and its supporting legal codes probably lead to greater injustice than those of most other "advanced" nations in the world today. Of course, the terms, justice and injustice, are matters of value judgment and definition is extremely difficult.[12]

Let us consider trial by jury. On the basis of solid factual evidence, apparently about the worst possible way of determining whether a person has or has not broken a law is to turn the decision over to a jury of his peers. In spite of the most careful selection techniques, juries are usually prejudiced for or against the accused before their selection. This is in part because the human animal tends to live by prejudice and also in part because of the habit of newspapers to try the accused and find him innocent or guilty before the trial takes place. Jurors also have their built-in prejudices—often archaic—of the nature of morality (which they tend to confuse with legal definitions of crime—an easy thing to do, since much legislation is based on moral precepts dating from earlier centuries).

When a jury is "hung," and its members are weary and frustrated, they have been known to make their decisions by tossing coins; by putting slips of paper each with a possible decision written on it, into a hat and then blindly selecting one; throwing dice; pulling cards from a deck; exercising extreme coercion, including threats of physical violence, on the one or two jurors who refuse to accede to the wishes of the majority, and so on.[13]

Now as to judges: There is good evidence that they are less saintly than most of the public believe, and often entitled to less respect than a bookie who makes good on his commitments. Some judges are old-fashioned moralists who have no conception of the difference between a judgment of fact and a value judgment. Some have no conception of rules of evidence. They share with juries the tendency to decide prior to

[12] For an excellent treatment on this subject, see Hans Kilsen, *What is Justice?*, University of California Press, 1958.

[13] For two classics in this field, see Jerome Frank, *Courts on Trial*, Princeton University Press, 1949; and Jerome and Barbara Frank, *Not Guilty*. Doubleday, 1957. Erle Stanley Gardner's *The Court of Last Resort*, Sloane, 1952, is also highly relevant.

a trial whether a man is innocent or guilty. Judges are well aware that they can, if they choose, sway the decision of the jury by the manner in which they treat the contending lawyers. Every shrewd lawyer knows that chances of winning acquittal for his client hinge very heavily on what judge he draws. Furthermore, judges can be "bought off"—the extent to which this happens is apparently much greater than even the most cynical would surmise.[14]

As to attorneys, the authors know of no scientifically valid study as to whether, on the average, their characters rate higher, lower, or equivalent to the public impression. Our opinion, and it is no more than that, is that the education of attorneys has improved immensely, that they show a continuous upgrading in sense of responsibility, and that ethical standards imposed by bar associations tend to become more stringent. The public very likely sells short this professional group.

What are some facts concerning the laws under which we live? It is our general thesis that many laws are designed to give one group of persons power over another in order to maintain the present power structure. Because this thesis seems rather new, documentation of it is an arduous task—too arduous for the authors to adequately accomplish here. There are some carefully done studies which seem to offer fairly conclusive proof that laws are heavily rigged in favor of organizations or persons of high or middle social position.[15] The owners of a corporation—i.e., the stockholders—cannot be held accountable legally for the misdeeds of corporate officials. When corporate officials commit criminal acts, they usually act with vision and operate on a grand scale. Such acts include fraudulent advertising, selling goods that do not meet the specifications of the buyer,[16] violating anti-trust laws, stealing patents, income tax evasion, and embezzlement—to mention only a few.

Sutherland contends that corporate crime contributes more to social disorganization and disintegration than any other category of crime. But the tendency of the federal government to settle most corporate crimes

[14] See Joseph Borkin, *The Corrupt Judge*, Potter, 1963. This adequately documented study deals only with federal judges, and elaborates their many criminal offenses, accepting bribes being the most common. Readers of the present book might wish to ponder the possible results of a study of the behavior of judges on state and local benches.

[15] See books such as Norman Jaspan and Hillel Black, *Thief in the White Collar*, Lippincott, 1960; and Edward H. Sutherland, *White Collar Crime*, Holt, Rinehart & Winston, 1961. The first focuses on individual crime committed by middle- and upper-class persons; Sutherland focuses on corporate crime.

[16] The "great highway scandal" is an excellent example; case after case has come to light of building contractors reaping fortunes by building roads that failed to meet the specifications of the federal highway program initiated during the Eisenhower administration.

out of court, and the tendency of the courts and laws together to permit, if not make mandatory, suspended sentences or infinitesimal ones (such as a fine limited to a few hundred dollars) furnishes strong evidence that the Legal Establishment is in fact a means of maintaining the power structure. In this instance, high corporate officials who have achieved membership in the power elite are virtually immune to punishment. What court dares punish severely a member of a group which either has direct power over the court or, in a more general sense, is simply higher than the court in the power hierarchy?

Crime among the middle- and upper-social classes occasionally takes the form of violent assault, rape, or murder. Often, it is theft in some form. Embezzlement is very common, as are numerous other crimes against property. Those who embezzle the greatest sums are those highest in the executive structure of business.[17] Probably at least 60 percent of white-collar theft is committed by executive or supervisory personnel; the remaining 40 percent is committed by accountants, store clerks, and store customers. The lower the social rank of the thief the more likely that punishment will be inflicted and the more severe it is likely to be.

The most wretched thief of all is the poorly educated, lower-class person who attempts robbery, armed or otherwise. He may get shot on the spot, he may be apprehended before he has succeeded in stealing anything, or he may temporarily abscond with some money—only rarely a large sum. He will almost surely get 15 to 20 years in a state or federal penitentiary.

The popular ideology that crimes of violence or of "immorality" tend to be committed mainly by lower-class persons contains a germ of truth —but not much more than a germ. The popular notion is misleading at many points. Crimes of violence among middle- and upper-class persons frequently do not lead to arrest and therefore do not enter into the statistics. The same is true of so-called crimes against morality—such as homosexual acts, statutory rape, drug addiction, and so on.

This leads us back to commentary on the nature of the law. Legislation, historically, has largely been under the control of the WASP (white-Anglo-Saxon-Protestant) majority in the United States. More specifically it has been the WASP middle-class which has controlled legislative bodies at national, state, and local levels. This group, with its historically puritanical leanings, has placed on the law books of every state —and in federal legislation as well—laws that uphold the puritanical— and basically Calvinist—traditions of the Western world.[18] This is why

[17] See Jaspan and Black, *op. cit.*

[18] See particularly Morris Ploscowe, *Sex and the Law,* Prentice-Hall, 1951; and Paul H. Gebhart, *Sex Offenders; An Analysis of Types,* Harper & Row, 1965. A

an upper-class executive who has stolen his corporation into bankruptcy and injured or ruined hundreds or thousands of persons is not severely castigated by the public; the middle-class public is horrified, however, by "crimes against morality." Upper-class persons obviously commit such so-called crimes, but they can buy their way out. Those at the bottom of the social heap cannot.

Some mention should be made of the capital-punishment issue. There is an abundance of literature in this field based upon empirical research. At one time, a chief argument for capital punishment was the need for vengeance ("an eye for an eye, a tooth for a tooth"); the chief argument now emphasizes capital punishment as a deterrent. The evidence in regard to its efficacy as a deterrent is conflicting. Most nations of Western Europe and Latin America have abolished, or carefully circumscribed, capital punishment and consider the United States "barbaric" because in almost three-fourths of our states it is still practiced. The homicide rate averages lower in those countries and those states in the United States which have abolished capital punishment than it does in those which have not. Not only is the homicide rate below the national average in those states which have abolished capital punishment; but in those states (all in the Southeast) which practice capital punishment with the most diligence, the homicide rates are the highest in the nation.[19]

There are other—and perhaps more potent—arguments against capital punishment. It is a firmly established fact that a rather large but unknown number of innocent persons are convicted of capital crimes each year and executed.[20] Furthermore, social-class membership plays a crucial role in determining who will be executed. A study of persons in penitentiary death rows indicates that with extremely rare exceptions they are lower-class "down-and-outers." A rich man is executed for murder approximately as often as a Harvard Ph.D. graduate seeks a career as a private in the Marines.[21]

---

study of the furor created in England by the Wolfendon Report is also enlightening; the same situation would apply in the United States except in greater extreme—the United States is far more backward than England in this respect.

[19] An excellent chart showing the homicide rate by states between 1948 and 1957 appears in Edmund G. Brown, *Message to the Legislature*, Sacramento, State of California, 1960. During that period, six states had abolished capital punishment. By 1960, the number had risen to nine; and by 1966, to ten with an unqualified ban on capital punishment, and three others permitting capital punishment only in special cases. See chart on "Methods of Execution in the United States," *Information Please Almanac*, Simon & Schuster, 1966, p. 319.

[20] See Frank, *op. cit.;* and Gardner, *op. cit.*

[21] For a rather personalized but highly insightful treatment, see Clinton T. Duffy, *88 Men and 2 Women*, Doubleday, 1963.

3.1 It appears to be an indisputable fact that the law and courts treat the "rich and well born" much more leniently than the impoverished for the same kinds of crimes. Do you think this is supporting evidence for the thesis stated earlier in the chapter that American law is designed to preserve the present power structure? Why or why not?

3.2 What do you think the term, justice, means? Conversely, what is injustice? Can you define either term operationally? Is a person talking nonsense when he uses such words?

3.3 What is the relationship between crime and morality? Between crime and sin? Is a proven criminal always a sinner?

DISCUSSION QUESTIONS AND EXERCISES

1. For purposes of discussion, assume the theory of the power elite is basically valid. Then try to answer questions such as these: Is a democratic state possible to maintain if a power elite exists? What counterbalancing forces might arise—with the help of an enlightened citizenry—to keep the power elite in check and perhaps make of it a constructive tool of democracy?

2. One of the tightest, most effective, special interest groups in the United States is the undertakers. Responsible students of funeral practices in the United States consider this one of our most disgraceful rackets. (See books such as Jessica Mitford's *The American Way of Death*, Ruth M. Harmer's *The High Cost of Dying*, and LeRoy Bowman's *The American Funeral*.) Investigate the provisions of your state code and try to decide what laws may have been passed at the instigation of undertakers' associations. Inquire from local undertakers what the cost of a "respectable" funeral is and compare the figures quoted. What control do you, as a citizen, have over such special interest groups?

3. Attend as many court trials as possible during the semester. Report to the class on your impressions.

4. Suppose you were apprehended on some charge, and whether or not innocent, you wished a nonjury trial. Investigate how you could secure such a trial and the procedures that would be involved.

5. How are juvenile offenders handled in your community? Ask that some student observe some trials at juvenile court and visit the detention home for juveniles and report to the class. How would you criticize present practices?

REFERENCES

ARENS, RICHARD, and HAROLD D. LASSWELL, *In Defense of Public Order: The Emerging Field of Sanction Law*, New York, Columbia University Press, 1961.

"Sanction law" refers to the imposition of sanctions (penalties) for infractions that damage the integrity of the social order. Sanctions may be imposed by law or in other ways. Unless they are considered as a whole, in relation to national goals and problems, social disorganization develops. The authors see the situation in the United States as chaotic.

BALTZELL, E. DIGBY, *The Protestant Establishment*, New York, Random House, 1964.

A study of the history, influence, and present status of what has come to be known as the WASP's—which Baltzell equates with the Republican Party. He forecasts their declining influence in the face of the rising influence of ethnic, religious, and racial minorities.

BURNHAM, JAMES, *The Managerial Revolution*, rev. ed., Bloomington, University of Indiana Press, 1960.

A highly controversial book on trends in government structure and function, which some have said had its inspiration in Mussolini's ideas of the "corporate state." It is interesting to compare the 1960 edition with the 1941 edition, in which Burnham forecast that Germany and its allies would win World War II.

BURNS, JAMES M., *Deadlock of Democracy; Four-Party Politics in America*, Englewood Cliffs, N.J., Prentice-Hall, 1963.

This book sets forth the hypothesis: We really have four major parties, not two; and government is possible only through coalitions—often unstable—as in other multiparty countries. The parties are; Republicans who identify with the Congress; Republicans who identify with the Presidential Office; Democrats who identify with the Congress; and Democrats who identify with the Presidential Office. The interests of the two Congressional parties often conflict with those of the two Presidential parties, making government complicated and difficult.

CARR, EDWARD HALLETT, *The New Society*, New York, Macmillan, 1951.

Carr, a British social theorist and historian of international reputation, has given us a book which has become something of a classic. It treats lucidly and profoundly twentieth-century social tendencies. The book has the virtue of brevity without superficiality.

FAULK, JOHN H., *Fear on Trial*, New York, Simon and Schuster, 1964.

A devastating book on how the power structure can destroy the life of a man who is suspected of not being sympathetic with the views of those in power. Faulk, a broadcaster for CBS, was fired because of a fraudulent attack by an organization named AWARE, Inc. Faulk was "blacklisted" in 1946, in 1964 won court vindication and a judgment of half a million dollars against his accusers.

FRANK, JEROME, and BARBARA FRANK, *Not Guilty*, Garden City, N.Y., Doubleday, 1957.

Two of the leading experts in the field examine 36 cases in which innocent persons were convicted, in most cases by "juries of their peers." This is the most recent (as of this writing) of a series of excellent books by Jerome Frank on court procedure in the United States.

GOODMAN, PAUL, *Growing Up Absurd*, New York, Random House, 1960.

Goodman views personal corruption as an expression of a broad and basic "structural immorality" of our culture which corrodes all of our social institutions, from church to race track. Relevant both to questions of power and law.

HAMILTON, WALTON H., *Politics of Industry*, New York, Knopf, 1957.

This is a very well done book by a person who is highly critical of the role played by big business in the United States. Although you may find Hamilton's opinions unacceptable, much of what he says about the extent to which large industrial firms maintain a "private government" affecting the lives of people both directly, and indirectly through pressures exerted on government, probably contains much that is factually correct, and which also supports the "power elite" thesis.

HUNTER, FLOYD, *Community Power Structure*, Chapel Hill, University of North Carolina Press, 1953.

An interesting description of the power structure in a small Southern Community. The top 40 businessmen make policy for the community; professional men execute their decisions; all others are the "ruled." Hunter stays clear of moral assessments.

JASPAN, NORMAN, and HILLEL BLACK, *Thief in the White Collar*, Philadelphia, Lippincott, 1960.

Considered by reviewers one of the best books on middle- and upper-class crimes against property. Heavily documented and highly detailed, but at the same time fascinating reading. The book implies much about both the power structure and the law in the United States.

KEY, VALDIMER O., *Politics, Parties, and Pressure Groups*, New York, Crowell, 1964.

A widely used political-science text which contains some novel hypotheses. Key defines politics as power relationships which "consist fundamentally of relationships of superordination and subordination, of dominance and submission. . . ." An excellent reference source, much of which is directly relevant to this chapter.

KOLKO, GABRIEL, *Wealth and Power in America*, New York, Praeger, 1963.

An important book on corporate wealth in the United States, written by an antagonist to the extent and use of the power it confers. Poverty is also an important theme, since Kolko contends—with good documentation—that the way wealth is distributed in the United States now is little different than it was 50 years ago.

KRONHAUSEN, EBERHARD, and PHYLLIS KRONHAUSEN, *Pornography and the Law*, New York, Ballantine, 1960.

They constitute a husband and wife team of psychiatrists who attempt to assess the meaning of the word, pornography, and to evaluate present legal means to control it. They conclude that the term has not been defined, and that statutes governing pornography are both meaningless and ridiculous.

LASSWELL, HAROLD, *Who Gets What, When, and How?*, New York, Mc-Graw-Hill, 1936.

A book on the American power structure as Lasswell saw it at that time. Still widely sold in paperback.

LASSWELL, HAROLD, and ABRAHAM KAPLAN, *Power and Society*, New Haven, Yale University Press, 1950.

Considered by most reviewers to be the best book written on the subject at that time. Since then, our system has changed in both obvious and subtle ways, particularly in the greatly enhanced power of the Presidency.

LEEDHAM, CHARLES, *Our Changing Constitution*, New York, Dodd, Mead, 1964.

One of the best accounts of how the original Constitution of the United States has been changed by amendments and legislation, and the difficulty and time lag which has usually accompanied such changes.

LIPSET, SEYMOUR M., *Political Man: The Social Basis of Politics*, Garden City, Doubleday, 1960.

Professor Lipset brings sociological analysis to bear on analyzing the conditions necessary for democracy. Although not without defects, this book is a fundamental contribution. One reviewer writes that "it should be compulsorily read by anyone who thinks American sociology is something written by Vance Packard." Not light, and probably best suited for advanced students.

MILLS, C. WRIGHT, *The Power Elite*, New York, Oxford University Press, 1956.

The late professor of sociology at Columbia sets forth his by now famous thesis that the nation is dominated in a selfish and often conspiratorial manner by an all-powerful military-industrial-political power center. Mills's arguments are criticized as overdrawn; in spite of this, the book is provocative, and has had considerable influence.

PLOSCOWE, MORRIS, *Sex and the Law*, Englewood Cliffs, N.J., Prentice-Hall, 1951.

A study of laws governing sexual behavior in all of the states. Reveals clearly the archaic, semantically innocent thought behind such laws, and is a biting commentary not only on law in the United States, but also on the chaos resulting from allowing each state and local community to legislate on such vital matters.

CHAPTER 14

Problematic Areas of Culture: Economics

Economic Thought in Modern America

LIKE OTHER problematic areas, economics is characterized by an extensive system of beliefs and attitudes which function very much as do religious dogmas. The present urgency of debates over government spending, inflation, wage policy, monopolistic practices, poverty, waste, free enterprise versus socialism, welfare programs, and the like attest to a strong interest among adults—and many high-school students—in economic matters.

Until after World War II, the leading economic beliefs of middle- and upper-class Americans reflected (not always consistently) the central ideas of "classical economics." Adam Smith's great book, *An Inquiry into the Nature and Causes of the Wealth of Nations* (1776), offered the first systematic analysis of the nature of economy in what came to be known as the classical pattern. Smith was followed by David Ricardo, Thomas R. Malthus, James Mill, and his son, John Stuart Mill. These men developed and refined a body of doctrine which was to influence economic thought profoundly to the present day.

The core of classical economic thought is the idea of the self-regulating or "laissez-faire" economy—an economy composed of a large number of independent producers in competition with one another. In such a system, supposedly, everyone seeks to do as well as he can—that is, to get as much as he can for what he has to sell and to give as little as he can for what he has to buy. As people follow this pattern, competing and bargaining as individuals, the "self-regulating market" appears.

This self-regulating market guarantees that resources will be used wisely and that people will get what they want. If demand for a certain product rises without a corresponding increase in supply, the price of that product will rise. The increase in price will reduce the number of customers and increase the number of producers (who rush in to take advantage of rising profits). Thus, through the mechanism of price, balance between demand and supply is restored. If demand for a product drops, prices fall; and demand rises again at the same time that supply falls (because falling prices will have bankrupted or discouraged the less efficient producers). According to this description of economy, supply

331

and demand tend to balance each other, and prices tend to fluctuate about a norm, which over the long run represents the lowest price at which products can be sold without ruining producers. Economists often refer to this picture of the economy as the "competitive model," meaning that it involves a large element of abstraction and simplification but at the same time contains the essential truth of the operation of a competitive economy as seen by classicists.

In order that the classical model may work, free competition is always necessary. Central to free competition is free pricing, not merely rivalry over quality of product or service given. Free pricing requires conditions such as these: numerous sellers and buyers, unaffected by any sort of monopolistic collusion; buyers and sellers informed at all times of market conditions; and complete freedom of labor and capital to move to new types of production or new geographic regions.[1]

Classical economic thought fostered a cluster of popular economic beliefs, some of which are as follows:

1. People do (or should) compete economically with each other. The essence of competition is free pricing.
2. Monopoly does not (or should not be permitted to) interfere with free competition.
3. The chief motive to behavior is the hope of economic gain (i.e., desire for money or goods).
4. The economy can operate successfully without central planning, which means government can, and should, keep hands off.
5. The laissez-faire system is harmonious with political democracy, because free competition prevents the emergence of any single individual or group with power over others.
6. Whatever economic problems may arise, they may best be handled by leaving them alone—letting nature take its course. (Business recessions can best be handled this way, for example.)
7. The economic system (if it functions properly) requires the right of private ownership and use of property, and the sanctity of contracts.
8. It is the private businessman, with his willingness to take risks in hope of profit, who supplies the mainspring of the economy.
9. The chief source of discouragement to private businessmen is govern-

---

[1] Those who wish to read generally competent descriptions of the "classical competitive model" may turn to almost any introductory textbook in economics published before World War II. For a lucid treatment in a few pages, especially good on the role of the price system, see John K. Galbraith, *American Capitalism: The Concept of Countervailing Power*, Houghton Mifflin, 1956, chaps. 2 and 3. More detailed but excellent is C. E. Ayers, *The Industrial Economy*, Houghton Mifflin, 1952, chaps. 1, 13, and 14.

ment interference in their affairs. (Another source of discouragement is labor unions.)

10. Currency is sound only when it is freely exchangeable for gold or other precious metal.

11. Governments should spend as little as possible and try always to operate on a balanced budget.

Probably in no other field of human interest is there a greater gulf between present understanding of experts and that of the lay public. Average citizens have never fully understood the structure and implications of the classical competitive model. They have never understood clearly that competition meant "price competition" nor have they grasped the conditions of price competition and the role of price competition in the market. They have not even understood that the competitive model implies an absence of protective tariffs and all forms of subsidies, and a ruthless disregard for inefficient producers.

To the long-standing confusion of laymen over the nature of a competitive economy a new source of confusion has been added. Academic economists generally, as well as most of the younger generation of business and political leaders, have adopted a new and radically different set of economic beliefs patterned after ideas of the late John Maynard Keynes. Ideas which are either Keynesian or fit the general Keynesian pattern include the following:

1. The federal government should use fiscal and other powers to ensure a steady rate of economic growth and full employment of all persons who are "employable."

2. The chief weapons to be employed are government spending designed to bolster purchasing power, tax reduction devoted to the same end, federal control over interest rates and other monetary policies.

3. Unconcern with limits over the size of the national debt, with major attention given to the most efficient ways of managing it—i.e., perpetuating it without its causing undue inconvenience.

4. Recognition that such competition as exists is based almost entirely upon quality and service, not free pricing; hence, dependence can no longer be placed on competition as a regulatory mechanism. This implies the application, as needed, of government price controls, either in the form of "lids" or "boosters."

5. Since the federal government is the only governmental unit which can create money and since only the federal government can coordinate effectively the allocation of human and natural resources on a national scale, it is the proper role of the federal goverment to be responsible for planning specific directions of development of the economy.

6. Since only the federal government can create money, it is accepted that the financing of needed state and local economic projects increasingly will be assumed by the federal government.[2]

It is very difficult in the United States for the federal government to pursue a rational and consistent economic policy because of popular misconceptions about economics. Whatever the government may try, even though it makes sense economically, becomes a subject of widespread and heated debate and an object of "movements" to change it. More often, policies which make the most economic sense are never tried because of opposition to them. An example of such enforced irrationality arises from the widespread hostility to income taxes as a means of raising revenue. This forces government to rely increasingly on sales and excise taxes, which do not seem to evoke such vigorous protest. The lack of protest probably stems from the facts that people do not feel that the visible taxes—e.g., the retail sales tax—add up to much in one day's purchases and are not aware of the existence of the invisible taxes—e.g., excises levied on goods before they reach the market. Yet, sales and excise taxes bear more heavily on the poor than on middle-income groups, more heavily on middle-income groups than on the rich. In short, they are "regressive." The great majority of the population therefore approves taxation policies that injure them the most and oppose taxation which, in immediate terms, seems to "hurt" the least. As every football coach insists, there is a difference between hurt and injury. Sales taxes "hurt" least but "injure" most.

Economically sound behavior would indicate a greater reliance upon income taxes than now seems possible. This should not be taken to mean that any approach to taxation should be fixed or dogmatic. As Galbraith pointed out, at the state and local level, increases in sales taxes, *especially on nonessential goods*, forces a reallocation of resources; it reduces spending for unnecessarily luxurious autos, jewelry, and homes, for example, leaving more for the public sector of the economy—schools, roads, hospitals, and the like.[3] But that we *could* make vastly heavier use of the income tax, if we chose, seems indisputable. As Stern demonstrates so well, if the numerous loopholes in the federal income tax law were eliminated, tax rates could be cut in half without reducing revenue—or, conversely, present tax rates could be kept as they are and the

[2] For a treatment of the "new economics," probably the most readable book is Harry Gordon Hayes, *Spending, Saving and Employment*, Knopf, 1945. For a more recent and comprehensive treatment, see Adolf A. Berle, *The American Economic Republic*, Harcourt, Brace & World, 1963.

[3] John Kenneth Galbraith, *The Affluent Society*, Houghton Mifflin, 1958, chap. p. 12.

revenue produced about doubled. As it now stands many millionaires pay no income tax whatsoever.[4]

Arguments over government ownership and operation of industry also illustrate the irrationality of economic policy and decision. The argumentation over government ownership in the production and distribution of electric power is one example. Here, the logical issue is, Who can do the job most economically? Electric-power installations are built to last a very long time and their monetary cost is amortized over a very long period. Private industry usually must pay about 6 percent interest for the money it "hires." The federal government pays about 3 percent interest—a rough approximation of the interest paid on government bonds. Interested students might wish to calculate the cost of financing a $100 million project over 30 years at 3 percent and at 6 percent and note the difference.

Even though most professional economists consider this a nation of "economic illiterates," there are good reasons why economic illiteracy should gradually decline. First, there is the test of experience. For example, even though people don't know *why*, they are aware that deficit spending by government seems to continue indefinitely without catastrophe. Second, each year an increasing proportion of the population graduates from college. A considerable number of these graduates are exposed to one or two introductory economics courses. The courses may or may not "take," but we are justified in assuming that they frequently will.

Five specific points of conflict and confusion in American economic thought will be considered in the following pages.

1. Government Frugality vs. Government Financing of Needed Projects

It is widely believed that the government should trim its expenditures as much as possible; but it is also widely demanded that government should finance all needed projects which otherwise could not be financed.

During the first administration of Franklin D. Roosevelt, a deliberate effort was made to reduce unemployment through federal spending. Judged by modern experience, government expenditures of these years were puny, though at the time they seemed gigantic. The economic effect of fiscal policy during these years is still debated. Some economists attribute the drift toward recovery between 1933 and 1939 to govern-

[4] Philip M. Stern, *The Great Treasury Raid*, Random House, 1964.

ment spending, and to bolster their case point out that a cut in spending in 1936 was followed by a sharp recession in 1937. But because recovery was so slow during all those years many conservative businessmen, who had always taken a dim view of government spending, began to say, "You can't spend your way out of a depression."

The quick recovery of 1941–1942 seemed so obviously a result of huge sums poured into the war effort that many more persons than before began to associate large-scale public spending with high-level prosperity. Thus, the belief "You can spend your way out of a depression, and the war experience proves it," came to oppose the belief "You can't spend your way out of a depression." The view now gained acceptance that a reason the government failed to achieve prosperity through spending during the 1930s was that not enough had been spent; if deficits of $20 or $30 billion or more a year had been incurred, prosperity would have returned in a hurry.

This conflict has probably been resolved on one level. Hardly anyone nowadays doubts that government spending contributes to prosperity; in this respect it is no different from any other kind of spending. But the issues now are rather different from what they were ten years ago. People seem unconcerned with what was once called "national bankruptcy." They are now concerned with the possibility of uncontrolled inflation —a direct "bread-and-butter" issue. Whether inflation is desirable depends on what side of the fence one is on: for a businessman, it means enhanced profits; for persons on fixed or slowly rising incomes, such as pensioners, persons in the military, civil service, teaching, anyone with investments which pay a fixed return, and the like, inflation may be painful.[5]

This discussion should not be concluded without mention of the economic role of the Military Establishment and our tendency to become engaged in a succession of cold wars or "hot" brush-fire wars. When war is concerned, the American public is willing to accept unlimited government spending. The government is expected to appropriate enough money to engage our troops in battle against Communist expansionism abroad or suppress any hint of a Communist conspiracy at home. Conversely, in the abstract they deplore large expenditures for the public sector of the economy (schools, hospitals, roads, parks, etc.) while at the same time demanding government expenditure for these things if something of local importance to them is at stake.

Most Americans understand vaguely the relationship between spend-

[5] Two excellent small books for student reading on the subject of government spending are Stuart Chase, *Where's the Money Coming From?*, Twentieth Century Fund, 1945; and, still better, Robert L. Heilbroner and Peter L. Bernstein, *Primer on Government Spending*, Random House, 1963.

ing for war and the existence of prosperity. Industrialists know this very well, as do financiers. The following UPI news release appeared in many papers on February 8, 1966: "Reports of a peace feeler from North Viet Nam brought a flurry of selling into the stock market today and drove prices down for a time. They recovered somewhat going into the final hour of trading." One writer argues that the basis of the American economy is militarism.[6] Shortly after World War II, an economist, Fritz Sternberg, published a book on the future of the American economy. After a period of initial prosperity caused by pent-up post-war demand, he forecast that the only way the economy could be kept afloat would be by major programs of deficit spending. He also expressed the fear that the only publicly acceptable means might be for armaments. Sternberg, a German, labeled an economic system which relies for prosperity on huge armament expenditures a *Wehrwirtschaft* economy—meaning literally a war-based, prosperous, but highly wasteful economy.[7]

1.1 If government spending is accompanied by prosperity, how do you explain the protests against spending by those whose material wealth is steadily increasing? Materially, Americans are living better than ever before, if we exclude the impoverished minority. In 1965, certain major corporations made the highest profits, in relation to investment, ever before made; yet, it is frequently the officials of these firms who argue most vehemently for reduced government expenditures. How do you explain this?

1.2 How is debt of the national government different from a private debt? Or is it? How can you explain why it appears that the government can operate "in the red" year after year?

1.3 How do you explain the almost universal willingness of the American people to accept deficit spending when its main purpose is to finance military operations? How do you explain their tendency to say "we can't afford" needed domestic expenditures?

1.4 Most people praised President Lyndon Johnson's promises of economy in government. When Secretary of Defense McNamara decided to close down a number of military bases because they were superfluous and expensive, people and Congressmen in the areas affected uttered cries of outrage. How do you explain this?

2. Taxes and Government Spending

It is believed that spending by government is a burden on the economy which must be borne by taxpayers; but it is also believed that spending

---

[6] Fred J. Cook, *The Warfare State*, Macmillan, 1963. Cook's biases and polemics get in his way but he makes for very interesting reading nevertheless.

[7] Fritz Sternberg, *The Coming Crisis*, John Day, 1947.

*by private corporations is not a burden and that private corporations
never tax the public.*

Americans dislike taxes to a point where tax evasion is a fine and
widely practiced art. They always assume that taxes are too high, and
that purchasing power and standard of living are lowered by the amount
of the tax. Government expenditures are thought to be essentially non-
productive, even when not inflated by graft and inefficiency.

On the other hand, it is generally assumed that corporations charge
for their services but never tax. When a corporation receives a price for
its product, a customer gets full value in return (if not, it is his own
fault). He has parted with his money, but he has received something
tangible in return. So, what corporations spend—unlike the expenditures
of government—is productive and not a burden to anyone.

Those are the beliefs. Actually, a tax per se is never a burden. The
government, in spending tax revenue, may channel some of our productive effort in directions which do not directly raise our material standard
of living. For example, if tax money is used to pay for national defense
or foreign military operations taxpayers get little in return. If tax money
is used to improve the national parks, taxpayers may get back only spiritual uplift. But if the government spends for public works of lasting
economic value, then such expenditures increase our material standard of
living and are productive in exactly the same sense that building a new
steel mill is productive. Also, taxes are not likely to detract from the
total dollar income of taxpayers. When the government spends tax
money (and it always does!) it becomes income, directly or indirectly,
for American taxpayers. Virtually all tax money is returned to the economy—even if it goes through the hands of foreign nations first.

Like government, private corporations may make expenditures which
do not increase our standard of living. In this category, perhaps, are
some kinds of advertising, padded expense accounts, unnecessarily high
remuneration for executives, and the production of goods of dubious
value. Some corporations—such as holding companies in certain situations—may never in any way contribute to our total production of
needed goods and services. It is wrong to assume that a corporation
never spends other than its "own" money. Actually, the money always
comes from the people in one way or another and the *function of this
money is not unlike that of any tax.* Corporations usually give their "taxpayers" (i.e., their customers and stockholders) something worth while,
but occasionally they may not:

Take the example of Paramount Publix. Here fifty thousand so-called in-
vestors contributed to the greatest public works project ever known in the
amusement field. In this project there was a maximum of what in government

would be called graft, but which in finance is recognized as legitimate tribute. Thus the directors voted themselves and the higher executive officers huge bonuses in order to encourage each other. The president of this principality took a salary and stock bonuses of more than a million and a half in 1930. The company lawyer got $75,000 a year and his assistants from $35,000 to $45,000. Kuhn, Loeb & Company, the bankers, received a huge present of stock simply out of gratitude. A list of relatives received fanciful sums for services of doubtful value.[8]

Another aspect of confusion over taxation is a general failure to understand the ways in which taxes can be used to produce greater economic stability. In periods of severe inflation, for example, certain kinds of taxes are among the most effective weapons available to bring prices down. Inflation presents people with a choice between higher prices and higher taxes, and often it would be to their advantage to take the latter. There is also much misunderstanding concerning the role of the graduated income tax—which cuts more deeply into high incomes than low. When our national income is rising, such a tax *automatically* increases the tax rate and when the national income is falling the rate is *automatically* lowered. This helps to dampen the effect of both inflation and deflation. Galbraith says of the graduated income tax, "It is doubtful . . . if any single device has done so much to secure the future of capitalism as this tax. . . . It works silently and automatically on the side of economic stability. Conservatives should build a statue to it and to its inspired progenitor, President William Howard Taft." [9]

2.1 What do people receive in return for the taxes they pay? What does the government do with tax moneys? What kinds of government expenditures tend to build up the productive capacity of the economy? Do these expenditures increase the living standard of the average American?

2.2 Do all expenditures by corporations tend to build up the productive capacity of the economy? Are corporation expenditures ever wasteful? Who pays the bill for wasteful or extravagant expenditures by corporations? How does the long-range economic effect of corporation expenditures differ from that of government expenditures?

2.3 In what way may it be said that taxes are a burden? Are taxes ever an economic burden, or is it only wasteful ways of using productive resources that can be burdensome?

3. Monopoly and Free Competition

It is believed that American businessmen like the idea of free competition and that most American industry is freely competitive; but it is also

[8] Thurman Arnold, *The Folklore of Capitalism*, Yale University Press, 1959 (paperbound ed.), pp. 302–303.
[9] Galbraith, *American Capitalism*, p. 188.

believed that much American industry is monopolistic, or tending in that direction, and that only by the vigilant enforcement of antitrust laws can we preserve free competition.

Most Americans, without bothering to define precisely what it is, believe they have a competitive economy. At the same time, large numbers of Americans curse "the monopolies." They seem to believe that much of United States industry is monopolized, or tending in that direction. And the United States is one of the few countries in the world where the people have shown enough awareness of the economic implications of monopoly to insist on antitrust legislation.

When monopoly is discussed as a problem, confusion, inconsistency, and irrationality triumph over logic. The difference between competition and monopoly is rarely understood. One person may insist that an industry is competitive but another, with much the same knowledge of the industry, may insist that it is monopolistic. Further, many people compartmentalize their beliefs to a point that they easily believe (1) that most prices are fixed by supply and demand and (2) that most prices are higher than they should be because of collusion among businessmen.

When price competition exists, prices are set by the market, and no individual producer has measurable control over the prices he may charge. This situation can hold only where the number of sellers is so great that each one's share of the total market is negligible. According to classical theory, the market of a self-regulating (laissez-faire) economy is governed by price competition. A twentieth-century advocate of laissez-faire says, "The price system will fulfill [its] function only if competition prevails, that is, if the individual producer has to adapt himself to price changes and can not control them." [10]

What is the situation in most of American industry today? The greater part of mining, transport, communication, power, and manufacturing industry does not practice competition in the classical sense. Control rests with a few gigantic firms having power over the market instead of being governed by it. In most cases, the leading three or four firms in an industry are responsible for more than two-thirds of the industry's production and sales. This sort of industrial structure is known technically as "oligopoly." Where oligopoly exists, any single firm can by its own decisions affect market price for the entire industry. Price competition in the classical sense is found only in a few American industries, and even in these it is adulterated with administrative decision.

Under oligopoly it is common for one firm in an industry to become a "price leader." As long as its decisions seem advantageous to the whole industry, other firms copy its prices. In industries with product differen-

---

[10] Alfred Hayek, quoted in Galbraith. *op. cit.*, p. 15.

tiation there may be some variation in prices—as between a Ford and a Chevrolet—but it is never extreme. When products are so similar that buyers have no strong preference for one over another, a price cut by one firm must be met by other firms. Thus a price cutter gains only temporary advantage. There is, therefore, a strong incentive under oligopoly not to practice price competition. In most American industries a convention against price competition exists, and habits of this kind cannot be prosecuted under the antitrust laws.

So-called "fair trade" laws are in effect, in one form or another, in 39 states. One provision of fair-trade laws is retail price fixing—the purpose of which is to prevent the more efficient retailers from selling a product with a registered brand name for a lower price than do the less efficient retailers. For example, in a given state you are likely to pay identical prices for a pack of cigarettes, a particular brand of whiskey, an electrical appliance, name-brand drugs, and the like. A popular Japanese camera of a certain make costs precisely $289.50 at every camera shop in the United States. The intent of "fair trade" is mitigated by the fact that many manufacturers have decided not to enforce retail price maintenance—hence, our discount houses. There are a number of ruses by which retailers, if they wish, can circumvent such laws. But this does not mean that fair-trade laws do not on the whole contribute to monopoly practice.

3.1 If American business were competitive in the classical sense, would you expect prices to be higher or lower than now? Would you expect depressions to be more or less severe? Would you expect business to be more or less efficient?

3.2 It is generally accepted among economists that American industry is more efficient each year. How do you explain this in light of the fact that American industry steadily becomes less competitive?

3.3 Which of the following do you believe to be destructive of competition: The closed shop? The quota system by which professions limit the number of new members? Fair-trade laws? Refusal of union plumbers to use pipe threaded at the factory? Destruction of fruit by farmers' marketing associations? Parity prices in agriculture?

3.4 Do you think businessmen generally prefer free competition? Why do they say that they do in their magazine ads? Does any group in our society prefer competition to a sure thing? What are the economic implications of the unpopularity of price competition?

4. Free Enterprise and Socialism

It is believed that free enterprise is the best possible economic system, and the only system compatible with political democracy; but it is also believed that under modern conditions government must play an increas-ingly large role in the economy, and that as time goes on the economy will almost certainly become more "socialistic."

First, the term, free enterprise, is a semantically empty term—quite undefinable. Free competition, as we have observed, can be defined rather precisely in terms of free pricing. Capitalism is a poor term with which to describe our system, because *any* economy which makes large-scale use of producers' goods (capital) is properly called capitalism. Neverthe-less, American people use the term, free enterprise, in daily discourse; and, whatever they mean by it, emotions run high in its defense. We shall use it in the following discussion to mean whatever readers want to read into it—perhaps simply the American system as it now appears to operate.

We can explore only a few of the many facets of the free enterprise-socialism conflict. In one aspect, there is an issue over the "workability" of capitalism (free enterprise) and socialism. Socialism, it is argued, sim-ply cannot work. Proponents of capitalism argue that socialism central-izes decisions in the hands of "bureaucrats." The meaning is not clear, but presumably a bureaucrat is an incapable political appointee who is-sues unreasonable manifestoes from behind a large desk in Washington. The economy is stifled when economic decisions are rendered by per-sons not competent to make them. Another aspect of this argument makes "human nature" a culprit: human beings are innately selfish and individualistic; their chief desire is for self-gain. A competitive system in which each person works for his own self-interest is the only economic arrangement compatible with human nature. If socialism requires a high level of selflessness and cooperation, it is bound to fail.

Another argument is that socialism is inconsistent with democracy. Socialism means great power concentrated in planning boards, and a cen-tral government with enough power to enforce its plans is undemocratic. Decisions which should be made by individuals become a function of the socialist state. The right to own and operate a business without petty in-terference, the right to accumulate as much property as one can, the right to choose an occupation and place of residence—all these are said to be usurped by a Socialist state. It is foolhardy to try Socialism even in small doses as an experiment because mild Socialism inevitably leads to extreme Socialism, which leads to Communism. There is only one direc-tion in which Socialism can creep. The process is as irreversible as preg-nancy. Socialism and dictatorship are thus identified in the public mind.[11]

[11] In connection with the general argument about free enterprise, the pro side is represented in Friedrich A. von Hayek, *The Road to Serfdom,* University of Chicago Press, 1945; and on a much lower intellectual level by Raymond Moley, *How to Keep*

In spite of the vigor with which these views are held, there is probably no issue on which Americans are more ambivalent or confused. We reviewed early in this chapter the steady progression of economic centralization in the federal government, and its diminishing condemnation and growing support. Although rejecting Socialism in the abstract, Americans of all persuasion not only want, but seem unable to avoid, increasing doses of it. We have only to mention social security; medicare; public schools; municipal ownership of water plants, bus lines, etc.; public ownership of roads, bridges, etc.; major hydroelectric complexes like the TVA and CVP (Central Valley Project, California; it also provides, as a main function, public irrigation); and the hugest industry in the country in terms of dollar investment, the manufacture of atomic materials for explosives, power, and radiation.

4.1 Which of the following countries have (or had) a free-enterprise system: pre-Communist China, India, Iran, Egypt, pre-Hitler Germany (Weimar Republic), Mexico, Canada, Sweden? Which of these are or were democracies? Do you find that only democracies have a free-enterprise economy?

4.2 Look up the Socialist platform for the national elections of 1912. How many of the proposed measures have not yet been enacted into law in this country? Why did the Socialist party in the United States die as a political force during the 1930s?

4.3 Would the law of supply and demand be allowed to operate in a Socialist system? How could one be sure under Socialism that the goods most desired and needed by the people would be produced? What means could be used to determine the price of goods under Socialism? The wages of labor? It has been argued tellingly that a Socialist economy must necessarily "allocate" labor to various industries and that this allocation would lead to "forced labor." Do you agree or disagree with this argument?

Prosperity and Population Growth

It is widely believed that it is good for a nation to have a rapidly growing population for the economic dynamism and other benefits it achieves; but it is also believed that one of man's most critical problems is overpopulation.

In a chapter on economics, we should stress the notion common among businessmen and others that the faster the rate of population growth the more rapidly will markets—and profits—expand; but we can

Our Liberty, Knopf, 1952. The pro-Socialism side is represented by a variety of authors, but for student reading we suggest Karl Polanyi, *The Great Transformation*, Oxford University Press, 1944; Joseph Schumpeter, *Capitalism, Socialism and Democracy*, Harper & Row, 1950; and the nontheoretical Venkata Ramanadham, *Problems of Public Enterprise*, Quadrangle Books, 1962.

hardly neglect the idea popular among religious fundamentalists that God's injunction to "populate and replenish the earth" has not yet been fulfilled and that large families are a religious obligation.

A rousing "booster" speech at a Chamber of Commerce meeting is likely to dwell on how to lure more people into the community—how to expand. We have never heard of a Chamber of Commerce campaigning for birth control, except for people on public assistance.

A woman with a remarkably large family, from seven or eight children up, is admired for her womanhood and her contribution to the national welfare. If a woman were to have three sets of quadruplets in a row, she would probably be recommended for the Congressional Medal of Honor. She certainly would make newspaper headlines and be treated as a national heroine.

The rate of population growth in the United States is high: it varies from year to year and there is little point in being specific. A rough way of calculating the time it will take a population to double is to divide the numeral 70 by the annual rate of population growth. Since the annual rate in the United States hovers around 2 percent, it is probable that our present 200 million population will double in 35 years. Forecasts are risky, however: any major breakthrough in the field of medicine, such as devising means to avert cardiovascular failure or cure cancer, would so lower the death rate that the rate of population gain might soar. Conversely, more convenient and dependable contraceptives—especially if furnished free to the poor—might cause a sharp decline in the birth rate.

More will be said about the dangers of uncontrolled population growth in the following chapter; we will confine our commentary here to the United States. Although most writers stress overpopulation in "backward nations" as being the legitimate source of major concern, a good case can be made for the argument that the United States is already seriously overpopulated.[12]

Statistically, the population to land-space ratio in the United States looks good, but vast land areas are uninhabitable—the "Great Western Desert" is incapable of supporting very many more persons than now live there. The habitable areas are progressively more crowded: The eastern seaboard is a vast urban clot, extending from New England halfway down the coast. The west coastal fringe is rapidly becoming the same, particularly in California south of the Tehachapis. The Great Lakes area is likewise densely populated. The Southeast is becoming more so, as is the Southwest excluding California.

Some of the problems already produced include: critical water short-

---

[12] See, for example, William Vogt, *People! Challenge to Survival*, Sloane, 1960.

ages; polluted rivers and water supplies; polluted air; an automobile problem which is almost out of control and which we seek to ameliorate by spending hundreds of millions on freeways, bridges, tunnels, etc.; health problems caused by crowding and polluted air and water; urban ghettoes of potential explosiveness; and, last but not of minor importance, destruction of the natural scene. The amount of genuine wilderness is virtually gone; and the rate at which we use many other natural resources promises a critical shortage before many decades have past.

5.1 It has been proposed that, if public support for such a measure should be gained, American parents be prevented from, or punished as a result of, having more than two or three children. Would you favor compulsory sterilization? What would be your attitude toward a reversed system of income tax exemptions? (That is, after two children, instead of exemptions, penalties would apply—say, an added annual $300 of tax for a third child, $600 for a fourth, $1000 for a fifth, etc.)

5.2 Overpopulation refers to the ratio between numbers of people and available resources (domestic or imported). What resources could we import? Clean air? Clean water? More water? More wilderness?

5.3 Overpopulation tends to require the substitution of one resource for another—e.g., if we are short on silver (as we are), we can attempt substitutes (a difficult problem because of silver's unique properties) or we can raise the price of silver to the point where presently unprofitable mines can be reworked again. In how many ways can you see that overpopulation may cause Americans to suffer an eventual drastic decline in standard of living? Algae and plankton can be substituted for foods we are accustomed to. Would you like algae soup and planktonburgers?

5.4 How do you account for the indifference on the part of the public to the population problem? Do you think that perhaps there is an instinctive urge to procreate which cannot be denied? If so, how long do you think man could survive?

DISCUSSION QUESTIONS AND EXERCISES

1. What periods or events in American history, or world history, are appropriately related to the study of current economic problems and issues?
2. Do you favor a required course in economics for every high-school student? Why or why not?
3. How do you explain the fact that the only kind of public spending the American public wholeheartedly condones is for the Military Establishment?
4. What would you do about the problem of too many people in relation to resources? Should this problem have first priority in our foreign-aid program?
5. If your students studied each of the economic conflicts described in this chapter, what difficulties would you expect to encounter?

6. What do you believe is the most crucial economic problem facing the American people today? Do you believe that the study of this problem should be incorporated in the high-school social-studies curriculum?
7. Have any of your economic beliefs been clarified by your reading of this chapter? If so, which ones, and in what way?
8. Make a list of economic data, sharply negative in form and quality, which you could use in order to cast doubt upon some of the economic beliefs discussed in this chapter.

REFERENCES

ARNOLD, THURMAN W., *The Folklore of Capitalism*, New York, Oxford University Press, 1937.

This remains an important work on the myths inherent in the American economic ideology. Arnold explodes with hard-to-answer arguments many popular beliefs about how the economy works.

ARNOLD, THURMAN W., *The Future of Democratic Capitalism*, Philadelphia, University of Pennsylvania Press, 1950.

Five "Benjamin Franklin" lectures given at the University of Pennsylvania by different persons. The lectures tend to be challenging and provocative, liberal, and sanguine about the future of the American economy.

AYRES, C. E., *The Industrial Economy*, Boston, Houghton Mifflin, 1952.

A useful reference on the history and present nature of the American economy. Ayres is an "institutionalist" economist somewhat in the Veblen tradition. His writings have a philosophical tone and are highly original.

AYRES, C. E., *The Theory of Economic Progress*, Chapel Hill, University of North Carolina Press, 1944.

In this oft-regarded classic—which is fully as relevant today as when published —Ayres condemns the identification of economics with price analysis and tries to approach economic theory from what Veblen called the "life process" of mankind. The book is dominated by overtones of the philosophy of John Dewey.

BERLE, ADOLF A., *The American Economic Republic*, New York, Harcourt, Brace & World, 1963.

Reviews our economic past, shows why nineteenth-century economic notions no longer make sense, and suggests how we might make our present "mixed economy" work better. He relegates both classical capitalism and Communism to the "museums of nineteenth-century thought and culture."

BERNSTEIN, PETER, *A Primer on Money, Banking, and Gold*, New York, Random House, 1965.

An understanding of money, banks, and gold is among the most difficult subjects teachers try to teach. This volume is particularly lucid in its analysis of the Federal Reserve System. Also of especial interest is Bernstein's discussion of the gold problem and balance of payments.

CALDER, RITCHIE, *After the Seventh Day: The World Man Created*, New York, Simon and Schuster, 1961.

A very useful book on the population explosion. Ritchie is a well-known demographer at Edinburgh University.

CAUDILL, HARRY M., *Night Comes to the Cumberlands: A Biography of a Depressed Area*, Boston, Atlantic-Little, Brown, 1963.

A description of poverty in one area of the United States. If readers think other countries are backward in relation to the United States, this well documented book may come as a shock.

DANIELS, ROBERT V., *Nature of Communism*, New York, Random House, 1962.

Generally considered the best book on the complexities of modern Communism. The author does a skillful job of showing all the different meanings that Communism has for people and reasons for the range of its appeal.

DRUCKER, PETER, *America's Next Twenty Years*, New York, Harper & Row, 1957.

Drucker writes in a scholarly but readable style and his articles by now should be well known to every reader of *Harper's Magazine*. He shies away from "isms" and with considerable originality tries to describe the development of what he sees as a unique potentially strong economy.

FRIEDMAN, MILTON, *Capitalism and Freedom*, Chicago, University of Chicago Press, 1963.

The author is a respected member of the "conservative school" at the University of Chicago, and one of the few scholarly laissez-faire economists we have left. As an anti-Keynesian, he is much less polemical and better grounded than Friedrich von Hayek.

GALBRAITH, JOHN K., *American Capitalism: the Concept of Countervailing Power*, Boston, Houghton Mifflin, 1956.

Galbraith sets forth his thesis that in a democracy when one economic power center becomes so powerful as to be oppressive, another arises to counterbalance it. Highly controversial.

GALENSON, WALTER, *A Primer on Employment and Wages*, New York, Random House, 1966.

How much unemployment do we really have? What kinds of unemployment are there? What determines wages? Are unions influential? Is full employment possible without inflation? These are only a few of the questions discussed in this brief introduction to the field.

HARRINGTON, MICHAEL, *The Other America,* New York, Macmillan, 1962.

A book on poverty in America. Harrington contends that even in the 1960s the poorest one-third of our population lives in a state of degradation.

HAYES, HARRY GORDON, *Spending, Saving, and Employment,* New York, Knopf, 1945.

This may well remain the most simple, lucid explanation of the "new economics." It is fundamentally Keynesian in outlook with a touch of Fabian socialism.

POLANYI, KARL, *The Great Transformation,* New York, Oxford University Press, 1944.

Draws upon anthropological and psychological data to demonstrate that human beings cannot tolerate a laissez-faire economy for long and historically have refused to do so. An exceptionally important book.

RAMANADHAM, VENKATA, *Problems of Public Enterprise,* Chicago, Quadrangle Books, 1962.

A description of socialist enterprise, focusing on Great Britain. A careful description of government-owned corporate enterprises which have worked and therefore might serve as models.

REAGAN, MICHAEL D., *The Managed Economy,* New York, Oxford University Press, 1963.

Describes the change from attempts to practice Adam Smith's laissez-faire economy to centralized control of the economy by big-business executives and government officials. Reagan is convinced that this is necessary and can be done within a democratic framework, but has some caustic remarks about corrupt corporate practices.

SCHUMPETER, JOSEPH, *Capitalism, Socialism and Democracy,* New York, Harper & Row, 1950.

Another oft-regarded classic with which all social-studies students should be familiar. A great laissez-faire economist, although deploring the trend, explains why he thinks socialism will eventually prevail over what we label free enterprise. Section I contains an exceptionally good critique of Marxist theory.

SHANNON, DAVID A., *Decline of American Communism,* New York, Harcourt, Brace & World, 1960.

In a well-documented book, Shannon describes the demise as an influential power center of the Communist party in the United States since 1945. This book is a "must" for all those who believe we are surrounded by a dangerous domestic Communist conspiracy.

SNIDER, DELBERT A., *Economic Myth and Reality,* Englewood Cliffs, N.J., Prentice-Hall, 1965.

This book discusses some of the possible misconceptions of Americans concerning economic matters. Snider treats money, taxes, debt, inflation, poverty, automation, unions, tariffs, foreign aid, free enterprise, and socialism.

CHAPTER 15

Problematic Areas of Culture: Nationalism, Patriotism, and Foreign Affairs

Our Nation "Right or Wrong"
—and Other Nations

THOSE beliefs, attitudes, and practices which we label nationalism appeared in Europe toward the close of the Middle Ages and marked the beginning of what we regard as "modern Europe." The appearance of nationalism was hastened by the erosion of feudalism and of a Christendom united under the international authority of one church. It was accompanied by formation of national states with strong central rulers, by development of national languages, and by a surging interest in commerce and industry. A motive for formation of national states was the need of the rising commercial and manufacturing interests for stable currencies, strong governments, and strong armies.

The Reformation was a potent stimulus to nationalism. Both Luther and Calvin turned to national states as bulwarks of Protestantism against the internationalism of the Catholic Church. Luther trusted to the state power to decide what was in accordance with the gospel, but Calvin insisted on supremacy of church over state. However, Calvin believed churches should be organized on a national, not an international, basis. The Protestant Church, organized along state lines and appealing strongly to the middle class, thus had immeasurable influence in uniting populations under the rule of a single monarch and in inducing them to think in national rather than international terms.

As Randall puts it, the concept of nationalism contained an acceptance of—if not hearty belief in—the growth of "independent, irresponsible, absolutely sovereign territorial states, the avowed sanction of whose acts is power." A chauvinistic and commercial patriotism developed which emphasized the slogans "For king and country," "For the glory of France," and "My country, right or wrong." [1]

Counterforces arose in the eighteenth century. Intellectuals, imbued

[1] John Herman Randall, Jr., *The Making of the Modern Mind*, Houghton Mifflin, 1940, p. 172.

with the spirit of the Age of Enlightenment, looked upon nationalism as irrational, unnatural, and harmful to human welfare. They condemned war and advocated unity of all mankind. In addition, the commercial groups had by now recognized that their interests were not served by mercantilistic nationalism. Businessmen began to favor international free trade, and this attitude had a corrosive effect upon nationalist sentiments.

The nineteenth century tells a different story. Sparked by a resurgence of nationalism which accompanied the French Revolution and the rule of Napoleon, the nineteenth century retreated from the humanitarian and internationalist thinking of the eighteenth. Nationalism became popular in Britain, France, Germany, and the United States. Randall tries to express the spirit of the age:

What, after all, is my country? Is she a group of discordant little men who have agreed to live together to serve their own selfish interests? Is she founded on an artificial contract, on a man-made and written constitution? A thousand times No! She is My Country! She is something sacred, something living, greater than any man, than all men now living, than all generations of men: she is an organic whole, one and indivisible, a past, a tradition.[2]

Patriotism became correlated with a blind, unreasoning love of country and obedience to national rulers. It came to have a mystical quality, to resemble a religion. One expressed his patriotism by undergoing appropriate rites, such as saluting his national flag, displaying it in respectful ways, and standing at grave attention when the national anthem was sung. Another common feature of patriotism was its tendency toward intolerance and ethnocentrism. All other countries were thought inferior to the fatherland. In some cases, every country but one's own was an object of contempt and hatred. Anyone within the fatherland who disregarded customary patriotic rites, or who advocated a philosophy of internationalism, was considered ignorant, depraved, or traitorous.

Nationalism and patriotism have continued as major forces into the twentieth century. Nationalistic feeling appears to rise during war and to remain at fever pitch for several years thereafter. These waves of ultranationalism are usually accompanied by conservative reactions in political, economic, and social thought, and by attacks on traditional ideas of free speech and right of dissent. An exception to this is the socialist-oriented nationalism of many new and so-called backward countries, as in Africa and Asia.

In the United States today, the following beliefs reflect our nationalistic outlook:

² *Ibid.*, pp. 433–434.

1. One's first loyalty should be to his country.
2. One should love his country more than life.
3. One should respect the symbols of national power and greatness (the flag, national heroes, the national anthem, patriotic documents, and the uniforms of our armed forces).
4. Peace without national honor is worse than war.
5. A nation's greatness is measured by its military strength and success.
6. The worst of all crimes is treason.
7. The United States is the greatest nation in the world and must always remain so.

A contrasting point of view, modifying or rejecting the ultranationalism just described, is essentially internationalist, antichauvinist, and critical of national institutions. Associated with the ideology of democratic liberalism, it has deep roots in the history of Western civilization. As we have seen, this viewpoint was introduced most conspicuously in the eighteenth century and lay largely quiescent in the nineteenth. A number of recent developments have contributed to its resurgence in the twentieth. One of these was "muckraking," which fostered a more critical attitude toward American heroes and institutions. Although muckraking represented a somewhat cynical manifestation of "scientific history," it approached that kind of historical research which stresses publication of unvarnished truth no matter whom or how much it hurts.

The liberalism of Populism and Progressivism was not internationalist in outlook; the former was largely unconcerned with the issue, and the latter, particularly as interpreted by Theodore Roosevelt, was frankly chauvinist. But these movements did help to prepare the soil for Wilson's New Freedom and the popularization of his brand of internationalism. World War II and the years following, in spite of a resurrection of extreme nationalism, were accompanied by a considerable movement which was internationalist in outlook and definitely hostile toward older nationalistic outlooks and saber-rattling patriotism.

A distinctive form of nationalism is "isolationism." Contributing to this movement was the debunking of World War I myths, performed with incisive skill by persons such as Sidney B. Fay and Harry Elmer Barnes and presented in popular version by Walter Millis. World War I was shown by these scholars not to have had the simple origins once supposed. Germans were shown not to be the ogres which American folklore had portrayed. Blame was placed upon the heads of Americans and the Allies as well as upon the Germans.

These interpretations, coupled with the unhappy aftermath of the war in Europe, led to development of an American pacifist and isolationist movement of major proportions. Whatever else this movement may have contributed, it did make millions of Americans more skeptical of government-sponsored propaganda and more critical of the point of view expressed in "My country, right or wrong."

Most of the liberal tendencies in American history were captured and synthesized under the intellectual leadership of Franklin Roosevelt during the New Deal era. The New Deal was broadly internationalist in outlook, critical of many of the old nationalist myths, yet willing to fight when the threat of fascist military victory in Europe became too compelling to ignore. It is notable that World War II was fought in a much more restrained emotional atmosphere than was World War I. Although feeling ran high against the enemy, especially the Japanese, there was a minimum of hysteria. Evidence of the new outlook was furnished by the enthusiastic part played by the United States in the founding of the United Nations.

Nor has this enthusiasm cooled substantially, unless it has been in the 1960s. Drawing again upon public-opinion polling, in numerous polls conducted between 1945 and 1954, approximately 80 percent of respondents approved the UN and never more than 13 percent favored our withdrawal. The public has usually had high hopes that the UN could help keep the peace (although, as we shall see, this optimism is tempered with respect to World War III). Seventy-five percent of respondents in 1960 wanted a UN police force in the Congo. Attitudes toward the effectiveness of the UN seem to be that it should be the first instrument used in "small" wars, whatever its ineffectiveness might be in a major confrontation.[3]

So far as foreign affairs in general are concerned, with few exceptions, the American people seem to have withdrawn from their historic isolationism. Although certain Americans have regarded the new internationalism from an idealistic "do goodism" point of view, there is no evidence that the power elite, including the Presidential Office, has anything in mind other than serving the selfish interests of the United States—which include, of course, corporate interests abroad. In fact, we appear to have entered into a new period of interventionism, reminiscent of that of the late 1890s and early 1900s. (Communists refer to this as "imperialism.")

For example, it is increasingly difficult for the Presidential Office to adduce evidence that our presence in Vietnam serves any of our national interests. The President and others overgeneralize when they "draw lessons" from Munich and the appeasement of the 1930s. The situation is almost totally different. Communism is not Fascism; furthermore, Communism takes a great variety of forms from country to

---

[3] Stuart Chase, *American Credos*, Harper & Row, 1962, chap. 4.

country, and is often intertwined with strong nationalistic impulses.[4]

Although withdrawal from Vietnam would be construed by many of the less sophisticated as a return to our old isolationist stance, most Americans seem confused as to just what we should do. The bland pronouncements from the Presidential Office that "all is going well" indicate either profound ignorance or attempts to conceal the truth. A hypothesis that demands attention is whether we have developed a *Wehrwirtschaft* economy, as Fritz Sternberg predicted we might (see page 337).

Americans are ignorant, ambivalent, and confused about foreign aid. To some, it means we are the most generous people on earth. During the latter 1950s and early 1960s, foreign aid averaged about $2.9 billions a year. Our gross national product, during the same period, ranged from $400 billion annually to, as of 1966, over $700 billion. Foreign aid in 1958 was about 0.6 of 1 percent of GNP; in 1964 it was about 0.4 of 1 percent of GNP. The facts tell us that we are not very generous after all and are becoming less so.

Compare this with foreign *military* aid, which is protested by very few.

Between 1956 and 1964, we spent a total slightly in excess of $34 billion on what was purported to be civilian aid; in the same period we spent $29.5 billion on aid which openly was labeled military. It should be noted that much foreign aid earmarked for humane purposes (economic development, medicine, education, etc.) is not used for that purpose exclusively. When a new road or bridge is built, who can say whether the motivation is to make the country more viable in a social or in a military sense? [5]

Each year, it appears increasingly difficult for the President to obtain congressional consent for the full amount of foreign civilian aid requested.

In the universe of foreign affairs, certain beliefs stand out:

1. The United States is the most powerful nation in the world.
2. The United States is the best nation in the world.
3. The United States has an obligation to protect all "free" nations against Communist aggression.
4. The "free world" is the non-Communist world. It includes Spain,

---

[4] Robert V. Daniels, *The Nature of Communism*, Random House, 1962, see especially chap. 6.

[5] Sources: Figures on foreign aid from *Information Please Almanac*, Simon & Schuster, 1966, p. 602 (original source: Office of Business Economics, U.S. Department of Commerce). Figures on GNP from *The Budget in Brief; Fiscal Year 1966*, The Bureau of the Budget, 1966, p. 76.

Portugal, South American dictatorships, South Africa, other African dictatorships, and the like.

5. If any new nation falls to Communism, we may assume that a kind of domino game is functioning. When dominoes are placed on end, sufficiently close to one another, then a push on the first causes all to fall.

Although apparently a majority of Americans hold some degree of commitment to most or all of the above statements of belief, a rising tide of cynicism is becoming evident. Educated Americans, adults and students alike, who are on the liberal, nonconformist "side of the fence," wonder if much of our anti-Communist pose is not truly a counter-revolutionary move—doomed to tragedy in the interim and failure in the end. There is a growing awareness that nothing is won on the basis of "anti-Communism" alone. A substantial minority know enough about Communism now to know that it takes forms indigenous to the countries in which it arises, that it goes through an evolutionary process so that there is, in fact, no such thing as a static concept of Communism which makes sense. The move to extend diplomatic recognition to China is burgeoning.[6] Opinion is perhaps best described as in a state of major flux—and confusion. Four major points of conflict and confusion follow.

1. War and Peace

Many Americans, commonly labeled the "hawks," like the idea of an escalated "hot war" with any nation labeled "Communist"; but at the same time it is believed by many others (the "doves") that armed conflict is futile and, if anything, drives more foreigners to support Communism than would letting matters take their course.

We have stated previously that Americans are a warlike people. The United States was largely responsible in instigating wars against Great Britain (1812), Mexico, and Spain—in each instance hoping to grab a large chunk of "real estate." We failed in our goal of obtaining Canada in 1812, but did succeed in acquiring substantial possessions of Mexico and Spain. Further, the American government has approved policies which were virtually guaranteed to drive the world into war.

The "revisionist" school of thought among scholars of the genesis of World War I sees our role as much different than we saw it at the time. Analysis of the causes of World War II will have to wait. But a case appears in the making that American tariff policies of the 1920s and early 1930s (especially the Smoot-Hawley tariff) provided a final blow to the

[6] Daniels, *op. cit.*

economies of Germany and Japan, helped bring Hitler and the Japanese militarists into a position of ascendency, and went far to precipitate their acts of expansionism.

When the United States enters a major war, it enters "all out." Americans seemed to derive some sort of psychological satisfaction from their participation in World Wars I and II—diversion from boredom, perhaps. Also, *no matter what the cause*, Americans fight to win. The world will never forget that it was the United States which dropped the first two airborne atomic bombs. Would any other nation be the first to do this, without prior warning and allowance of time for the enemy to evacuate its civilians? (Our tradition of violent, rather than peaceful, settlement of domestic disputes seems somehow to fit this total picture; in certain states, anyone has been free to murder a Negro without conviction of crime or punishment; instead his reward has been heroism.)

There are sincerely peace-loving Americans. Much of the time they are in trouble. These people baffle the "hawks," as, for example in the nonviolent civil rights movement instigated by Negroes. What must a Bull Connor think when he has to use force against an "enemy" which refuses to use force in return? Asian Indians gained freedom from colonial status by using the same baffling tactics against the British. Although life for a sincerely peace-loving person is difficult in the United States, many have had the courage during the middle 1960s to make the sacrifice. There is a tiny minority who think that refusing to kill has something to do with Christianity and the other major religions which preach nonviolence. But this is a very hard position to maintain, and punishment of some sort is inevitable.

Anyone who is inclined toward nonviolence must be prepared to suffer grave punishment. Persons who oppose serving in the armed forces recognize this full well. Suppose a man does not want to kill others, no matter what their race, creed, or nationality—because he simply does not like to kill. He can claim "conscientious objector" status, but claiming it and getting it are two different matters. Apparently, such a person must be able to prove that he is a member of an "off-beat" religious sect which contains in its doctrine opposition to killing others. But suppose a young man does not belong to such a religious sect? Suppose he has only philosophical grounds for despising murder? In that case, he finds it virtually impossible to gain CO status. A gun with bayonet is thrust into his hands and he is taught survival—a euphemism for killing one's opponent before he kills you.

On the other side of the coin, we pretend—probably with full sincerity—that we are a peace-loving people. Cartoonists like to display an American as a dove carrying an olive branch in its beak. We talk peace incessantly. We have remained uninvolved in many armed conflicts in which we could, perhaps, have defended involvement. We are generous almost to a fault in lending aid to nations *we have fought successfully*. We have a peculiar bent for wanting to whip someone, then help him up, render first aid, and pay for his hospitalization.

Paradoxically, we "think" peace, regardless of what we "do." Recently the following newspaper report appeared:

WASHINGTON (AP)—The United States has sold arms to both Israel and the Arab nations to help them meet "legitimate defense needs," the State Department said in a policy statement made public today.

"United States military sales have been on a selective basis and in support of our objectives of maintaining friendly relations with all the states of the area while seeking to advance peace, progress and stability," the department said.[7]

1.1 How would you explain the ambivalence of Americans concerning war and generosity to the foe? American soldiers, after dropping napalm on a Vietnam village and subduing it, give candy and chewing gum to the surviving children, food and hospital care to the remaining population. What motivation operates in such cases?

1.2 It is perhaps inescapable that troops on both sides of a conflict tend to reach the same degrees of cruelty. In subduing the Philippines, American soldiers used exceptionally brutal methods. One of their intents was to *Christianize* the Filipinos—but they were already mostly Roman Catholics. Explain this.

1.3 Man is the only species of animal who seems intent on destroying, with conscious aforethought, other members of his species. Lower on the phylogenetic scale, two males may fight to the death over a female—but it is unlikely that they consciously want to kill one another. What hypothesis can you imagine which would explain the difference between man and the so-called "lower" species? The bottle-nosed dolphin is one of the most peace-loving of mammals. Is this species "superior" to man?

2. National Honor and Foreign Commitments

It is widely believed that national honor is more valuable than life and that any sacrifice of "foreign commitments" which would endanger it is intolerable; but there seems to be a growing suspicion that the concept of national honor is meaningless and not worth fighting for.

Defending national honor has been a time-honored cause for war. It has been used as a slogan in probably every war since the beginning of nationalist sentiments. Although one of the chief motivations of the War of 1812 was to grab Canada from England (we had "hawks" then just as

---

[7] *The Fresno Bee*, February 16, 1966.

we do now), the war was fought for "national honor." A great issue was made of the burning of Washington, even though our forces, with no better excuse, had previously burned a major Canadian city.

In the war with Mexico, our national honor was at stake in saving Texans who had moved—largely unwanted—into Mexican territory. Then there was the battle of the Alamo, and Americans ever since have taken great pride in the heroism of their soldiers there—"Remember the Alamo!" The Mexicans have a rather different view of the subject.

In regard to the war with Spain, all competent historians are aware that the Spanish government had previously acceded to virtually all our demands. "Yellow journalism," wanting something saleable to write about, pressed for war. The sinking of the battleship *Maine*, under extremely mysterious circumstances—probably from an explosion inside the ship—served as a convenient trigger. The slogan immediately became, "Remember the *Maine*." President Roosevelt had probably also had a lifelong yearning to charge up a hill. When the war was clearly won, President McKinley was forced to decide how much Spanish real estate, in addition to Cuba, our country should grab. Of his method of decision, Charles and Mary Beard said:

> The intellectual and moral methods by which he resolved his perplexity the President later explained. . . . "I walked the floor of the White House night after night," he said, "and I am not ashamed to tell you, gentlemen, that I went down on my knees and prayed Almighty God for light and guidance more than one night. And one night late it came to me in this way—I don't know how it was, but it came—. . . . There was nothing left for us to do but to take them all, and to educate the Filipinos, and uplift and civilize and Christianize them. . . ." [8]

In World War I, the arms-carrying passenger ship, *Lusitania*, was clearly warned not to sail. The Germans placed an advertisement in New York newspapers to that effect. Americans ignored this violation of the then commonly accepted rules of war. The ship sailed and was sunk by torpedo. Probably more than any other act, this aroused Americans to a warlike mood—never a difficult undertaking. We probably had legitimate reasons for entering this war, but this particular "cause" was of the most irrational sort.

What is national honor? Most people find the term very difficult to define. It appears to be something like oriental "face saving"—but, again, what does that mean? To maintain an elusive and undefinable "national honor," we are willing to sacrifice thousands—or if necessary millions —of young men. Great Britain, step by step, has loosed its colonies and

---

[8] Charles A. Beard and Mary R. Beard, *Rise of American Civilization*, Macmillan, 1930, vol. II, pp. 375–376.

given them the choice of becoming free or remaining within the Commonwealth. Great Britain has been adulated for this all over the world. France and Belgium relinquished their colonies in Southeast Asia—the French by military defeat, the Belgians by voluntary withdrawal. France, risking civil war, freed Algeria from colonial status. There are many other records of such withdrawals by major powers. Typically, they have led to admiration and respect—not loss of a mystical "national honor." Americans appear to favor peace—but only "peace with honor." This is all quite meaningless and indicates a deep-seated irrationality as well as semantic innocence.

As of this writing, many prominent Americans—including Senator Fulbright, Walter Lippmann, John Emmett Hughes, and Eric Sevareid, seem equally puzzled as to what it means to defend one's national honor. Added to this list are numerous intellectuals of all sorts, students, and laymen. Unfortunately, some of these persons wear beards; and respectable, middle-class conservatives equate beards with Communism. On this matter, people were far more rational 75 years ago.

2.1 Do you believe that man has an "instinct" for war? Since the definition of instinct is "genetically-derived behavior patterns applicable to all members of a species," how would you explain the peace-lovers? Was Ghandi human?

2.2 According to one theory, at periodic intervals nations get psychological satisfaction out of war. It relieves boredom, serves as an excuse for breaking constraining mores, and affords a deep sense of purpose. Do you, therefore, think that war is inevitable?

2.3 According to another theory, historically war has served several important functions in addition to those we have already mentioned. It has, so it is claimed, reduced population growth and weeded out the unfit. It has also built courage and patriotism. How do you react to these arguments?

2.4 What meaning do you assign to the term, nationalism? How nationalistic do you think Americans are compared with other peoples?

3. Self-Determination of Nations and Puppet Governments

It is widely proclaimed that our foreign policy is based on the self-determination of nations but it is also increasingly believed that we support unpopular governments against the wishes of the people in the countries involved.

In 1821, the British foreign secretary proclaimed that it was the privilege of all nations "to be left free to manage their own affairs, so long as they left other nations to manage theirs." This doctrine was not popularized until the end of World War I, when Woodrow Wilson's famous "fourteen points" strongly connoted the idea of self-determination of nations—particularly in his aims for a League of Nations, one provision of which was to guarantee political independence to all nations desiring it. The notion that it was a moral obligation of every nation not to meddle in the affairs of another was proclaimed steadily by many prominent figures in the United States, particularly Franklin D. Roosevelt, Harry Truman, Dwight D. Eisenhower, and John F. Kennedy. Respective Secretaries of State and other cabinet members, as well as numerous members of Congress have made similar pronouncements. On an abstract level, hardly anyone seems to disagree. It may be said, therefore, that one of our central points of foreign policy is nonintervention in the affairs of other states.

But we have a considerable group of cynics who feel that this stated policy is nothing more than hypocrisy. They have nothing more to go on than such events as the following:

1. The destruction of the American Indian "nations."

2. The Monroe Doctrine, which proclaimed that Latin American nations could not, even if they wished, form alliances with or accept guidance from, any power but the United States.

3. In 1853, Commodore Perry, with gunboats threatening, "opened" Japan to Western trade.

4. In 1893, marines were landed in Hawaii and, with the probable connivance of Secretary Blaine and the sons of missionaries, deposed Queen Liliuokalani, and the islands became ours. However, in spite of government by Americans, consciences were salved by referring to the islands as the "Republic of Hawaii."

5. In 1888, the United States acquired rights, along with Great Britain and Germany, in Samoa; by 1900 France was pushed out; and after World War I the Samoans were ours.

6. In the 1880s, James G. Blaine recognized that we had a problem with South America. The perverse countries of this area were purchasing most of their manufactured products from Europe even though the United States was buying Latin American raw materials—almost 90 percent of them duty free. Our self-interest demanded that the Latin American countries reduce tariffs on U.S. manufactured goods, so that the Latins would buy from us. Blaine's invitation to the Latin Americans to establish a "Pan-American customs union" (to our advantage) seemed, in the words of Samuel Morison and Henry Commager, like "the invitation of the spider to the fly." But with the Dingley Tariff of 1897, the goal was believed established; the Senate, however, refused to ratify it.

7. In 1895, President Cleveland announced his intention to determine the boundary between Venezuela and a British colony. In this connec-

tion, a pronouncement of Secretary of State Olney alarmed Latin America and insulted Canada. It read, in part, "Today the United States is practically sovereign on this continent, and its fiat is law upon the subjects to which it confines its interposition. . . ."

8. In addition to the acquisitions mentioned above, in the 1890s the United States secured possession of Puerto Rico, Midway, Wake, Guam, Tutuila, and the Philippines, and established protectorates over Cuba, Panama, and Nicaragua. The landing of American Marines was often required and fighting in the Philippines was of extraordinary cruelty. One missionary journal was moved to announce that "to give the world the life more abundant both for here and hereafter is the duty of the American people by virtue of the call of God."

9. A Cuban revolution occurred in 1895. This was an outcome of the imposition by the United States of a 40 percent tariff on Cuban sugar, which resulted in extreme poverty and a strong desire of the Cubans to be free from foreign domination (they were then a Spanish colony). United States corporations had by that time invested over $50 million in Cuban mining and sugar. In response to a growing demand for war in the United States, Spain finally cabled that the Cuban question could be settled in accordance with American demands. But, luckily, the Battleship *Maine* blew up in a Cuban harbor. The American people desperately wanted war—hence, the Spanish-American "affair."

10. Students may be interested in exploring the number of times, and places, American Marines have been landed to protect American corporate interests. They may also want to add the number of times in the twentieth century that the United States has interfered in the internal affairs of other nations. It might be worth while to investigate United States shenanigans in China: In 1899, Jon Hay, in collaboration with the British, announced the "open door" policy for China—which meant, in effect, that China, which had long been up for grabs, would be subjected to the additional economic exploitation of these two powers. The Boxer Rebellion followed, some 300 foreigners (mostly missionaries) were put to death, and the United States sent 5000 soldiers into China. China was forced to pay an indemnity to the United States of $24,000,000—half of which was eventually returned (because we are a kindly, generous people).

3.1 Are our present pronouncements about wishing for Southeast Asia only "self-determination" hypocritical? If not, what motives are at work?

3.2 Has the principle of "self-determination" been a myth throughout both our history and that of other countries? Has any such principle ever been applied anywhere by a major power?

3.3 What governments can you name that might properly be labeled "puppet governments" maintained in power only by the strength of American military power or economic sanctions?

4. Patriotism as Obedience and Patriotism as Critical Inquiry

It is widely believed that patriotism consists of serving government wishes, whether right or wrong, in time of emergency; but it is believed also that the best kind of patriotism is constructive criticism of one's government.

This issue is particularly timely as we now write. The nation is involved in an undeclared war in Vietnam. Already about 500,000 troops are committed, and this may double or triple by the time this book is off the press. (Or, conversely, the war may be over.) The point is, among both soldiers and persons on the home front, who are the more patriotic—those who criticize our involvement in Vietnam or the way we are discharging it, or those who give unquestioning support to every decision of the Executive Office, Congress, and members of the power elite influential enough to sway these arms of government?

There is no point repeating the verifiable facts of the Vietnam story. However, several aspects of this situation must be noted. Other nations, and the journalists of those nations, tend to place an entirely different interpretation on our presence in Vietnam and the way we are or should be conducting the war than do our own government and our own journalists. The point is made in the foreign press that the executive head of the Viet Cong is not a Communist, even though many in his staff are, and that the typical Viet Cong soldier is not even aware of the ideological issues between Communism and democracy. Foreign interpreters also tend to interpret the war in South Vietnam as a *civil war*, motivated in large part by widespread detestation of a succession of incompetent and callous governments. These writers also emphasize the complexity of the entire situation, since the population of South Vietnam consists of a combination of Catholics, Buddhists, and the religiously passive; and, politically, of persons who want to maintain present vested interests in spite of majority opposition, of those who espouse a militant opposition to vested interests, and of those who only want to be left alone to work their rice paddies. We hear stories of unnecessary brutality on the part of American soldiers, as well as on the part of South Vietnamese soldiers. We are told by foreigners that we proclaim that all we want is self-determination for the South Vietnamese; but that in any *free* election, since a majority of them probably would vote for a Communist regime, the outcome will be the same no matter how long we remain involved. Foreign writers and observers point out that our involvement is intrinsically illogical.

They likewise criticize the so-called "domino" theory to the effect that if South Vietnam becomes Communist, then so will all of Southeast Asia, country by country—and they use present antiCommunism in Indonesia to bolster this point. Some suggest that in the long run all of Southeast Asia will become Communist anyway, so that any war, now or later, to quell this trend can have no more effect than to squander thousands of lives and disrupt civilian life—all to no end.

Some point out that the Chinese, who to some degree support the North Vietnamese Communists and the Viet Cong with supplies, weapons, and military advisors, have every reason to hate Americans and want them ejected from all of Asia. In this connection, it is pointed out, the Chinese have good memories: They recall the Boxer Rebellion and many other matters which would incense any nation. Chinese involvement, therefore, may not be primarily political: It may be based on a long-standing list of grievances.

The foregoing is only a beginning of what we are told by those who disagree with our way of handling the situation in Asia. But it illustrates an important point. American involvement in Vietnam is, in the eyes of the world, highly controversial. It is inevitable that these same controversies enter into discourse and influence behavior in the United States. We now have a large number of critics of our involvement in Vietnam. They include both the young and the old, both men and women, both Republicans and Democrats. They include well-informed, highly prominent persons—such as several members of the Senate Foreign Relations Committee and other congressmen. Some of these persons at times, in addition to speaking loudly, form picket lines and carry placards.

It is quite clear that the Presidential Office, a majority of congressmen, most members of the power elite, and a probable majority of United States citizens, do not like criticism of our war in Vietnam. There is a general feeling that even if some of the critics are right on specific points, they should keep quiet because everything they say encourages the enemy to fight with more determination and to refuse the bids of our government for negotiation. President Johnson has himself seemed quite touchy about criticism, as have Secretary of State Rusk and Secretary of Defense McNamara. Criticism of how the United States conducts its foreign policy is being proclaimed by many as "unpatriotic." The critics are being urged to keep quiet and let the government get on with the war. So far, we have no sedition laws which would legally punish critics, but the passage of such would be in harmony with some previous actions in United States history.

The critics, on the other hand, feel that they are more patriotic than the passive—or, if not quite passive, silent—supporters of government action. They are convinced that a democracy can function only by the full exercise of the right of dissent. They believe the government and people are misguided about Vietnam. They feel it a moral obligation to try to "set the record straight." Most of them probably feel that they are more patriotic than the noncritics, and feel this sincerely.

4.1 How would you define patriotism? Is it love of country? "Country" is an abstraction. Can a rational person be in love with an abstraction?

4.2 Young men who claim conscientious-objector status in wartime are always suspected of unpatriotic motives. What do you think? Should it be made easier or harder for a person to receive conscientious-objector status?

4.3 In a communication with a friend, Thomas Jefferson once wrote that he felt it might be good for a nation to have a revolution every twenty years. It would keep the nation on its toes, he felt. Was this an unpatriotic assertion?

4.4 Prior to and during the American Revolution against England, the colonists disobeyed laws and said many insulting things about King George and the British government. We now call these colonists patriots. Do you think the British government thought so? Were the loyalists patriots?

DISCUSSION QUESTIONS AND EXERCISES

1. What is the social function of such patriotic ceremonies as saluting the flag, pledging allegiance to the flag, singing the national anthem, and holding memorial services for the war dead? Do these ceremonies make citizens more patriotic? More democratic?

2. Is loyalty to the United Nations incompatible with loyalty to the United States? Why, or why not?

3. Should public-school teachers teach American youth to support the United Nations? Or should they merely teach *about* the United Nations? Should public-school teachers teach American youth to support the Constitution of the United States? Or should they merely teach *about* the Constitution of the United States?

4. To what extent, if any, should the teaching of history have as one of its purposes the building of patriotic sentiments? Can one teach patriotism at the same time that he teaches the truth about his country?

5. Every nation has a body of myth or legend concerning its past. One of the purposes of historical research is to determine the relative amounts of truth and falsity incorporated in any nation's myth and legend. What attitude toward myth and legend should a history teacher foster? Is it possible to teach patriotism without teaching that certain myths and legends are true?

6. Is the myth and legend approach to teaching patriotism essentially different

from the ritual approach? If so, what is the difference? Do these two approaches have anything in common?

REFERENCES

COOMBS, PHILIP H., *The Fourth Dimension of Foreign Policy: Educational and Cultural Affairs,* New York, published for the Council on Foreign Relations by Harper & Row, 1964.

Coombs writes a highly useful book on what he regards as our "big goof"—that is, to funnel a disproportionately large amount of our foreign aid into military, political, and doubtful economic projects.

DECONDE, ALEXANDER, *A History of American Foreign Policy,* New York, Scribner, 1963.

Focuses on post-World-War II diplomacy. This review of the political, social, and economic developments which have shaped American foreign policy is useful to students studying in this area.

DOOB, LEONARD W., *Patriotism and Nationalism: Their Psychological Foundations,* New Haven, Yale University Press, 1964.

Doob's book is based on field work in the German-speaking South Tyrolean section of Italy, but is intended to have general application. Although not without faults, the book provides a useful model for the phenomenological analysis of patriotism. The only book of its kind.

DULLES, FOSTER RHEA, *America in the Pacific; a Century of Expansion,* 2nd ed., Boston, Houghton Mifflin, 1958.

As is usual with Dulles' writing, this book is eminently readable as well as scholarly. Students who wonder why the people of the Far East don't love Americans can find much of the story here.

DULLES, FOSTER RHEA, *America's Rise to World Power, 1898–1954,* New York, Harper & Row, 1955.

A largely historical treatment of American foreign policy. Especially informative on analysis of intellectual currents, of sectional and partisan attitudes, and of public opinion in general. Dulles has a gift for being exceptionally readable at the same time he is scholarly and penetrating.

FEIS, HERBERT, *Foreign Aid and Foreign Policy,* New York, St. Martins, 1964.

A Pulitzer prize winner for his *Between War and Peace,* Feis raises serious questions about American foreign aid. He considers it not an isolated issue, but an integral plan, if properly used, to strengthen the needy and reinforce democracy. Dollars are not the prime ingredient; rather we should contribute essential material equipment and expert advisers—even though this is hazardous unless done wisely. Part I of book is best.

FINLETTER, THOMAS K., *Foreign Policy: the Next Phase*, New York, published for the Council on Foreign Relations by Harper & Row, 1958.

Finletter is a former Secretary of the Air Force. The book is based on lectures, given by him before the Council, in which he reviews our postwar diplomatic history and attempts to diagnose its ills. Among our major errors, Finletter thinks, was our failure to recognize diplomatically the Red Chinese regime, and to see clearly that although the risk of a major nuclear confrontation might diminish, we were likely to become involved in a series of more-or-less small "brush fire" wars.

FROMM, ERICH, *May Man Prevail? An Inquiry into the Facts and Fictions of Foreign Policy*, Garden City, Doubleday, 1961.

Less easy to read than some other books on this list, Fromm's work has attracted much attention. It takes an entirely different approach to foreign analysis—that of an eminent social psychiatrist. Fromm questions seriously whether the human race will survive, and places a share of the blame on United States foreign policy since World War II.

Fund for the Republic, Inc.. *Foreign Policy and the Free Society*, New York, 1959.

Two essays on the implications of our foreign and military policy by Walter Millis and Jesuit theologian John C. Murray, followed by discussion of the essays by a panel of eight, chaired by Robert M. Hutchins. The essays are stronger than the remarks of the panel; nevertheless, many cogent issues are brought out, including abundant criticism of our foreign and military policy. A stimulating and valuable book.

HALLE, LOUIS JOSEPH, *Civilization and Foreign Policy; an Inquiry for Americans*, with an introduction by Dean Acheson, New York, Harper & Row, 1955. (English title: *Nature of Power*.)

An interpretation of American civilization and its ways by an Englishman. He sees the aim of the power of foreign policy as civilization in conquest of barbarism and not democracy against Communism. He rejects isolation and colonialism in favor of coalitions based on consent and leadership. Controversial, but meaty and thought provoking.

KOHN, HANS, *American Nationalism*, New York, Macmillan, 1957.

Difficult to read, but like all of Kohn's books, scholarly, brilliant, and of enduring importance. Kohn seeks to capture the form and movement of America—what might be called its "style."

KRAMISH, ARNOLD, *The Peaceful Atom in Foreign Policy*, New York, published for the Council on Foreign Relations by Harper & Row, 1963.

This book deals with one of the most disastrous aspects of both our domestic and foreign policy—the peaceful use of the atom. Of his three major themes, two are domestic atomic use, the other relates to improving the international use of nuclear energy for peace.

LEDERER, WILLIAM J., *A Nation of Sheep*, New York, Norton, 1961.

Using his usual hard-hitting style, Lederer gives his impressions of the major mistakes of United States foreign policy during the period since World War II. Short, readable, perhaps overdrawn—but worth looking into.

MILLS, C. WRIGHT, *The Causes of World War III*, New York, Simon and Schuster, 1958.

Mills, in a highly controversial and at times emotional volume, reviews his theory of the power elite and its likely intentions in relation to foreign policy, and ends by arguing that World War III is inevitable unless certain fundamental—and probably unattainable—changes occur. One of his most controversial claims: If the holocaust begins, it will be the United States that will start it.

SCHAAR, JOHN HOMER, *Loyalty in America*, Berkeley, University of California Press, 1957.

An important book on loyalty—which is to say, patriotism in its less-blind sense. Schaar lifts the concept from the strictly political arena and comes at it with sociological, anthropological, psychological, and legal data. As a peculiar American phenomenon, the loyalty demanded stems from emphasis on conformity and is a menace to democratic process. The only kind of loyalty which makes sense is "shared experience," as propounded by John Dewey.

SULZBERGER, C. L., *What's Wrong with U.S. Foreign Policy?*, New York, Harcourt, Brace & World, 1959.

Sulzberger, foreign correspondent for the *New York Times*, in a highly readable and personalized fashion, criticizes many aspects of United States foreign policy which have produced the "mess" of the 1960s. Having visited five continents and talked with hundreds of foreign statesmen, he deserves a hearing; and any impartial reader must concede he makes a strong case and one that is only now coming to be understood by a few of our leaders in Washington.

CHAPTER 16

Problematic Areas of Culture: Social Class

Social Class as an Area of Contradictory and Irrational Belief

PROBLEMATIC aspects of social-class behavior may best be understood against the backdrop of the American creed of equality, which will be considered again briefly in Chapter 18.[1] When asked about their class affiliation or that of their acquaintances, many people say, "We have no classes here. In this community everyone is equal." The average American, especially of a small town or rural area, regards class as something alien and undemocratic. He is loath to admit that classes exist in his community.

One reason for this attitude is popular identification of class with the social structure of Europe and England. Probably most Americans think of a class system as having sharply delineated status levels, from which it is virtually impossible to move. They associate class with hereditary position. When conceived in these terms, the idea of class seems so contradictory to American ideals of democracy that to many persons it is highly unpalatable, if not actually menacing.

Nevertheless, Americans behave daily as if classes exist. Research conducted by W. Lloyd Warner, Allison Davis, John Dollard, Robert J. Havighurst, and many others has told us a great deal about the class structure of the United States, and about thinking and behavior related to class membership.

A social class is an aggregation of persons having a given social ranking in a community. Membership in a social class represents one form of status, but there may be bases of status other than class—sex and age, for example. The definition of class most commonly used among social scientists is largely objective; that is, it assumes that a person's rank depends not on what *he* thinks it is but on what *others* think it is. It is possible to develop objective criteria for ranking persons which will assign them with great accuracy to the class to which most other members of the

[1] For a summary statement of the American Creed, see Gunnar Myrdal, *An American Dilemma: The Negro Problem and Modern Democracy*, Harper & Row, 1944, pp. 8–12.

community assign them.[2] Social classes tend to differ in income level and occupation, manners and customs, beliefs and attitudes. No sharp lines can be drawn between classes, however, since they shade into one another at their upper and lower borders.

Originally, students of social class applied a five- or six-class scale in describing all those who are classifiable at all. This scale consisted of (1) lower-lower class; (2) upper-lower class; (3) lower-middle class; (4) upper-middle class; (5) upper class; and in those communities—mainly in the East and Southeast, where an old-line aristocracy exists—the upper class was broken into two groups, lower uppers and upper uppers.

As we review these studies from the vantage point of the 1960s, it seems clear that the foregoing system was faulty. Although it was conceded in the period between the 1930s and the 1950s that many persons are unclassifiable by any method yet devised, it was not clearly recognized that there is an additional group—greatly expanded since World War II—which must be delineated within the structure. It seems clear that the lower-middle and upper-middle bifurcation is grossly oversimplified. There is now a *middle-middle* group of major importance. This group is composed largely of the "new technicians," mostly educated since the war, who are essential to industry and the space and war effort. There are thousands of types of jobs in this category and we will name only a few for illustration: computer programmers, electronics engineers, rocket-motor technicians, nuclear technicians, designers of military hardware, and so on. Many persons who were once located in the lower-middle class have moved up without yet obtaining upper-middle status. These include beauty-shop operators, school teachers, sales persons, and numerous other categories of persons in the "service industries." The foregoing is incomplete and hence oversimplified, but it should give students a notion of this new middle-middle group.

Where six identifiable classes exist (according to the old system of classification), the upper class divides into two groups, according to age of family: an "old" and a "new" aristocracy. Very often lower uppers have more money, but they cannot boast the ancestral lineage of upper uppers. They are the *nouveaux riches*. The upper-middle class consists

[2] Warner and associates have used two fundamental methods of "placing" individuals classwise. One is known as the Index of Status Characteristics, and assigns scores to individuals according to their occupations, sources of income, house types, and dwelling areas. Each of these criteria is weighted and a total score derived for each person. Class membership is determined according to a score table. The second method is the method of Evaluated Participation; it consists of techniques which expose a person's rank by getting at what other community members think of him and how they behave toward him. See W. Lloyd Warner, *American Life: Dream and Reality*, University of Chicago Press, 1953, pp. 60–66.

of solid community citizens, persons successful in business and professions, who are prosperous but not wealthy. The lower-middle class is chiefly made up of persons with white-collar jobs who do not make much money: clerks, salespeople, stenographers, and farmers of moderate means. The upper lowers are mainly skilled and semiskilled workmen, persons who work in blue collars but are thought respectable. There is a marked range of income within this group, and many upper lowers have higher incomes than most lower middles. The lower-lower class consists of unskilled or semiskilled workers who are thought by others to be ignorant, dirty, and immoral. Warner and associates sometimes refer to the upper-middle and upper classes as the "level above the common man," the lower-middle and upper-lower classes as the "common man level," and the lower-lower class as the "level below the common man."

In communities studied, from 3 to 4.2 percent of the population are upper class, approximately half of them upper uppers, except in communities where there is no upper-upper group. The upper-middle class may include from 10 to 22 percent of the population, lower middles from 28 to 35 percent, upper lowers from 28 to 41 percent, and lower lowers from 10 to 25 percent. The "level above the common man" includes from about 13 to 26 percent of the population, depending upon the community. The "common man level" comprises from 60 to 70 percent.[3] Since we do not know the extent to which changes since World War II force revision of these figures, they are mainly of historical interest.

Although class has been defined objectively, classes exist in an identifiable form only on the basis of what people *believe* about class. That is, Americans hold a complex pattern of beliefs which *assume* that classes exist and which tend to call forth overt class-oriented behavior. Both ideology and behavior are in direct contradiction (much of the time) to professed beliefs in equality.

Persons may, and often do, experience moral conflict in the area of class behavior, as will be shown later in this chapter. Warner points out that "It is clear to those of us who have made studies in many parts of the United States that the primary and most important fact about the American social system is that it is composed of two basic, but antithetical principles: the first, the principle of equality; the second, the principle of unequal status and of superior and inferior rank."[4] Although antithetical, these two principles are not considered by Warner to be necessarily inconsistent if properly balanced; on the other hand, Warner and others recognize that class phenomena may produce frequent and serious conflicts for individuals. Because most persons believe

---

[3] *Ibid.*, pp. 58–59.
[4] *Ibid.*, p. 104.

and behave in contradictory ways where class is concerned, because for the most part they are unaware of these contradictions, and because these contradictions often lead to irrational and confused behavior, social class is properly included in our list of problematic areas.

The existence of class-related beliefs complicates the problem of describing ideologies in other problematic areas. Classes vary considerably in their beliefs about sex, economic matters, religion, politics, nationalism and patriotism, and etiquette. As a result, we do not have on most of these matters *an American ideology*, but several ideologies which are different in important respects.

However, belief patterns are less chaotic than they seem at first glance. There is a general American culture which cuts across class lines. This includes not only the American creed of equality and liberty but also a number of almost universally accepted beliefs—that it is proper to wear clothes, that murder is undesirable, that monogamy is the best form of marriage, etc. And, although each social class has its own characteristic beliefs about a number of matters, it is not improper to refer to the United States as a "middle-class nation." Although the lower class outnumbers the middle class in many communities, the middle class tends to set the ideological standards of the culture. For example, upper-lower-class persons tend to emulate middle-class standards, presumably because they hope to rise some day to middle-class status. Lower-upper persons typically accept many middle-class beliefs and attitudes, partly because most of them rose from the ranks of the middle class, partly because they wish to be "democratic," and partly because upper uppers, whom they are trying to imitate, also share many traditional middle-class thought patterns. Although media of mass communication sometimes express upper-class sentiments, they generally promote a middle-class outlook.[5]

Here are a few of the middle-class beliefs which so profoundly affect American life:

1. Economic beliefs are typically conservative. They follow the free-enterprise ideology described in Chapter 14. They emphasize "getting ahead," which means getting better jobs, making more money, and living more comfortably than previous generations. Although the middle class places more emphasis upon thrift and prudent management than does either upper or lower class, middle-class persons usually try to "keep up with the Joneses," which requires compromise in the valuing of thrift.

2. Standards of sex behavior are rather puritanical, but, as we shall see in Chapter 19, are changing rapidly.

3. Parents tend to supervise their children closely, commonly restricting their play activities and choice of associates. They often nag their

[5] *Ibid.*, chap. 10. See particularly the analysis of a "soap opera," pp. 216–234.

children in an effort to keep them physically and morally clean, safe, and in good company. They insist on early toilet training and on early learning of respectable language and manners. They are also willing to make major sacrifices for their children.

4. Church membership and attendance looms high, and patriotic organizations and ceremonies receive support.

5. Honesty, fair play and sportsmanship characterize all relationships where a strong person is dealing with a weaker (as expressed in the saying, "Never kick a man when he's down"). This belief is honored mainly in the abstract and in special circumstances (see the analysis in Chapter 13).

One might summarize the dominant middle-class beliefs and attitudes by saying that they uphold "success," "respectability," and "morality," all defined in a traditional and essentially Calvinist sense.

Although middle-class ideology tends to dominate American thinking, beliefs and attitudes of both upper and lower classes do differ sharply at certain points. For example, both upper- and lower-class persons tend to be less puritanical and inhibited where sex is concerned. A fairly large proportion of lower-class persons, especially those of the lower-lower class, are frankly irreligious and unpatriotic. Upper-class persons usually belong to a church but seldom attend, and often hold very liberal religious views; they are also usually cold to patriotic ceremonies. Lower-class persons often do not take seriously middle-class beliefs about fair play, honesty, cleanliness, and respectability. Both upper- and lower-class persons often regard middle-class persons as stuffy and hypocritical.

Because of these differences, members of each class except the lower lower look down upon and in various ways discriminate against members of "inferior" classes. Discrimination may take the form merely of avoidance. It may go further and involve actual manipulation of people for personal ends, as when an upper-lower employee is fired to make room for the son of an upper-middle acquaintance of the boss, or when a lower-class girl is ousted as drum majorette because of pressures put upon a principal by upper-class parents.

Social-class problems are basically problems in intercultural or intergroup relations. Since each class tends to have its own characteristic beliefs, it is reasonable to view classes as *subcultures* within the broader framework imposed by the "American creed" and other nationally held beliefs and attitudes. Prejudiced beliefs, and discrimination directed toward an inferior class are not unlike those directed at an ethnic minority (except where caste behavior is involved).

Class discrimination is felt very sharply in most American public schools. At least 94 percent of public-school teachers identify themselves with the middle class and may be judged to be middle class according to objective criteria. But about 60 percent of the student body of a typical school is lower class.[6] Probably many problems experienced by lower-class children in school arise from the fact that schools prize middle-class culture and penalize manifestations of lower-class culture wherever these happen to deviate markedly. Curriculums and activities are arranged, for the most part, to favor middle- and upper-class children.[7]

Although the total program of most schools is weighted against lower-class children and youth, readers should not get the impression that nothing is being done to help the lower-class school population. In the 1960s, the federal government, in collaboration with state governments, adopted a series of programs for underprivileged youth which is so vast and complex that as of this writing most schoolmen do not understand it very well. Although numerous congressional measures have been designed to lend help in some manner, the three major pieces of legislation are the Vocational Education Act of 1963, the Economic Opportunity Act of 1964, and the Elementary and Secondary Education Act of 1965. In 1966 more than $2 billion had been allocated to implement these Acts.

The extent of this effort can best be indicated by reviewing hastily the total program. The primary purpose of all aspects of these programs is *education*—the assumption being that this, in the long run, is the most effective way of striking at poverty and improving the social mobility of the poor. It is not necessary for our purposes here to go into minute detail concerning which Act has which purposes, or the mechanics of finance and administration. Students who want the particulars can secure large numbers of pamphlets from the U.S. Office of Education, the U.S. Office of Economic Opportunity, and the Superintendent of Documents, Washington, D.C.

The first program of major interest is schooling for children of pre-kindergarten age. The guiding theory for this program, named *Operation Head Start* is that by the age of 4, enough of an individual's basic personality structure has developed to account for about 50 percent of his score on IQ tests later in life (by the time he is 8, environmental factors will have accounted for another 30 percent of his IQ score). Although many other factors are involved, IQ score correlates to a significant degree with how well a youngster does in school and whether he will become a dropout. Preliminary data suggest that Head Start may increase IQ scores as much as 30 points.[8]

[6] *Ibid.*, p. 177.

[7] For an interesting account of discrimination among high-school students see W. Lloyd Warner and associates, *Democracy in Jonesville*, Harper & Row, 1949, chap. 6.

[8] See *Education, An Answer to Poverty*, U.S. Office of Education and U.S. Office of Economic Opportunity, Washington, D.C. (no publishing data given; either 1955 or 1956).

At least seven different programs have been provided for lower-class children of the primary and kindergarten years. These include programs to improve oral and written language skills, involvement of parents, large-scale experimentation in new techniques of teaching, furnishing visual and printed materials, summer programs for migrant children, and so on. At least as many programs have been made available for children in grades 4 through 6. These include programs similar to the primary ones, the addition of more remedial programs, and the beginning of a guidance and counseling program.

Teen-age programs include the *Job Corps* for unemployed youth between 16 and 21. This includes work for pay and combined job-training programs. For lower-class teen-agers still in school, there is a greatly expanded emphasis on courses of direct vocational utility to those occupations now in greatest demand for which these youth may be suited. There are continued remedial programs for those still in school. There are combination work-school programs, in which youth combine the two and receive pay for their out-of-school employment. These programs for youth still in school have been labeled *Operation Fair Chance*.

Although much is made of the extent to which schools are receiving federal aid, the Military Establishment, the space effort, and other kinds of expenditures not only have priority but involve spending on such a vast order that aid to schools is quite negligible by comparison. As a people, we are "education minded" in one sense but in another sense almost everything else has financial priority—especially at the federal level.

In spite of what seems to be a massive program of aid, we can forecast with some assurance that psychological conflicts of lower-class youth in a middle-class school will remain. The new programs are unlikely to change the middle-class values of teachers—the fundamental value clash will remain. There is also a risk that stigma will be attached by middle-class students and by teachers of academic subjects to the new programs. Lower-class parental involvement would seem to have an uncertain future: These parents are already too hostile and alienated to be likely to change much.

Children experience conflicts when they observe that their own behavior does not square with American ideals of equality and liberty. Children of lower ranks experience conflict when they try to conform to middle-class standards pressed upon them by the school, since such conformity often means violating the standards of their home and neighborhood. Conflicts arise also when children reject friends of their own class in order to take advantage of friendships offered them by children of a higher class.

Some of the contradictions and confusions in belief and behavior which define social class as a problematic area will be considered in the following sections.

1. Rank in a Classless Society

It is believed that there are no social classes in America; but it is also believed that some persons are better than others and entitled to more of the rewards of life.

First in our equalitarian ideology is the belief that "All men are created equal," sometimes stated, "All men are equal in the sight of God." We may identify a cluster of beliefs which support or logically follow from this basic proposition: All occupations are to be respected, even the most lowly. Honest toil, earning one's bread by "the sweat of one's brow," is honorable and respectable. The poor have special virtues seldom found among the rich (we may sometimes identify a kind of doctrine of inverted status—hard-working laborers are thought the true aristocracy, and the rich regarded as parasitical, profligate, and immoral). A social climber—anyone who "puts on airs"—is contemptible, and to be shunned rather than admired. It is only the "cheap" and the "small-minded" who "lord it" over those who are less fortunate. Such persons put on a "false front" by living in ways they "cannot really afford."

We shall comment on but one other example of our equalitarian ideology. A rich man who behaves like a common man, who has the language and manners of a plain person, who is willing to associate with plain persons, is much admired. He is a "regular guy," as "common as an old shoe." Persons who are socially inferior report glowingly on their "democratic" associations with the great man. Similarly, when young Mr. Van Swank marries Sadie O'Leary from the other side of the railroad tracks, he is much admired by middle- and lower-class persons. Such a marriage proves, it is thought, that America has a truly classless society.

Alongside the foregoing beliefs are an equal or greater number which assume that classes exist, or ought to exist. These are less widely held by lower-class than by middle- and upper-class persons; but even members of the lower-lower group may accept some of them. Foremost is the notion that some persons and some families are better than others. One constantly encounters statements such as, "He comes from a fine family," "She is a nice girl, but her family doesn't rate," "I wonder why Jack and Ted run around together—Jack is such a well-bred young man," "The trouble with joining the club is that some of the people in it you would want to associate with, and some you wouldn't." Occasionally one hears statements which suggest that superiority-inferiority is a function of heredity, and blood is the carrier of hereditary qualities. "Blood will tell" communicates this idea. One also hears the expressions "blue blood" and "fine-blooded family." The saying "You can't make a silk purse out of a sow's ear" probably assumes a hereditary basis for upper-class status. Expressions referring to inherited superiorities occur more often among upper-class than among middle- or lower-class persons.

It is commonly believed that some behaviors are "vulgar," "coarse," "crude," "awkward," or "unrefined." By contrast, other behaviors are "correct," "polished," "stylish," "well bred," or "proper." Whenever behaviors are so labeled, persons using them are likely to be categorized as either "high type" or "low type," which is equivalent to assigning class rank.

Some jobs, some clubs, some schools, and some churches [9] are thought better than others—not objectively, according to money earned, physical facilities, or usefulness, but in terms of greater "social respectability."

Since most individuals accept to some degree both the American creed of equality, with all that it implies with respect to social class, and a class-accepting group of beliefs, it is obvious that in the area of social class there is much inconsistent and compartmentalized thinking. For example: Persons who dislike to think of our culture as class structured work very hard at acquiring and displaying symbols of status. A wife of an equalitarian professor is likely to prefer that her children not associate with children who display lower-class traits, such as "smutty" talk or use of the word "ain't." Even though she regularly denounces upper-class persons as snobs, a middle-class housewife is likely to be very pleased to be invited to a tea given by an upper-class woman. Even though there may be plenty of food and a vacant place at the table, a middle-class person of equalitarian philosophy is still not likely to invite into the house for a meal a laborer who comes to tend the lawn.

Those who are most class conscious are most likely to become entangled in inconsistencies of the above sort. Certain groups, identifiable by sex, status, or occupation, usually take class more seriously than do other groups. Women tend to be much more class conscious than men. Newspaper society pages are read chiefly by women, it is primarily women who organize social functions in which symbols of class are conspicuously displayed, and women are more prone than men to snub or ostracize persons of a lower class. In contrast, men of all class levels are often able to associate harmoniously in a veterans' organization, church,

[9] In Jonesville, for example, churches rank socially from high to low as follows: Federated (Congregational and Presbyterian), Methodist, Lutheran, Catholic, Baptist, Free Methodist, and Gospel Tabernacle. Warner, *Democracy in Jonesville*, p. 153.

or club. Probably class consciousness increases among both sexes as one moves upward in the class hierarchy, upper uppers being the most aware of class distinctions although sometimes exhibiting more outward democracy in their behavior than lower uppers.

Certain occupational groups seem largely to escape class entanglements and discriminations; they are "outside" the class system, so to speak. Examples are artistic and scholarly professions and government service. Small children are not at first class conscious, but evidence sugggests that they steadily become so as they mature, and over two-thirds of sixth-grade children are able to rate other children in terms of conventional symbols of social class.[10]

1.1 How do you define social class? How does a class differ from a caste? Are social classes necessary?
1.2 What would a classless society be like? Would any of the following have a role in such a society: stylish clothes, correct English, proper etiquette, formal teas, tuxedos, sororities, finishing schools?
1.3 Is it possible to have equality and social class at the same time? How would each have to be defined in order for them to coexist without conflict?

2. Earned Success and Fortuitous Success

It is believed that the United States is a land of opportunity and that anyone can get ahead if he tries hard enough; but it is also believed that a person cannot move upward nowadays unless he gets lucky breaks or knows the right people.

The first belief has such a long tradition and such wide currency that it needs but little comment. It perhaps reached its zenith in popular acceptance in the late nineteenth century, when "success novels" achieved a circulation of millions of copies.[11] The belief is accompanied by a cluster of optimistic notions of the following sort: America is a classless society. Since ancestry and childhood circumstances are irrelevant to success, it is no real handicap to be born poor or on the wrong side of the railroad tracks. Anyone can move upward if he has what it takes. If a person is of high character, works hard and conscientiously, and saves his money, reaching the top is virtually guaranteed. If he fails to reach

---

[10] For an interesting study on class attitudes of children see Celia Burns Stendler, *Children of Brasstown*, University of Illinois Press, 1949.

[11] Horatio Alger wrote more than one hundred novels on the "rags-to-riches" theme, most of which were widely read in the late nineteenth and early twentieth centuries.

the top, it is because he did not try hard enough, or showed moral weakness, or did not have what it takes. The life of Abraham Lincoln has come to symbolize the dream of American opportunity, with the result that Lincoln is perhaps the greatest of all American folk heroes.

A belief in equal opportunity may be associated—as demonstrated by some of the beliefs just mentioned—with a belief in the essential equality of individuals. If one assumes that everyone is created equal, then success becomes a matter of *effort*. On the other hand, a belief in equal opportunity may be associated with a belief in the essential *in*equality of individuals: Social status and success are a manifestation of "survival of the fittest." Persons who feel that those who get to the top do so because of superior biological endowment, and that those who fail do so because they are biological weaklings, properly eliminated through natural selection, are ideological descendants of the "social Darwinists" of the nineteenth century.[12]

Whether one's philosophy of opportunity assumes that people begin the race as equals or as unequals, it usually maintains that everyone should try to rise as far as he can, should make maximum use of his powers.

Countering ideas such as those above is the more cynical notion that America is no longer a land of opportunity except for a fortunate few, and that one joins their ranks chiefly as a result of "lucky breaks" or "knowing the right people." Warner reports that a considerable, and in his opinion a growing, proportion of people feel that opportunity for the average person is declining in the United States.[13] Students should remember, however, that the state of the economy is highly influential in determining beliefs. The relatively sustained period of business prosperity since World War II very likely invalidates Warner's earlier conclusions. The opening of new industries and expansion of the old have created rather remarkable opportunities for upward mobility. This is particularly true for all who have the ability and can afford a college education; and probably doubly so for those who can manage a stint in graduate school. Such young persons enter—almost automatically—the middle-middle group described earlier. This is one reason, no doubt, why all upper lowers and lower middles plan, if possible, a college edu-

[12] This group, writing between about 1860 and World War I, included such names as Herbert Spencer, Walter Bagehot, and Francis Galton. See the excellent volume, Richard Hofstadter, *Social Darwinism in American Thought*, Braziller, 1959.

[13] For example, see Warner, *Democracy in Jonesville*, chap. 6. The Lynds also reported this trend in the second of their Middletown studies (Robert S. and Helen Merrill Lynd, *Middletown in Transition*, Harcourt, Brace & World, 1937). See also Richard Centers, *The Psychology of Social Class*, Princeton University Press, 1949, p. 147.

cation for their children, and why education—the more the better—is now regarded as the royal road to success.

Our success ideology produces a number of contradictions and conflicts in thought and behavior. People are likely to believe, on an abstract level, in the prevalence of opportunity, and in the obligation and possibility of "making good." These same people may in concrete situations attribute success to lucky breaks, as when they say, "No wonder Jones made foreman—his and the boss' kids were in the same outfit during the war." Upper-class persons tend to attribute their success to biological superiority; lower-class persons, on the other hand, who are less successful, often attribute succcess to lucky breaks.

A belief checklist administered by one of the authors to a group of college sophomores seemed to indicate that a number of students attributed membership in the upper class to biological superiority, and membership in the lower class to faulty environment. Gorer sensed the same discrepancy in the thinking of American adults.[14] If this inconsistency is widespread, it represents an interesting amalgamation of "social Darwinism" and modern sociology.

Another contradiction is apparent when persons, who preach the doctrine of success to their children and to adults less successful than they, criticize their former equals who have managed to outdistance them in the race. Since getting ahead usually means moving into a higher social class, and since this almost inevitably means the abandonment of old friends, those who get ahead are likely to be accused by their former friends of "getting a swelled head" or "getting uppity." In short, "getting ahead" is often advocated by the same persons who feel that social climbers are contemptible.

Probably the chief conflict is that between the ideals of success and social reality. Although we believe that everyone should try to be successful, and that failure is a result of personal inadequacy, it does not require much thought to see that everyone cannot reach the top. The upper class comprises no more than 3 or 4 percent of the population, and the upper-middle class comprises from one-tenth to one-fifth of the population. Many persons would be satisfied to move upward only a notch or two—let us say, from upper-lower to lower-middle status. We have pointed out that for those who can achieve sufficient education, opportunity for upward mobility is increasing. There remain good chances—so long as prosperity lasts—for persons with only a high-school education or a BA to move far. In spite of this, approximately the lower third of our population remains in poverty and their chances for upward

[14] Geoffrey Gorer, *The American People; a Study in National Character*, Norton, 1948, p. 168.

mobility in this generation seem dubious. Kolko's study seems to indicate that the *distribution* of wealth is approximately the same in the 1960s as it was fifty years previously.[15] Distribution aside, however, our upper two-thirds live on a vastly higher material standard than fifty years ago, as do a few of the lower one-third.

2.1 Take a poll to find what proportion of your classmates hopes to enter professions or become business owners or executives. Then try to find statistics on what proportion of the population is in these occupations. Do you think that most of your classmates can achieve their occupational goals?

2.2 What determines the level which each individual reaches in life, heredity or environment or both? What data do you need in order to answer this question?

2.3 How do you explain the tendency to explain success as a result of inherited superiority, and failure as a result of poor environment? Is it consistent for one to explain success and failure in these terms?

3. Success and Happiness

It is believed that everyone should try to be a success; but it is also believed that the happiest persons are those who learn to relax and take it easy.

Although in special situations "success" may be defined as formation of good character, it is usually correlated with occupational and social advancement. Success is a relative concept; at the very least it means achieving wealth and status beyond what a person was born into, but for many it is always just out of reach because it is defined as a step higher than present attainment, whatever the latter may be. Thus, a member of the lower-middle class by birth who becomes a member of the *nouveaux riches* may feel deep frustration because he cannot expect to become a member of the *anciens riches* during his lifetime. In our culture, a person is expected never to feel satisfied with present attainment; he should strive always for a higher place.

At the same time, those who are struggling up the ladder of success may sincerely envy those who are, by conventional standards, failures. One often hears statements such as "Old Joe never made anything of himself, but he is a lot happier than some top executives I know," or "The Scrogginses never had a cent ahead, but look how content they are." In more general form, the belief is expressed as "Lower-class people are usually happier than the rich." Envy for the unsucccessful who

---

[15] Gabriel Kolko, *Wealth and Power in America*, Knopf, 1957.

at the same time appear to enjoy life issues from an ambivalance of motives which is apparently very common among those who are working to improve themselves. This ambivalance is expressed, on the one hand, in a craving for the self-esteem which accompanies occupational and social advancement and, on the other, in a craving for stability, relaxation, and freedom from excessive responsibility.

The literature of psychiatry frequently offers the opinon that the conflict most often observed in patients is that produced by a desire for "success," on the one hand, and a desire for stability and security, on the other. Social realities tend to make impossible the achievement of both goals; yet many persons find it emotionally difficult deliberately to choose one to the exclusion of the other. An eminent psychiatrist, Franz Alexander, describes this conflict as follows:

> The [explanation] . . . is to be found in the culturally determined internal inconsistency of our social standards; the traditional one-sided worship of individual success in a complex and interdependent society and the exaggerated emphasis on independence in times of great insecurity. . . . The prestige attached to independent achievement on the one hand and the longing for security, love, and belonging to somebody or some group on the other are the two poles between which patients are torn in a futile struggle. . . .
>
> . . . The analyst sees his patients . . . engaged in a Marathon race, their eager faces distorted by the strain, their eyes focused not upon their goal, but upon each other with a mixture of hate, envy, and admiration. They would all like to stop but dare not as long as the others are running. . . . If one of them finally stops and begins leisurely to whistle a tune or watch a passing cloud or pick up a stone and with childish curiosity turns it around in his hand, they all look upon him at first with astonishment and then with contempt and disgust. They call him names, a dreamer or a parasite, a theoretician or a schizophrenic. . . . They not only do not understand him—they not only despise him but "they hate him as their own sin." All of them would like to stop . . . [but] they do not dare . . . lest they lose their self respect, because they know only one value—that of running for its own sake.[16]

In Alexander's opinion the chief dread of the American male is that he will not make the grade in life, that he will not be "a success." Alexander believes this anxiety to be the most common cause of mental breakdown and neurosis among men in the United States.[17]

3.1 How does a person determine whether he is a success? What are your criteria for success? Is a person successful if he is merely happy? Is a lower-class person a success if he is happy? Is it possible for a person to be both a success and a failure?

[16] Franz Alexander, *Our Age of Unreason: A Study of the Irrational Forces in Social Life*, Lippincott, 1942, pp. 309-310.
[17] *Ibid.*, pp. 307-308.

3.2 Would it be a good idea to quit teaching children that "everyone should try to get ahead"? What alternatives are there to the goal of "getting ahead"? What would be the effects upon our nation if people generally ceased to pursue wealth and social position?

3.3 What has been the effect upon the United States of the "gospel of success"? What has been the effect of the "gospel of democracy"? Are these two gospels in any way conflicting?

4. Liberal vs. Vocational Education

It is believed that children of the upper class should have a liberal education and that children of the lower class should have a vocational education; but it is also believed that all children should have an equal opportunity for an education which fits them for citizenship and cultured living.

According to the first belief, the best place for an upper-class child to get an education is a private liberal-arts college, preferably one which is old enough to have traditions. Many upper-middle-class parents include their own children among those deserving of a liberal-arts education. Prerequisite to this kind of education is a college-preparatory course in a public high school, or in a private secondary school.

Those who hold this view of what is proper education for upper-class children usually believe that a liberal education is beyond the capacity of lower-class children, and that furthermore they have no practical use for philosophy, literature, music, and the fine arts. Acquaintance with these fields might even make them unhappy and dissatisfied. A much better education for lower-class children is one which emphasizes vocational training.

These beliefs date from the ancient world. They are explicitly stated in Plato's *Republic* and characterize the educational thought of many Greek philosophers. They have had wide currency in Europe to the present day and were generally accepted in colonial America. They are still held by a considerable number of persons in all walks of life but have been reinterpreted in the modern world so that their meaning is different from Plato's. Whereas Plato meant that the recipients of liberal education were to be an "aristocracy of brains" and not an aristocracy of wealth, it is assumed today that an aristocracy of wealth is an aristocracy of brains. In fact, the modern tendency is to judge a man's intelligence by how much money he has been able to accumulate.

The notion that liberal education should be reserved for upper-class children is part of an aristocratic traditon. It is a logical corollary of the assumptions that some individuals are intellectually superior by virtue of heredity, that these persons are destined to become a governing class, and that a liberal education is the best means for equipping our natural leaders. It develops the mind, and those who are to rule should achieve the greatest possible mental development, while those who are to follow need only enough to understand what their leaders require.

Since a liberal education has been historically associated with high social position and superior intelligence, middle- or upper-lower-class children are often encouraged by parents, or they desire independently, to pursue in high school a college-preparatory course, the nearest thing to a liberal education which one can get in a secondary school. Parents of moderate status may also encourage their children to attend a liberal-arts college or to take a liberal-arts course at a state university.

In contrast to these ideas is a belief that all children should have essentially the same education. In a democratic society, it is held, all children are citizens and as adults will share in political control. Therefore all need the same basic education for citizenship and have an equal right to the benefits of cultured living, usually taken to include acquaintance with good books, music, and art, and development of a variety of intellectual interests.

This idea may stem from basically different philosophical outlooks. For example, a contemporary group of liberal-arts professors in the United States, often called humanists, feel that "true education" requires the same subject matter in every situation, and that all educable children should receive the same kind of education. This group would not limit a liberal education to the wealthy; they feel that it is good for everyone. If there are those who are incapable of learning the liberal arts, it is because they are ineducable. In opposition to the humanists are various branches of another philosophical tradition which advocate a core of common learnings. Within this general framework are at least two groups— followers and interpreters of Bode and Dewey, and followers and interpreters of Kilpatrick. Although the two groups may have divergent views concerning what the core of common learning should be and how it should be taught, they agree that the traditional liberal-arts curriculum, and its high-school counterpart, has not succeeded very well in liberating human intelligence.

Emotional conflict arises when upper-class children who are not academically inclined are pressed by parents and school authorities to complete a college-preparatory program in high school or a liberal-arts program in college. Parents may believe that a vocational program would be more practical, or that its pursuit would make children more happy and useful, but they dare not dishonor the family name by letting a child take such a program. A lack of interest in, or an inability to master, the content of a liberal-arts course (as traditionally organized and taught) is not evidence of stupidity in a child except for those parents who have been victimized by an aristocratic tradition, in which case both child and parent suffer. Very frequently parents fail to recognize that it is social status they want rather than education of their children.[18]

Teachers become entangled in the patterns just described. Being aware that somehow a college-preparatory program is more "respectable" than other programs, they tend to favor college-preparatory students and often in subtle ways discriminate against vocational students. It is easy to assume that the latter are less bright and less gifted than the former. Teachers may vacillate between the attitude expressed in "If only those dumb kids who ought to be in the shops full time were not in my history class, teaching would be a pleasure" and the attitude reflected in "Some of my students don't learn much history, but they *need* it just as much as anyone else so I'll teach them all I can."

4.1 Is it true that some students are incapable of profiting very much from a liberal-arts course? If so, why? Can a liberal-arts course be redesigned in both content and method so as to benefit more fully greater numbers of students? Can this be done without "watering down" its traditional content?

4.2 What revisions, if any, in a liberal-arts course would increase its value to lower-class students? If such revisions were carried out, would the program still be "liberal arts"?

4.3 If we assume that the new federal programs for the lower-class make them more upwardly mobile and provide them with language, dress, and other middle-class habits, without lowering living standards for the remaining classes, would we be moving in the direction of a classless society? Would this be good or bad? The aim of theoretical Communism is a classless society. Would this make us Communists?

DISCUSSION QUESTIONS AND EXERCISES

1. On July 28, 1964, President Lyndon Johnson said the following: "If we are learning anything from our experiences, we are learning that it is time for us to go to work, and the first work of these times and the first work of our century is education." As of then, the federal government had decided to spend $2 billion a year to assist state and local governments in educating the poor. Look up the latest estimates of the cost of our "man-on-the-moon" program, for which the President is enthusiastic. How do the expenditures compare? How do you explain the President's statement?

2. If a school is given comparatively large sums to increase its library, add to

[18] It must be recognized, however, that while not displeased by the status-conferring qualities of a liberal-arts education, many parents do value genuinely the kind of education which a liberal-arts program is capable of giving.

its shop facilities, hire consultants, buy audiovisual equipment, etc., will this necessarily improve the quality of education? What if the school has no defensible long-range philosophy of education? Could all these new federally supplied "goodies" operate like the famous leaf-raking projects of Franklin Roosevelt's administration, in which the poor were bought *new rakes* in order to rake leaves from one side of a public park to another and back again all day?

3. Assume you are teaching in a school in which the social-studies subjects are taught separately, and that somewhere you want to insert a unit on social class. In which subject would you place it? Would it be advisable to include such a unit if your classes included lower-class students?

4. What current beliefs about social class could be studied—and perhaps tested —in connection with "standard" topics of American history such as the following: the American Revolution; the cotton economy of the South; sectional disputes between North and South; the rise of big business; the growth of organized labor; populism, free silver, and progressivism; the New Deal; the Great Society?

5. As a college or university student, you have had many opportunities to participate in and observe campus life. In your opinion, how does social class manifest itself on a college campus? Could you arrange your sororities and fraternities according to a "social hierarchy"?

REFERENCES

Clark, Kenneth B., *Dark Ghetto: Dilemmas of Social Power*, New York, Harper & Row, 1965.

A powerful book, in which the author says that what he writes is a "summation of my personal and lifelong experiences as a prisoner within the ghetto long before I was aware that I was really a prisoner."

Davis, Allison, *Psychology of the Child in the Middle Class*, Pittsburgh, University of Pittsburgh Press, 1960.

Allison Davis is one of the foremost authorities on patterns of child rearing. He is known for his thesis that social pressure and resulting tension is greater for the preschool middle- than for the preschool lower-class child.

Davis, Allison, *Social Class Influences upon Learning*, Cambridge, Harvard University Press, 1948.

Draws from studies which indicate that social class membership rather than genetic factors are crucial in determining how well students do in school.

Eells, Kenneth, *et al.*, *Intelligence, and Cultural Differences*, Chicago, University of Chicago Press, 1951.

Although Eells' conclusions have been criticized as exaggerated, his basic thesis still stands; i.e., that lower-class children tend to score relatively low on commonly used intelligence tests for reasons other than inferior intelligence.

FANON, FRANTZ, *The Wretched of the Earth*, Constance Farrington, trans., New York, Grove, 1965.

This important book grapples with the connection between violence and freedom in the context of colonial revolution. Relevant to the *Prologue*, as well as to this chapter.

GORDON, MILTON H., *Social Class in American Sociology*, Durham, Duke University Press, 1959.

A stock taking of theory and research from Weber to the middle 1950s. A solid, informative book which analyzes, compares, and relates the work of persons such as Lynd, Warner, Hollingshead, West (Withers), Dollard, Kaufman, and Goldschmidt.

HOLLINGSHEAD, AUGUST B., and FREDERICK C. REDLICH, *Social Class and Mental Illness*, New York, Wiley, 1958.

Based upon a study made in metropolitan New Haven over a ten-year period. This book is Part I of the total report; Part II is found in Jerome K. Myers and Bertram H. Roberts, *Family and Class Dynamics in Mental Illness*, New York, Wiley, 1959.

HOLLINGSHEAD, AUGUST B., *Elmtown's Youth*, New York, Wiley, 1949.

On how our class structure affects high-school youth. Fascinating, easy reading, and not outdated.

HUSGAR, GEORGE B., ed., *The Intellectuals: A Controversial Portrait*, Glencoe, Ill., Free Press, 1961.

This book of readings is a potpourri with no unifying theme. It includes selections from the writings of intellectuals of the past two centuries which focus on the subject of what an intellectual is.

KAVALER, LUCY, *Private World of High Society*, New York, David McKay, 1961.

Illuminates in chatty prose the current *life style* of the *haut monde* and, if you wish and are in a position to make the assault, how to "arrive." Kavaler not only sympathizes with this group, but seems serious about helping persons who want to get on the "social register." Interesting—but it may irritate prospective school teachers.

KEATS, JOHN C., *The Crack in the Picture Window*, Boston, Houghton Mifflin, 1957.

A witty, readable, but at the same time, slashing attack on modern suburbia. See also Auguste Spectorsky, for a description of the land beyond suburbia.

LASCH, CHRISTOPHER, *The New Radicalism in America (1889–1963): The Intellectual as a Social Type*, New York, Knopf, 1965.

The author is considered an extraordinarily creative historian of ideas. He ties together persons with a wide range of talents and personality types into a subculture, and the results are most interesting.

LIPSET, SEYMOUR M., and REINHARD BENDIX, *Social Mobility and Industrial Society*, Berkeley, University of California Press, 1960.

A synthesis of international research on social mobility, including a report on empirical studies in Oakland, California. Rather tedious, but lightened by some very bright spots; Parts I and III are best.

MILLS, C. WRIGHT, *White Collar*, Oxford University Press, 1951.

A provocative study of the American middle class at midcentury. Mill's interpretation tends to be critical and to reflect his socialist orientation; nevertheless, the book is powerful.

SELBY, HUBERT, *Last Exit to Brooklyn*, New York, Grove, 1964.

A realistic book about ghetto life by one who has experienced it. A fascinating personal testimony which rings of truth but might shock the squeamish.

SPECTORSKY, AUGUSTE, *The Exurbanites*, New York, Lippincott, 1955.

Describes the land beyond suburbia. A more sophisticated book than that of Keats.

SUTHERLAND, ELIZABETH, ed., *Letters from Mississippi*, New York, McGraw-Hill, 1965.

A remarkable collection of letters written by the volunteers who spent the summer of 1964 in Mississippi working for equal rights for Negroes. A powerful book that hits one where it hurts.

WARNER, W. LLOYD, "The Warner Library." This is our terminology and is not meant to imply that all the books bearing Warner's name were published by the same firm or constitute any sort of formal collection. To our knowledge at least 17 titles have been published bearing Warner's name—either by him singly or by Warner and associates—all in the area of social class.

There is the famous *Yankee City Series*, which comprises four titles. We prefer Warner and Lunt, *The Social Life of a Modern Community*, *The Status System of a Modern Community*, and the final volume, by Warner, *The Living and the Dead* (very good). Students should browse among all the other titles and decide what they like best. Since Warner's works on social class range from 1941 (*Color and Human Nature*) to 1963 (*The American Federal Executive*) there is no point listing them all here.

YOUNG, MICHAEL D., *Rise of the Meritocracy, 1870–2033*, New York, Random House, 1960.

A British sociologist takes us on an excursion into the future, in which he attempts to show the logical outcome of selecting the "brainiest" students for special education. Among the questions he raises are: Would this result in a society in which the only thing that counts is "intellectual merit"? If so, what about other human virtues such as empathy, kindness, and generosity?

CHAPTER 17

Problematic Areas of Culture: Religion and Morality

Religion and Morality in Modern American Society

THE situation with respect to moral education in our public schools was reviewed in Chapter 6.[1] Public schools have tended to ignore those moral issues in which youth are most vitally concerned. When moral issues have been treated, they have been most commonly handled on an unreflective level.

Many people feel that religious and moral instruction cannot be separated, and for this reason, have urged that religious instruction be installed in public schools. In spite of Supreme Court rulings ordering that sectarian religion not be advocated in the public schools, a larger portion of the public school curriculum than most persons realize is, in fact, highly sectarian. It is sectarian, obviously, to offer a Christmas program with a Christian theme. In fact, the entire WASP slant of our middle-class schools is fundamentally Calvinist and therefore sectarian. When any "moral issue" arises, the public schools tend to revert to WASP values. They ignore Jews, Buddhists, Bahais, and other non-Christian students; more than this, they ignore the rapidly increasing number of nonreligious students.

Nearly all public schools offer some instruction *about* religion. This kind of instruction is legal, and it does not conflict in any way with the constitutional barriers separating church and state. World-history courses deal with the history of Judaism and Christianity; some include a comparative treatment of the world's great religions. Courses in United States history normally include some treatment of the history of religion

---

[1] The issues we have considered in each of the problematic areas are moral in their nature. Unfortunately, most citizens do not see them as moral. In this chapter we are concerned with exploring some of the more traditional conceptions of morality. Morality in the lay sense usually points to issues involving alcohol, card playing, gambling, sex, and church attendance. In this chapter sex will not be treated, since it will be given rather full attention in Chapter 19.

in this country. Senior-problems and problems-of-democracy courses ordinarily have a unit on religion. Units of this kind usually stress aspects of the psychology and sociology of religion and may include a brief review of church history in the United States. All these types of religious instruction are the almost exclusive responsibility of social-studies teachers.

There can be little doubt that the study of morals and religion deserves a much larger place in the public-school curriculum. If increased study is to be effective in changing attitudes and behavior, it will be necessary to approach religious and moral issues more reflectively. Whether reflection has a function in the religious and moral area is itself an issue. Many argue that religion is a matter of faith, and that reflective thought tends to undermine faith. This argument implies that faith is "believing what you know ain't true." It also implies that someone has to determine the substantive content of a religious faith, and the common man's duty is to accept this content uncritically. In any case, given the present state of religious thought in the United States, adolescents are very likely to develop religious conflicts whether or not a study of religion is included in the curriculum. Only through reflective analysis can they be resolved democratically. It is true that such reflection may undermine particular beliefs; but it is equally true that many religious and moral beliefs will be sustained by reflection, and a given faith will be better understood and more likely to influence behavior.

Another argument against reflective study of religious beliefs claims that they include metaphysical assumptions not susceptible to scientific verification. For example, how is one to test the assertion that "The Devil is the cause of all evil"? We have discussed in Chapter 6 the question of whether the reflective method can function in the area of moral judgment. In most cases, beliefs of the so-called metaphysical kind can be analyzed according to the rules developed in that chapter.

Contemporary religious thought in the United States is profoundly affected by early Judaism and Christianity. One of the leading contributions of the ancient Hebrews was their conception of God. They came to believe that there was only one true God, Yahweh. Yahweh was regarded as a tribal god, in the sense that the Hebrews believed themselves to be his "chosen people." The important point for our purposes is the conception of the character of Yahweh which developed, since this has colored our thinking about God to the present day. First, the Hebrew God was anthropomorphic—that is, described in essentially human terms; even though just and righteous, he was also capable of great anger and harsh vengeance. Second, God was much concerned with the moral behavior of men. He was the source of ethical principles which man was expected to follow. Third, although God was the source of everything in nature, he governed and manifested himself directly rather than through natural law. God was thus thought to talk to persons directly, to inflict droughts or plagues as punishment, to raise the dead and smite the wicked, and to perform various other miracles. Man's relation to God furnished the theme of the Old Testament.

Although Christ was a Jew and sympathetic to many aspects of Hebrew religion, he introduced a new group of insights which distinguish early Christianity from the Hebrew religion which preceded it.[2] Like the Hebrews, Christ taught that God was a sovereign moral personality, ruling the universe with perfect justice and righteousness. But Christ, much more than earlier Hebrews, emphasized the loving and forgiving nature of God. According to Christ, God has no favorites. He is the God of rich and poor, and of all races and nationalities. No person, said Jesus, is natively unworthy of God's grace or man's fellowship. Men are to live religiously oriented toward God as sons toward a father, and toward each other as brothers. Christianity thus implies both equality and brotherly love as guides to social living. Christian teaching softened the sternness of God and introduced greater tolerance and sympathy into moral codes.

Further changes in religious belief occurred during the first three centuries A.D., chief of which was adoption among church fathers of asceticism as an ideal of life on earth. Asceticism as an ideal developed from a growing belief in dualism of matter and spirit. Whereas Jesus had "apparently accepted the body as functionally integrated with the mind and spirit in a working unity,"[3] by the time of Augustine it was believed that the soul was in bondage to the flesh, which was thought corrupt. The only way the spirit could be freed from lusts of the flesh was through self-denial. Some authorities feel that the ascetic ideal was a perversion of Christ's teaching. For example, Noss states "[Jesus] . . . was no ascetic. He enjoyed wedding feasts and banquets. He never suggested that the body is inherently corrupting and defiling, or that the soul is foully imprisoned in the flesh."[4] The idea that the body is vile seems to have been borrowed from pagan belief systems of the Middle East. For Example, Augustine was greatly influenced by a Persian philosophical system known as Manichaeism, which combined elements of Zoroastrianism, Buddhism, Judaism, Gnosticism, and Christianity.

---

[2] Some Bible scholars doubt that Christ intended to establish a new religion called Christianity. They attribute this achievement to St. Paul. Other scholars doubt that Christ ever lived.

[3] John B. Noss, *Man's Religions*, Macmillan, 1949, p. 587.

[4] *Ibid.*, p. 587.

Manichaeists stressed the dualism of light and dark, good and evil, spirit and matter.[5] Augustinian thinking also stressed mystical experience and blind reliance upon faith, with a result that intelligence was all but excluded as a guiding force in life.

Medieval religious thought was influenced strongly by Greek philosophy. Thomas Aquinas adopted virtually all of Aristotle's thought except where it conflicted irreconcilably with beliefs central to Christianity. Aristotle had advocated substitution of reason for blind faith, and use of sense observation to establish the truth of propositions. He had urged that man learn all he could through intellectual inquiry. Aquinas tried to reconcile and synthesize the uncritical reliance on faith which characterized Augustine and the appeal to reason which characterized Aristotle.

By the time of the Reformation, Christianity had thus come to combine aspects of the thought of Greece and the Middle East, and of Old and New Testament teachings. This amalgam was distilled and bolstered by authority of the Church. The religious system which developed constituted a world-outlook. Stripped of minor and incidental aspects, the Christian world-outlook embraced three major ideas, as follows:

Belief in a personal God of stern but loving character, who created man and the universe and who governs them according to his will.

Belief in a purposeful universe. It was thought that the universe and every thing and event in it are part of a divine plan—consequently man and nature are moving inexorably toward an end already determined by God.

Belief in moral order—that is, belief that moral ideals exist in the universe as absolutes, universal and unchanging. Man's duty is to ascertain these moral values and try to follow them.

Protestantism arose as a protest against the means by which the medieval Church had asserted that individuals may gain religious understanding and salvation. Both Catholics and Protestants assume that early prophets and apostles were instruments of divine revelation. Roman Catholics believe it is a role of the pope and bishops to interpret this revelation to men and a duty of men to accept submissively their authority. Protestants strongly reject the Catholic attitude toward this role of the Church. They assume that all guidance necessary for man's salvation is provided in Holy Writ. They assume that men can directly approach God without mediation by church or priesthood. Contrary to Catholicism, Protestantism came to advocate individualism and personal freedom in religious affairs. Early Protestantism also rejected the Thomist attitude toward natural reason and adopted an extreme Augustinianism

---

[5] *Ibid.*, p. 633 n.

which denied competence to human reason and relied upon faith alone. Although this was Luther's position, Calvin modified it somewhat to allow a place for natural theology. To this day, orthodox Protestants place faith or mystical experience above reason as a means of knowing God and interpreting his will.[6]

During the past generation we have come to refer to orthodox or traditional Protestantism as fundamentalism. Although Calvin's *Institutes of the Christian Religion* (1536) remains perhaps the outstanding systematic formulation of Protestant orthodoxy, present-day fundamentalists have in various ways modified the strict tenets of Calvinism. For example, many fundamentalists have abandoned Calvin's doctrine of predestination. Yet fundamentalists continue to share a strict core of belief which includes the following: [7]

1. God is sovereign in the universe, and although his will may sometimes seem inscrutable, his character is righteous and his decisions just.
2. Man is possessed of a certain natural knowledge of God, but this understanding is dimmed by innate depravity and he needs the aid of revelation of the Scriptures.
3. Man is subject to a hereditary corruption which makes him obnoxious to God. The original source of man's defilement was Adam's sin.
4. In spite of his predilection for sin, man can gain salvation through God's grace. He needs only to repent his sins and accept Christ as his savior.
5. On Judgment Day, Christ shall return to earth and the dead shall be resurrected. The saved shall enjoy eternal bliss in heaven and the damned eternal torment in hell.

Beliefs such as these led to formulation of a distinctive social and moral code and encouraged development of particular economic and political doctrines. As we have seen, Protestant religion implied a belief in freedom of mind and conscience. Although early Protestantism was highly intolerant, gradually it came to recognize that freedom of individuals to interpret the Bible according to conscience leads to considerable diversity in belief—a diversity to be not only expected but tolerated. Furthermore, Calvin insisted that the first allegiance of man is to conscience rather than to any temporal ruler. (It is difficult to know whether to laugh or cry over the fact that, after this assertion of belief, Calvin had many persons burned to death for disagreeing with him.)

Protestantism led not only to religious individualism but also to repub-

---

[6] *Ibid.*, p. 144.

[7] For an excellent description of the leading tenets of Calvinism, see Noss, *ibid.*, pp. 668–669. The first three items in the following list follow Noss closely.

lican political institutions. And Calvin's emphasis on faithful pursuit of one's calling elevated thrift, hard work, and enterprise to the status of cherished values. Hence, Protestantism was a stimulus to rising capitalist institutions. Historically, it has defended virtually unlimited freedom for businessmen, even being charged with allying itself with predatory business interests and against laborers. Protestantism has also advocated strong national states and overseas imperialism because in this way the interests of business could best be served, but at the same time it has emphasized softer and more humane values of family loyalty, charity, and personal integrity.[8]

Although intellectual freedom and religious tolerance became a part of the Protestant heritage, moral tolerance did not. A liberal interpretation of the Bible, combined with a tendency to construe as sinful many acts not clearly condemned in the scriptures, has produced an elaborate and rigid moral code which makes a life free from sin practically impossible. Orthodox Protestants tend to define sin in Old Testament terms, and to denounce vigorously persons who deviate from traditional sexual codes, or who drink, gamble, and carouse.[9]

On many basic questions Catholics, orthodox Jews, and Protestant fundamentalists are in agreement. All three subscribe wholeheartedly to the three central elements of medieval religious philosophy: God the Father, a purposeful universe, and an eternal moral order. These three groups accept as literally true the moral injunctions of the Bible and add their own interpretations of sinfulness to behavior not specifically condemned in scripture.

Differences between Protestant fundamentalists, orthodox Jews, and Catholics are much less significant than differences between any orthodox faith and any naturalistic philosophy. Naturalism denies the existence of supernatural forces of any kind. It substitutes the reign of natural law for rule by a personal God, natural causation for teleological explanations. The belief that moral law is made by man is substituted for the belief that moral ideas are suprahuman and eternal. Naturalism as an outlook originated in ancient Greece. It all but disappeared during the medieval period but emerged more strongly than ever in the seventeenth and eighteenth centuries.

The rise of modern science between the sixteenth and nineteenth centuries provided a renewed impetus to naturalistic philosophy. It is by now common knowledge that certain scientific discoveries have tended

[8] For the classic treatment of the relation between Protestantism and economics, see R. H. Tawney, *Religion and the Rise of Capitalism*, New York, Harcourt, Brace & World, 1962. Mentor paperback, 1947.

[9] Edwin A. Burtt, *Types of Religious Philosophy*, Harper & Row, 1939.

to undermine orthodox religious interpretations. Yet none of these specific discoveries is as important as the growing acceptance of a naturalistic world-view. Stace puts the issue when he says:

> While it cannot be doubted that these shocks have had a powerful effect in the way of undermining religious faith, it must be pointed out that this is on the whole a very superficial account of the conflict between religion and science. The real antagonism lies much deeper. It is not between particular discoveries of science and particular dogmas of religion at all. It is rather that certain very general assumptions which are implicit in the scientific view of the world conflict with basic assumptions of the religious view—any religious view, not merely the Christian view—of the world.[10]

The assumptions of the scientific (or naturalistic) view of the world, if they did not exclude God altogether, produced a feeling of the remoteness of God. God was now seen, if at all, only as a first cause, who ruled the universe quite impersonally through natural law. This was a central belief of the deism of the late 1700s. As a result of this trend, interest in religious affairs waned. In America, for example, many prominent persons were deists, and the masses likewise lost interest in religion. One writer says, "It was not uncommon for missionaries to report . . . that a whole region [of the frontier] was destitute of religion. . . ." [11]

Among established churches, liberalizing influences appeared. Although a reaction to the forward march of a scientific world-view occurred in the nineteenth century, a scientific view seems to have established itself solidly in the twentieth. "Modernism," a religious movement developed in the twentieth century, makes numerous concessions to it. Whereas Protestant fundamentalists maintain that religious truth is independent of science, and authoritative over it, modernists generally assume that scientific method is the more reliable—and perhaps the only —means of ascertaining truth. Some modernists explicitly renounce belief in the supernatural. Although the same tendencies which have produced Protestant modernism have been apparent within Catholicism, Pope Pius X condemned the movement and it was suppressed among Catholics early in the century. Among Jews, modernist tendencies have also produced a retreat from orthodoxy. Primarily, however, modernism is a phenomenon of Protestantism.[12]

At present, the Roman Catholic church is in a ferment. Pope John (successor to Pius) injected a remarkably liberal and flexible view. The Vatican Councils have permitted debate on many issues central to the

[10] W. T. Stace, *Religion and the Modern Mind*, Lippincott, 1952, p. 53.

[11] William Warren Sweet, *Religion in the Development of American Culture*, 1765–1840, Scribner, 1952, p. 211.

[12] One of the best short treatments of modernism is in Burtt, *op. cit.*, chap. 8.

church. The issue of most concern as of this writing is what stand the church should take on birth control. We suspect that a major issue in the future will be the doctrine of papal infallibility. Nor should we fail to mention the church's internal furor caused by the writings of the Jesuit priest, Pierre Teilhard de Chardin, which introduced a new theological basis for Catholicism.

What do modernists believe? Although modernism is a tendency rather than a position, it is possible to identify a group of beliefs commonly a part of it. Modernism places scientific methodology above faith, intuition, and authority. It employs scientific procedures in Biblical criticism and as a result rejects belief in the literal truth of the Bible. On social issues many modernists are politically liberal. They believe in social reform, international cooperation, social-welfare programs, and a morality which is congenial to fundamental human impulses. They tend to favor relatively easy divorce, liberalization of sexual codes, practice of birth control, and a frank acceptance of sexual relationships between man and wife as contributing toward higher values of love and friendly harmony. They seem to be moving toward a morality more pragmatic than that which has characterized earlier religious outlooks.

There is impelling evidence that the religious beliefs of Americans have undergone rather fundamental change since World War II. The study of beliefs at Fresno State College only confirms numerous other studies. Fresno State students are, in general, not seriously interested in religion. It is a common topic of conversation but the conversation does not indicate deep interest or conviction. Except for a small Mennonite group and a few other fundamentalists (mostly Southern Baptists), students question the existence of God, reject a belief in heaven or hell, question the efficacy of prayer, and in general do not care one way or another. Few go to church regularly. Their main interest lies in sex, courtship, and marriage; and religion, although a popular subject of discussion, is not a major concern. Further, students seem to have rejected the concept of "sin," and to have separated religion and morality.

Some specific points of conflict and confusion in American moral and religious ideology will be discussed in the following sections.

1. Religious Belief and Practice

It is believed that persons should take their religion seriously and try to understand and believe its teachings in order to practice them in daily living; but it is also believed that anyone who tried seriously to practice the philosophy of Jesus would not get very far in today's world, and besides, extremely pious individuals are usually somewhat "nutty."

The first belief above was so widely held in America that until recently, anyone who openly derided it was likely to be rebuked. Most Americans verbally uphold such purportedly Christian values as honesty, love and kindness, forgiveness, charity, generosity, and humility. If asked, most Americans assert that they are Christians and accept as true the central teachings of Jesus. Furthermore, most Americans feel, at least most of the time, that they practice a Christian philosophy in daily life. When they admit lapses, they are usually quick to say, "But I try to be a good Christian."

On the other hand, many beliefs and practices which contradict the philosophy of Jesus are prevalent. For example, "Business is business" seems to mean, in some situations, that anything goes in business—"Let the buyer beware." A businessman must learn to buy cheap and sell dear, to use whatever advertising and selling techniques will sell the most goods, to cover his hand when competitors or customers become too curious. Another principle with unchristian implications is expressed in the general rule "Don't let others shove you around." As a nation, we are ready at a moment's notice to defend national honor by fighting "aggressive foreigners." Carrying a chip on the shoulder is widely condoned, even though it is inconsistent with turning the other cheek. Under another popular belief, "People should get what's coming to them," we condone punishment for wrongdoers and try to adjust punishment to fit an offense. If a wrongdoer escapes the law but loses his fortune or becomes ill, we say, "It is good enough for him." This general point of view is scarcely in harmony with Jesus' espousal of sympathy and forgiveness.

These and other unchristian points of view are upheld so insistently that it is easy to understand why many persons agree that "Anyone who tried seriously to practice the philosophy of Jesus would not get very far in today's world." A result is that many attend church on Sunday and verbally espouse Christian doctrine but relegate these ideas to the background on weekdays and behave not as Christians but as hardheaded, practical Americans.

A standard device for reducing conflict is reinterpretation of Christian teaching to fit the needs of a situation. We say, "I don't think Christ really meant what he seems to have said. He must be taken for what he meant, not literally." Nowhere is this approach better illustrated than in the writings of Paul Elmer More (1864–1937). More was sharply critical of equalitarianism and humanitarianism. He wished to teach respect for authority, the past, the elite, and the institutions of private capitalism. The teachings of Christ, he maintained, supported this position. More said one part of Christianity has a purely spiritual phase, and this is what is expressed in the terms *faith*, *hope*, and *love*. "But faith, hope, and love, in this spiritual sense, have no direct bearing on the social question we are here considering. . . . They are of the spirit and not of this world. Even love, which at first might seem corroborative of humanitarian equality and is no doubt so interpreted, is in this spiritual sense *a state of mind, not a rule of action.*" [13]

The ability of many Americans consciously to violate Christian ethics because they are "impractical," or to reinterpret them to suit a situation, is an indication of how lightly they take religion. That ours is basically a secular society is borne out by a fairly common belief that an extremely devout person is a "crackpot," "odd," or "crazy over religion." Devout laymen are likely to try to conceal their true attitudes because of this notion.

1.1 Do you consider any of the following practices unchristian? Fraudulent advertising, reckless driving, cheating on tests, petting, drinking, snubbing a lower-class acquaintance, selling shoddy goods? Why or why not?

1.2 What do you consider to be the essence of Christ's teachings? Are the central ideas applicable in the modern world? Could they be applied if people were willing to try? How many persons do you know who regularly apply them?

2. Science and Religion

It is believed that although this is an age of science many problems cannot be handled scientifically and require a return to faith; but it is also believed that all problems, including moral ones can be studied scientifically.

ALSO

It is believed that science and religion often conflict; but it is also believed that there is no conflict between science and religion because the former deals with means and the latter with ends.

In popular thought, the leading issues involving religion stem from the relationship between science and religion. Two common ones are stated above. Both involve the question of proper spheres of religion and science. Many persons assume that science is a legitimate tool for the study of nature, including all animals below man, but always fails when applied to a study of human affairs. The willfulness of man makes prediction of human behavior impossible. Furthermore, they posit an eternal and universal moral law; the truths embodied in such law, once discovered

[13] Shelburne Essays, Quoted in Willard Thorp, Merle Curti, and Carlos Baker, eds., *American Issues,* Lippincott, 1944, p. 885. (Italics ours.)

through divine revelation, need only to be followed. It would be sense-less and sinful to seek for better behavior through science.

The naturalistic tradition, in sharp contrast, assumes that any problem is potentially susceptible to scientific solution, or that it is unreasonable to reject science until it has been given a fair trial. If science does not work in certain areas, its failure may be due to lack of human knowl-edge. The studies of sexual behavior by Alfred Kinsey and his associates are examples of investigations consistent with a naturalistic tradition. Al-though Kinsey tries to avoid conclusions concerning what is "right" and "wrong," the studies are evidently conducted in hope that their findings will provide more adequate bases for making moral decisions. It would be hard to justify them on any other ground. Nevertheless, many per-sons oppose the studies because they believe not only that science lacks competence in the field of sexual values but also that traditional values are of divine origin and thus eternal.

A variation of this conflict is expressed by those who believe that the discoveries of science conflict with established religious truths. For ex-ample, science's theory of the creation of the universe and man, although not claiming to explain "first causes," differs fundamentally from the story of Genesis. Another example is the belief that historical criticism casts serious doubt upon the literal truth of the Bible. Some persons also believe that science can produce no evidence that God has ever willfully interfered with natural law in order to answer prayer (as would be the case if God, in response to prayer, caused rain to fall when it could not have according to our understanding of natural law).

There is a school of thought which believes that all controversy of this kind can be avoided. It assumes that means and ends are separable, that science deals exclusively with means and religion exclusively with ends, or the purposes, of life. Accordingly, one seeks ends in life by turning to the Scriptures or consulting a priest; once ends are deter-mined, it is appropriate to use scientific means to achieve them. If this position is to be tenable, religious dogma must confine its remarks to statements of value and avoid attempts at description of man and the universe, or at least insure that any such descriptions conform to the findings of science. A common solution denies to religion any compe-tence to describe the natural universe, which in turn means a rejection of the Scriptures as a source of literal truth. Modernists hold to this view, and for them religion becomes a search for social ideals.

Confusion is enhanced by a tendency to mix and blend these various positions: "There is really no conflict between religion and science, but if they do conflict, religion must take precedence over science," or, less commonly, "In case of conflict, science must take precedence." It is highly confusing for anyone to take the position that "There is no con-flict, but if there is, then . . . !"

Whether there is a necessary conflict between religion and science—and this is a difficult question, depending in part on how the major terms are defined—many persons experience a conflict which is real to them and can involve genuine emotional pain. Children reared in fundamen-talist homes may wish to accept the Bible as a source of literal truth but find it necessary to accept, as they pursue their education, scientific in-terpretations which are inconsistent with certain interpretations of the Scriptures. Children who have been taught by their parents that science should not tamper with certain types of problems are upset when re-quired to study and understand certain scientific investigations. Hollings-head describes vividly such conflicts among fundamentalist Lutheran youth in Elmtown.[14]

2.1 Can you name any problems which an American might have to face but which cannot be solved or understood if studied scientifically?

2.2 How do you explain church groups who appear to accept a religious world-view but who also encourage scientific research? Are such church groups consistent or inconsistent? Give reasons for your answer.

2.3 Is it consistent for a church group to oppose historical criticism of the Bible and at the same time insist that youth learn the facts of history?

2.4 Are most scientists in the United States religious persons? If so, what kind of religion would you expect them to hold?

3. High Pleasures and Low Pleasures

It is believed that the highest and most desirable satisfactions result from subordinating sensual to spiritual pleasures; but it is also believed that life is short and that we should live fully while we can.

Prominent among religious beliefs is the notion that pleasures of soul, or mind, are "higher" than pleasures which involve physical sensations alone. "Higher" in this case probably means "more pleasing in the sight of God." It may also imply that a person who experiences spiritual plea-sures feels a greater rapture, or receives more lasting satisfaction, than he would feel from any sort of pleasurable sense stimulation. This general position stems from dualisms assumed by early Church fathers—partic-ularly the idea that man consists of two discrete parts, flesh and spirit, and flesh is evil whereas spirit is pure and good, or can be made so.

Beliefs about pleasure include the following: The fullest ecstasy

[14] August B. Hollingshead, *Elmtown's Youth: The Impact of Social Classes on Adolescents*, Wiley, 1949, chaps. 10, 12.

known to man occurs during deeply religious experience, as when the soul establishes communication with the eternal. Prayer and religious meditation provide deep spiritual satisfaction. A source of great pleasure is any service performed for the Lord—such as missionary service, ministering to the sick, or giving alms. Next in satisfaction to purely religious experience is meditation, contemplation, speculation—in short, any sort of "philosophizing." An existence which emphasizes such experiences is called a "life of the mind." High pleasures also include enjoyment of art, literature, and music. One is more likely to experience high pleasures if he subordinates to them all pleasures of the flesh. Poverty, chastity, and physical discomfort are often viewed as necessary or helpful means for experiencing high pleasures.

In contrast to "high" pleasures, many "low" or "vulgar" pleasures are enjoyed by those who lack spiritual perspicacity. Although low pleasures may involve mental satisfactions, most of them indulge only the physical senses. The more they indulge the senses the lower they are. Thus, copulation performed solely for erotic delight is the lowest pleasure of all. Drug addiction is low for similar reasons. The use of tobacco and alcohol is also suspect—these substances "dull the spiritual sensibilities." High living of any sort is condemned. Attending horse races, visiting taverns, watching burlesque, playing poker, using perfumes and cosmetics, and eating exotic foods are all objectionable. Plain loafing—"sleeping in the sun"—is criticized if practiced habitually. Low pleasures are not thought to be lasting, genuine, or deep. Habituation to them conditions one against the enjoyment of higher pleasures and is likely to make a person self-centered, brutish, and unable to commune with God.

Despite such beliefs about vulgar pleasures, a growing number of people are embracing a frankly hedonistic outlook. They argue that man has but one life to live, and it behooves him to live it well. "High living" is enjoyed by most persons who can afford it and some who cannot. The poor must be content with cheap liquor, roll-your-own cigarettes, and low-stake crap or poker games. But on all social levels there is a search for adventure, variety, and spice. Commercialized recreation has blossomed. Night clubs, race tracks, amusement parks, and liquor stores flourish; and on Sundays highways are crowded with persons pleasure bent. Occasionally someone pauses long enough to remark that "Americans are too materialistic," but this comment seldom engenders in its speaker or anyone else a serious yearning for a monastic existence.

Acceptance of the idea that pleasures can be classified as high or low, along with acceptance of the idea that "You only live once" can produce inconsistency, confusion, and conflict. Often the ideal of spiritual pleasure is accepted only on an abstract and verbal level. Gestures are made during seasons of fast to revoke a few—but never all—worldly pleasures.

Hardly anyone really denies himself. Fundamentalist ministers continue to inveigh against card playing, alcohol, sex, gambling, tobacco, and cosmetics; but the influence of such persons is usually slight and temporary. It is often difficult to decide which pleasures are proper, and many people feel guilty for practicing a condemned activity. High-school youth are likely to develop emotional conflict as they try to decide whether they should smoke, drink, gamble, visit taverns, or drive recklessly. Parents, although enjoying some of these recreations, usually wish to deny them to sons and daughters as long as possible. Therefore, conflicts develop between adults and youth, particularly during adolescence, when youth have a strong desire to "grow up" and to seem adult.

Other emotional conflicts result from the fact that certain "low pleasures" are status symbols in American culture. For example, it is a symbol of status to serve martinis before dinner, to eat exotic foods, to use good perfumes, to smoke good cigars, to attend horse races, and to visit night clubs. Another type of inconsistency arises when hedonistic upper- or upper-middle-class persons urge simplicity and moderation upon the poor, in the belief, no doubt, that if the poor are more content with their station in life they will make less trouble for their social superiors.

Again turning for evidence to the study of college-student beliefs at Fresno, it appears that tolerance is increased and conflict somewhat diminished by the time an individual has passed through adolescence and entered college. With respect to the so-called low pleasures, the most prevalent student belief seems to be "Live and let live." Some of the most common responses are summarized below. (More will be said in Chapter 19 about the opinions of college students concerning low pleasures.)

a. Smoking is a health and not a moral issue; students who decide they are willing to risk the health hazards certainly have a right to smoke if they wish.

b. Almost all college students drink; this is not a moral issue except when students become drunk to the point of being obnoxious. Most boys prefer that girls they plan to marry drink only moderately, but try to get thoroughly "stoned" girls they are out to seduce (who are the girls *other* fellows plan to marry).

c. Feelings are mixed about swearing, the use of "obscene expressions," and telling risque jokes. Boys about divide down the middle as to whether it is proper for boys to do these things in mixed groups; they are perfectly all right, of course, in stag groups. Girls show the same ambivalence, a majority conceding that girls in unmixed groups (as at a sorority house) tend to use such speech habits to no harm, but an apparent majority feel somewhat uneasy about such speech in mixed groups. At the same time, they do not want to appear as "prudes" and rarely condemn a boy verbally for "rough" language.

d. Reading "dirty books." A typical comment, "Good heavens—we all have to in our upper-division literature courses!" A favorite remains the classic, *Lady Chatterley's Lover,* which is considered "beautiful," "touching," "art, not smut," etc.

e. Almost all students have no objection to gambling, but say they can't afford it.

3.1 The following behaviors have been variously described as morally harmful, damaging to health, or sinful: drinking, smoking, card playing, gambling. Which do you consider immoral, which sinful, and which physically harmful? Is there a difference between immorality and sin? How can one determine whether an act is immoral? Whether it is sinful?

3.2 Do you believe there is a divine law which rates pleasures as "high" or "low," and "respectable" or "unrespectable"? How does one determine what this law decrees? Does the Bible have anything to say about the use of alcohol? About smoking? Gambling? Petting? Use of cosmetics? Visiting night clubs? Have ministers ever made claims about sin which could not be substantiated with Scripture?

3.3 Is it possible that a person might achieve what is usually considered a "high pleasure" through indulgence in a "low pleasure"? Could a person experience religious ecstasy while under influence of alcohol or drugs? Could a person develop a feeling of love and kinship toward mankind while drunk? Could a person meditate and philosophize in a tavern?

4. Democracy and Religion

It is believed that Christian religion is the basis of democracy and that democracy cannot function successfully except among a people who are deeply devout; but it is also believed that democracy is a secular philosophy and that some well-known democrats have been irreligious.

The first position has it that Jesus laid the foundation for democracy when he affirmed that all men are equal in the sight of God and all men are brothers on earth as well as in heaven.

But the equalitarianism taught by Jesus is not thought the chief reason that Christianity is essential to democracy. It is usually assumed that democracy cannot survive without widespread and voluntary acceptance of certain Christian moral ideals—for example, the golden rule. It is further assumed that acceptance of this or any other moral ideal is improbable without religion. The source of moral ideals is thought to be an eternal moral order, established by God and interpreted for man by Jesus. Survival of democracy is therefore commonly linked with Christianity and vice versa.

On the other hand, some persons argue that democracy is a secular and not a religious philosophy and that its origins are to be found in motives which are strictly human.[15] Modern democracy is an outgrowth of a long historical process associated with emergence of a middle class in Europe and its colonies. The struggle of merchants and manufacturers for freedom from feudal controls could be won only through establishment of representative forms of government. The divine rights of kings, a thoroughly Christian concept at the time, was one barrier to the achievement of representative government. Those who argue that representative government entered the world scene at the same time as free enterprise (except for a few isolated and temporary experiments with republicanism, as in ancient Greece) do not deny that certain religious ideas, especially those associated with Protestantism, have helped greatly in establishing representative government. Protestantism, in defending individual freedom, property ownership, and a money economy, undoubtedly gave the rising capitalist class an invaluable assist. But the primary motives behind the attacks on feudalism and aristocracy, these persons contend, were *economic;* and availability of religious ideas consistent with political liberty was a fortuitous circumstance, not a decisive cause.

It is pointed out that democracy as a social ideal became widely understood and accepted only after the scientific world-view reached ascendancy among intellectual leaders. Exponents of political-intellectual liberty in the eighteenth century were, for the most part, either "supernatural rationalists" or deists. The former included Descartes, Newton, and Locke; the latter Diderot, Voltaire, and Hume. Locke was a leading exponent of constitutional government, and his ideas, supplemented by those of Montesquieu, were appropriated by such American revolutionary leaders as Thomas Jefferson, John Hancock, and Thomas Paine (all deists). It should be remembered that democracy, in its modern sense, was not popular even in revolutionary France and America except among a small group of intellectuals and lower-class persons whose opinions were not influential. But many people believe that it was the eighteenth-century intellectual, usually unorthodox in his religion, who established the groundwork for modern democracy and whose theories continue to form its ideological underpinning. For example, Randall suggests that modern ideas of democracy can be traced to Locke, Rousseau, and Jefferson.[16]

In late twentieth-century America, although some spokesmen for democracy are Christian or Jewish theists, many are philosophic natural-

[15] See Norman Cousins, ed., *In God We Trust*, Harper & Row, 1958. By reproducing excerpts from their writings, Cousins clearly demonstrates that our "founding fathers" in the main were *not* theists or much interested in religion.

[16] John Herman Randall, Jr., *The Making of the Modern Mind*, Houghton Mifflin, 1940, pp. 349-357.

ists. It would be indefensible to say that one group is more sincerely and effectively democratic than the other. The issue, as stated at the head of this section, is such that many individuals will find intrapersonal conflict to some degree inescapable. If one's minister asserts that no atheist can be a sincere democrat, and one then becomes acquainted with an atheist who is sincerely democratic, confusion is likely to result. On the other hand, a person reared in a naturalistic tradition, who has been taught that democracy is a secular philosophy and that all religions are to some extent authoritarian in outlook, may be troubled when he meets a devout individual who seems honestly dedicated to the cause of democracy. A further problem may arise when a person who has been taught to believe that only Christians can be sincere democrats finds that some nonChristians are more democratic than some Christians.

4.1 It is assumed that any social ideal, including democracy, must have a moral basis. Is it possible to defend any moral system except in religious terms? Can a person be a moral individual and still be irreligious? Would abandonment of traditional Christianity lead to moral deterioration?

4.2 What sort of moral ideals are consistent with democracy? How does a democratic person behave? Does democracy imply a whole way of life? Does the idea of democracy apply to operation of a school? Are parochial schools generally more democratic than public schools?

4.3 Does democracy apply to running a home? To associations with one's friends? If so, what are the basic moral principles involved?

DISCUSSION QUESTIONS AND EXERCISES

1. Some who favor religious instruction in public schools believe that clergy rather than public-school teachers should give this instruction. Without regard to questions of constitutionality, analyze this argument and locate relevant assumptions in educational philosophy and learning theory.

2. Is it possible to study ideas in the problem areas of sex and economics without also studying certain ideas in religion? Some have argued that critical thinking in economics is desirable but that such analysis in religion is unfair. How could one limit his critical thinking to economics so that it would not tread upon religion? What would be the consequences of such limitation? How would one's understanding of economics be affected?

3. One man's meat is another man's poison. Likewise, one man's religion is another man's superstition. Is there any rational and objective basis for distinguishing between religion and superstition?

4. There are those who fear that democracy as a social philosophy will replace traditional Christianity as a primary source of moral ideals. Is this change likely to occur? What would be the consequences of such a change?

5. Morally, do you believe the younger generation is "going to the dogs"? Do

you think that, at the same age in life, their parents were much the same in belief and behavior?

6. With respect to "high pleasures" versus "low pleasures," do you think this is a valid or a false distinction? Can you name any major "spiritual leaders" who enjoyed, and participated in, the so-called low pleasures? How would you know?

REFERENCES

ABELS, JULES, *The Rockefeller Billions*, New York, Macmillan, 1965.

About the life of John D. Rockefeller I—a hymn-singing Calvinist and Sunday School teacher who stayed home from the Civil War to begin the accumulation by questionable means of one of the nineteenth century's greatest fortunes. Ironic, cynical, and factual.

BRINTON, CRANE, *History of Western Morals*, New York, Harcourt, Brace & World, 1959.

This famous student of the history of thought treats moral belief from the ancient Near-East to the mid-twentieth century. He combines exceptional scholarship and readability—very likely the best book in the field.

CHILDS, MARQUIS, and DOUGLASS CATER, *Ethics in a Business Society*, New York, Harper & Row, 1954.

Somewhat of a classic by now, this book develops the implications of Christian premises for the operation of business. Based on a study financed by the Rockefeller Foundation—an ironic touch.

ECKHARDT, ARTHUR R., *Surge of Piety in America*, New York, Association Press, 1959.

The Head of the Department of Religion at Lehigh University and himself religiously dedicated, Eckhardt feels that the apparent "religious awakening" after World War II has been a return to "folk religion"—largely in the interests of conformity.

FAGLEY, RICHARD M., *Population Explosion and Christian Responsibility*, New York, Oxford University Press, 1960.

A Congregationalist minister discusses the tendency of church groups to feel a Christian obligation to install modern medicine in backward countries, but at the same time, to refuse to take steps toward population control. The result: an acceleration of the population explosion and greater hunger and misery than before.

GOODMAN, PAUL, *Growing Up Absurd*, New York, Random House, 1960.

A provocative and rather frightening book about the moral emptiness of the world's most affluent culture, with special reference to problems of youth.

GUIRDHAM, ARTHUR, *Christ and Freud*, New York, Macmillan, 1960.

A psychiatrist shows how certain beliefs and practices of traditional religion lead, in many persons, to mental disorders. Guirdham is convinced that, in the context he perceives, religion can be an important therapeutic agent.

HALSEY, MARGARET, *The Pseudo-Ethic*, New York, Simon and Schuster, 1963.

Author Halsey argues that in our culture all other values are subordinated to the support of business and private profit. Controversial, but very thought provoking.

HERBERG, WILL, *Protestant, Catholic, Jew: An Essay in American Religious Sociology*, New York, Doubleday, 1955.

By the virtual consensus of reviewers, and in the opinion of the present authors, this is one of the most useful books ever written on the sociology of religion in the United States.

LEWY, GUENTER, *The Catholic Church and Nazi Germany*, New York, McGraw-Hill, 1964.

Drawing upon painstaking research into hitherto unpublished sources, this shattering book is written around the call that went out to German Catholics when Hitler began World War II to "keep calm and not to 'lose sight of the welfare of the church as a whole.' "

MARTY, MARTIN E., *New Shape of American Religion*, New York, Harper & Row, 1961.

A dedicated Protestant, who would like to see this faith regain its former vitality, discusses post-war religion in America and decides it has nothing to do with authentic religious commitment.

MEYER, DONALD, *The Positive Thinkers*, New York, Doubleday, 1965.

On the tendency among many religious writers to link piety with business profit, personal pleasure, and political power. The book abounds with case studies, from the nineteenth century to the present.

MURTAGH, JOHN, and SARA HARRIS, *Who Live in Shadow*, New York, McGraw-Hill, 1960.

In a popularly styled book, a prominent judge and a sociologist examine—and attack—the whole approach used toward the handling of drug addiction in the United States.

SCHNEIDER, LOUIS, and SANFORD DORNBUSCH, *Popular Religion*, Chicago, University of Chicago Press, 1960.

Two sociologists analyze 46 best-selling books on the subject of religion and conclude that what the public wants religiously is a placebo—an easy religion which will solve all their problems with no sacrifice in return—especially the sacrifice of having to think.

SHAPLEY, HARLOW, ed., *Science Ponders Religion*, New York, Appleton-Century-Crofts, 1961.

An eminent scientist brings together a collection of readings written by American scientists in which they state their own beliefs. Views range from open hostility to attachment to unorthodox naturalistic opinions.

SMITH, HUSTON, *Religions of Man*, New York, Harper & Row, 1958.

An important book on comparative world religions. Treats impartially Christianity, Buddhism, Hinduism, Confucianism, Islam, Judaism, and Taoism.

SPENCE, HARTZELL, *Story of America's Religions*, New York, Holt, Rinehart & Winston, 1962.

Compiled from what was originally a series of articles in *Look* magazine. Very impartial and readable.

TILLICH, PAUL, *The Eternal Now*, New York, Scribner, 1963.

Tillich is considered among the three or four most influencial theologians of the century. This book is a collection of his shortest and easiest readings—some of which students will not find particularly easy.

WELLS, DONALD A., *God, Man, and the Thinker*, New York, Random House, 1963.

The Chairman of the Department of Philosophy at Washington University writes a well-balanced review of some of the major historical issues which have beset religion. He also treats some different theories of religious motivation.

ZAHN, GORDON C., *In Solitary Witness: the Life and Death of Franz Jägerstätter*, New York, Holt, Rinehart & Winston, 1964.

Although the main theme of this book is the proclivity of Christians for war, from Constantine to the present, it effectively uses as a case study the life of a German Christian who martyred himself by refusing to fight in Hitler's army.

CHAPTER 18

Problematic Areas of Culture:
Race and Minority-Group Relations

The Problem of Prejudice in the United States

AFTER making the most exhaustive study which had yet been undertaken of relations between whites and Negroes in the United States, Gunnar Myrdal and associates concluded that the "Negro problem" is primarily moral as experienced by both whites and Negroes.[1] The Negro problem as well as most problems related to intergroup relations, comprises a large measure of intrapersonal conflict with attendant feelings of personal inadequacy and frustration. Intrapersonal conflicts in the area of group relations result from contradiction between democratic and religious ideals and specific beliefs, attitudes, and behaviors which violate these ideals.

Most Americans are in some way involved in problems of intergroup relations. (Some years ago, studies suggested that at least four out of five white Americans have prejudices directed at some minority group.[2]) High-School students may become involved when, after a life in contact with ideals such as the brotherhood of man, the dignity and worth of every individual, and equality before the law, they become aware that prejudice and discrimination are typical of most adults.

Beliefs and attitudes held by a majority toward a minority are commonly referred to as *prejudices*. Defined strictly from derivation, a prejudice is a prejudgment—i.e., a judgment made before examination of evidence. It is not unusual for social scientists to use the term in a more popular sense, as "attitudes and beliefs which serve to place the objects of the attitudes and beliefs at an advantage or disadvantage."[3]

Prejudice may involve beliefs and attitudes of which the holder is barely conscious. It may be incidental and peripheral, and not integrated with a person's central cognitive structure. Prejudiced beliefs and atti-

---

[1] Gunnar Myrdal, Richard Sterner, and Arnold Rose, *An American Dilemma: The Negro Problem and Modern Democracy,* Harper & Row, 1944.

[2] David Krech and Richard S. Crutchfield, *Theory and Problems of Social Psychology,* McGraw-Hill, 1948, p. 475.

[3] *Ibid.,* p. 444.

tudes are usually inconsistent and poorly understood; many prejudiced persons act according to one belief or attitude in one situation and contradictory ones in other situations. Prejudices may be held so lightly that their holder reacts against members of a minority only by avoiding their company; in some cases he may strongly reject openly discriminatory behavior.

Because the structure of prejudice in individuals is ordinarily rather haphazard, and because of a tendency to turn prejudices on and off according to the situation, it is hardly correct to say that most prejudiced persons have an ideology of prejudice—except, perhaps, in the Southeast. It is difficult, for example, to identify in the area of race a core of beliefs, widely and popularly held, which compare with the ideology of laissez-faire capitalism described in Chapter 14.

Some persons do intellectualize their prejudices to the point of developing a conscious and often elaborate philosophy (*racism*) regarding racial and ethnic groups; and use this philosophy to justify some overt action against the groups in question. Beliefs of racists almost always correspond to widely held beliefs in the culture, but they are held with greater-than-average intensity and are likely to be integrated with the racists' core of beliefs. Racists *value* their prejudices; they are not passive products of a culture pattern.

All human groups appear to be ethnocentric. That is, each group accepts its own way of life as best and assumes that ways of other groups are inferior. Although ethnocentrism was common in ancient times, it was not then based upon race. Ancient Greeks, for example, considered all outsiders culturally inferior, and worthy of the name *barbarian*. But it was the *culture or way of life which was thought inferior, and not people as biological organisms*. It is rare to find in the ancient world examples of discrimination based upon the idea that some people are inferior because of heredity.[4]

With expansion of Europe in the sixteenth and seventeenth centuries, Europeans first began to have widespread contact with peoples of other cultures. Although Europeans usually thought them inferior, it was not because of their racial origin but because of their paganism. Conversion brought a pagan inside the fold of humanity, gave him, at least in principle, the rights and privileges of nonpagans. During the earliest period of colonization by Christian powers, for example, it was common to free those slaves who accepted Christianity. Spanish, Portuguese, and French explorers, traders, and colonists regularly married converted native women. The English were an exception.

---

[4] Material presented here on history of prejudice draws heavily from Ruth F. Benedict, *Race: Science and Politics*, Viking, 1945, pt. II.

As colonialism developed, the practice of freeing slaves merely because they became Christians ceased to be good business. Although keeping slaves in spite of their conversion became the rule, actual practice with respect to freeing slaves and their status after manumission varied from place to place depending upon the traditons of the colonial power. In Spain and Portugal, there was a tradition of slave law, resulting from the practice of slavery prior to the period of overseas colonization. Persons enslaved in Spain, for instance, included Negroes, Moors, Jews, and Spaniards. Both Spanish and Portuguese slave law was based upon the Justinian Code, which assumed that slavery was a condition of *legal bondage* unrelated to any imagined biological or moral inferiority of slaves. A slave was seen as a human being reduced by misfortune to a condition of servitude. Upon manumission, he became in principle a person with all the rights of his former master.

The situation in English colonies was quite different. By 1500 the Anglo-Saxon world had lost all vestiges of slavery and slave law.[5] There was no legal provision for slavery, and no tradition for handling slavery on a legal basis. Planters of the southeastern United States found themselves in a legal vacuum and, as the ruling class of the region, were free to innovate legal definitions and rules as they pleased. It is not surprising that they chose to define slaves as *chattels* and not as persons, and made no provision for reinstatement of slaves to the position of free men. Because of their position as chattel, not human beings, a family structure among slaves in the United States became all but impossible. At an early age, children were sold from their parents. Parentage was unique: slaves were bred for the market as we now breed cattle. A husband and wife relationship was a rarity. Daniel P. Moynihan, an expert on this particular subject, considers the North American form of slavery the worst the world has ever experienced and a key factor in certain current racial problems.[6]

If human beings are defined as chattels, legally comparable to mules and bales of cotton, it is difficult later to recognize freed slaves as fully human and moral beings. The idea grew, furthermore, that only Negroes could be slaves, as they were the only slaves Americans knew. If Negroes alone are slaves, logically one may justify this condition by assuming that they are subhuman and incapable of fully responsible and moral behavior. In the United States, Negroes came to be regarded as biologically inferior to whites. In countries which began as colonies of Spain or Portu-

---

[5] *Ibid.*

[6] His confidential policy paper, *The Negro Family*, written for the federal government (1965), is the source from which we draw. See also *Newsweek*, December 6, 1965, p. 38; and *The New York Review of Books*, October 14, 1965, pp. 39 ff. More will be said about his thesis later.

gal, Negroes are not regarded as biologically inferior, little prejudice is directed toward them by whites, and intermarriage is common.[7]

Racism was given its modern and classical form by European and American writers between 1853 and 1930.[8] According to one racist of the period, there are three different races of mankind (white, yellow, and black); and they differ from one another in physical, intellectual, and moral qualities. Only the white race has "reflective energy," "perseverance," "instinct for order," "love of liberty," and "honor." The only example of a truly white race is the blond "Aryan." Europeans as a whole are a hybridized lot, Alpine types being of "yellow extraction" and Mediterranean types of "black extraction." Aryans are the natural aristocracy of Europe, and the group best fitted to rule.[9]

Near the beginning of the twentieth century the idea of race became attached to nationality. It became popular to speak about the "English race," the "German race," and the "French race." Although the French and Germans appeared to make it more of an issue, each nationality more or less assumed it was superior to the rest. When nationality became equated with race, it was necessary to define race by other than surface physical characteristics. Obviously the German nation included persons of many different physical types. A solution was found in a concept of race which was based almost exclusively upon "inner qualities." Thus, all Germans were said to have certain innate moral qualities which, irrespective of physical appearance, mark them as Germans. Under Hitler, this notion was developed to the point where a person could be a German without having been born in Germany and without ever having lived there—"a German soul in a non-German body." [10]

Racist literature in the United States during the last half of the nineteenth century and the early twentieth followed European racism and was aimed chiefly at "inferior" southern Europeans who were flocking to the United States in great numbers.[11]

[7] The interpretation given here of why there is a "Negro problem" in the United States and none in countries such as Brazil and Cuba follows Frank Tannenbaum, *Slave and Citizen: The Negro in the Americas*, Knopf, 1947.

[8] The year 1853 marks the first publication of an influential work which was to inspire later racists, Count de Gobineau's *Essay on the Inequality of Human Races*.

[9] Gobineau, quoted in Benedict, *op. cit.*, pp. 115–118.

[10] Among writers who claimed that a nationality may correspond to a race, one of the most influential was Houston S. Chamberlain, *Foundations of the Nineteenth Century*, London, 1911. Chamberlain became a German by adoption. He advanced the theory that Teutons are the chosen people, and that in Germans Teutonic blood is to be found in its purest form.

[11] American racists include Madison Grant (*The Passing of the Great Race*, 1916), Clinton S. Burr (*America's Race Heritage*, 1922), and Lothrop Stoddard (*The Revolt Against Civilization: the Menace of the Under Man*, 1922).

Today, popular beliefs in the United States about the meaning of race and proper relationships between different races and ethnic groups reflect the above history of racism. However, persistence of racial prejudice on a wide scale, and of racism among certain groups, cannot be explained wholly in terms of historical developments. Much prejudice today appears too strongly motivated to be simply a result of hereditary belief. Ethnocentric feelings now often have a pathological quality, and inherited beliefs are useful chiefly in justifying discrimination which would have been practiced anyway.

MOTIVES OF PREJUDICE

Social scientists have identified a number of possible motives of prejudice.[12] It may be a characteristic response by most persons to the existence of out-groups; i.e., ethnocentric behavior involving prejudice may typify normal human relationships. Racial prejudice may be a means of helping a person to identify with his group, and thus to feel accepted and wanted. In some cases, adoption of prejudiced beliefs may be in response to a need to find an understandable interpretation of some social situation. For example, one who lacks an understanding of war and its causes may clarify the problem to his own satisfaction by accepting the idea that "international Jews" promote war for their own profit. The motive in this case is the need common to everyone to make sense of his world. In still other cases, economic or other forms of competition may explain prejudice. If there is not enough of some wanted thing to go around, then an individual may reason, "Unless I assert my own strength, *they* will take what I want."

Although such motives may help to explain the persistence of prejudice from one historical period to another, they are not adequate to explain the pathological level of prejudice typical at certain times and among certain groups. A more promising hypothesis which has a great deal of presumptive evidence in its favor treats this pathological level of prejudice as a *personality disorder*. It is now believed by many social scientists that a highly prejudiced person is to some degree mentally ill. Such persons may be normal at most times, but occasionally, victimized by temporarily frustrating circumstances which generate intense aggressive impulses, they direct their aggression at minorities. Other persons may have deep frustrations of a more permanent nature stemming from parental rejection, repressed needs, or other causes. The result is a personality structure which includes a "need" for "inferior persons" who can serve as objects of aggression.

---

[12] For a summary of motives which have been found to operate in connection with racial prejudice, see Krech and Crutchfield, *op. cit.*, pp. 447 ff.

THE AUTHORITARIAN PERSONALITY

It is now customary to call the type of individual who has a deep and permanent need to persecute weaker persons the *authoritarian* personality type.[13] A tendency toward prejudiced belief is not the only conspicuous trait of this type; it is one trait among many which together compose a distinctive pattern. One had best be cautious in use of this concept since many persons who are basically democratic may occasionally exhibit authoritarian traits, and relatively few authoritarian individuals have all the traits associated with the type. Furthermore, some persons who exhibit many authoritarian traits show them only to a mild degree. With these cautions in mind, the authoritarian personality structure is believed to have such traits as the following:

Hierarchical Orientation. This leads to an admiration of, and submissiveness toward, persons who are strong (strong in the sense of having political, economic, or social status), and contempt for weak persons. The authoritarian tends to exploit and manipulate the weak, often in cruel and callous fashion. Because he sees society as a hierarchy, he is often a ruthless social climber given to fawning on superiors and abusing inferiors.

Conventionality and Pseudo Conservatism. To gain respect in his community, he is likely to want his wife to dress modestly, to stay at home, and to send the children to Sunday School (although not everyone who does these things is an authoritarian). His political and economic beliefs are best described as pseudo conservative because he admires the power of big business and strong but reactionary political leaders and accepts violence and expediency as necessary means for preserving his "one hundred percent Americanism." As Adorno observes, he is characterized by "conventionality and authoritarian submissiveness on the ego level, with violence, anarchic impulses, and chaotic destructiveness in the unconscious sphere."[14]

Tendency to View Other Persons as Means. The authoritarian tends toward an "exploitive-manipulative type of power orientation." He sees others as tools for furthering his ends. He regards marriage, for example as a way to gain wealth, status, and respectability. He judges his wife and children according to how they make him look in the community.

[13] For one of the best treatments of this subject, see Erich Fromm, *Escape from Freedom,* Farrar & Rinehart, 1941. Perhaps the most ambitious studies of the authoritarian personality were sponsored by the American Jewish Committee and published under the general title *Studies in Prejudice.* Among the volumes published, the one most pertinent to our thesis is T. W. Adorno *et al., The Authoritarian Personality,* Harper & Row, 1950. Discussion on following pages draws heavily from this source.
[14] Adorno, *op. cit.,* p. 675.

Repression of Instinctual Tendencies. An authoritarian is seldom able to enjoy the erotic or sensual. He may be cold and prudish; or he may pursue a crude, compulsive kind of promiscuity lacking in any real satisfaction; or he may lead a dual life, exhibiting great conventionality on the surface but pursuing numerous extramarital affairs.[15] Male authoritarians tend to idealize women on an abstract level ("American motherhood," for example) but be incapable of establishing warm and affectionate relations with them.

Exaggerated Ethnocentrism. This may lead to fear of, and hostility toward, all groups which are "different." The authoritarian tends to see every group as an out-group except his own inner circle and the power groups with which he identifies. A conspicuous aspect of his ethnocentrism, contrasted with more normal ethnocentrism, is the *generality* with which he rejects others. Levinson points out that to the ethnocentric or authoritarian type "The social world . . . is arranged like a series of concentric circles around a bull's eye. Each circle represents an ingroup-outgroup distinction; each line serves as a barrier to exclude all outside groups from the center, and each group is in turn excluded by a slightly narrower one. A sample 'map' illustrating the ever-narrowing ingroup would be the following: Whites, Americans, native-born Americans, Christians, Protestants, Californians, my family, and finally—I." [16]

Mental Rigidity and Tendency to Think in Stereotypes. The authoritarian often rejects science as a method, and in view of his frequent rejection of cultural interests he may be called anti-intellectual as well. Although exhibiting a closed mind most of the time, he may be gullible and suggestible when under the influence of persons or groups of superior power. He rejects critical analysis of any sort, particularly self-criticism. For this reason, the typical authoritarian is usually more ignorant and confused about social affairs than most other persons. He tends to generalize on the basis of scanty or nonexistenct evidence. A result of this habit is stereotypy, in which he attributes certain traits to "all Jews," "all Armenians," "all socialists," or "all professors."

Self-Glorification and Projection. The authoritarian male typically boasts of obstacles which he has overcome (in Horatio Alger pattern), and of possessing all the most admired traits of a virile American male. He may boast of his morality, of his sexual conquests, of his conservatism, and of his associations with the "right people." At the same time, he usually blames his failures on others. He projects his difficulties on

[15] *Ibid.,* pp. 393–397. Studies by Frenkel-Brunswik and Sanford of a group of college coeds indicate a significant correlation between anti-Semitism and sexual repression. See "Some Personality Factors in Anti-Semitism," *Journal of Psychology,* 20: 271–291, 1945.

[16] Adorno, *op. cit.,* pp. 147–148.

whatever scapegoat is convenient, and often his anger is focused on a minority group.

The authoritarian is a person of deep frustrations, who finds little pleasure in life. Typically, the adult authoritarian was reared in a home where love and mutuality were lacking, where the father was an auto- crat, where conventional mores were enforced with an iron hand. As a rule, some aspect of his adult life is also highly unsatisfactory. He may be a member of a depressed group, as a white sharecropper in the South; or a clerical worker who finds it impossible to rise from a routine and unrewarding job; or a businessman frustrated by an inability to keep up with the Joneses. Authoritarians are usually rootless, unintegrated with the culture around them, lacking in a sense of purpose, and facing obstacles which are too great for them to surmount. They are fodder for any sort of "movement" which gives them adventure and a feeling of importance.

The studies of authoritarian personalities indicate that solutions to the problem of intergroup prejudice will necessarily include serious attention to the emotional atmosphere within which intellectual reorganization is to be undertaken. Group-leadership techniques, as described in Chapter 7, can help create this atmosphere. Several studies have suggested that children's attitudes become more democratic when teachers are sensitive to the social-emotional needs of children—the needs for belonging, achievement, and love.

In the area of social relations, there are numerous points of contradiction and confusion concerning race and minority groups. Some of these will be discussed in the sections that follow.

1. Racial Differences and Human Similarity

It is believed that there are distinct races of mankind which differ from one another physically, intellectually, and morally; but it is also believed that race is only skin deep and that all men are brothers.

The assumption that there are different races of mankind which differ in physical, mental, and moral characteristics has already been described. There is value, however, in reviewing some widely held associated beliefs. Many persons, for example, assume that all persons speaking a particular language, or languages of a related group, are of the same race. An example is use of the term *Aryan* to designate a race. Originally this term referred to a group of languages which included Sanskrit of ancient India and languages of ancient Persia. Later it came to designate a large language group which included the above and also German, English, Latin, Greek, Armenian, and Slavic. These are the Indo-European languages. Historically persons whose ancestors spoke any of these languages were members of the "Aryan race."

Another common belief is that race and culture are related—that is, persons of a particular race show certain cultural preferences because "it is in them" to be that way. Conversely, when persons show certain cultural characteristics, these are supposed to represent hereditary differences attributable to "racial influences." The belief in a Jewish race is rooted in assumptions such as these.

In contrast to a belief in fundamental biological differences which separate men into races composed of superior and inferior beings is a belief that all men are essentially alike, that race is "only skin deep." This equalitarian idea sometimes has a religious basis. Many believe that the human race sprang from Adam and Eve, and so all people have common ancestors. Closely related is the belief that, since all human beings have souls, and all souls are composed of the same primal stuff (the universal soul-substance), human beings are necessarily alike in their most important characteristics. The belief that all races are essentially alike is also rooted in (a) eighteenth-century liberalism, which furnished background for Jefferson's proposition in the Declaration of Independence, "All men are created equal"; and (b) a scientific-naturalistic outlook which makes no reference to religion or the ideals of the Age of Enlightenment.

There is evidently considerable popular confusion over the meaning of the term *race*. Most persons probably have a nebulous conception of race, and their actual opinions in this area undoubtedly shift a great deal from one occasion to another. A general understanding of what science knows to be true of race would not in itself eliminate patterns of discrimination, but it would be a necessary step in that direction and would certainly reduce ambiguity in popular conceptions of race. The following are some of the scientific facts.

It is clear to all scientists that all men belong to a single species. There are no divisions within mankind such as divide the different species of lower animals. Compared to their similarities, differences between races are insignificant. Yet men do differ; a Norwegian and an Australian bushman are clearly distinguishable one from the other.

However, attempts to classify human beings into races have always encountered difficulty. It is possible to compile a list of widely shared characteristics for a given group, such as skin or eye color, hair texture, or head shape, and to describe generally a "typical" individual of that group. But very few, if any, members of a given race correspond in all respects to the average type. Each individual in a given race has unique characteristics. Many individuals of a given race show traits which are more to be expected in some other racial grouping. There are some grounds for saying that every individual belongs to a race of his own; but it would not be helpful to define race in this way.[17]

As previously suggested, it was once believed that blood carries hereditary characteristics. So far as we know now, this is complete nonsense. Hereditary characteristics are carried by a cooperative arrangement of DNA and RNA molecules, and perhaps other unknown factors, in the germ cells. (For DNA molecules, we can still, with some respectability, use the old term *genes*.) DNA molecules retain their identities for countless generations; this is one of their most significant features—i.e., a DNA molecule which contributes toward a particular shade of brown eyes will continue to do so generation after generation. Occasionally, a small part of a specific DNA molecule becomes altered by mistake; and when this occurs, the characteristic with which it is associated may be altered. It is only by mishap to a particular DNA molecule (known as mutation) that a particular hereditary characteristic can change.

Another crucial aspect of DNA molecules is that they are transmitted independently. Those that produce tall stature may occur with hereditary factors which produce black or white skin, long or round heads, narrow or broad noses, blond or dark hair, blue or brown eyes, and so on. Thus, generally, any hereditary physical or mental trait may appear in conjunction with any other trait. Nevertheless, much remains to be known about how the basic heredity stuff functions.[18]

Genetic principles may give meaning to the following definition of race: "Races are populations which differ in the relative commonness of some of their genes."[19] Thus, in a particular race a given trait, such as tallness, may occur more often than in some other race. A particular shade of skin may be more common in one group than in another. This does not mean that genes capable of producing traits quite different from the usual ones are absent from a race. Rather, there are "majority traits" which are sufficiently common to make most members of a race look different from most members of another race.

Even this definition presents difficulties. A problem remains of deciding which traits to use in defining a particular race. Obviously, combination of characteristics is called for. If we use only one characteristic, such as dark skin color, and assume that everyone with this characteristic belongs to a "black race," we must include peoples who differ markedly from one another in other characteristics (e.g., Asian Indians, Melanesians, and Africans). It is necessary, therefore, to use several traits which

[17] L. C. Dunn and Theodosius Dobzhansky, *Heredity, Race, and Society*, New American Library, 1952, p. 114.

[18] For a readable and very well written book on the general subject of heredity, see Ruth E. Moore, *The Coil of Life*, Knopf, 1961.

[19] Dunn and Dobzhansky, *op. cit.*, p. 125.

are easily measured and which tend to occur in combination. Anthropologists have used skin color, hair color and texture, eye color, head shape, and stature. Such classificatory schemes usually produce several hundred races (e.g., Nordic, Alpine, Mediterranean, Armenoid, and Hindi). Anthropologists have also identified primary races (sometimes called stocks). Primary races are usually limited to three: Caucasoid, Negroid, and Mongoloid.

Students are likely to forget, however, that it would be just as logical to classify persons according to traits not now commonly used. Distribution of blood types in a population is one such trait, as is distribution of color blindness, or ability to taste phenyl-thio-carbamide.[20] Yet if any of these clearly hereditary and easily measurable traits were used, present classifications would be completely changed. It is correct to say, therefore, that the present scheme for classifying people into races is arbitrary. Dunn and Dobzhansky also believe that it has only limited usefulness: "When we say that two populations are racially different we are not saying very much." [21]

With increasing scientific information, even stronger positions are now taken. Morton H. Fried, Columbia University professor of anthropology, argues with great force that the word *race* is completely meaningless and should no longer be used in discourse which is meant to communicate. He points out that ". . . there is no white race. . . . Also, there is not now and never has been either a black race or a yellow race."

He suggests there was no great difference between Neanderthal man and other contemporary members of *homo sapiens*. The Neanderthals disappeared by biological integration, not extermination. In fact, the conception of Neanderthal man is a myth, "invented in the nineteenth century." It was the hunting down, killing, and making of slaves of non-European peoples "to which most of our twentieth-century mythology about race can be traced." Fried states, "At best, a racial category is a statistical abstraction based upon certain frequencies of genetic characters observed in small samples of much larger populations . . . *but it cannot be displayed by an individual.*" And ". . . some of our best known and noisiest Southern politicians undoubtedly have some 'Negro' genes in their makeup." Fried concludes that *race* is undoubtedly the most vicious of all four-letter words in our vocabulary.[22]

[20] *Ibid.*, pp. 121–122.
[21] *Ibid.*, p. 125.
[22] Morton H. Fried, "A Four-Letter Word That Hurts," *Saturday Review*, October 2, 1965 (our italics). See also Harrison Weiner, *et al.*, *Human Biology*, Oxford University Press, 1964; Ashley Montagu, ed., *The Concept of Race*, Free Press, 1964; and Frank B. Livingston, "On the Non-existence of Human Races," *Current Anthropology*, *3:* 3, 1962.

1.1 What meanings have been given to the term *race?* What is the scientific meaning? How many races are there? Does race, scientifically speaking, relate in any way to cultural achievement, or nationality?

1.2 How does science account for the fact that some whites have darker skins than some Negroes, that some Swedes are brunet and short, that some Chinese do not have high cheekbones?

1.3 In countries which were once colonies of Spain, such as Brazil, persons of mixed white and Negro ancestry are commonly regarded as white but in the United States, they are usually classified as Negro. How do you explain this inconsistency in racial classification?

2. Negro Inferiority and Negro Capacity

It is believed that of all races the Negro is lowest on the evolutionary scale and least capable of a high order of civilized living; but it is also believed that all human beings should have equal rights and opportunities, and that Negroes have been treated more unfairly than any other minority.

The anti-Negro ideology of American whites places the Negro in a *caste.* A caste is a group permanently set apart in that it is not allowed the right of intermarriage or of full social intercourse with the majority group. A *class,* in contrast, represents a status position which is not necessarily permanent, since members of one class may move with some freedom into another, and classes may intermarry without serious affront to the mores.

The basis of a Negro caste in America is assumed biological inferiority. Negroes are believed to be unassimilable because their ancestry is different from that of whites and inferior to it. One of the cruder beliefs holds that Negro blood infects the white race, and intermarriage will weaken the white race. Miscegenation is a threat to "racial purity" and "contrary to nature." [23]

An anti-Negro ideology exists on both sides of the Mason-Dixon line but there are some differences between North and South. Although many citizens of the South are more democratic than some of their northern neighbors, in the South one is more likely to find die-hard acceptance of the belief that amalgamation of races will forever remain intolerable. Northerners and southerners share many beliefs about the traits of Negroes but northerners are more likely to attribute these traits to environmental influences, southerners to biological inheritance.

The South commonly believes that Negroes are less intelligent than whites, and more ignorant and superstitious; that Negroes are lazy and,

---

[23] Myrdal, *op. cit.,* p. 55.

when they do work, do so more slowly and casually than whites; that Negroes are happy-go-lucky, childish, and irresponsible, more emotional, less stable, and more inclined to behave impulsively. There is a pretty general assumption that Negroes are more suceptible to disease, and that they have a distinctive, ineradicable odor. The notion that Negroes are subject to congenital physical weakness applies with special force to mulattoes, who often are believed to be sterile, inharmoniously proportioned, and more susceptible to disease than are "full-blooded Negroes." Oddly, the achievement of successful mulattoes is usually attributed to their white ancestors. It is also thought that Negroes are endowed with a more powerful sexual drive than are whites and possess greater sexual capacity and skill. Negroes are said to be loose in their morals, and frequently to become criminals. It is even believed that they cannot learn to speak clear and correct English.[24]

Northern whites are more likely to feel that Negroes are entitled to the same rights and the same justice as other citizens, but the differences between North and South can be, and usually are, exaggerated. Most northerners are willing to extend certain rights to Negroes provided "equal rights are not abused" or "carried too far." Schermerhorn summarizes the beliefs of northern whites by saying, "With regard to results, the northern ideology accents subordination while it minimizes segregation. Internally it is composed of moral idealism with a touch of complacency, indifference unless circumstances force the issue, withdrawal to prevent occasions that might test a real concern, and practical ignorance of the Negro as a human being or of his culture. . . ." [25]

Another group of popular beliefs attributes especially desirable traits to Negroes: they are gifted in music, art, dancing, and acting; they are superior to whites in handling animals, or, sometimes, children; they make loyal and reliable servants; they are happier, more relaxed, and more free from tensions; they are capable of more emotional warmth and can take sorrows and disappointments more easily than whites; they are more religious.[26] These more favorable beliefs do not imply unqualified admiration of Negroes and neither do they imply that they are "as good as whites." Their function seems to be to define a Negro's "place" since one of the most general beliefs of all is that "Negroes are all right in their place."

On page 409, we observed that slavery in the United States was relatively unique in the world because of its destruction of the family and that Daniel Moynihan had researched this more thoroughly than anyone

[24] Ibid., pp. 106–108.
[25] R. A. Schermerhorn, These Our People, Heath, 1949, p. 137.
[26] Myrdal, op. cit., p. 108.

else. Moynihan, meaning well for American Negroes, argues that they are distinctively different culturally because of their background and that many steps we now try to take to ameliorate the position of the lower-class Negro is fruitless because of this background. It is true that the rate of crime, illegitimacy, desertion, unemployment and other problems is higher among underprivileged Negroes than among underprivileged whites. At present, because of their cultural background, many Negroes are disqualified from equal opportunities. Their central problem is what Moynihan calls the *matrifocal* family, in which the male is a "transient who provides neither a regular income, consistent discipline and direction, nor an example to his sons of what they might hope to become as adults . . . [the] problems generated by matriarchy are getting worse, not better." [27] Logically, Moynihan's proposal is not that we abandon present attempts to assist the underprivileged Negro, but that we add a new program—that of trying to rebuild the Negro family structure into a psychologically more satisfactory form. It is unfortunate that his thesis has been attacked by Negro leaders who feel that it makes worse the present Negro image.

In the past, the chief moral conflict of whites undoubtedly has been that, on the one hand, they feel Negroes—more than other minority groups—are biologically inferior and incapable of ever reaching the achievement of whites. And, on the other hand, they have espoused the idea of the "brotherhood of man" and have felt severely guilty over the obvious mistreatment of Negroes. This conflict still exists among many persons.

The situation has changed greatly in recent years. Educated whites, now aware of the scientific facts about race, no longer try to promote the "biological inferiority" argument. Arguments against giving Negroes full rights with Whites are now based on cultural grounds—"The blacks haven't had a chance yet to earn equal status." The same notion also provides arguments for doing everything possible to give Negroes equal opportunities—if not fully equal status. This was the prevailing student opinion exposed in the study of student beliefs at Fresno State College. Currently, although a considerable minority do believe in offering full rights *now*—even including social integration (and miscegenation), 1966 and 1967 data suggest a possible resurgence of traditional White prejudices.

Much of the old mythology about "Negro" differences appears to have disappeared since the spread of scientific views through the mass media and a greater intermingling of the races on a social basis. It is no

---

[27] See *Newsweek*, December 6, 1965, p. 38 ff.; and Christopher Jencks, "The Moynihan Report," *The New York Review of Books*, October 14, 1965, pp. 39 ff.

longer startling to read in the paper of a white coed, "Why, many of my friends run around all the time with Negroes. Why should anyone think anything of it?"

In fact, among some of the white intelligentsia a kind of reverse ideology about Negro-white relationships is appearing. In parts of the country, such as Los Angeles and the deep South, whites have carried on their traditional way of settling disputes through violent rather than democratic means. For a few years, Negroes, through their policy of nonviolence of a Ghandilike pattern, led many Whites to wonder if Negroes did not possess some kind of unique moral superiority. However, the "Black Power" movement of 1967 has apparently caused some reversal of this view.

2.1 How do you explain that in the United States anyone with a Negro ancestor is considered a Negro, but offspring of white-Indian marriages are thought to be white? If a person with Negro ancestry who "looks white" is able to "cross the color line" and is freely accepted as white by whites, is he still a Negro? If he marries a white, would his children be Negroes?

2.2 Is it possible to combine segregation and equality of treatment? Is segregation in itself a form of discrimination? If an employer provided separate rest rooms for Negroes and whites, and if those for Negroes were the cleaner and more modern, would you say that anti-Negro discrimination was being practiced? Anti-white discrimination?

2.3 It is argued that Negroes like paternalism (i.e., kindly domination by whites). It is also argued that Negroes must be kept in their place. If Negroes like paternalism, why would it be necessary to take pains to keep them in their place?

3. Jewish Greed and Jewish Radicalism

It is believed that Jews control most industry and money in the United States; but it is also believed that most Jews tend to be radical and Communistic in their political philosophy.

This contradiction is only one of many central to anti-Semitism in America. Anti-Semitism probably is declining in the United States but still exists. It appears to be stronger in rural areas than in cities, and stronger among lower, and lower-middle- than among upper- or lower-class persons. It correlates with ultraconservative political and economic beliefs; reactionaries, unless they are Jews, are usually anti-Semites. Beliefs about Jews which are widespread among Christians include the following: [28]

[28] For data on the ideology of anti-Semitism, see Schermerhorn, *op. cit.*, pp. 31-32; and Adorno, *op. cit.*, pp. 94-100.

a. There is a Jewish "race," easily identifiable by certain physical characteristics: a prominent hooked nose, a dark and oily skin, black—often
wavy—hair, and a narrow jaw.

b. Jews are grasping and greedy. Their chief aim in life is to make money,
and they will resort to the most unethical business practices in order
to do so.

c. Jews are aggressive and power seeking. They have too much power,
especially in the economy, and will gain more as they can.

d. Jews adopt radicalism and intellectualism (which are thought to be the
same). They lean toward all kinds of radical doctrine. They tend to be
atheists, to believe in moral relativism, and to approve modern art and
music.

e. Jews are morally impure, are sensual, and often practice perversions.

f. Jews control most industry in the nation. Through their control of
banks they also control the money supply. Jewish international bankers
control the world economy.

g. Jews are industrious and intelligent, but their intelligence is characterized by a shrewdness and craftiness unappealing to decent persons.

h. Jews are clannish; they do not welcome non-Jews into their circle and
make no attempt to adopt customs of people around them.

It is unlikely that anti-Semitism creates in the minds of Americans the
same dilemma as does discrimination against Negroes. Discrimination
against Jews is much less conspicuous than that against Negroes. Jews
are refused lodging at some resorts and hotels, yet a Jew can go almost
anywhere in the United States and secure first-class hotel lodging and
restaurant service. Jews may be admitted to universities according to
quota, but there are few institutions of higher learning which altogether
exclude them. Jews are discriminated against in employment, yet many
of them manage to attain high positions in business and the professions.
Anti-Jewish discrimination is—much of the time—a quiet, "gentlemen's
agreement" sort. Therefore, Americans do not sense a "Jewish problem," nor do many of them feel moral qualms about present treatment
of Jews.

Anti-Semitism dates at least as far back as the pre-Christian era, when
Jews were persecuted for political and cultural reasons. It increased during the late Roman and medieval period, when it was largely based upon
religious differences; and began to function as a political weapon in the
latter half of the nineteenth century. Apparently the only country prior
to Nazi Germany to use anti-Semitism as a state policy was czarist Rus-
sia. However, the Roman Catholic Church, until its most recent Council,
has been basically anti-Semitic on the grounds that the Jews crucified
Christ (who was a Jew). This fundamental attitude has not everywhere

been prevalent but appears to have had an extremely strong influence during World War II.

In the United States, restrictions were first placed upon Jews in the 1870s. Anti-Semitism developed gradually in this country until the 1920s, when it received stimulus from the Ku Klux Klan and the anti-Semitism of prominent figures, among them Henry Ford. By the late 1920s, Americans were generally familiar with the idea that the Christian world was under the power of Jews, and that Jews were radical and dangerous.

Because it has a long history and is prevalent in almost every Western country, anti-Semitism is a special kind of problem in prejudice. It cannot be explained in the same way as prejudice against Negroes, Japanese, and Chinese. Jews, more than any other minority, are economic and intellectual competitors of those who mold public opinion. However, this fact does not explain all anti-Semitism. A psychoanalytic explanation has been offered, and it seems to be winning acceptance among social scientists. For a review of some of its chief points, see pp. 412 and 413 above.[29]

3.1 A *Fortune* survey showed that among the anti-Semites in a poll sample 45 percent belong to the lower-middle class. How do you explain this? Are middle-class persons more frustrated than other groups? Why would resentment be directed against Jews? Are lower-middle-class persons upwardly mobile? Would there be any tendency for the lower-middle class to regard Jews as competitors?

3.2 It is easy to find facts to refute the belief that our economic system is controlled by Jews. Why are these facts not distributed more generally? Why is it that one who criticizes a Jewish capitalist is rarely called a Communist, but those who criticize non-Jewish capitalists are likely to be so labeled?

3.3 Negroes are criticized for stupidity and laziness. Jews are criticized for shrewdness and industry. How do you explain this difference, and what is its significance?

4. Catholic Conservatism and Catholic Liberalism

It is believed by the Catholic hierarchy—especially in the United States —that Catholic liberals are destroying the Church; but it is also believed that the Church is medieval in outlook and its survival as a major influence depends on fundamental reform.

It is significant that the Catholic hierarchy in the United States is one of the most conservative there is. At the upper echelons, it tends to follow the pronouncements of the Roman Curia, of which even the present

[29] Typical of the psychoanalytic explanations is Nathan W. Ackerman and Marie Jahoda, *Anti-Semitism and Emotional Disorder*, Harper & Row, 1950. See also Adorno, *op. cit.*

Pope, Paul VI, is wary. Many see Catholicism in the United States as the most conservative, the most rigid, and the most unpopular in the world. On the other hand, among the younger priests we find a humanism in outlook rather characteristic of Unitarianism and other Liberal Protestant churches.[30] And there is developing a young Catholic set of both priests and laymen who bitterly oppose the dictates of the top American hierarchy.

The Catholic Church formally published lists of "banned" books and motion pictures; Catholic laymen read the books and went to the pictures with delight. Catholic laymen (if we can take birth rates seriously) ignore the Church's dictates regarding contraceptives. Magazines such as *Commonweal* and *Ramparts*—published by Catholic laymen—are among the most liberal magazines.

In the United States, as elsewhere, the basic conservatism of the Catholic Church presents a serious problem for Catholicism. The priests feel, for the most part, obligated to follow the conservative "party line." Their Catholic lay audiences do not. Hence, perhaps more than in any other church group, Catholic laymen disdain the priesthood and violate its dictates. There are, also, rebellious priests, such as Father Dubay who was purged from Los Angeles. (Although priests of his point of view assume heroic stature in the United States, they have been fully accepted in France and Italy for many years.)

4.1 Major religions have risen and fallen in strength. Once Spain was largely Moslem. Do you feel that the Catholic Church may at some time become minor? Even if it retains large numbers of nominal lay members, do you think its intellectual influence will wane?

4.2 What is your opinion of any church group dictating motion pictures, television shows, or books that you may watch or read? Defend your position.

4.3 Why do you think certain church groups—either Protestant fundamentalist or Catholic—tend to work toward "thought control"? Is this proper? Do they derive their authority from Holy scriptures? Did Christ condemn contraceptives? Did he condemn much that the fundamentalist churches now condemn?

4.4 Do you think that orthodox religious thought is virtually dead in the Western Hemisphere? Why or why not?

DISCUSSION QUESTIONS AND EXERCISES

1. Most studies of attitude change indicate that high-school students, over a four-year period, change very little in their prejudices. The same results

[30] See Will Herberg, *Protestant, Catholic, Jew: An Essay in American Religious Sociology*, Doubleday, 1955.

have been found among college students over a four-year period. How do you explain this almost complete failure of higher education to develop more democratic attitudes?

2. Some teachers will not encourage a class to discuss problems of racial prejudice if the class includes both white and Negro students. Why do you suppose they do this? Is this practice sound?

3. Which do you believe is the most significant difference to be taken into account when a couple are contemplating marriage? A religious difference between them; a social-class difference; a racial difference; a difference over whether they want children.

4. The teachers in an elementary school learned how to recognize and meet some of the emotional needs of their pupils: the need for belonging, for achievement, for affection, and for sharing in decisions. It was found that these children became less prejudiced toward minorities as they became more and more secure. At no time did the teachers promote among the children an intellectual examination of racial attitudes and beliefs. Why did these children become more democratic? Does this experiment question the value of a reflective approach to racial prejudice among children? Would you expect the same results with high-school students?

5. Would you expect a straight factual course on racial characteristics and differences to produce changes in racial attitudes? Why, or why not?

REFERENCES

ASHMORE, HARRY S., *Epitaph for Dixie*, New York, Norton, 1958.

The editor of the *Arkansas Gazette*, Little Rock, attempts to show why—mainly because of long-range economic forces—integration must occur in the South. Several reviewers of the book say, "The best book about the South ever written by a southerner."

BALDWIN, JAMES, *Nobody Knows My Name; More Notes of a Native Son*, New York, Dial, 1961.

One of the best prose stylists in the country, Baldwin, a Negro, writes his own personalized, emotional, extremely powerful, and often shocking message.

BENEDICT, RUTH, *Race: Science and Politics*, New York, Viking, 1945.

The late Ruth Benedict, one of the world's greatest anthropologists, produced a classic in this book. It is highly recommended reading.

BERRY, BREWTON, *Almost White*, New York, Macmillan, 1963.

Berry writes of a little-known minority, the Mestizos, a biological mixture of white, Negro, and Indian, who are caught in a sociological no-man's-land. Rebuffed by everyone, unable to identify with anyone, they have lived in small isolated groups near the East Coast.

BIBBY, CYRIL, *Race, Prejudice and Education*, New York, Praeger, 1961.

In this small volume, which emerged from a UNESCO study, Bibby writes a valuable book on measures schools can take to educate against prejudice.

BROOM, LEONARD, and NORVAL D. GLENN, *Transformation of the Negro American*, New York, Harper & Row, 1965.

These two sociologists write a remarkably powerful book about what has happened to the Negro in recent years, with a focus on urban ghetto life. Each chapter may be taken as an entity in itself.

BUTCHER, MARGARET J., *The Negro in American Culture*, New York, Knopf, 1956.

Probably the most useful book on the contributions of Negroes to American culture in literature, art, music, theatre, education, and politics. Fascinating reading, as well as a valuable reference source.

CAMERON, JAMES, *The African Revolution*, New York, Random House, 1961.

Cameron, drawing his thesis from a statement made by DuBois in 1909, contends that the world of the future will be made by dark-skinned people. Good food for thought for those "whites" who don't realize that they are a small minority in the world's population and have no monopoly on brains.

CAYO, PATRICIA, *Spanish Harlem*, New York, Harper & Row, 1965.

The author spent time in East Harlem to study the Puerto Ricans first hand. In spite of the unbelievable squalor she found there, Cayo decides that the Puerto Ricans are on the move, slowly, but upward. Basically optimistic, without pulling punches.

CLARK, KENNETH B., *Dark Ghetto: Dilemmas of Social Power*, New York, Harper & Row, 1965.

Clark, a product of a Negro ghetto and now a social psychologist, writes a powerful book about ghetto life. The book, he writes, "is a summation of my personal and lifelong experiences as a prisoner . . . long before I really knew that I was really a prisoner."

EHLE, JOHN, *The Free Men*, New York, Harper & Row, 1965.

A study by an expert of problems related to integrating a supposedly liberal town, Chapel Hill, N.C., home of the state's university. A remarkably well-done case study. The "free men" are a core of student leaders who were willing to accept harassment and prison for their cause.

GREENBERG, JACK, *Race Relations and American Law*, New York, Columbia University Press, 1960.

Greenberg presents convincing evidence that the passage of laws can change attitudes and that legislation can be a potent weapon in furthering social change.

HERSKOVITS, MELVILLE J., *The Myth of the Negro Past*, New York, Harper & Row, 1941.

Herskovits was a noted anthropologist. Drawing upon evidence about ancient civilizations, Herskovits demonstrates that at certain times and in certain places Negroes had highly advanced civilizations, in terms of complexity, ingenuity, art forms, etc.

KROEBER, THEODORA, *Ishi in Two Worlds; a Biography of the Last Wild Indian in North America*, Berkeley, University of California Press, 1961.

The wife of one of the world's greatest anthropologists, Alfred Kroeber, drawing upon her husband's records, writes a tragic biography of the last member of the Yahis, southern-most tribe of the Yana Indians of the western Sierra Nevada Mountains. In the nineteenth century, these Indians were so brutally mauled by white Californians that they went into hiding and remained in complete isolation for generations. Ishi, the last surviving member, starving, stumbled into a foothill town in 1911. Kroeber rescued him, and Ishi became a live exhibit in the museum of the University of California at Berkeley—a mutually satisfactory arrangement. A best seller of great power which reflects most unfavorably on "Christian" Caucasians.

LaFARGE, OLIVER, *Pictorial History of the American Indian*, New York, Crown, 1956.

LaFarge, an anthropologist and one of our leading experts on American Indians, writes a panoramic portrait of North American Indians from 1492 to the middle of the 1950s. The book makes no attempt to conceal LaFarge's anger at what he considers the sadistic treatment administered to Indians by whites. LaFarge is always readable and many of his pictures are stunning.

MALCOLM X, with the assistance of ALEX HALEY, *The Autobiography of Malcolm X*, New York, Grove, 1965.

Provides insights into the Black Muslim movement. The review in the November 11, 1965, issue of *The New York Review of Books*, although lacking all the details, is in itself almost as valuable as the book.

MONTAGU, ASHLEY, *Man's Most Dangerous Myth: The Fallacy of Race*, 4th ed., Cleveland, World, 1964.

Rather polemical, but one of the best source books available. There is a sixty-page bibliography.

MYRDAL, GUNNAR, *An American Dilemma: The Negro Problem and Modern Democracy*, New York, Harper & Row, 1944.

This book remains *the* classic study of white-Negro relations in the United States. It provides not only a brilliant analysis of the Negro problem—which is really the "white" problem—but a similarly brilliant analysis of many aspects of American culture. Myrdal is a Swedish social scientist with an international reputation in more than one field.

PETTIGREW, THOMAS F., *A Profile of the Negro American*, Princeton, Van Nostrand, 1964.

In a short but jampacked volume, Pettigrew writes what may be the single most useful book for students today. He treats the personality of the North American Negro, scientific facts about race, and the protest movement. Contains a reference list of 565 titles.

SENIOR, CLARENCE, *The Puerto Ricans*, Chicago, Quadrangle Books, 1965.

A good description of Puerto Rican life in Harlem, with an essentially optimistic tone. Slum life is still terrifying, but not quite as bad as at the turn of the century when Jacob Riis described it.

WARREN, ROBERT PENN, *Who Speaks for the Negro?* New York, Random House, 1965.

Warren, famous for other writings, interviewed more than a score of Negro leaders and many dozens of participants in the civil rights movement. His conclusion: No white man really speaks for the Negro.

WILLIAMS, JOHN A., *This Is My Country*, New York, Harcourt, Brace & World, 1965.

A Negro's deeply felt introspection concerning a cross-country journey in which he is provided with a luxurious new car and an abundant supply of the most respectable credit cards. There are surprisingly few nasty incidents—but some—and Williams reacts to them in a rather paranoid way.

WILLIAMS, ROBIN M., JR., *et al.*, *Strangers Next Door: Ethnic Relations in American Communities*, Englewood Cliffs, N.J., Prentice-Hall, 1964.

An intellectually heavy but important book. Taking its beginning from the now famous Elmira study, the authors include twenty more communities, six for depth studies. Their focus primarily is on relations of Negroes, Jews, Mexican-Americans, and Italo-Americans. They expose much about American ideology as well as almost every aspect of intercultural relations. They conclude that only a small proportion of our population are "rigid hostility-ridden bigots" but that half the population is prejudice prone.

CHAPTER 19

Problematic Areas of Culture: Sex, Courtship, and Marriage

American Sexual Ethics and Their Implications for Education

Aｌｔｈｏｕｇｈ millions of American adults apparently believe that sex education is desirable, it is one of the most neglected subjects of study in the secondary-school curriculum. Neglect of sex education may be attributed to lack of preparation (both emotional and informational) among teachers, and to a belief among many parents that what sex education is needed is better given in the home. However, demand for sex education in the schools appears to be growing, stimulated probably by a belief that, however good their intentions, many parents fail to give children the help they need in this area.

Present sex education typically has two emphases: (1) dissemination of facts concerning the physiology of reproduction and (2) attempted inculcation of traditional middle-class attitudes. The first is usually a responsibility of biology or health-education teachers, or boys' and girls' counselors. The second task may be performed by health, physical-education, home-economics, and social-studies teachers, or by counselors.

In the opinion of many persons sex education, even where most fully developed, remains grossly inadequate. Dissemination of physiologic facts may be reasonably satisfactory, but ordinarily an attempt is made to inculcate traditional sexual ethics in uncritical and authoritarian fashion. This approach does not help students to resolve conflicts they may have developed in the area of sex. As in other problem areas, teaching of this sort is likely to intensify conflicts and make them less manageable than would instruction emphasizing reflection and clarification.

If one knows the origins of traditional middle-class sexual ethics, he is likely to understand them better. Some present-day notions have been in the Western culture stream since the development of early Mediterranean civilizations. For example, certain attitudes toward sexual practices are expressed in the Egyptian Book of the Dead, the Code of

Hammurabi, the Talmud, and the Old Testament; and most of them continue to be held by many Americans today.

Since Hebrew and Christian scriptures are the most important sources of our traditional sexual ethic, it is helpful to examine their pronouncements regarding sex. Premarital coitus is severely condemned in the Old Testament, as are also adultery and homosexuality. The Old Testament condemns every type of sexual experience except marital intercourse, and decrees the harshest of punishments for those who transgress.

Extreme asceticism, however, was not associated with ancient Hebrew culture. It remained for early Christianity to develop the ideal of asceticism, and in so doing it borrowed heavily from oriental paganism. For St. Paul, existence was a struggle of desires of the spirit against desires of the flesh; victory of spirit could come only as demands of the flesh were subdued: "It is good for a man not to touch a woman. . . . I say therefore to the unmarried and widows, It is good for them if they abide even as I. . . . But if they cannot contain, let them marry: for it is better to marry than to burn." [1]

By the fourth century A.D., asceticism had become an ideal to most Christians. The monastic system translated the ideal of celibacy into a way of life. The notion that sexual desire and fulfillment are intrinsically evil, and that the surest road to salvation is denial of the flesh, thus became instated during the Middle Ages.

One finds in the ancient and medieval world the origin of contemporary beliefs such as these:

1. Virginity is to be prized above all else. A virgin is nearer spiritual perfection than any nonvirgin can hope to be.

2. Sexual relations, although regrettable under any circumstances, are permissible only between man and wife. The chief end of sexual relations should be procreation, not recreation.

3. Adultery is a mortal sin, deserving severe punishment. But it is worse for a woman to commit adultery than for a man.

4. Since sex is evil, everyone should avoid experiences which arouse sexual desire. It is best for people not to talk or think about sex any more than necessary, and children should be protected from knowledge of sex.

5. Any type of sex experience except marital intercourse is a mortal sin. Perversions are abominable, as is masturbation.

Certain other beliefs may be traced straight to ancient times. The paternalistic culture of Judea, Greece, and Rome gave rise to beliefs that a husband should be head of his household, that wives and children

[1] Corinthians 7:1, 2, 7, 8, 9.

should be submissive and obedient, and that woman's place is in the home.

The influence of Hebrew and Christian ideas upon sex, marriage, and the family has fluctuated from time to time and place to place. With the rise of Puritanism in England and its spread to the New World, the Christian sexual ethic was pursued with intense vigor. In Puritan England, fornication was once classified a felony, punishable by death. In Puritan New England, adultery was punishable by death, and fornication by fine and corporal punishment. Later, adultery was punished by requiring an offender to wear a letter *A* sewn on the outside of his upper garments, or, as in Connecticut, by having a letter *A* branded on his forehead with a hot iron.[2] The Puritan code was relaxed in the eighteenth century but underwent a powerful resurgence in the late nineteenth.

We have offered the foregoing brief historical résumé in part to indicate what many of the older generation still thinks, but also to vivify the contrast between the old ethics and those of the young today. Lower-class youth have changed but little—they never were impressed by the traditional mores. The most conspicuous revolution in thought is within the middle class. It is more noticeable among the well educated than the less-well educated, among middle and upper middles, and particularly among the present generation of college students. The beginning of the revolution may perhaps be traced to the feminist movement of the nineteenth century; but it surged forward only after World War I. Major wars upset culture and greatly accelerate some kinds of change. For this reason, some writers believe that another surge occurred after World War II, and they speak of not one, but two sexual revolutions in this century.

(We use the term *sex* broadly: not only are we describing changes in thought about restricted matters such as premarital intercourse, but lovemaking in all its forms both before and during courtship and after marriage. We refer, also, to changing sex roles, changing ways in which men and women relate, what is considered appropriate after marriage [the business of "affairs"], and even the rearing of children.)

We shall describe some of the new belief patterns in this section of the chapter, but first we want to indicate that they *remain* under sharp attack. The new codes continue obnoxious and frightening to the fundamentally religious, the elderly, and a considerable number of the lower-middle class. The mass media take an ambivalent attitude. The "lovelorn columnists" always find ways—no matter how far-fetched—of defend-

---

[2] Morris Ploscowe, *Sex and the Law*, Prentice-Hall, 1951, pp. 143–144.

ing many Victorian beliefs, such as the ideal of premarital and extramarital chastity. Among the most conservative of all are many school teachers, administrators, and boards of education; and of these it is the elderly spinster teacher who is most shocked by new ways of thought and behavior. It is inescapable, therefore, that many of the young feel conflicts in the area of sex. The specific nature of some of these conflicts will be treated later in the chapter.

One obvious and extremely significant trend of this century is the virtual breakdown of censorship. Censorship of books appears to have all but disappeared; it is on its way to disappearing in motion pictures; and has been greatly relaxed on television. Confronted as they are by unexpurgated realism in print and on the screen, it follows that young people see no cause for restraint in either their topics of conversation or the language they use. Freely available sex manuals have become so frank and detailed that one writer has been led to write an amusing satire of such manuals.[3]

As a consequence, the young as well as the old converse with great frankness, often using without inhibition the old "prohibited" four-letter words. The young are in the process of coining an entirely new four-letter vocabulary, to the considerable confusion of curious adults who don't know what the kids are talking about. This frankness of speech is not limited to sexually segregated groups.

It is all very apparent that sex in all its ramifications is no longer as much of a closed area as it was even a decade ago. Nor is there any reason to suppose the trend will change. Operating in its favor is the basic secularization of society, the long-range trend toward a more open-minded morality, and the increasing tendency of persons to travel (we must not forget that, in most aspects of sex, almost all cultures are far more "open" than ours). Yet, sex cannot be excluded as a closed area or as a source of intrapersonal conflict. Many people in other parts of the world—motion-picture producers, for example—regard America as the chief remaining stronghold of prudery in the world.

A few of the trends which appear to have emerged or to have accelerated in the past decade are:

1. Increased openness concerning sex at most age levels, as described above.

2. Increased permissiveness in behavior.

3. Increased interest in matters sexual. This is difficult to explain, since one would expect the new permissiveness to cause most persons to "take

---

[3] Sussman, Gerald, *The Official Sex Manual*, Putnam, 1965. Sussman coins many of his own words—such as conginutal for conjugal—and in general has great fun. See particularly his diagram of the "Erroneous Zones of the Female."

sex as a matter of course." The intentionally humorous comment of British Malcolm Muggeridge is pertinent here: "America is drenched, if not submerged in sex. . . . Young lovers arm themselves with birth pills and the Kama Sutra, and engage in erotic exercises which might have seemed excessive in the pages of *Les Liaisons Dangereuses;* middle-aged couples swap partners . . . and disturb the suburban night with their strident love cries. . . ." [4]

4. Related to the foregoing, steadily increasing use of sex in advertising and in much business practice: It is commonly taken for granted that business corporations are not reluctant to employ call-girls to soften potential customers.

5. Increased acceptance of nudity or seminudity: The topless stage performer or waitress is now commonplace in some parts of the West. (Social innovations that occur in California have a way of gradually infiltrating other parts of the nation.)

6. Again related to the point above, we have developed "the cult of the large breast." Quoting from *Newsweek*, October 25, 1965, p. 112A, we read: "Down from the ceiling of San Francisco's Condor Club slides a small pedestal bearing blond Carol Doda doing a wild Watusi. She's topless and so top-heavy she seems in imminent danger of toppling onto the customers' tables. . . . 'Unbelievable!' gasps an onlooker. Not at all, replies the 26-year old Miss Doda, who has escalated her measurements from 36–24–36 to 44–24–36 with injections of liquid silicone. 'Science has invented all these new wonderful things,' she explains, 'why shouldn't we use them?' The article reports that the physician who treated Carol has a six-month waiting list.

7. General acceptance among the young that it is "all right if that's the way you feel about it" to engage in premarital intimacies. This becomes a complicated issue. Once "heavy petting" meant practices such as deep kissing (of the mouth), kissing the neck, or nibbling the ears. Now heavy petting at the least involves fondling and kissing the breasts—but usually the pelvic region is involved. (These data are from the study of student beliefs at Fresno State College.) As one girl put it in her paper, "Nowadays, after a few kisses to distract you, the first thing a girl knows, the boy has his hand in her crotch. . . ." Although data are lacking, presumably high-school students engage increasingly in similar intimacies. Sexual intercourse is a common but not necessary result; many college students satisfy themselves through mutual masturbation. As one girl wrote, "The girls don't object on moral grounds to 'going all the way' but they fear pregnancy. This other way they get the same kicks without the risk."

[4] *Newsweek*, July 19, 1965, p. 62. Muggeridge's original article appeared in the *New Statesman.*

8. "Going steady" may have increased in recent years and very likely begins earlier—e.g., at the age of 13 or 14. Going steady for two or three years virtually guarantees a steady build-up of intimacy. The rate of premarital pregnancy between the ages of 17 and 20 has greatly increased. Marriage is a frequent way out of these premature catapultings into "adulthood," especially when money is not available for an abortion. Sociologists in general deplore going steady prior to an age when maturity makes a successful marriage somewhat more likely.[5]

9. The chief changes in marriage patterns seem two: (a) more acceptance of divorce as a proper way of solving problems of marital unhappiness (in some circles, divorce may be a prestige-conferring behavior); and (b) acceptance of the "affair" as often a desirable means of saving a boring marriage[6] —or, in more extreme instances, "wife swapping."

We could continue with many more such trends, but space does not permit. A few may be reversible but the authors are skeptical of that—with the possible exception of the present tendency toward "going steady." Too many deep-seated cultural factors related to industrialization, urbanization, secularization, new knowledge about birth control and treatment of venereal disease, higher educational standards, and the like, are operating to prevent much reversal—the moralists to the contrary. The following sections will consider some of the contradictions and confusions in American sexual beliefs and attitudes.

The following sections will consider some of the contradictions and confusions in American sexual beliefs and attitudes.

1. Purity Versus Experience

It is believed that sexual experiences before marriage are always sinful; but it is also believed that sexual experience is good preparation for marriage.

We have related origins of the first belief. Some specific and supporting beliefs include the following: Men prefer to marry virgins. Men lose respect for any girl who submits to them. Persons who have premarital intercourse are likely to develop a taste for it which will lead to adultery in marriage. Any sort of love making which arouses sexual passion should be avoided. It is the girl's responsibility to see that things don't go too far on a date. Continence is neither physically nor psycho-

---

[5] One of the best treatments of this subject is Edgar Z. Friedenberg, *The Vanishing Adolescent*, Beacon, 1960.

[6] See John F. Cuber and Peggy Harroff, *The Significant Americans*, Appleton-Century-Crofts, 1965.

logically harmful. Persons who enter marriage as virgins are more likely to have a happy and successful marriage. The best preparation for the sexual relationship of marriage is complete avoidance of it until the wedding night. One premarital sexual experience is decisive—a once unchaste woman is a fallen woman (or as a minister expressed it to one of the authors, "You never saw a girl who was only half-way a sinner, did you?").[7]

Even among relatively conservative adults there is one situation which allows some exception to the general stand expressed above. If a couple are desperately in love, and if they are engaged and soon to be married, sexual liberties are considered a little more tolerable. Although such liberties are not to be encouraged, they will be understood and condemned only mildly. Marriage will "cleanse the couple of sin."

The second of our dichotomous beliefs takes more than one form. In its older form, it referred to males only and was thus an expression of a double standard. Sometimes it was stated as "Men who sow their wild oats before marriage make the best husbands." One ground for this belief was a common opinion that men are naturally unsatisfied with one woman, that all men want experiences with as many women as possible. It was believed by many women that it is better for a man to work the edge off his polygamous instincts through premarital affairs than to establish adulterous connections later. Another possible ground for this notion may be a belief that an experienced male is a better lover, that he will be able to afford his wife more physical satisfaction in the bedroom than will an inexperienced man.

The double standard in sexual belief and behavior is disappearing. Those who believe that premarital intercourse is desirable now commonly feel that if it is good for a male it is also good for a female. Some reasons cited for premarital coitus include these. Sexual experiences bring lovers closer together and make them love each other more. Sexual relations before marriage prove sexual compatibility; if compatibility is absent, it is better to find out before marriage. Tension produced by long-enforced continence among lovers is damaging to their physical and mental health. In reducing tensions and bringing lovers closer together, sexual relations also reduce friction and quarreling.[8]

[7] For traditional arguments against premarital experience see Gladys D. Shultz, *Letters to Jane*, Lippincott, 1947. For arguments offered by subjects of one scientific study, see Ernest W. Burgess and Paul Wallin, *Engagement and Marriage*, Lippincott, 1953, pp. 380–384. For a compilation of arguments from other sources, see Alfred C. Kinsey, *et al.*, *Sexual Behavior in the Human Female*, Saunders, 1953, p. 308.

[8] These reasons follow closely those given by persons who have engaged in premarital coitus, as reported by Burgess and Wallin, *op. cit.*, pp. 373–374. See also Kinsey, *op. cit.*, pp. 308–309.

There is a tendency for many persons to vacillate between liberal and conservative positions. Ellis, generalizing from his analysis of attitudes expressed in mass media of communication, says:

> . . . Twentieth-century attitudes toward fornication are certainly disapproving enough if we are to believe some of the most authoritative and widely read, seen, and heard sources of the day; but at the same time these identical sources leave ample room for the inclusion of attitudes that are often frankly, insinuatingly, sophisticatedly or romantically pro-fornicative.
>
> To confuse the issue still further, a considerable portion of the published and broadcast literature of today seems to have accomplished the noteworthy feat of, in precisely one and the same breath, accepting *and* rejecting premarital sex relations.[9]

This ambivalence is reflected in actual behavior. Almost everyone is verbally opposed to fornication and strongly in favor of chastity. Yet studies by Kinsey and others show that virginity at marriage is not as widespread as verbal endorsement would lead us to expect. Among predominantly middle-class samples, about 85 percent of married males and 50 percent of married females had premarital intercourse. These percentages would probably have been much higher had the samples studied contained a normal proportion of lower-class persons or contemporary college students.[10]

There is every reason to believe, however, that as a greater proportion of the population is subjected to "the college experience," and as other trends (mentioned on pages 432 and 433) develop, not only will this ambivalence lessen, but premarital relations will become so acceptable—perhaps even felt necessary—that finding a virgin at marriage will be equivalent to finding a living Dodo.

1.1 Considering the nature of American society, what are some advantages of remaining chaste until marriage? Is a person more comfortable if he confines his behavior to what is socially approved? Or does one have more fun, and is there more zest to living, when conventions are flouted?

1.2 Are there any satisfactory substitutes for premarital sexual intercourse? Are any of the following acceptable substitutes? Masturbation, necking, petting? What do we know about the effects of each? Would complete continence be better than any of these substitutes?

1.4 How do you explain the fact that in the area of sex what we do does not always conform with what we say? Is inconsistency between behavior and belief a sign that sex codes are changing? Is such inconsistency typical of any period of transition?

[9] Albert Ellis, *The Folklore of Sex*, Liveright, 1951, p. 32.

[10] For conflicting data on the consequences of premarital sexual relations, see Burgess and Wallin, *op. cit.*, pp. 324, 366, and Kinsey, *op. cit.*, pp. 316–319, 386–387.

2. Chastity and Peer-Group Status

It is believed that premarital sexual relations are immoral; but it is also believed by many youth that demonstrations of seductive ability and capacity as a lover are among the best means for gaining status and popularity among peers.

Havighurst and Taba have reported that the sexual ideology of typical high-school students is conventionally middle class.[11] Gorer has commented on a tendency of American girls to lead a man on only to refuse intercourse.[12] In the late 1960s, although a belief in the wrongness of premarital relations appears to be held by a minority of youth, high-school students have a background of parental beliefs shaped at a time when, Margaret Mead maintained, most middle-class girls of high-school age, and possibly a majority of boys, valued chastity and managed to maintain it.[13]

Despite these conservative pressures and some conformity to them, American middle-class youth, both male and female, have strong motives to prove maturity by demonstrating sexual prowess. It is thought to be manly to try to seduce the girl one is "going with"—although attempted seduction is often a game, indulged in for the sake of appearances and not seriously intended to lead to sexual intercourse. It is considered womanly to behave seductively, to seem sexually experienced and sophisticated. A high-school girl is thought most mature who emphasizes her sexual charateristics in her dress, speech, and manner—although obviously this can be overdone to the point where she is regarded as a real hussy instead of merely a girl trying to look and act like a hussy. An immediate aim of adult-appearing behavior is not adult status but peer-group status.

That this pattern places youth in a difficult situation scarcely needs stressing. The sexual drive of males soars at adolescence and reaches its peak during high-school years. The sexual drive of females seems to develop more slowly, if we are to accept Kinsey's evidence; perhaps in part because of inhibitions imposed by middle-class notions of what is proper behavior for a girl. Freedom which is accorded modern youth tends to undermine these inhibitions. It is certain that practically all high-school boys and a substantial proportion of high-school girls are erotically aroused, as a result of their dating practices, and feel strong impulses

[11] Robert J. Havighurst and Hilda Taba, *Adolescent Character and Personality*, Wiley, 1949, p. 36.

[12] Geoffrey Gorer, *The American People*, Norton, 1948, pp. 116–117.

[13] Margaret Mead, *Male and Female*, Morrow, 1949, p. 285.

toward fulfillment. All available evidence suggests that, despite possible adult disapproval, as well as that of the peer group (if a reputation for promiscuity develops), an apparent majority of middle-class youth do pet to the point of orgasm and increasingly feel few qualms about "going all the way" by having intercourse.

Even with the emerging ultrapermissiveness in the area of sex, there remain many reasons why most youth are likely to experience conflict in this area. Peer-group expectations vary according to the particular sub-culture to which a youth belongs. Although teen-agers generally achieve prestige by seeming liberal, free, and appearing "sexy," this may meet with parental disapproval. It is more likely to meet with such disapproval in rural, "bible-belt" areas and among the urban lower-middle class than it is among middle-middle, upper-middle, or upper-class urban or sub-urban dwellers. Thus, a high-school boy or girl may be torn between loyalty to parental teaching and to peer-group expectations.

Furthermore, even our most "modern thinking" adults—especially among the middle class—enforce certain punishments for youth who prematurely become pregnant. These punishments are not as severe as they were a decade or so ago; and, if the parents have enough money, such problems can be taken care of quietly, with little more verbal chas-tisement than, "Why couldn't you have been more careful?" Punish-ment falls most severely on the lower-class girl who becomes pregnant out of wedlock. She and her child are likely to become public charges and to have the finger of shame pointed at them. There is nothing more effective than poverty to label a person a moral leper.

2.1 What are some of the bases of popularity among high-school students? Is sophistication and acting grown up one of them? What does "acting grown up" mean in the sexual area?

2.2 Why do high-school students pet? Is this a method for getting popularity? Does petting, since it is accompanied by unchaste thoughts, violate the chastity ideal? Is petting good or bad preparation for marriage?

2.3 Why are people strongly motivated to behave as their associates do? Do most high-school students "go along with the crowd"? To what extent should high-school students conform to peer-group behavior if it violates parental teachings?

3. The Nice Girl Versus the Good Sport

It is believed that women should not be interested in sex as men are, that their minds and behavior should remain on a higher and cleaner plane; but it is also believed that women should have the same right as men to enjoy life, and that men dislike prudish women.

The double standard which decrees that what is proper for a male is improper or sinful for a female may be found originally in ancient Hebraic law, where it is ordered that women should be punished more harshly than men for certain immoralities. The following notions express or uphold a double standard between the sexes: There is, first of all, the concept of the "nice girl" or "good woman," sired by man's desire to idealize womanhood and to attribute to women traits which are more refined, more delicate, more gentle, and more spiritual than those of males.

A nice girl (or good woman) does not have very much interest in sex except for procreative purposes. She never really desires sexual experiences, does not consider sex a proper source of pleasure. If a man makes an "indecent" suggestion, she blushes, and perhaps even forcefully slaps his face. If a nice girl falls in love and becomes engaged, she resists suggested intimacies, but if she and her fiancé engage in intimacy at all she is extremely reluctant and guilt ridden. Her surrender is not supposed to represent any desire for sex, but only a service or gift to the man because she "loves him very much" or "feels sorry for him." However, a nice girl who weakens under these circumstances will probably lose the respect of her fiancé, and he will probably break the engagement.

A nice girl is always refined in her behavior. If she does discuss sex, it is discreetly with members of her own sex. In such conversation she persistently avoids words of one syllable, preferring instead to use approved medical terms. But a really nice girl—unless forced to—will not discuss sex at all. She never tells "dirty" jokes, and if one is told in her presence, she shows embarrassment or, if she is extremely nice and the joke very dirty, indicates that she has been insulted. When a nice girl gets married, it is thought proper that her husband initiate their sexual relations with as much tact as possible. She is to wait passively, submit passively, and make no show of pleasure—always remembering that a lustful woman is a depraved woman. So go the cultural beliefs about the nice girl.

A double standard assumes that a female will be a virgin at marriage, but no such assumption is made for the male. It is much worse for a wife to commit adultery than for a husband to do so. A double standard applies also to children. Small girls should be protected from sex to a greater degree than small boys. A small girl who innocently shows an interest in her genitals, or in any kind of sexual experience, is shamed or punished more severely than a small boy.

Recent years have seen a growing assumption of equality in all respects between the sexes. The twentieth century has brought the emergence of a new philosophy which grants to women rights and privileges traditionally reserved for men. If a man is to "sow wild oats," then an equal privilege should be accorded a woman. If woman is to remain chaste until marriage, then so is man.

With the rise of a single standard has developed a concept of the woman who is a "good sport." A good sport is not shocked by earthy language in men; she uses it herself. She understands a dirty joke, laughs at it, and then tells a better one. She fits in at a poker party, knows how to act at a bar, and will accompany a male friend to a "topless" show. She reads risqué novels; she can talk about sex intelligently and without embarrassment. She may smoke and drink; she is not modest in attire; and she does not blush every time she leaves for the powder room. A good sport pets, but not necessarily indiscriminately. She often indulges in premarital sexual intercourse or heavy petting just for the sheer fun of it.

In the Fresno State College study, one girl, forgetting that she was supposed to be "tattling" on other students, unabashedly began her paper by saying, "I am writing on sex because it is not only interesting but I personally enjoy it. It is good, clean fun. After all—I'm normal." This girl is a good student, conscientious, honest, kindly—an example, one supposes, of the 1967 version of the "nice girl."

That this kind of change could occur as rapidly as it has without the generation of moral conflict is very unlikely. Many men are uncertain in their attitudes toward women. They cannot decide whether they want their women to be old fashioned or modern. Many of them indulge their desire for a "good sport" through associations with women who are not their wives—secretaries, girl friends, prostitutes. They may feed their desire for "naughty women" by reading salacious literature or patronizing risqué shows. Women also are ambivalent. They want to be "good sports" for the fun of it, but they find it difficult to do so without developing feelings of guilt. Moreover, they are not sure whether men really want them to assume this role. Apparently many women receive vicarious pleasure from reading sexy fiction and watching television soap opera, most of which includes at least one woman who is a "good sport."

A late-twentieth-century good sport would have been considered a fallen woman in the nineteenth century—and indeed still is by many persons. Yet she is usually not promiscuous; she may have a strong sense of responsibility in accepting consequences; she may be honest, generous, and selfless. She is, in short, an emancipated woman who, in her values and conduct, is very similar to the men with whom she associates.

An increasing number of men not only accept a "good sport" but prefer her to the "nice girl," as indicated above. Many boys of today may actually criticize their girl friends, including girls they regard as nice, for not being better sports. Many husbands are critical of wives for being too prudish and inhibited. The proportion of men who demand that their wives be virgins at marriage is probably decreasing, although data on this matter are inadequate.[14] Despite the fact that a double standard is still very much alive for many persons and still has legal sanction, its erosion is obvious; for a large segment of our population it has practically ceased to exist.

3.1 Are there any good reasons why women should not follow the same moral standards as men? Are women more likely than men to be harmed by smoking and drinking? Is a woman more likely than a man to want to "go too far" in petting? Is a woman more likely than a man to abuse the practice of premarital intercourse?

3.2 What are the origins of the double standard? Was the double standard developed by a patriarchal, by a matriarchal, or by an equalitarian society? Do you think we would have a double standard if women had been in a position to make the rules? Why do men wish to deny to women privileges which they regularly claim for themselves?

3.3 Since World War I an increasing proportion of American women appear to conform to the "good sport" pattern. Do you think they are more likely than the "old-fashioned" girls to fail as wives? Is the rise of modern woman responsible for the increase in divorce rate which has occurred since World War I? Are American women going to the dogs?

4. Modesty and Sex Appeal

It is believed that lack of modesty is shameful and immoral; but it is also believed that an attractive woman would be a fool if she did not reveal some of her charms, and that clothes should be designed for comfort and healthful living rather than for concealment.

The first belief is as old as Genesis, in which it is told how Adam and Eve were made ashamed of their nakedness. A belief in modesty is logically related to a belief that things of the flesh are "unclean" and "indecent." In the United States, a belief that the human body is shameful, and that sexual organs are the most shameful part of all, dates from colonial Puritanism. It continues to be widely believed by the elderly that the body, except for the extremities, should remain clothed at all times. A person who exposes himself is considered either unbalanced mentally or depraved morally. West reports that in Plainville many married adults have never seen the nude body of their spouses.[15] The law regularly punishes night-club artists who strip to the raw. Completely nude bath-

[14] Kinsey, *op. cit.*, p. 323, referring to his studies of American males, says that over 50 percent do not insist that their wives be virgins at marriage. From what is known of attitudes fifty years ago, this represents a marked shift.

[15] James West, *Plainville, U.S.A.*, Columbia University Press, 1945, p. 177.

ing is prohibited on public beaches, and many states outlaw sun-bathing societies. Anyone who appears unclothed in public is arrested, and in many places European-style bikini bathing suits are illegal. Hollywood, television, and the stage have strict—but increasingly less strict— rules concerning the extent of undress permitted.

There are certain qualifications to the taboo on exposure of the human body. Nakedness is permitted in small infants, although many believe that it is best to keep a nude infant belly-down. Nude modeling is permitted under properly controlled conditions. It is considered proper for a trained nurse or physician to see nude bodies of patients of the opposite sex. A few states permit sun-bathing societies to operate legally.

Americans are amusingly, and at times tragically, inconsistent in their attitudes toward modesty and nudity. They consider the human body in full view somewhat indecent but at the same time they strive to see as much of it as possible. Seminudity has become a fetish. Nudity carried as far as the law allows is practiced on beaches, in night clubs, on the stage, in popular magazine art, and even in fashions and styles. Although it is considered decent to conceal tabooed parts of the body with clothing, or some type of adornment, it is also proper, and even socially necessary, to wear clothing and adornment which *calls attention to and exaggerates the sexual characteristics of the body.*

In the past decade, major cultural and technological breakthroughs have occurred. Newspapers have advertised inflatable bras "that defy detection by sight or touch" (literal quote from a newspaper ad for Trés Secrète bras). Clothing has been designed which seems to defy all laws of gravity—it stays in place, as a bumble bee flies, by laws not understood by man.

Scanty or semitransparent clothing is now "high fashion"; a matter which provides continuous copy for the public press and fantastic opportunities for the imagination of journalists. One article, summing up the situation was entitled, "Bulls Vs. Bares: Sin and Skin Battle Still Rages." [16] After following a years-old policy of airbrushing navels out of bikini-clad girls, the magazine, *Seventeen*, finally decided this was too unrealistic, giving a journalist a chance to entitle his article "Navel Treaty." [17]

The "no-bra bra" has provided writers fun and advertisers conflict. This transparent mesh "undersupport"—designed for use with evening gowns with an equally transparent mesh top—must be advertised, but how? In an article (with pictures) one writer came up with "Vogue—and Vague" and described how *Vogue* magazine unhesitatingly used

[16] *The Fresno Bee,* December 2, 1965. The bares seem to be winning.
[17] *Newsweek,* October 18, 1965, p. 79.

realistic photographs in its ads but the staid *New York Times* used a vague, rather surrealistic picture which left much to the imagination.[18] Once upon a time, girdles were designed not merely to "shape up" but to conceal certain portions of the anatomy. A recent Macy's ad depicts a girdle named "Fancy *That*," which accentuates the cleavage between the buttocks. Their ad includes the words, "Something's been added behind your back. . . ." A New York advertising man could not resist impishly urging the admen to include "add more wow to your wiggle . . . with fanny falsies." [19]

Taboos with respect to modesty obviously create confusion, inconsistent behavior, and moral conflict. Enjoyment of seminudity—as practiced in night clubs, theaters, and the public press—may be accompanied by guilt feelings. Among couples engaging in petting or sexual relations exposure of the body may be painful and a source of later remorse. Within families, attempts to enforce severely the traditional taboos regarding modesty may lead children to regard their own bodies as indecent and make it difficult for them, as adults, to adjust to normal sexual relationships. Conflicts may also result from differences between lower-middle and upper-class attitudes toward nudity. Probably lower-class persons are most prudish about nudity, middle-class persons somewhat less so, and upper-class persons least of all.

Whereas taboos on exposure of the body may produce embarrassments of various kinds, as well as feelings of guilt, the American cult of exposing as much of the body as possible and insisting that exposed portions be "alluring" also creates conflicts. A small, flat-chested male may have trouble getting a girl, though not as much as a thin, flat-chested girl will have in getting a boy. A "glamour-girl" pattern is firmly established in the culture, and woe betide a girl who cannot in at least small ways measure up.

4.1 How do you explain the American craze for partial nudity, coupled with firm insistence that nudity not be complete? Is there any difference in morality in the night-club entertainer who strips completely to the waist and an entertainer who wears tiny bits of cloth over each breast? Would the law punish one and not the other? Is the law rational?

4.2 How do you explain the fact that, among the vast majority who do not object to the publication of pictures of the most revealing paintings and statues, there are some persons who have serious reservations about publishing pictures of living nudes? Do you consider it rational that we consider it much more acceptable to publish photographs of living nudes if they are dark-skinned, "primitive" people than if they are of a modern

---

[18] *Newsweek*, March 22, 1965, p. 90.
[19] *Newsweek*, February 15, 1965, p. 78.

culture? The only portion of the human anatomy which cannot be portrayed in photographic reproduction is the front pelvic area of adults. Why is the front of the pelvis more "indecent" than the rear? Why is pubic hair considered "indecent" when at the same time we consider lack of hair on the head embarrassing?

4.3 What is "sex appeal" and how important is it? To whom and for what is it important? Is it a means of gaining social status? To what extent is "sex appeal," its manufacture and sale, a profitable American industry? How much does an average American girl or woman spend on items designed to enhance "sex appeal"? How much profit is made by American merchants and manufacturers on sale of such items? Is the "glamour-girl" idea publicized in American advertising for mercenary purposes?

5. Career Versus Housewifery

It is widely believed that women owe it to themselves and society to enter a career and pursue it as a main interest in life; but it is also widely believed that a "woman's place is in the home."

Although this issue is old, it has gained new life since World War II. One recent precipitating force was publication of the best-selling *The Feminine Mystique* by Betty Friedan. It is unlikely that this book would have created the furor that it did if there had not been a large backlog of frustration among women. It was reviewed and discussed with great heat at women's book clubs the nation over. Friedan's contention, basically, is that women have the same competence, if developed, to perform successfully in the professions and other occupations as do men; that they represent a vast reservoir of presently wasted talent; that women cannot find self-fulfillment in the home—only in creative effort in the world of work. A plethora of magazine articles and other books on the same subject appeared, including considerable written material designed to help the "kitchen slave" live with her situation and find real delight in home life—as in creative dish washing, creative diaper washing, creative husband pampering, and creative mopping.

More than one-third of the nation's women work outside the home for pay, either part- or full-time. This proportion increases each year. Most are not in what might properly be called a "profession;" but a rather large proportion are in some well-defined occupation in which they will stay during their working life—such as secretary, saleslady, or beauty-shop operator. Each year a larger proportion of female high-school graduates go on to college, but many of these frankly are seeking a husband—not an education or a career. Many of those primarily seeking a husband, however, are also seeking an education and a permanent career—or, if not the latter, a saleable skill to which they could turn if their husbands died, became incapacited, or a divorce occurred. As in the case of males, it appears to be only a matter of time until all girls who have the necessary intellectual capability will want to attend college.

The frustrations of men and the traditions of Western civilization to the contrary, it appears that there *will* be an increasing proportion of women working for financial gain outside the home. And women in general may be destined to suffer major frustrations and emotional conflict,

One major source of conflict is likely to stem from an obvious biological difference—women have babies. Even most career women say that for their "self-fulfillment" they want to have two or three babies. To have children without social stigma requires marriage, so the career woman must marry. This means that in addition to the responsibility of children, she will have the responsibility of a husband—which is much worse. Although a husband is a major chore—often almost unbearable to the career woman—he *may* offer a source of regular and socially acceptable sexual satisfaction.

Another situation that may lead to serious conflict for both the man and the woman arises when the career male's career wife knows of his "affairs," in which case she is forced into certain choices which, among others, include: ignoring the whole business and pursuing her career, and perhaps herself seeking a lover or lovers—in which case her husband may become jealous and cause trouble; working out an arrangement by which she and her husband will go independent ways but remain married as a matter of convenience—"for the sake of the children," or seek a divorce.

Of course, the career woman always has the choice of remaining single—and childless—as many do. In this case, if she needs male companionship, she is free to form as many liaisons as she chooses—an arrangement which seems increasingly acceptable in our culture. This choice may lead to conflict because she is denied the opportunity to have babies unless she is a woman of rare courage or extreme carelessness, although cultural trends suggest that even this "out" may in due time cease to carry stigma. Many persons feel that a more civilized society would offer a woman complete freedom to choose whether or not to rear children in an unmarried state. (If this comes to pass, child psychologists will suffer great mental anguish became of their belief that without a strong and permanent father image with which a child can identify, the child will be emotionally deformed.)

In any case, on the basis of data we now have, it seems clear that it is not easy to be a career woman, or a housewife, or to combine the roles. Housewifery today becomes increasingly demanding and frustrating. A housewife is supposed to combine more roles than is possible for any individual human being. She is supposed to be a housekeeper (cook, laundress, cleaning maid, etc.); a childbearer and mother, with major responsibility for children until they are through college and out of the home; a community servant ("Will you please canvass your block for funds for the Heart Association this year?"); a hostess to visiting friends; an intellectual companion to her husband; and his delectable bedmate. Her roles continue to increase: we are now coming to add gardener, fixer of broken appliances, interior decorator (painting walls from a stepladder), and many more. Probably one of the most puzzling questions of the 1960s is why women, on the average, live longer than men.

5.1 Try to think of some better compromises to the dilemma described in this section than were mentioned. It is clear that we will have more career women and the problem has to be managed somehow. How?

5.2 What is your opinion of women, without social stigma of any sort, being permitted to bear and rear children whether or not they are married? Should this be considered a "basic human right"?

5.3 Is the idea of encouraging women to enter permanent occupations outside the home good? Even though it appears that most will, should we try to slacken this trend as much as possible? Is a woman's place within the home? What are the moral issues involved?

DISCUSSION QUESTIONS AND EXERCISES

1. Certain aspects of sex education in the public schools are offered on a segregated basis—girls in one class, boys in another. Do you believe conflicts such as are described in this chapter can or cannot be discussed in mixed groups? Why or why not?

2. The conflicts described in this chapter are not the only ones relating to sex, courtship, and family which young persons are likely to have. Nor are they necessarily the most important ones. What are some other problems which might be an appropriate part of education in this general area?

3. How will a person's religious and social-class background influence the kind and degree of his sexual conflicts? Can a teacher who is deeply religious and steeped in middle-class values help youth understand their sexual conflicts? Can a teacher who has serious conflicts over sex help youth with sex problems?

4. Not everyone who is exposed to the conflicts and contradictions of America's sexual ideology incorporates these inconsistencies into his personality. Why?

5. Procure as many teaching materials as you can relevant to the general topic of sex, courtship, and the family. (Movies and filmstrips, pamphlets, and books are available.) Evaluate these materials in terms of their usefulness for reflective learning.

6. Some countries have made notable attempts at providing government programs to help women combine careership and housewifery at the same

time. These include the U.S.S.R. and Sweden. Study the steps taken in one of the countries—preferably Sweden because its problems are more like our own.

REFERENCES

BLOCH, HERBERT A., and ARTHUR NIEDERHOFFER, *Gang: A Study in Adolescent Behavior*, New York, Philosophical Library, 1960.

The authors point out what they see as the similarities between primitive puberty rites and many of the practices of modern teen-agers. Our society makes inadequate provision for inducting youth into adult status—gang behavior being one result.

BORGESE, ELISABETH M., *Ascent of Woman*, New York, Braziller, 1963.

This author contends that, based on the study of historical sex roles in relation to the collectivization of society, the female personality is better adapted than the male for living in a crowded, industrial culture. Hence, in future life, women will play an increasingly important role. Very controversial; good for discussion purposes.

CUBER, JOHN F., and PEGGY B. HARROFF, *The Significant Americans: A Study of Sexual Behavior Among the Affluent*, New York, Appleton-Century-Crofts, 1965.

Cuber is a prominent sociologist, who with his wife, (Peggy Harroff) conducted depth interviews with a total of 437 eminent persons. These included artists, lawyers, legislators, judges, and military officers. Their aim was to uncover the kinds of conflicts in personal life which result from eminence. Extraordinarily readable and revealing.

EHRMANN, WINSTON W., *Premarital Dating Behavior*, New York, Holt, Rinehart & Winston, 1960.

Ehrmann reports research done with a sample of over 1000 male and female college students in a large university. He develops a six-stage "intimacy scale." Your authors feel proper labels for the extremes would be "no holds at all" to "no holds barred."

ELLIS, ALBERT, and ALBERT ABARBANAL, eds., *The Encyclopedia of Sexual Behavior*, 2 vols., New York, Hawthorne Books, 1962.

In 1059 pages, these writers have put together the most comprehensive compendium of studies concerning sex ever available. Probably the most useful reference source available. The authors seem to feel that sex still has quite a future.

FITCH, ROBERT E., *Decline and Fall of Sex; with Some Curious Digressions on the Subject of True Love*, New York, Harcourt, Brace & World, 1957.

The Dean of the Pacific School of Religion (Berkeley), drawing on novelists and social scientists, describes with considerable objectivity contemporary sexual beliefs and practices. But he wants no part of it: to Fitch, sex should be strictly for procreation and his attack on today's beliefs and practice is blistering. For an amusing rejoinder, see Philip Wylie's review in the *Saturday Review*, August 3, 1957.

FORD, CLELLAN S., and FRANK A. BEACH, *Patterns of Sexual Behavior*, New York, Harper & Row, 1951.

This excellent and comprehensive study is still timely. It contains much material which cannot be found elsewhere.

FRIEDAN, BETTY, *The Feminine Mystique*, New York, Norton, 1963.

A long-time best seller which provoked tremendous controversy; in addition to her hard-hitting and controversial comments on the role of women, she offers an abundance of pretty solid cultural analysis.

FRIEDENBERG, EDGAR Z., *Coming of Age in America: Growth and Acquiescence*, New York, Random House, 1965.

Friedenberg's account of his impressions of the growing-up process, based on personal interviews with students from a number of schools. Objective, but at the same time he concedes his own bias—namely, that children and youth do not fare well in our culture. An excellent book.

FRIEDENBERG, EDGAR Z., *The Vanishing Adolescent*, Boston, Beacon, 1960.

This significant book should be in the library of every social-studies teacher. Friedenberg, among other things, attacks the early heterosexual socialization now so common in our culture and promoted by both parents and school authorities.

GEBHARD, PAUL H., *et al.*, *Pregnancy, Birth, and Abortion*, New York, Harper & Row, 1958.

After Kinsey's demise, Gebhard assumed direction of the Kinsey studies. Although reporting from the same sample used for the first two books, Gebhard points out some of the sampling defects. A more cautious and generally better volume than the first two, it offers a wealth of highly useful factual information.

GEBHARD, PAUL H., *et al.*, *Sex Offenders: An Analysis of Types*, New York, Harper & Row, 1965.

The fourth and best in the Kinsey series, this is a most valuable book. We find, for example, that many persons who are "legal offenders" are harmless types unlikely ever to injure individuals or harm the social order. It is rich in implications with respect to how our present archaic and inhuman sexual codes should be reformed. This is the first "Kinsey book" to dig deeply into psychological factors.

GREENWALD, HAROLD, *Call Girl: A Social and Psychoanalytic Study*, New York, Ballantine, 1958.

A psychiatrist depicts an interesting series of case studies and concludes that the life of a "high-class" call girl, although lucrative, is not a happy one. His subjects suffered many serious conflicts. On the other hand, Dr. Greenwald may be ignoring the fact that only a small minority of call-girls go to psychiatrists—the rest may lack serious psychological problems.

KARDINER, ABRAM, *Sex and Morality*, London, Routledge, 1955.

In a short and readable book, Kardiner discusses various aspects of sexual morality, which he points out, is based on customs that at one time in history served a useful purpose but for which centuries later people can give no sensible reasons. Sexual morals are undergoing an irreversible revolution and we should establish careful guidelines for change. The book's aim is to suggest such guidelines.

KINSEY, ALFRED, *et al.*, *Sexual Behavior in the Human Female*, Philadelphia, Saunders, 1953.

This book uses essentially the same approach as the 1948 volume on males and the same commentary applies.

KINSEY, ALFRED, *et al.*, *Sexual Behavior in the Human Male, Philadelphia*, Saunders, 1948.

Only an entymologist would approach the study of sex like this—in coldly quantitative terms with no concern for qualitative factors. Nevertheless, it remains one of our most useful reference sources.

McGINLEY, PHYLLIS, *Sixpence in Her Shoe*, New York, Macmillan, 1964.

Of the direct rebuttals to Betty Friedan, this is probably the best. It is readable, amusing, and effectively pokes holes in many of Friedan's arguments.

REISS, IRA L., *Premarital Sexual Standards in America*, Glencoe, Ill., Free Press, 1961.

A provocative but "culturally in tune" book in the sense that Reiss argues persuasively for "pre-marital relations *with affection*." The main body of the book is an analysis of American premarital standards, with data drawn from many sources, including Kinsey, Ehrmann, Burgess and Wallin, and Terman.

SEWARD, GEORGENE H., *Sex and the Social Order*, New York, McGraw-Hill, 1946.

This old timer remains one of the best studies of sex we have. Compared with many other books in the field it seems readable, balanced, and reasonable.

TAYLOR, GORDON R., *Sex in History*, New York, Vanguard, 1954.

Taylor, who in previous writings has dealt with economics and industrial relations, broadens his scope to write a hard-hitting book on the evolution of ideas about sexual behavior in Western civilization. Although loaded with well-documented facts, this is no ordinary history of ideas. It includes many quotable stories and also the author's own strong opinions—to the effect that the guilt-breeding Western tradition has been tragic for man.

Indexes

INDEX OF NAMES

INDEX OF SUBJECTS